New Perspectives and Developments in Chinese Semantics

Xu Wen · Ruiliang Tang

New Perspectives and Developments in Chinese Semantics

清華大學出版社
Tsinghua University Press

Springer

Xu Wen
Southwest University
Chongqing, China

Ruiliang Tang
Southwest University
Chongqing, China

Translated by
Junfang Mu
Hebei University
Hebei, China

ISBN 978-981-95-1729-9 ISBN 978-981-95-1730-5 (eBook)
https://doi.org/10.1007/978-981-95-1730-5

Jointly published with Tsinghua University Press
The print edition is not for sale in China (Mainland). Customers from China (Mainland) please order the print book from: Tsinghua University Press.

Translation from the Chinese language edition: "语义学新发展研究" by Xu Wen and Ruiliang Tang, © Tsinghua University Press 2021. Published by Tsinghua University Press. All Rights Reserved.

This Springer imprint is published by the registered company Springer Nature Singapore Pte Ltd.
The registered company address is: 152 Beach Road, #21-01/04 Gateway East, Singapore 189721, Singapore

Preface

Foreign Language and Literature constitutes an essential part of China's Humanities and Social Sciences. Since 1862 when Tongwen Guan (Imperial College for the Propagation of Learning in Peking) was first founded, China's Foreign Language and Literature Studies has already existed for over one hundred and fifty years. For more than a century, the discipline of Foreign Language and Literature Studies has been growing and thriving in tandem with national development and societal transformations. It has driven social progress, promoted the development of several undertakings like politics, economy, culture, education, science and technology, and diplomacy, and strengthened exchanges, communication, and cooperation with the international community. Each stage of this discipline's development has embodied the requirements and characteristics of the times.

Before the twentieth century, the focus of Chinese language studies was primarily on philology and Chinese exegetics (xun gu xue, a branch of traditional Chinese philology focusing on the interpretation of ancient texts). At that time, grammatical analysis often treated the meaning of isolated words as the basic criterion. This was due to the central role that studies of "characters" (or hanzi, the logographic Chinese characters) played in linguistic studies. Consequently, there was a notable absence of grammatical criteria specifically tailored for differentiating parts of speech in Chinese. In 1898, China witnessed the publication of its first grammatical monograph, *Ma Shi Wen Tong*. Although studies of "characters" continued to dominate, this book marked the announcement of grammar as an independent discipline. This signaled the dawn of a new era for linguistics, a field that was previously uncultivated and now ready to flourish. The May Fourth Movement of 1919, an anti-imperialist and anti-feudal uprising, sparked a wave of enthusiasm for the Chinese New Culture Movement, which in turn contributed to the thriving development of Language and Literature Studies, including Foreign Language and Literature Studies. Since the founding of the People's Republic of China, and particularly the Reform and Opening-up, the discipline of Foreign Language and Literature Studies has exhibited a sustained and rapid momentum of development. By the end of the twentieth century, its academic system had become increasingly sophisticated, with research philosophies, methods, and instruments becoming more scientific and advanced. This progress almost achieved synchronization with international leading research levels. As a result, remarkable achievements were made, significantly driving the establishment of Humanities and Social Sciences. These achievements also supported and served the development of the Reform and Opening-up and various social undertakings.

Similarly, during the transitional period around the "May Fourth Movement", translation emerged as a prominent discipline, serving as a crucial gateway and pathway for understanding foreign culture, thought, education, science and technology, politics, and society, and functioning as a valuable tool for transforming old China. During that period, translators shifted from the periphery to the center of Chinese academia. A group of renowned thinkers and translators cultivated Chinese modernity through the translation and introduction of Foreign Language and Literature publications and works. Their academic contributions were monumental and would be passed down through history, making significant contributions to the fostering of Chinese academia. Many western academic theories and disciplines have become familiar to and accepted by Chinese universities through translation. For example, Wang Guowei translated foundational textbooks on education and agriculture, while Wu Mi translated works on neo-humanistic aesthetics by Irving Babbitt of Harvard University, and so on. These translated texts contributed to the development and refinement of China's higher education disciplinary system in one aspect, with sociology, anthropology, folkloristics, aesthetics, pedagogics, and so on, all founded and developed almost during this period. Translation services have played an indispensable role in cultural exchanges and integration, as well as in promoting mutual recognition among civilizations. Meanwhile, translation studies has become increasingly mature after undergoing turns toward philology, linguistics, cultural studies, and so on. Nowadays, translation studies are undertaking important missions and responsibilities in letting China understand the world and letting the world understand China, especially in the context of the "Belt and Road" Initiative, the construction of a community with a shared future for mankind, telling China's stories well and conveying China's voice effectively. The task is arduous and the road is long.

In the early twentieth century, foreign literature profoundly influenced the shaping of China's modern literature. As Lu Xun aptly put it, one should emulate Prometheus by stealing the "fire of heaven" for China's traditional literature, thereby issuing a clarion call for literary revolution in China. This played an irreplaceable role in confronting life, healing souls, and transforming society. Consequently, a vast amount of foreign advanced culture was introduced into China, playing a pivotal role in shaping China's modernity. Starting from the late Qing Dynasty, especially after the May Fourth Movement, the introduction and translation of foreign literature became a widespread phenomenon. Through the relentless efforts of several generations of translators and scholars, numerous achievements were made in translation, commentary, research, and education. After the Reform and Opening-up, foreign literature studies flourished even more. Studies of foreign writers and their works gradually deepened, while studies and writings on the history of foreign literature became increasingly mature. In terms of the translation and introduction of literary theory and criticism, as well as the continuous innovation of international trends in literary ideology, China has basically kept pace with European and American academia.

The profound significance of translating and studying foreign literature lies in exhibiting the fine traditions of world literature, manifesting vitality and dynamism in deepening literary themes, diversifying expressive forms, enriching genres, and drawing upon critical methodologies. This endeavor has notably inspired the Chinese literary community to continuously forge new literary perspectives, thereby enriching contemporary and modern Chinese literary creation with abundant artistic resources. Simultaneously, it has vigorously propelled academic studies in related fields within universities.

Entering the twenty-first century, China's foreign linguistic studies have achieved unprecedented development. It has not only promptly introduced the latest achievements of Western linguistic studies but also applied these theories to the practice of Chinese language studies. The theories were not only introduced, evaluated, and criticized, but also they were drawn upon and absorbed in a critical way. Comparative studies between English and Chinese language have received unprecedented attention and gained remarkable achievements, greatly improving the phenomenon of "two skins". This phenomenon, often referred to as "two separate skins", described the isolated functioning of English and Chinese language studies, which lacked communication and cooperation. Furthermore, in disciplines closely related to contemporary science and technology, such as psycholinguistics, neurolinguistics, and cognitive linguistics, foreign linguistic scholars took the lead in sharing new achievements and discoveries in linguistic studies with the world. Some advanced ideas in foreign language teaching, as well as study achievements in language policy, have made positive contributions to the country's formulation of foreign language education policies and development strategies.

General Secretary Xi Jinping has stated, "We should prioritize the enhancement of international communication capabilities, innovate external publicity methods, and reinforce our discourse system. Our goal is to create new concepts, categories, and expressions that bridge Chinese and Western cultures, effectively telling China's stories and conveying China's voice, thereby strengthening our international discourse power". To fully implement this directive, the Ministry of Education has recently announced comprehensive advancements in the construction of new engineering disciplines, new medical disciplines, new agricultural disciplines, and new liberal arts education. The concept of "new liberal arts" has officially gained recognition from Ministry of Education and has been endowed with new connotations and positioning. Against the backdrop of the global new technological revolution, new economic development, and the new era of socialism with Chinese characteristics, new liberal arts breaks through traditional liberal arts thinking and construction systems. It establishes a theoretical framework and research paradigm that resonates with the new era, new ideas, new technologies, and new cultures. Combining the characteristics of traditional liberal arts with interdisciplinary approaches, new liberal arts emphasizes science and technology, strategic innovation, and integrated development. It is deeply rooted in China while embracing a global perspective.

The concept of new liberal arts education has set forth new goals, tasks, requirements, and a new landscape for the development of Foreign Languages and Literatures discipline. Specifically, under the banner of new liberal arts education, the development goals of Foreign Languages and Literatures are as follows: to serve as the knowledge framework for the national education development strategy, to cultivate the ability to meet the challenges posed by the new technological revolution, to demonstrate the deep integration between humanities and interdisciplinary studies, to strengthen the construction of general education courses covering Chinese and foreign politics, culture, society, and history, to establish an interdisciplinary and cross-field learning mechanism, and to adopt a multi-dimensional and interactive teaching model. These new elements of liberal arts education will facilitate the thorough implementation and realization of the spirit, connotation, and philosophy of the new liberal arts in educational practice. Consequently, more foreign language talents in the field of Humanities and Social Sciences, who possess innovative and integrated professional skills, possess a global perspective, and understand and are proficient in the humanities, history, geography, and language of the target country, will be cultivated for the nation.

As we enter the new era, our country has witnessed tremendous changes in the education, teaching, and research of foreign language and literature, resulting in remarkable achievements among the exploration and innovation of theory, the discussion and application of methods, as well as specific experiments and practices. Reviewing, summarizing, organizing, and refining the academic development of an era, especially when conducting research from theoretical, methodological, and practical perspectives, holds significant discipline and academic value, as well as realistic and profound implications.

Given the aforementioned concepts and reflections, we planned, organized, and compiled this series of books titled "Research Series on the New Development of Foreign Language and Literature in the New Era". The aim of this series is to analyze and summarize the construction of significant theories within the discipline of Foreign Language and Literature in China, the exploration of research fields, the discussion of core issues, the investigation of research methodologies, as well as the application and practice of achievements across various fields in China over the past decade. Through this endeavor, we have identified the major shortcomings in current research and provided discipline-specific strategies for the development of the Foreign Language and Literature discipline. We hope that the publication of this series will assist researchers, learners, and enthusiasts in this field to understand and grasp the latest developments at the forefront of the discipline. It will enable them to become familiar with and comprehend the current situation, acknowledge the existing problems, and explore development trends and pathways. Ultimately, we aim to support Chinese scholars in constructing a discourse system that integrates both Chinese and foreign perspectives, using academic achievements to narrate China's stories. Consequently, we envision the emergence of a Chinese school that can stand tall and prominent among the academic forests of the world.

The book series, collaboratively organized and developed by the China Association for Comparative Studies of English and Chinese (CACSEC) and Shanghai Times Education Publishing Research Center, was collaboratively created by 29 secondary branches under the research institute through innovative collaboration. Luo Xuanmin and Zhuang Zhixiang oversaw the entire manuscript outline, while over twenty experts, engaged by the Secretariat of the Research Institute, individually reviewed and revised the book draft outlines. Huang Guowen conducted the final review and made corrections to most of the outlines. Composed predominantly of renowned scholars and young to middle-aged academic leaders, the authors have undergone rigorous academic training, possess profound academic attainments, and have achieved substantial research outcomes in their respective fields. Their contributions are among the most resource-intensive research projects in their areas to date. This series encompasses five core fields: "Foreign Linguistics", "Foreign Literature", "Translation Studies", "Comparative Literature and Cross-Cultural Studies", and "Country and Regional Studies". It showcases the latest theoretical, methodological, and practical research achievements in each field, encompassing theoretical definitions, research scopes, perspectives, methodologies, and paradigms, while also addressing existing issues and outlining future prospects. In essence, leveraging the five main directions of Foreign Language and Literature discipline, this series scientifically and systematically generalizes, summarizes, sorts out, and refines the past decade's development history, current research status, and future trends of the field. It achieves this through the integration of basic and applied studies, the complementary nature of synchronic and diachronic studies, and the effective fusion of quantitative and qualitative studies. Presenting highly visible study results, it aims to contribute to the high-quality construction and development of the Foreign Language and Literature discipline in China, undertaking significant missions and responsibilities in enhancing national soft power and building a community with a shared future for mankind.

Gratitude is given to strong support of Tsinghua University Press and Shanghai Time Education Publishing Research Center. We hope, through the combined efforts of the research association, the publishing house, and the research center, to create a set of academic masterpieces in Foreign Language and Literature studies, offering a sincere and valuable gift for the 100th anniversary of the founding of the Communist Party of China.

Xu Wen
Southwest University
Chongqing, China

Ruiliang Tang
Southwest University
Chongqing, China

Acknowlegments Three postgraduates supervised by Professor Junfang Mu—Yun Liu, Tianpeng Wu, and Rui Huang participated in the proofreading of the translation.

Competing Interests The authors have no competing interests to declare that are relevant to the content of this manuscript.

Prologue

Semantics is not only an essential component of linguistics, but also the core content of linguistics studies. The exploration of language inherently involves the study of meaning, a pursuit that has fascinated humans for a long time. From ancient times onward, both Eastern and Western civilizations have exhibited a profound interest in the nature of linguistic meaning. For instance, ancient Greek philosophers such as Heraclitus, Democritus, Socrates, Plato, and Aristotle penned works dedicated to delving into the meanings of language. They endeavored to clarify intricate matters like understanding the essence of names and the intricate relationship between objects and their corresponding names. Furthermore, this intellectual pursuit sparked a contentious dialogue between the concepts of "essentiality" and "prescriptiveness". Semantic studies also hold a long-standing and prominent position in ancient China. For example, as early as the second-century BC, a specialized monograph titled *Erya* (*Classic of Etymologies*) was compiled, dedicated to explaining word meanings. During the pre-Qin period, philosophers such as Xunzi, Mozi, and others engaged in discussions on the relationship between "names" and "realities", offering detailed argumentation on the connection between linguistic labels and their corresponding objects in the real world. In the Eastern Han Dynasty, Xu Shen's *Shuo Wen Jie Zi* (*Explanation of Script and Elucidations of Characters*) emerged as the first reference book in China to systematically analyze the form, origin, and evolution of Chinese characters. This monumental work was also one of the few dictionaries in existence worldwide at that time. Furthermore, the disciplines involved in semantics in ancient China primarily encompassed Critical Interpretation of Ancient Texts, as well as Logic and Argumentation Studies.

Semantics, having evolved significantly, has become a core and frontier discipline within language studies, alongside phonetics and syntax, collectively constituting the three major branches of modern linguistics. After entering the twenty-first century, with the continuous elevation of the status of linguistics studies, the issue of linguistic meaning has also garnered increasing attention from other disciplines. The study of modern semantics has become a hot topic and difficult point in studies of logic, linguistics, philosophy, semiotics, and other disciplines, and also entered a multi-dimensional and diversified stage. The multidimensionality of semantic studies is reflected in the increasing interdisciplinary studies. For example, in cognitive linguistics, the exploration of semantic issues often combines the theories and study methods of different disciplines such as philosophy, psychology, anthropology, and neuroscience. In addition, the wide employment of methods based on corpus and linguistic statistics has brought about an empirical turn in semantic studies, such as collostructional analysis, distributional semantic analysis, and multi-factor analysis based on statistical analysis model. The combination of semantics studies and modern statistical methods has not only enabled the verification of previous introspective discoveries, but also provided opportunities for further exploration of the deep-seated rules behind semantic phenomena. In the future, much more study methods and theoretical perspectives from other disciplines need to be urgently introduced to semantics studies, and consequently the studies will continuously develop in both theoretical level and methodological level. Moreover, with the constant development of language teaching, machine translation, human-computer interaction, linguistic information processing, and artificial intelligence, semantic issues will gain more attention. The diversification of semantics studies is manifested in expanding study fields and rapid development of sub-fields. Semantic studies have evolved from traditional lexical semantics, sentence semantics, and discourse semantics to speech acts and theories of meaning, with studies increasingly refined. It can even be said that modern semantics has encompassed the study domains of traditional pragmatics.

Since the new era of China, tremendous changes have taken place in all walks of life and various fields, and the education, teaching, and study of foreign language and literature are no exception. In the past decade, domestic semantics studies have achieved many excellent results in theoretical exploration and innovation, methodological investigation and application, as well as specific experiments and practices. When reviewing, summarizing, organizing, researching, and extracting the development of semantics studies in China, it can be seen that its studies have both disciplinary and academic values, as well as practical significance. Based on the study findings of semantics in China over the past decade, this book focuses on the study content such as lexical semantics, sentence semantics, discourse semantics, formal semantics, cognitive semantics, semantic change and the application of semantics, and sorts out the innovation and development of semantics in China. At the same time, the development trends of the future research in semantics are proposed. Studying and showcasing the new developments of semantics studies in China over the past decade can assist researchers in this field to understand and grasp the latest academic and disciplinary achievements. This can help semantics researchers familiarize with the current situation and recognize existing issues so as to explore the future development trends and paths of semantics. Moreover, this book can provide a reference for linguistics postgraduates and linguistics enthusiasts in their study and research. Additionally, 2021 will be the 100th anniversary of the founding of the Communist Party of China, and the publication of this book will also be a valuable and meaningful commemorative contribution.

This book is the result of collective efforts. Chapter 1, "Introduction", is written by Wen Xu. Chapter 2, "Lexical Semantics Studies", is contributed by Wu Shuqiong. Chapter 3, "Sentence Semantics Studies", is authored by Si Lianhe. Chapter 4, "Discourse Semantics Studies", is penned by Cao Duxin. Chapter 5, "Formal Semantics Studies", is written by Ma Junjun. Chapter 6, "Cognitive Semantics Studies", is jointly written by Cheng Jun and Chen Xiyi. Chapter 7, "Semantic Change Studies", is authored by Tang Ruiliang. Chapter 8, "Semantics Applied Studies", is contributed by Wang Huijing. Due to the rush in compilation and the limited ability of the compilers, if there are any omissions or errors in the book, we sincerely request readers' understanding and corrections.

December 2020 Xu Wen

Contents

Chapter 1
Introduction

1.1 Prologue

Semantics constitutes an essential component of linguistics and serves as a discipline dedicated to studying language meaning (linguistic meaning). Alongside phonetics, lexis, and syntax, semantics represents a component of language, a level within language, and a highly significant phenomenon in human society. For instance, renowned French scholar A. J. Greimas remarked, "Essentially, the human world is probably the world of meaning. A world devoid of meaning could never be termed the world of "humans"".

Humans have long paid attention to the meaning of language, and numerous disciplines are involved in this exploration. When ancient Greek philosophers studied philosophical questions, they inevitably touched upon issues related to linguistic meaning. For example, the philosophical monographs of Socrates, Plato, and Aristotle all once explored the meaning of language. In ancient Europe, disciplines such as logic, eloquence (or rhetoric for persuasive speech), rhetoric (in a broader sense encompassing the art of effective communication), and philosophy of religion, among others, also addressed the issue of language meaning from various perspectives. In ancient China, the disciplines primarily concerned with semantics were Chinese exegetics (xun gu xue, a branch of traditional Chinese philology focusing on the interpretation of ancient texts) and Logic and Argumentation Studies (ming bian xue, an important branch of ancient Chinese philosophy that delves into logic, argumentation, reasoning, and the relationship between language and thought). Furthermore, ancient Chinese disciplines like philosophy, logic, Buddhism, Neo-Confucianism, and literary theory also demonstrated great interest in the issue of linguistic meaning. Many modern European disciplines, such as philosophy, logic, semiotics, psychology, and anthropology, have explored semantics from different perspectives and contributed to its development. However, none of these disciplines have treated semantics as their primary study focus, nor have they conducted systematic inquiries into semantic issues. It is semantics (as a discipline in its own right)

X. Wen and R. Tang, *New Perspectives and Developments in Chinese Semantics*,
https://doi.org/10.1007/978-981-95-1730-5_1

that has placed the study of meaning at the forefront, treating it as its direct and fundamental study object, and conducting comprehensive and systematic studies on it.

It is generally believed that semantics emerged as an independent discipline in the early nineteenth century. In 1838, the German scholar K. Reisig advocated for the establishment of the study of word meaning as an independent discipline, which he termed Semasiologie (a combination of semasio, meaning "meaning", and logie, meaning "science"). However, his proposal did not gain much attention at the time. In 1893, the French linguist Michel Bréal first used the term sémantique (semantics) and published his work *Essai de Sémantique* in 1897. From then on, semantics gradually separated from lexicology to become a new branch of linguistics.

In the development history of semantics, semantics has manifested two significant aspects: on the one hand, as a part of linguistics, semantics concerns itself with the meaning of words and their evolution; on the other hand, as a branch of philosophy, semantics focuses on the reference of symbols. These two aspects have actually shaped three important stages in the development of semantics: historical semantics, structuralist semantics, and formal semantics. Historical semantics primarily investigates the meaning of words and their evolutionary patterns, while structuralist semantics mainly concerns itself with the relationships between meanings. Formal semantics, on the other hand, focuses on the logical and mathematical aspects of meaning. However, from the perspective of study angles and scopes, semantics can also be categorized into three broad classes: linguistic semantics, logical semantics, and philosophical semantics. Linguistic semantics primarily examines the meaning of words and their evolution, with a particular emphasis on studying the causes and laws of lexical semantic changes from social and historical perspectives, such as issues like the broadening, narrowing, and shifting of word meanings. Logical semantics delves into issues such as designation, truth-value, and satisfaction conditions in formalized languages. Philosophical semantics, or semantics philosophy, advocates that language is the sole, or at least the primary, object of philosophical analysis. Neopositivism, also known as logical positivism, is a representative and a school within semantics philosophy. It posits that philosophy is an analytical activity, specifically the logical analysis of scientific terms and sentences. Neopositivism argues that viewing philosophy as the logical analysis of language represents a new philosophy and a turning point in philosophy.

In the 1930s, amid the Neopositivist Movement and the evolution of linguistics, philosophical semantics emerged as a branch of logic, dedicated to studying the relationship between symbols and the referents of propositions, while disregarding etymology, cultural, and psychological factors. Although semantics achieved considerable success within formal logic, this came at the expense of abandoning cognitive research. It could be said that for a considerable period after the 1930s, an important trend in the development of semantics was the separation of language from cognition, leading to the simplification of cognitive theories of semantics into logical or purely linguistic theories. Evidence of this trend can be found in contemporary philosophy, particularly in analytical philosophy. Until the 1950s and early 1960s, due to the dominance of structuralism in linguistics, linguists' attention was primarily focused on the formal structure of language, while semantic studies received scant attention. For instance, the American structuralist linguistic school, known as descriptive linguistics, consistently shied away from semantic studies, with semantic studies remaining relatively weak from the time of L. Bloomfield through C. Hockett to N. Chomsky. Consequently, semantics was derisively labeled as the "poor relation", the "neglected sibling", or the "garbage can of syntax" within linguistics at that time. However, after the mid-1960s, interest in semantic studies surged in the linguistic community, transforming semantics into the "Cinderella" of linguistics. As the renowned British linguist G. Leech stated in the preface to his book *Semantics* (1983), "Semantics has become increasingly important in language studies and is now the focus of study, a view that most people now agree with". The emphasis on semantic studies in modern linguistics is, on the one hand, a logical outcome of the internal laws governing the development of linguistics; the deeper the studies into language, the more significant semantic issues become apparent. On the other hand, this emphasis on semantics is also an inevitable result of the new challenges and topics posed by social practice to linguistics. Many disciplines, such as philosophy, logic, semiotics, psychology, anthropology, computer science, artificial intelligence, and phonetics, have provided rich nourishment for the development of semantics. In turn, semantics has borrowed from these diverse fields, continuously refining and enhancing its own theoretical framework. Many theories in semantics, such as referential theory, idea theory, use theory, and behavioral theory, originate from philosophers and logicians. The componential analysis theory in semantics stems from anthropological methods of analyzing word meaning, while the binary opposition idea in the dichotomy of semanteme analysis is derived from phonetics. Due to its openness and inclusiveness, semantics has flourished since the mid-twentieth century, giving rise to numerous schools of thought, including interpretative semantics, generative semantics, Montague semantics, conceptual semantics, situation semantics, psycho-semantics, cultural semantics, and cognitive semantics.

In the late twentieth century, cognitive science had a profound impact on the fields of linguistics, logic, and artificial intelligence. These study domains necessitated not only a mastery of calculus but also an insight into "working models of the human mind", essentially understanding how the human mind operates. Consequently, scholars raised questions such as: why is the mind indispensable in linguistic analysis? Notably, linguistic and artificial intelligence studies into topics like speech acts and reasoning spurred comparisons among diverse forms of semantics and ignited a strong interest in the cognitive dimensions of semantics. Thus, cognitive semantics emerged onto the historical stage in response to the demands and advancements of the times, quickly becoming a focal point and a prominent discipline within the realm of semantic studies.

1.2 Introduction to the Content of All Chapters

Based on China's semantic study achievements over the past decade, this book focuses on the applied study areas of lexical semantics, sentence semantics, discourse semantics, formal semantics, cognitive semantics, semantic evolution, and semantics in general. It reviews the innovation and development of semantics in China and proposes future study trends in this field. This book comprises eight chapters. This Chapter, "Introduction", is written by Wen Xu. Chapter 2, "Lexical Semantics Studies", is contributed by Wu Shuqiong. Chapter 3, "Sentence Semantics Studies", is authored by Si Lianhe. Chapter 4, "Discourse Semantics Studies", is penned by Cao Duxin. Chapter 5, "Formal Semantics Studies", is written by Ma Junjun. Chapter 6, "Cognitive Semantics Studies", is jointly written by Cheng Jun and Chen Xiyi. Chapter 7, "Semantic Change Studies", is authored by Tang Ruiliang. Chapter 8, "Semantics Applied Studies", is contributed by Wang Huijing.

Chapter 2, "Lexical Semantics Studies", provides an overview of the general study landscape in lexical semantics, summarizes the core theories, major study topics, and methods of lexical semantics, and offers insights into future study trends in this field after reviewing representative study results from academic monographs and periodicals in China over the past decade. This chapter first elucidates the relationship among lexical semantics, lexicology, and semantics, emphasizing that lexical semantics primarily focuses on word meaning. From the perspective of disciplinary classification system, lexical semantics is a branch of semantics rather than traditional lexicology. Using the scientific data visualization and bibliometric software CiteSpace, based on publication data from China National Knowledge Infrastructure (CNKI), the author conducts a review and summary of the disciplinary status, study content, and methods of lexical semantics in China over the past decade. Through bibliometric analysis, the author identifies that word meaning, semantic evolution, semantic differentiation, polysemy, comparison of meanings, and semantic representation are the hot points of current studies in lexical semantics. The author provides an overview and analysis of the study results achieved in the main topics of lexical semantics over the past decade, focusing on four aspects: the interface study between lexical semantics and syntactic semantics, the study of word meaning relationships (including antonymy, synonymy, and polysemy, among others), study of semantic processing of vocabulary, and cross-lingual comparative studies of lexical meaning. This chapter also summarizes the main approaches to lexical semantic studies in the last decade, primarily including corpus-based studies and experimental methods. Finally, the author forecasts the future direction of lexical semantic studies. From an interdisciplinary perspective, as the study of cognitive typology deepens and expands, the author posits that there is still considerable room for growth in interdisciplinary studies combining cognitive typology and lexical semantics. Additionally, the social turn and empirical quantitative turn in lexical semantic studies deserve special attention.

Chapter 3, "Sentence Semantics Studies", summarizes in detail the major achievements in the field of sentence semantic studies in China in the past decade, highlighting the fruitful achievements and advancements in nearly all previously explored related fields. The study in this field is rather thorough. Moreover, the author believes that when applying Western sentence semantic theories to solve specific problems, Chinese scholars have also been able to criticize and innovate, proposing several theories with strong explanatory power, such as Case Grammar and Meaning Ontology. Acknowledging the existing study achievements in sentence semantics, the author also points out that future sentence semantic studies exhibit the following development trends. Sentence meaning analysis continuously develops in a micro-level and meticulous manner. For instance, the analysis of sentence meaning structures is becoming increasingly detailed, and the classification of arguments is becoming more nuanced. Increasing attention will be paid to the communicative aspect of sentences, shifting from an isolated focus on static sentence meaning to a focus on dynamic discourse meaning. Studying simple sentence meaning changes into studying meaning within texts, continuously broadening the scope of study. In the future, there will be an increasing reliance on cognitive linguistic theories to study sentence meaning, and the trend of integrating cognitive theories with sentence meaning studies, which possesses powerful explanatory power, will become increasingly evident.

Chapter 4, "Discourse Semantics Studies", primarily centers on three key issues: the definition of "what is said", the processing of generalized conversational implicatures, and the interpretation of pragmatic processes. Given the scarcity of related studies in China at present, the author begins by introducing and reviewing the latest foreign studies on these three topics. Building upon this foundation, the author then focuses on discussing the future development trends of related studies in China, aiming to clarify the intellectual progression and theoretical differences among the various main schools of utterance meaning studies. This is intended to provide researchers with practical observation perspectives and analytical methodologies. As for the future study trends, the author initiates a discussion on the profound insights gained from the contentious debate between contextualism and semantic minimalism in the post-Gricean pragmatics era. These insights are mainly reflected in the following five aspects: the definition and reconstruction of "what is said", the new interpretation of the "pragmatic enrichment" approach, contextualism's rejection of truth-conditional semantics and semantic minimalism's reflection on it, the transition from monotonic logic to non-monotonic logic, and the leap from the modularity hypothesis of language to holism. The author further proposes that there are several key development trends that should be prioritized in future domestic studies on utterance meaning: (1) there are numerous controversies or mysteries surrounding unarticulated constituents triggered by non-linguistic systems, such as the pragmatic mechanism of their repetition and how to restrict their over-generation; (2) the ontological status of generalized conversational implicatures and the pragmatic process urgently require fair and objective theoretical explanations; (3) studies of meaning representation also needs to integrate relevant findings from cognitive science and psychology, thus exploring a theoretical model that aligns representation and inference; (4) based on the "pragmatic richness" of the Chinese language, future domestic studies of utterance meaning will promote meaning interface studies from a typological perspective by continuously uncovering new factual evidence from corpora.

Chapter 5, "Formal Semantics Studies", first conducts a review of formal semantic theories and methodological studies. The review mainly covers two aspects: context dependency, semantic experimentation, and semantic diagnosis. Then, focusing mainly on linguistics-oriented formal semantic studies, this chapter reviews the achievements in formal semantics over the past decade by selecting representative literature such as journal articles and dissertations, with a focus on typical Chinese language topics. Through an overall review of the literature, the author discovers that domestic studies mainly focuses on the following three aspects: (1) the introduction, translation, and elucidation of the development history, fundamental theories, and basic content of formal semantics; (2) research on the syntax and semantics of Chinese discourses from levels of description, analysis, comparison, and experimentation, mainly involving the syntax and semantics of Chinese quantifiers, the Chinese quantificational adverb "dōu", and other domains of static formal semantics; (3) the application of Discourse·Representation Theory (DRT) and Segmented Discourse Representation Theory (SDRT) in Chinese, exemplified by Chinese discourse structure's rhetorical formats, Chinese complex sentences, sentence groups in Chinese, dialogue relations studies, Chinese donkey sentences, conditional sentences, and other domains of dynamic formal semantics. Through the review of domestic formal semantic studies in the past decade, the author points out that disciplinary barriers and boundaries still exist between linguistics and logic studies. Additionally, a broader scope of linguistics-oriented formal semantic studies awaits our exploration and expansion. And the development of formalized studies in China lags behind the development of other linguistic study paradigms or approaches in general. As for the future development trend of domestic formal semantic studies, the author points out that future studies should delve into broader topics while paying attention to typical topics, conduct dynamic semantic studies while paying attention to static semantic studies, and carry out studies of experimental semantics while also considering studies of formal pragmatics alongside formal semantics, while paying attention to exploring the scientific principles of formal semantics.

Chapter 6, "Cognitive Semantics Studies", first points out that cognitive semantics has been a hot study topic in the domestic linguistic academia over the past decade. A large number of excellent scholars have emerged during the past decade, conducting thorough and detailed studies in various aspects such as semantic theories, linguistic phenomena, and Chinese ontology, and achieving a series of accomplishments. This chapter begins by briefly introducing the fundamental theoretical propositions of cognitive semantics, primarily covering guiding principles of cognitive semantics, the "usage-based" linguistic perspective, conceptual metaphor and metonymy, prototype theory, the typicality effect, and other cognitive linguistic theoretical propositions. Moreover, this chapter also conducts an overview of hot topics related to cognitive semantics over the past decade and summarizes important results cognitive semantics has attained in the recent decade, which specifically can be classified into three major fields: conventional study topics, unconventional study topics, and Chinese cognitive semantic studies. Domestic scholars' studies of conventional topics in cognitive semantics primarily cover conceptual metaphor, conceptual metonymy, category theories, mental spaces and conceptual blending, etc. Unconventional topics mainly refer to cognitive discussion of synecdoche, semantic research based upon Embodied-Cognitive Linguistics (ECL), multimodal metaphors, meaning construction, and so forth. Additionally, the author conducted a specialized discussion on syntactic and lexical studies in domestic Chinese cognitive semantics over the past decade, which mainly involves two fields of cognitive semantic studies including syntax and vocabulary. Cognitive semantic studies of Chinese vocabulary primarily involve the semantic evolution and cognitive mechanisms of Chinese vocabulary, comparisons of meanings and cognitive mechanisms between Chinese and other languages, as well as the study on Chinese quantifiers, etc. The cognitive semantic studies of Chinese syntax have also made some breakthroughs in recent years, among which studies of new construction with "bèi" attract most attention. Finally, the author also points out that while domestic cognitive semantic study has achieved numerous theoretical accomplishments, it lacks empirical research to verify the validity of various hypotheses. The author offers an outlook for the future development trends of domestic cognitive semantics from two directions: data-driven cognitive semantic studies (such as corpus-driven semantic prosody studies, corpus-based studies on metaphor and metonymy) and cognitive semantic studies from the perspective of language typology (such as intralingual cognitive semantic studies, interlingual cognitive semantic studies).

Chapter 7, "Semantic Change Studies", having had the important topic of historical linguistics studies—semantic change as study subject, and conducted a preliminary review of the 100-year vicissitudes of the status of studies on semantic change discipline, gives a summary of literature concerning domestic linguistic change studies through bibliometric methods. Based on CNKI retrieval, the author has discovered that the top three scholars in terms of publication count on semantic change studies in China over the past decade are Wu Fuxiang (with 13 articles), Jin Xiaodong (with 6 articles), and Chen Manjun (with 4 articles) and Zhou Hong (with 4 articles). In terms of the languages covered in the study, it primarily encompasses seven languages: Chinese, English, Japanese, Uyghur, Manchu, Russian, and Turkic. Among these, Chinese semantic change serves as the primary study focus, accounting for the vast majority (88.48% of the total). In terms of study topics, the author thinks that new results and new trends of linguistic change study in China over the past decade are mainly demonstrated in the following five aspects: the study of content words' semantic changes, study on semantic evolution from the perspective of construction grammar, the law and path of semantic changes study, the study of motivations and mechanisms of semantic changes, and study methods of semantic changes. The study of content words' semantic changes mainly focuses on two big issues which are the grammaticalization of content words (including the grammaticalization of verbs, adjectives, and nouns) and the non-grammaticalization of content words. In the recent decade in China, study on semantic evolution from the perspective of construction grammar has been gradually developing under the huge influence of construction grammar theory, making significant contributions to overcoming the limitation of traditional semantic change study's being restricted to lexicology or Chinese exegetics. Moreover, large amount of studies concerning the law and path of semantic changes in China provide sufficient historical evidence for such a controversial topic as the regularity of semantic change. Meanwhile, many results also explicitly prove that the law of semantic change is not supposed to be absolute but should display a gradient and flexibility. Over the past decade, while conducting semantic change studies, scholars in China also constantly accept and try various corpus-based new study approaches or paradigms. These approaches or paradigms are mainly embodied as diachronic collostructional analysis, semantic map, and others. The author puts forward that although semantic change studies in China have a rather long history and good tradition, and a great amount of significant study results and experience have been accumulated in this field over the past decade, the deficiencies and defects of studies remain noticeable and there are still huge space to expand. Specifically, these deficiencies and defects can be concluded as follows: too narrow study scope, unsuitable study framework, insufficient theoretical discussion, scarce cross-language perspective, simplistic study methods, insufficient comparative studies between Chinese and other languages, etc. The author continues to propose that the development trend of future semantic change studies should mainly attach attention and thought to these three aspects as innovating semantic change study methods, broadening study perspective, and strengthening comparative study on the semantic change of Chinese and other languages. Additionally, researchers should notice that while learning from related theories and methods abroad, they should combine the Chinese cultural and typological characteristics of Chinese language, break through academic barriers abroad, and develop the semantic change studies with Chinese characteristics.

Chapter 8, "Semantics Applied Studies", points out that in the recent decade, the development momentum of applied studies in semantics in China has mainly exhibited the characteristics of multiple perspectives, multiple levels and interdisciplinary integration, with rather fruitful results achieved especially in the fields of translation studies, foreign language teaching, and the compilation of dictionaries. The author mainly recalls domestic semantics theories in the recent decade, especially paying attention to major results cognitive semantics theories have achieved in these three fields. The application of semantics in translation studies mainly focuses on theories of frame semantics, conceptual metaphor, and conceptual metonymy. The theoretical proposals of cognitive semantics conform to the development trend of translation studies and provide novel perspectives for translation strategies, translation process, and the translation of Chinese classical texts, thus boosting the development of translation theories. In the field of foreign language teaching, the application of cognitive semantics theories mainly involves teaching of translation and vocabulary, which not only improves teaching methods and strategies, but also promotes more in-depth development of teaching studies. Then emerge new study focuses. Moreover, cognitive semantics has become tightly integrated with the compilation of dictionaries and lexicography. From the theoretical perspective, "the symbolic meaning view" in cognitive semantics has exerted significant influence on lexicographic theory. In view of the specific work of lexicography, numerous theoretical ideals of cognitive semantics (such as frame semantics, categorization theory, metaphor theory) have been proven to have the capability of handling core issues like the classification, arrangement and explanation of polysemy lexical items. On the basis of recalling the existing studies, the author also points out that there still exist deficiencies and defects in current domestic applied studies in semantics, with still huge development potential for fields of application like translation studies, foreign language teaching, and lexicography.

Chapter 2
Lexical Semantics Studies

2.1 Introduction

Language is "the language of words", and words determine other language units (Saussure, 1916). The core of words lies in their meanings, which have always been a significant topic of lexical semantic studies. "Lexical semantics is the development of traditional semantics and a branch of modern semantics" (Zhang Zhiyi & Zhang Qingyun, 2012: 9). Lexical semantics studies semantic issues related to words at the lexical level.

In recent years, lexical semantic studies have achieved fruitful results. This chapter primarily summarizes the overall study situation in lexical semantics by combing through representative study findings from domestic academic monographs and periodicals in the recent decade. It outlines the core theories, major study topics, and methodologies in lexical semantics, grasps the latest development directions in this field, and provides an outlook on study trends in this area. The aim is to offer some references for lexical semantics and related studies.

2.2 The Relationship Between Lexical Semantics, Lexicology, and Semantics

Lexicology, semantics, and lexical semantics are three closely-related concepts. Lexicology is the comprehensive study of lexicon in language, which includes etymology, morphology, and social, religious and dialectal variations in the vocabulary (Geeraerts, 2010; Hanks, 2007). Semantics is the discipline concerned with meaning. And lexical semantics mainly studies "word meaning" (Paradis, 2012; Taylor, 2017). It pays attention to issues like what is the meaning of a word, why is there such a

X. Wen and R. Tang, *New Perspectives and Developments in Chinese Semantics*,
https://doi.org/10.1007/978-981-95-1730-5_2

meaning, and the representation approach of meaning in the speaker's brain. Therefore, according to disciplinary classification system, lexical semantics is not the branch of traditional semantics but the branch of semantics.

Lexical semantics as an academic discipline in its own right originated in the early nineteenth century (Geeraerts, 2010). Cruse's *Lexical Semantics* (1986) is the first monograph named after "Lexical Semantics", which adopts contextual paradigm to conduct a systematic study of lexical meaning, thus laying a foundation for the subsequent development of lexical semantics. Afterward, a set of monographs and literature collections expanding on lexical meaning emerged abroad, among which *Theories of Lexical Semantics* (2010) written by Dirk Geeraerts from University of Leuven in Belgium is a monumental lexical semantic monograph. This book conducts a comprehensive and systematic overview of the tradition, evolution, and contemporary situation of lexical semantic development starting from the nineteenth century, presenting five theoretical frameworks in lexical semantic studies from chronological perspective: historical-philological semantics, structuralist semantics, generative semantics, neostructuralist semantics, and cognitive semantics.

There are also numerous books regarding lexical semantic studies in China, with *The Analysis and Description of Word Meaning* written by Fu Huaiqing (1996) first coming out, followed subsequently by a surge of seminal works such as *The Study of Chinese Word Meaning* by Su Xinchun (1992), *Modern Chinese Lexical Semantics* by Cao Wei (2001), *Lexical Semantics* by Zhang Zhiyi and Zhang Qingyun (2001), *English Lexical Semantics* by Wang Wenbin (2001), and *Treatise on Lexical Semantics* by Chen Shumei (2006). Among these works, *Lexical Semantics* coauthored by Zhang Zhiyi and Zhang Qingyun (2001) was the first domestic monograph named after "lexical semantics". This book gives a systematic illustration of the relationships among Chinese word meanings, and builds a theoretical framework of lexical semantics in modern linguistics, thus greatly boosting the development of China's lexical semantic studies.

2.3 Overview of Lexical Semantics Studies in the Past Decade

2.3.1 General Trends in Lexical Semantics Studies

This chapter employs CiteSpace, a citation visualization quantitative software, to perform a full-sample analysis and produce Figures of literature's overall diachronic distribution and keywords' synchronic distribution. The data of the Figures come from CNKI, a Chinese website that stores the world's largest information load and is the most valuable. The writer conducted the search using "word meaning" and "lexical meaning" as keywords for the title, with time span set from January 2010 to December 2019 and literature source category chosen from core journals and CSSCI journals. The initial search produced 352 papers, which finally had 338 papers left

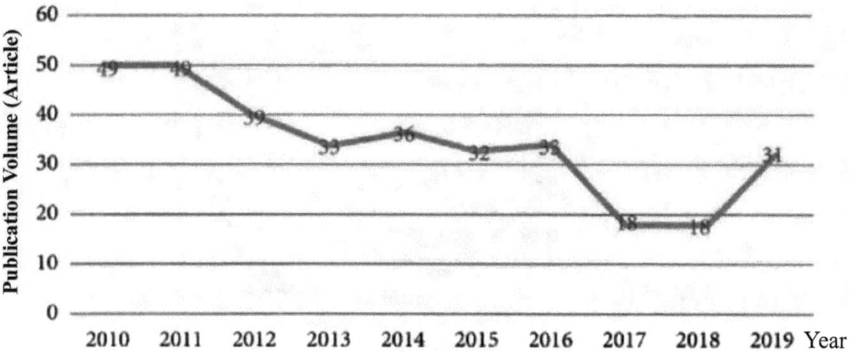

Fig. 2.1 Distribution of annual publication volume of papers concerning lexical semantics

after getting rid of 14 papers unrelated to content through manual examination and screening. This distribution Figure (Fig. 2.1) objectively exhibits the overall development situation of lexical research in the past decade. It assists us to grasp research hot spots and investigate clearly the development frontiers, providing references for related research in lexical semantics.

According to the annual publication volume of papers shown in Fig. 2.1, the volume reached peaks respectively in 2010 and 2011. It took on a trend of gradual decrease from 2011 to 2013, and started to increase in 2014. From 2014 to 2016, the volume was rather stable. It decreased to the least point from 2017 to 2018 (only 18 papers were published every year), but increased dramatically from 2018 to 2019. In general, the publication volume of papers concerning lexical semantics fluctuates rather dramatically in 10 years. However, the number of core journals and CSSCI journals released every year all maintained over 18, suggesting that this study topic has always been a major point of attention to scholars.

Keywords are highly concentrated and summarized representations of the content of an article. Keywords of high frequency demonstrate scholars' current focus and focal points in this field of study. Nodes in Fig. 2.2 represent keywords. The occurrence frequency of keywords is reflected by the size of nodes, and there appears a positive correlation between them. The higher the frequency of keywords' occurring together, and the larger the nodes are, then the correlation among keywords becomes closer and these keywords are more capable of representing focal topics. Lines linking all nodes represent the interrelation of various study subjects. It can be observed from Fig. 2.2 that in lexical semantic studies, the frequency of "word meaning" as a keyword is the highest, with that of "semantic evolution" and "semantic differentiation" as keywords following subsequently. "Semantic evolution" is tightly related with "cognition", "metonymy" and "metaphor", suggesting fruitful accomplishments that have been attained in studying word meaning from cognitive perspective. Studies of "semantic differentiation" are quite plentiful and were closely related with corpus-based studies and synonym annotation studies. Additionally, "comparison of lexical meanings" is also a focal point of research, and "semantic representation", "second

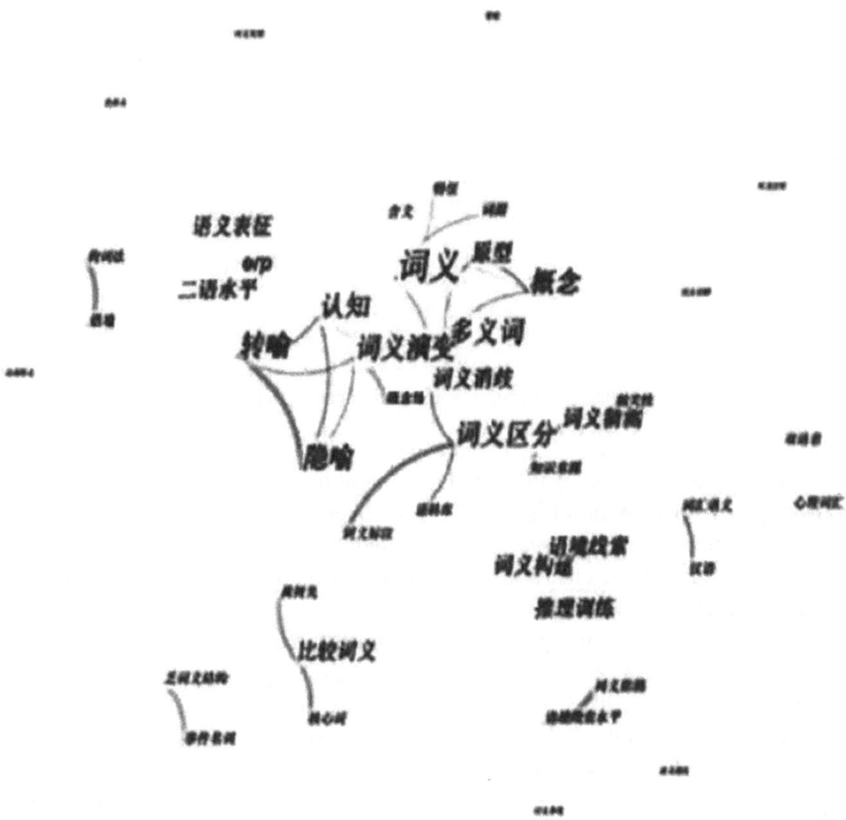

Fig. 2.2 Distribution of nodes of word meaning keywords

language proficiency", and "polyseme" are all high-frequency keywords. In view of this, keywords such as "word meaning", "semantic evolution", "semantic differentiation", "polyseme", "comparison of meanings", and "semantic representation" are rather obvious in the Figure, all of which have become the focal points of lexical semantic studies over the last decade.

2.3.2 *Core Theory in Lexical Semantics Studies: Cognitive Semantics*

Lexical semantics is a branch of modern semantics. Cognitive semantics is a theory developing in the course of the 1980s. Its guiding principles are: conceptual structure is embodied; semantic structure is conceptual structure; meaning representation is encyclopedic; meaning construction is conceptualization (Evans & Green, 2006). In cognitive semantics, vocabulary is the perfect starting point in cognitive semantic studies. For example, prototype categorization theory originated from the observation of lexical categories, which later expanded into grammatical categories (Shao Bin, 2014). Cognitive semantics holds the embodied view, the encyclopedic view, and the contextual view, which play a significant role in boosting the development of lexical semantics. As a branch of cognitive semantics, cognitive lexical semantics observes the fundamentals of cognitive semantics and adopts basic theories and methodologies of cognitive semantics. Specifically, through adopting the cognitive approach in cognitive semantics, depicting the internal structure of lexical categories, analyzing semantic relationships, as well as illustrating theoretical motivations of semantic change, cognitive lexical semantics thereby uncovers the nature of human cognitive activities. According to Geeraerts (2010), the distinction between cognitive lexical semantics and traditional lexical semantics primarily lies in the following aspects: first, by focusing on differences of salience between members of categories, innovative ways of analyzing the internal semasiological structure of words are put forward; second, a renewed interest in the semantic relations between the elements of such semasiological structures triggers a reconsideration of metonymy and metaphor and their interaction; third, by highlighting the importance of conceptualization phenomena that transcend the level of the individual lexical item, studies into regular patterns of polysemy and semantic change are boosted.

Alongside the booming development of cognitive semantics, fruitful accomplishments of studies into cognitive lexical semantics have been attained. Structuralist semantics treats semasiology and onomasiology as two fundamental principles of linguistic structure. With form as a starting point, semasiology focuses on various meanings conveyed by one linguistic form; while starting from studying concept, onomasiology focuses on which kind of linguistic form to illustrate a concept. Cognitive lexical semantics primarily make efforts in these two aspects to develop structuralist semantics (Geeraerts, 2015). As far as semasiology is concerned, cognitive lexical semantics primarily concerns the internal semantic structure of words and semantic representations. The focal point of study falls on typical models of lexical semantic structure: (1) typical study into monosemic context with prototype structure of words as analysis focal point; (2) typical study in the context of polysemic context, with radial network model of polyseme as analysis focal point. In terms of onomasiology, cognitive lexical semantics primarily concerns semantic structure and relations of words. On the one hand, it discusses the internal structure of words and the cognitive mechanism of semantic evolution based on conceptual metonymy, conceptual metaphor, and frame semantic theories. On the other hand, it discusses onomasiological salience, that is to say, the typical models of categories.

Main study topics concerning cognitive lexical semantics can be summarized as follows: (1) the internal structure of lexical categories; (2) the relations between words' polyseme structure and senses; (3) the cognitive mechanism of the formation, evolution and extensions of word meaning; (4) the dynamic interpretation of word meanings; (5) semantic change mechanism that goes beyond the lexical level; (6) models of words' lexicalization and grammaticalization. Theories of Cognitive Linguistics used to depict and illustrate these issues primarily include: prototype categorization theory, theories of conceptual metaphor and metonymy, conceptual blending theory, image-schema theory, frame theories, idealized cognitive models, subjectification, construction grammar theory, and others (Shu Dingfang & Tang Shuhua, 2008; Zhou Qiqiang & Xie Xiaoming, 2009).

Over the past decade, studies of cognitive semantics integrated with word meaning have also gradually become the major trend of lexical semantic studies in China. Among them, the majority of studies put emphasis on illustrating lexical derivation approaches and semantic evolution rules by using theories of cognitive semantics. And Shi Chunhong's studies have developed a school of his own. He integrates semantic analysis mode of lexical semantics with conceptual cognition-based analytical mode, applying cognitive perspectives to various levels of the formation, derivation, and lexicographical definition of lexical meanings. In the article "The cognitive foundation of the lexical meaning structure and the principles of lexicographical definition" that he published in *Studies of the Chinese Language* in 2012, he analyzed the cognitive foundation and process of the formation and derivation of lexical meanings. With examples, it is proved that the formation of the lexical meaning results from the structuralization of the cognitive process, and the derivation of the lexical structure presents topological characteristics. He combines cognitive semantics, structuralist semantics, and the analytical concepts and operating principles of lexical semantics. This analytical mode is refreshing, which significantly pushes ahead with the development of lexical semantic studies.

2.3.3 Primary Topics of Lexical Semantics Studies

1. **Interface Studies of Word Meaning and Syntactic Meaning**

Traditional linguistic theory holds the view that vocabulary exist independently of syntax and they are seen as two parts completely separate from each other (Chomsky, 1957). Word is not only a basic unit in lexicology, but also a basic unit in syntax. As the primary study object of grammatical units, there exists a phenomenon of overlap and integration between lexical studies and syntactic studies.

As for interface studies of the lexicon and syntax, scholars at home and abroad primarily focuses on studying: first, what kind of word meanings influence sentence structure; second, the ways of word meaning impacting sentence structure (Liu Yuhong, 2010). In the studies of how lexicon influences syntax, scholars primarily analyze the relationships between the argument structure of verbs and the thematic structure of syntax, with Case Grammar put forward by Fillmore as a representative. On the basis of Case Grammar, he put forward frame semantics, proposing that based on the relations between event participants, a sentence activates relevant semantic characters in the scene through verbs and specific sentence patterns it administers (Ungerer & Schmid, 1996). He discovered that when irregular structure units or commonly-used phrases correspond to single framework, this framework was called syntactic construction while structure chunks in the syntactic construction were called construction elements (Liu Yuhong, 2010).

Based on such viewpoint, Fillmore further put forward construction grammar theory with idioms as the study object. According to construction grammar, grammar is the form-meaning pairing or symbol unit which integrates the knowledge of lexis, semantics, syntax, phonetics, and pragmatics (Evans, 2019). On the basis of the interaction between verbs' participant roles and argument roles, Goldberg (1995) proposes the view of the interaction between verbs and constructions and the view of generalizations across constructions. She argues that constructions are a grammatical phenomenon, and all languages exhibit such phenomena—meaning that everything from individual words to abstract grammatical and syntactic rules can be represented as constructions. Accordingly, Diessel (2019) argues that there is an interactive relationship between word classes and constructions. As significant components of constructions, closed-class words are closely related with constructions while the relationship between content words and constructions is subject to changes; he also proposes that in the studies based on constructions, scholars often assumed that constructions include open slots for specific content words and these open slots generally calculate the association strength between constructions and specific content words in a probabilistic way.

Semantic interface studies of the lexicon and syntax primarily discusses the relationship between lexical semantics and syntactic structure. In China, studies in this field have achieved abundant results. *Semantic Interface Research: Lexical and Syntactic Interactions* authored by Sun Daogong (2011) is the first monograph. In this book, the author conducted a thorough study in terms of the restrictions of Chinese lexical semantics on syntactic semantics and the interaction mechanism between lexical semantics and syntactic semantics. He elucidates variation rules governing the process of single lexical unit developing into a syntactic combination, and realizes the integration between lexical semantics and syntactic semantics, providing a new model of lexical and syntactic interface studies. This book stresses the integrated study of lexical semantics and syntactic semantics, eliminates the oppositions between both sides, and is a classic among those studies of semantic interface studies on the lexicon and syntax. In his monograph *The Syntax-Lexical Semantics Interface,* Gao Mingle (2018) analyzes the intimate relationship between verbs' lexical semantics and syntax, examines Chinese language's syntactic features and grammatical nature, eventually discovering the corresponding law existing between Chinese lexical semantics and syntax, and establishing an effective interactive model. Apart from studies paying attention to interface relations between the lexicon and syntax form traditional theoretical dimension, studies dedicated to discussing relations between the lexicon and syntax from the perspective of construction grammar also gradually increased. For instance, Liu Yuhong (2010) analyzes the interface model and construction grammar model of traditional lexical semantics and syntax, and puts forward the model of causal meta-construction. The lexicon is quite closely correlated to syntax. The effective combination of them contributes to insightful discovery of complex language phenomena, thus having a broad study scope.

2. Studies of Word Meaning Relationships

"The primary task of lexical semantics is to study and analyze the relations between words and word meanings" (许余龙, 2010: 75). For a long time, word meaning has consistently been the core theme of cognitive semantic studies (Evans & Pourcel, 2009), but the study of lexical relations has been subject to great negligence. In recent years, with the widespread application of empirical study approaches such as corpus-based study method and experimental method, semantic relations weathered its developmental downturn and achieved a set of fruitful accomplishments. The latest development of lexical semantic studies was particularly embodied in the studies of antonymy, synonymy, and polysemy.

(1) Studies of Antonymy (Opposite Meaning Relationships)

Early studies view antonymous relation as the paradigmatic relation of words. However, antonymous relation is not only the alternative relation along the axis of conglomeration (Syntagmatic), but also the co-occurrence relation along the axis of combination (Jones et al., 2012). Charles and Miller (1989) studied antonym co-occurrence earliest. They primarily examined the frequency of antonym co-occurrence, and thought that the semantic association among antonymous words originates from their high-frequency co-occurrence in the same syntactic context. In the recent decade, antonym co-occurrence has gradually become a heated topic of study on antonymous relations and achieved fruitful results. These results can be summarized mainly into the following four aspects: (1) the syntactic framework of antonym co-occurrence (such as Davies, 2013; Jeffries, 2010; Lobanova et al., 2010); (2) the function of antonym co-occurrence in the text (such as Jones, 2002; Jones et al., 2012; Muehleisen & Isono, 2009; Murphy et al., 2009); (3) the ordering law of co-occurrence antonym. Studies of Kostié (2015), Wu (2017) and others suggest that co-occurrence antonym usually takes on a certain advantageous order; (4) the semantic explanation of specific antonym co-occurrence construction. Some scholars carried out studies of the cognitive mechanism of semantic change of antonym co-occurrence construction. For example, Panther and Thornburg (2012) analyze the semantic reasoning process of antonym co-occurrence construction such as "X and Y alike"; Wu (2014) analyzes the antonym co-occurrence construction "you X you Y", and discovers that metonymy is the premise of semantic explanation of antonym co-occurrence construction through his studies.

Domestic scholars primarily conducted a case study of specific antonym co-occurrence constructions. Zhang Yuan (2015) analyzes construction features of antonymous adjectives' co-occurrence construction "Adjective 1 + Adjective 2" from the perspective of cognitive grammar. The study analyzed conceptual motivations of the semantic and grammatical category transformation as well as relevant boundary collocations of "Adjective 1 + Adjective 2". Wu Shuqiong and Qiu Huan (2017) conduct a detailed analysis of syntactic and semantic features of Chinese antonym co-occurrence construction "X de Y de". Among these, two-character antonym compounds are a hot topic of study. Scholars conducted an analysis of Chinese antonymous compounds from both diachronic and synchronic perspectives.

Study focuses have been conducted in aspects of the classification, ordering rules, lexicalization, semantic changes of Chinese antonym compound. And great emphasis has been put upon studying one type of modal adverbs, namely antonymous mood adverbs. Zhang Jinzhu (2015) analyzes the lexical categories of Chinese antonymous compounds. He posits that antonymous compounds have a special status in the whole lexical category, as an atypical word form, occupying the transition zone of verb/noun continuum, and presenting a nominal tendency. Zhang Jinzhu (2018) attaches focal attention to analyzing the internal semantic expressions and conceptual hierarchical characteristics within three types of antonymous compounds such as category "N + N", category "A + A", and category "V + V". The study reveals that the internal semantic structure of antonymous compounds does not align with their grammatical structure, nor is it a simple combination of the two constituent morphemes. Instead, they exhibit a "typical universal reference" semantic function, manifesting three distinct levels of conceptual hierarchy: universal exhaustive reference, arbitrary exhaustive reference, and collective exhaustive reference. Liu Yuqian and Meng Kai (2019) examine the factors influencing the semantic interpretation of antonymous compounds from the perspective of second language acquisition. They argues that the type of semantic relationship and the native language writing system affect how second language learners interpret the meanings of antonymous compounds, and accordingly proposes pedagogical recommendations for teaching such compounds. In the study of adversative modal adverbs, based on Zhang Yisheng's (2004) analysis of eight adversative modal adverbs—fǎn zhèng ("anyway"), gāo dī ("no matter what"), héng shù ("in any case"), zuǒ yòu ("one way or another"), sǐ huó ("by all means"), hǎo dǎi ("for better or worse"), zǎo wǎn ("sooner or later"), and chí zǎo ("eventually")—scholars have conducted case studies on their semantic features, pragmatic functions, and formation mechanisms. Cheng Wenwen and Zhang Xiancheng (2018) analyze the lexicalization process of zǎo wǎn, identifying two distinct pathways in its lexicalization evolution.

(2) **Studies of Synonymy**

Compared with other theoretical frameworks, cognitive linguistics is more suitable for studying synonymy (Divjak, 2010). According to Divjak (2010), studies of synonymy primarily deal with the following three core themes: (1) how to describe synonymous word classes? In other words, what information do language users need to determine whether the meanings words express are similar? (2) What is the internal structure of synonymous word classes? What methods can be used to measure the degree of similarity among synonymous words? (3) How can the internal semantic distinctions among synonyms be differentiated? Over the past decade, advancements in the study of synonymy have mainly been reflected in the following two aspects.

First, the conceptual nature of synonymy.

Structuralist semantics posits that two words are synonymous if one can be substituted for the other without altering the truth-conditional meaning of the utterance. However, cognitive linguistics rejects this supposition, arguing that no such necessary and sufficient conditions exist. Storjohann (2010) investigates the conceptualization and construction of synonymy in actual discourse, revealing that synonymy is not merely a lexical relationship between two word forms. Rather, it is a relation of meaning equivalence dynamically constructed by speakers during language use, based on shared linguistic and extra-linguistic knowledge as well as cognitive principles. Thus, synonymy is neither a relationship between words nor between meanings, but rather between lexical representations mapped onto the same conceptual structure. In other words, synonymy is conceptual in nature, and its construction constitutes a dynamic process.

Cognitive linguistics posits that study of semantic relations essentially involves investigating variations in entrenched form-meaning pairings. It defines synonymy as "an entrenched functional and conceptual relationship between symbolic forms and non-symbolic forms" (Glynn & Robinson, 2014: 14), encompassing both concrete forms and schematic forms. The former refers to lexical synonym while the latter denotes grammatical synonymy. Consequently, cognitive semantic research on synonym has progressively expanded from focusing solely on lexical synonym to incorporating grammatical synonym as well.

Domestic scholars recognize the conceptual nature of synonymy relatively late, and studies in this area remain limited. Wang Tongwei (2009) is the first to introduce cognitive linguistics into the study of Chinese synonyms, proposing that synonymy is cognitively motivated. He argues that prototype theory, typicality effects, and family resemblance theory could provide more plausible explanations for Chinese synonymy phenomena that were difficult to account for under traditional categorical approaches. Pang Yang and Zhang Shaojie (2012) investigate lexical synonymy from pragmatic and cognitive perspectives, suggesting that lexical synonymy is constructed as a form of cognitive similarity established in context through relevance principles. Later, Pang Yang (2016), building on the ad hoc category theory from cognitive psychology, proposes that ad hoc categories both constrain and activate the online construction of lexical synonymy. He posits that cognitive similarity between words emerges through pragmatic inference mechanisms and ad hoc categorization. These studies demonstrate that the study of the conceptual nature of synonymy in the Chinese context still requires further deepening.

Second, semantic and usage variations within synonym groups.

Distinguishing synonyms remains the core topic in synonymy research, with particularly fruitful findings in this area. Early studies employed various approaches: Hanks (1996) differentiates urge and incite through distributional patterns. Partington (1998) examines usage distinctions among absolutely, completely, and entirely. Gries (2001) analyzes collocational overlap in adjectives with end of -ic and -ical. Recent decade has witnessed a surge in corpus-driven studies leveraging big data and multivariate statistics to investigate co-occurrence patterns in discourse and semantic preferences of synonyms. Studies examining the similarities and differences in synonym usage have been increasingly conducted. For example, Wu (2018) carries out a corpus-based quantitative study on Chinese approximate synonyms "shàng xià"" ("up and down"), "qián hòu" ("front and behind"), and "zuǒ yòu" ("left and right"). Given the inherent consistency between corpus study methodology and the fundamental principles of cognitive linguistics. Namely, people comprehend word usage by observing how words are employed in phrases, sentences, and other contextual environments. Researchers are now able to perform more nuanced analyses of synonyms' semantic structures and usage patterns. This is achieved by combining authentic linguistic data with advanced statistical tools.

Domestic scholars have conducted substantial studies on the semantic and usage variations within synonym groups. Zhang Jidong and Liu Ping (2005) propose a corpus-based approach for distinguishing synonyms, including methods such as analyzing frequency distribution differences across registers and identifying significant collocational patterns. Tang Jing and Lei Rong (2015) take the near-synonyms rob and steal as examples, employing cognitive linguistic theory to examine syntactic-semantic asymmetries between them. Wu Xiaofang and Xiao Kunxue (2016), grounded in cognitive linguistic theories of categorization and construal, combine corpus analysis to investigate the differentiation mechanisms among English walk-class near-synonyms. They argue that variations in these verbs primarily arise from different construal operations within the same basic-level category.

(3) **Studies of Polysemy**

Polysemy, as a universal phenomenon in human language, has long been a focal topic of study among scholars worldwide. According to Gries and Divjak (2009), the key challenges in polysemy studies primarily include: the prototypicality of senses in polysemous words; the degree of sense-distinctions in polysemous words; the net-representation of semantic relations in polysemous words; the semantics-morphosyntax interface. In the past decade, domestic scholars' studies of polysemy can be broadly categorized into three main approaches: studies on individual polysemous words; investigations into polysemy patterns within word classes; studies on constructional polysemy.

Studies of individual polysemous words represent the most substantial body of work among domestic scholars, with studies adopting diverse theoretical perspectives. For instance, Huang Yuehua (2012) employs the regular polysemy approach to construct the semantic network of the Chinese directional verb "guò", analyzing its derived meanings through both experiential bases and pragmatic processes. Hou Ruifen (2015) investigates the polysemy of "bù" in compound words, concluding that its multiple meanings stem primarily from its characteristics of "subjectivity", manifested specifically as "highlighting conflict" and "expressing euphemism". Zhu Yan (2016) conducts a meticulous analysis of the polysemous system of the Chinese verb "gǎn" using image schemata, demonstrating the crucial role of image schemata in semantic categorization. Liu Hui and Yu Linlong (2019) examine the polysemy of the Chinese noun "shí jiān" within the Lexical Concepts and Cognitive Models (LCCM) framework, validating their findings through corpus-based collocational and semantic preference analysis.

Some scholars have investigated polysemy within specific word classes. Peng Yi and Bai Jiehong (2010) explore the polysemy of adjectives, arguing that the interpretative differences between domestic and international scholars primarily stem from divergent research perspectives and analytical levels. Peng Yuhai and Yu Xin (2013) analyze the cognitive metaphorical mechanisms underlying meaning extension in Russian mental verbs from the perspectives of cognitive similarity and semantic misplacement. Other researchers have examined constructional polysemy. Wu Weishan (2012), adopting a cognitive-functional grammar approach, analyzes three sub-types of the "NP-patient + VP-transitive + QM" construction in Modern Chinese, demonstrating their shared constructional motivation. Zhang Xiufang (2014) investigates the cognitive basis for the polysemy of the "V-lái-V-qù" construction, proposing that the semantic extension derives from the reduplicative verb pattern, and the aspectual and quantificational schemata formed by grammaticalized directional verbs "lái" and "qù". Yu Jianliang (2017) applies prototype categorization theory to syntactic constructions, clarifying two fundamental types of event-based constructions and usage-based constructions while revealing their distinct meaning-generation mechanisms.

3. **Studies of Lexical Semantic Processing**

In international studies, lexical semantic processing encompasses studies on second language acquisition and factors influencing automatic semantic recognition and processing. Such studies frequently employ psychological experimental software and instruments like DMDX, E-Prime, and eye trackers to analyze learners' lexical processing mechanisms. The author conducted a search in the CNKI database for core journals and CSSCI-indexed publications from 2010 to 2019 using "lexical semantic processing" as the key term, identifying 228 relevant articles. A comprehensive analysis of this decade-long research yields the following conclusions. First, regarding lexical processing, studies primarily focus on: specific words, idioms, or word classes; collocational patterns; bilingual/multilingual comparisons; lexical activation mechanisms; mental lexicon establishment. Second, in pragmatics and discourse analysis, there has been increasing studies conducting logical and cognitive analyses of lexical processing. Third, lexical processing study demonstrates clear interdisciplinary tendencies, showing strong integration with fields like linguistics, psychology, second language acquisition, translation studies, foreign language teaching, and cross-linguistic studies. Particularly noteworthy is its close integration with cognitive science and psycholinguistics, such as applying eye-tracking technology to language testing and translation studies. Within this domain, the study examining lexical semantic processing from cognitive science and psycho-linguistic perspectives has grown significantly. Representative scholars in this field include Zhang Jijia, Wu Shiyu, and their respective study teams.

Zhang Jijia and his team mainly explored semantic processing methods from the perspective of psychology, combining psychological experiments and cognitive linguistic knowledge, and have produced numerous publications in this field. Zhang Jijia and Lu Aitao (2010) employ a picture-word congruency judgment experiment to investigate the automatic activation of phonology and orthography in the semantic processing of action pictures and their temporal courses. They find that during picture representation, the activation of verb phonology occurred earlier than orthographic activation. Zhang Jijia et al. (2014) utilize a semantic priming paradigm and category judgment experiment to examine the saturation effect in semantic processing among Chinese-English bilinguals, with results supporting the theory that semantic saturation effects occur at the stage of linking word forms to semantics. Wang Juan and Zhang Jijia (2016) adopt behavioral experiments and eye-tracking technology to investigate the influence of semantic radical category consistency and family size on semantic processing of pictophonetic characters, discovering that the role of semantic radical family features is modulated by the category consistency between the semantic radical and the whole character. Wang Xinxiao et al. (2017) employ an embodied cognition paradigm to examine spatial and weight metaphors in the semantic processing of words for peers and relatives, comparing the concepts of seniority and cultural differences between the Korean and Han ethnic groups.

Wu Shiyu and her team's study focuses on exploring vocabulary processing methods in the field of second language acquisition. Wu Shiyu and Ma Zheng (2015) conduct a cross-modal priming experiment to investigate the role of inhibitory mechanisms in second language vocabulary processing, verifying the "facilitation without inhibition" effect observed in previous semantic integration experiments in second language listening comprehension, and thereby analyzing the allocation process of learners' cognitive resources. Wu Shiyu and Yang Feng (2016) further study the "cross-word interference effect" in second language vocabulary processing, helping second language learners and their teachers understand the root causes of the "foreign language listening syndrome" and the organization of the second language mental lexicon as well as second language reading disabilities. Wu Shiyu et al. (2017), within the theoretical framework of the revised hierarchical model, investigate the development patterns of vocabulary and conceptual representation for Chinese English learners at different learning stages, discovering that lexical association remains a crucial channel for Chinese English learners in processing word meanings.

4. **Cross-Linguistic Contrastive Studies of Lexical Semantics**

Cross-linguistic contrastive studies of lexical semantics is a classic topic in lexical semantics. In the past decade, most domestic scholars have mainly focused on the comparison between English and Chinese, addressing two major areas: lexical morphology and lexical semantics, which encompass research on vocabulary, its development and evolution, word formation, word meaning, lexical/semantic relationships, and morphemes. Within the trend of conducting English-Chinese contrastive studies of word meaning based on linguistic theories, studies utilizing cognitive linguistic theories have gradually increased. For example, Mao Haiyan (2010), from the perspective of frame semantics, explores the methods and procedures of English-Chinese lexical contrast by comparing the semantics of emotional frame vocabulary in both languages, thereby constructing a model for lexical semantic contrast. Jia Dongmei and Lan Chun (2010), based on conceptual metaphor theory and the principled polysemy analysis approach in cognitive lexical semantics, conduct a comparative analysis of the prototypical and extended meanings of "water" in English and Chinese, presenting their similarities and differences in meaning, conceptual elaboration, and grammatical structure through semantic extension network diagrams. Sun Chengjiao (2015), based on Talmy's lexicalization pattern theory, compares English and Chinese hand verbs related to "taking" and concluded that the lexicalization degree in Chinese is lower than in English, while also demonstrating that both English and Chinese lexicalization patterns follow the "action + manner/cause" structure. Lu Weizhong (2015) constructs a theoretical framework for contrastive cognitive lexical semantics, elucidating the theoretical foundations, content methods, and future directions of this discipline. Zhang Weiyou's (2010) *A Comparative Study of English and Chinese Lexicon* analyzes various aspects of English-Chinese lexical contrast through four sections: an overview of English-Chinese lexical contrast research, a comparison of morphological structures, a comparison of lexical meanings, and a comparison of English and Chinese idioms, covering a wide range of content. Feng Guoxin's (2016) *A Comparative Study of Chinese and English Lexicon*, based on the Chinese character-centered theory, conducts a comparative study on fundamental issues of Chinese and English words, such as the nature of words, their structure and definition, word formation, and compound words. This book emphasizes examining lexical phenomena from the perspective of differences between Chinese and English, with a focus on Chinese lexical phenomena. Shao Bin's (2019) *A Comparative Study of English and Chinese Lexicon* is a new work in the field of lexical contrast study. This book comprehensively reviews the development trajectory and methods of English-Chinese lexical contrast study, with a particular focus on the comparative analysis of morphological and semantic differences between English and Chinese words.

Besides the comparison between English and Chinese, there have also been numerous achievements in lexical semantics studies involving Chinese and other languages. For example, Sun Shufang (2015), based on Russian semantic theories, applies cutting-edge ideas and methodologies from Western semantic studies to conduct a comparative analysis of lexical semantic phenomena in Russian and Chinese, thereby uncovering both commonalities and distinctive features in lexical semantics between the two languages. Li Meixiang (2015), from the perspective of holistic word meaning, takes the homographic verbs "chǔ lǐ" (deal with) and "zhěng lǐ" (arrange) in Chinese and Korean as examples to compare and analyze the semantic correspondence of homographic words in Chinese and Korean from the angles of word meaning, typical collocation semantic categories, and corresponding translations. She was the first to propose a research approach that integrates multiple factors to measure the semantic correspondence degree of homographic words in Chinese and Korean, as well as a method for classifying semantic correspondence levels.

2.3.4 The Main Methods of Lexical Semantics Studies

Traditional lexical semantic studies primarily employed introspection. To overcome the limitations of introspection, there has been a usage-based empirical shift in cognitive linguistic studies (Geeraerts, 2006). In recent years, this shift has led to a substantial number of empirical studies in cognitive lexical semantics, mainly including corpus-based study method and experimental method (Wu Shuqiong, 2019).

1. **Corpus-Based Study Method**

In linguistic studies, lexical semantics is likely the field where the corpus method is most extensively utilized (Gries, 2010). The main assumptions underlying corpus-based study in lexical semantics are as follows: the distributional characteristics of a linguistic form reflect its semantic and functional properties. There are typically two corpus-driven study methods for word meaning studies: collocation analysis and feature analysis (Glynn & Robinson, 2014).

Collocation analysis is based on observable formal structures, aiming to identify the co-occurrence characteristics of these linguistic forms within a given sample and use them as indices for understanding their meaning structures. Collocation study is a mainstream study method in corpus linguistics, focusing on the co-occurrence features of linguistic forms in naturally occurring language. The renowned father of lexical collocation study, Firth (1957: 12), once stated, "You shall know a word by the company it keeps". In other words, the meaning of a word is reflected in the words it co-occurs with. Based on this, collocation analysis primarily examines the strength of the association between a target word and its co-occurring words. Among these methods, collostructional analysis (CA) (Gries & Stefanowitsch, 2004a, 2004b; Stefanowitsch & Gries, 2003) belongs to this study approach. This method mainly employs quantitative techniques such as Fisher's exact test to reveal the strength of the association between co-occurring morphemes in one or more slots of a construction and the construction itself. It examines the degree to which semantic slots in a construction attract or repel lexical items, thereby exploring the meaning of the construction or the differences in meaning between similar constructions. Collostructional analysis includes collexeme analysis (Stefanowitsch & Gries, 2003), distinctive collexeme analysis (Gries & Stefanowitsch, 2004a), and covarying collexeme analysis (Gries & Stefanowitsch, 2004b). Collostructional analysis primarily involves creating a contingency table from the co-occurrence frequencies of constructions and verbs, comparing the observed frequency of a verb in the target construction with its expected frequency, and quantifying the significance of the difference to explain the strength of collocation or the degree of association between the construction and the verb. Applying collostructional analysis to statistically determine the strength of collocation between constructions and verbs helps identify the prototypical verbs of constructions and summarize their prototypical semantics (Zhang Dong, 2019). Therefore, this method has gradually gained attention in the field of lexical semantics.

Feature analysis is a quantitative analytical method. This method employs corpus-based study approaches, utilizing manual analysis techniques combined with multivariate statistics to obtain usage features of words. Originating with Geeraerts et al. (1999) and Stefanowitsch and Gries (2003), this method does not have a long history in mainstream corpus linguistics but is widely applied in the field of cognitive linguistics. Divjak and Gries (2006) and Gries and Divjak (2009) refer to this method as the "corpus-based behavioral profile approach" (BP for short), while Glynn (2009) calls it "multifactorial usage feature analysis". Feature analysis typically involves four steps: (1) retrieving all instances of a word from a corpus; (2) manually analyzing and annotating the features of each category of words in the concordance, referred to as ID tags, including morphological (tense, aspect, mood, person, number, etc.), syntactic (sentence type, clause type, modifiers, etc.), semantic (types of nominal arguments, types of verbal arguments, etc.), and other features (acceptability, collocation, etc.); (3) transforming this data into a co-occurrence frequency table that includes the relative frequency of each word co-occurring with each ID tag, where the vector of co-occurrence proportions for each word constitutes its behavioral profile; (4) analyzing the contents of the table using statistical methods. Compared to past corpus-based research methods, feature analysis employs statistical techniques such as cluster analysis, correspondence analysis, regression analysis, and multi-dimensional scaling analysis to quantify and analyze corpus data, and presents the results visually using visualization technologies, thereby revealing subtle differences between variables and enhancing the reliability of research conclusions. In recent years, this method has been widely used to analyze synonymy (e.g., Divjak, 2010; Liu, 2013), polysemy (e.g., Glynn & Robinson, 2014; Jansegers & Gries, 2017), and antonymy (e.g., Gries & Otani, 2010; Paradis et al., 2015). The corpus-based behavioral profile approach reflects the usage-based view of language in cognitive linguistics and has gradually become one of the main methods in lexical semantic studies (Wu Shuqiong & Liu Dilin, 2020).

In domestic studies over the past decade, there has been a gradual increase in the use of corpus-based methods to study word meanings, primarily encompassing review articles and empirical applications. In review articles, scholars such as Zhang Weiwei and Liu (2015), Zhang Weiwei and Liu Nian (2016), Fang Yinjie (2016), Xu Jiajin (2020), and Wu Shuqiong and Liu Dilin (2020) have introduced the concepts and methods of multi-factorial analysis. Among these, Xu Jiajin (2020) systematically introduces multi-factorial analysis from the perspectives of its origins in probabilistic multi-factorial contextual co-selection research, its main study topics, statistical methods, current status, and future prospects. Wu Shuqiong and Liu Dilin (2020) elaborate on the background, theoretical foundations, and operational processes of behavioral profile analysis, introduce relevant research in lexical semantics, and evaluate its strengths and weaknesses. Hu Jian and Zhang Jiayi (2012), Fang Yinjie (2018), and Zhang Dong (2019), among others, have written articles introducing the constructional collocation analysis method. Hu Jian and Zhang Jiayi (2012) are the first to provide a systematic introduction to constructional collocation analysis, outlining its background, main analytical methods, advantages, and relevant application studies. Zhang Dong (2019), based on corpus-based quantitative research in construction grammar, focuses on argument structure constructions, elaborating on the principles and application value of corpus-based quantitative methods such as constructional collocation analysis and multi-factorial analysis, highlighting issues in their relationship with usage frequency and prototypicality, as well as statistical methods, and proposes a study approach that integrates corpus methods, experimental methods, and introspection for multi-angle cross-validation. In addition to introductory articles, empirical study in corpus-based cognitive semantics by Chinese scholars has also gradually emerged, including the study findings of scholars such as Shao Bin et al. (2012), Tian Zhen (2012), Fang Zichun and Chen Jianlin (2014), Shao Bin and Wang Wenbin (2014), Shao Bin et al. (2017), Yang Lili (2020), and Tian Xiaoyu and Zhang Weiwei (2020). For example, Shao

Bin et al. (2012) use a corpus-based approach to quantitatively analyze the usage patterns of English "carbon family compounds" and provide an in-depth explanation of the results from a cognitive metaphorical perspective, exploring the feasibility of corpus-based cognitive semantic research. Shao Bin and Wang Wenbin (2014) treat "-friendly" as an emerging affix, conducting quantitative and qualitative analyses of the word-formation power, semantics, and evolution of N-friendly based on the Contemporary American English Corpus (COCA), and explore the cognitive mechanisms behind this evolution using a constructional morphology framework. Fang Zichun and Chen Jianlin (2014) use the behavioral profile analysis method to compare and analyze the semantic and usage differences among six synonymous adjectives meaning "huge" (immense, enormous, huge, massive, tremendous, and vast), focusing on their collocational patterns with nouns, predicative usage, and register distribution. Shao Bin et al. (2017) use constructional collocation analysis to examine the association strength between English adjectives and the "intensifier + adjective" construction, and visually presented the semantic distribution differences of superlatives through cluster analysis and correspondence analysis. Tian Xiaoyu and Zhang Weiwei (2020) enrich the study of Chinese analytical causative constructions and variations in Chinese varieties by examining syntactic, semantic, and language variety factors influencing the choice of causative verbs "shǐ", "lìng", and "ràng" within a cross-linguistic variant corpus, using multinomial logistic regression. Yang Lili (2020) conducts a case study on "cause-purpose" constructions in Chinese, analyzing the constructional meaning, frequency differences among synonymous constructions "chū yú X", "wèi le X qǐ jiàn", and "wèi X ér Y", and establishes framework semantic relations between different schematic slots within the same construction.

2. **Experimental Method**

As one of the empirical study methods, the psychological experimental method, although not as widely used as the corpus method, has long been regarded as a common study approach in cognitive linguistics (Geeraerts, 2006). In the field of lexical semantics, early researchers who employed the psychological experimental method include Deese (1965), Gross et al. (1989), and Sandra and Rice (1995), among others. "The psychological experimental method has the advantages of being relatively objective, reliable, and verifiable" (Zhong Shouman & Wu Anping, 2015: 10), and can provide data for linguistic description that is closest to natural language processing. Currently, scholars mainly utilize psychological experimental software and instruments such as DMDX, E-prime, and eye trackers to study the processes of lexical recognition, processing, and learning.

In recent years, in addition to the psychological experimental method, the neuro-experimental method has also gained attention from scholars abroad. Among them, Event-Related Potentials (ERP) and functional Magnetic Resonance Imaging (fMRI) are commonly used study tools. Through a literature survey conducted on CNKI, the author finds that the number of study outcomes applying the neuro-experimental method to the study of word meaning has gradually increased. Zhang Yu et al. (2012) use ERP technology, employing a semantic priming experimental paradigm, to investigate the cognitive processes and neural mechanisms underlying the semantic processing of familiar and unfamiliar idioms. The results indicate that the familiarity of idioms significantly influences their processing. Wang Tao and Yang Yiming (2017) utilize fMRI technology, employing a picture-naming task, with 18 highly proficient Chinese-English bilinguals as participants, to study the neural mechanisms of noun and verb processing in Chinese-English bilinguals. Yu Jue and Zhang Hui (2019), from the perspectives of contextual expectation and semantic integration, employ ERP technology to explore the neural mechanisms of high-proficiency and low-proficiency learners in processing English phrasal verbs. The experiment shows that the neural cognitive mechanisms related to high-proficiency learners are still not fully developed, while those related to low-proficiency learners need to be established, indicating that second language proficiency influences the neural mechanisms of learners in processing phrasal verbs. These studies suggest that experimental methods are gradually gaining attention in domestic research on word meaning and have broad development prospects.

2.4 The Future Direction of Lexical Semantics Studies

2.4.1 Interdisciplinary Shift in Lexical Semantics Studies

Dabrowska and Divjak (2019) point out that cognitive linguistics has undergone an interdisciplinary shift, with increasing attention from the academic community on cross-disciplinary studies with linguistic typology. The complementarity between cognitive linguistics and linguistic typology has led to their mutual reinforcement and gradual integration, giving rise to a new discipline in language studies known as cognitive typology (Chen Lixia & Sun Chongfei, 2012). Cognitive typology integrates the theoretical assumptions of cognitive linguistics with the strengths of formal description in linguistic typology, based on the theoretical foundation of the relationship between cognitive conceptual spaces and cross-linguistic forms, and is dedicated to explaining differences and commonalities in cross-linguistic form-meaning relationships (Yu Xiujin & Jin Lixin, 2019).

The study goal of lexical typology is to reveal universal characteristics at the level of semantic representation in lexical systems from a cross-linguistic perspective. Lexical typology study primarily proceeds from the following three perspectives (Koptjevskaja-Tamm, 2012): (1) the semasiological perspective, which examines which meanings or features can be encoded as independent lexical items and the differences in how the lexical systems of different languages encode the same cognitive domain; (2) the onamasiological perspective, which investigates the relationships between word meanings and the semantic derivation paths among these meanings; (3) the perspective of the interaction between lexicon and grammar, which examines the syntactic representation and syntactic encoding of vocabulary in specific semantic domains. Currently, foreign lexical typology study mainly focuses on basic conceptual words such as kinship terms, color terms, body part terms, and motion verbs, and explores their universal tendencies and individual characteristics through cross-linguistic comparisons. In domestic studies, there were more studies on syntax from the perspective of linguistic typology in the past, while studies on word meaning have been relatively scarce. In recent years, numerous research achievements in lexical typology have emerged. They primarily explore typological characteristics of onamasiological expressions (i.e., one meaning, multiple forms) from a cross-linguistic perspective, based on the interaction between lexicon and grammar, to illustrate the lexical characteristics of Chinese. However, there has been less exploration of lexical typological features from the semasiological perspective (i.e., one form, multiple meanings).

The international academic community has achieved significant results by adopting the cognitive typology approach, with research objects encompassing both words and sentences. Among these studies on lexicon, Talmy is one of the representative scholars. He proposes that within the realm of lexical patterns, languages can be categorized into verb-framed languages and satellite-framed languages (Li Fuyin, 2017). In China, few scholars have delved into cognitive typology, which is still in the stage of being reviewed and introduced, with limited empirical studies. Only Zhang Li (2010) has conducted an analysis of the Chinese particle "le" from the perspective of cognitive typology, drawing on Japanese characteristics. Therefore, within an interdisciplinary framework, as cognitive typology study continues to deepen and expand, there is substantial room for growth in the cross-disciplinary studies between cognitive typology and lexical semantics.

2.4.2 Social Turn in Lexical Semantics Studies

With the emergence of the social turn in cognitive linguistics, lexical semantics studies have also embarked on a social turn. The social turn in cognitive linguistics primarily follows two major study paths: cognitive sociolinguistics and sociocognitive linguistics (Divjak et al., 2016; Wen Xu, 2019).

Cognitive sociolinguistics, a fusion of sociolinguistics and cognitive linguistics, is dedicated to providing a more rational and productive analytical framework for issues of concern in sociolinguistics (such as language variation and variant studies) from a cognitive linguistic perspective (Wen Xu, 2019). Cognitive sociolinguistics primarily focuses on language variants, lexical variation, and their cognitive representations (Geeraerts, 2010; Kristiansena & Dirven, 2008), and explores the reasons behind language variation from sociolinguistic perspectives such as cross-linguistic communities, cross-regional, and cross-cultural angles. Lexical variation is one of the important study areas in cognitive sociolinguistics, encompassing three main aspects (Geeraerts, 2015): (1) semasiological variation, where the same linguistic form expresses different meanings in different dialects; (2) formal onamasiological variation, where different forms are used to express the same conceptual category;

(3) conceptual onamasiological variation, where different conceptual categories are chosen to refer to the same entity. Currently, many foreign scholars study lexical variation from a sociolinguistic perspective. For example, Robinson (2010) establishes a correspondence between polysemous components and social variables using the adjective "awesome" as an example, demonstrating the variability and dynamics of word meanings and proving the advantages of integrating cognitive linguistics and sociolinguistics in explaining polysemous categories. Ho-Abdullah (2010) conducts a comparative study on the variations of the prepositions "at", "in", and "on" in Malaysian English, New Zealand English, and British English based on cognitive linguistic theories. In domestic studies, the intersection of lexical semantics and sociolinguistics is mainly reflected in studies on variant vocabulary such as buzzwords, advertising language, gender appellations, public signs, and dialects. In the integrative studies of cognitive linguistics and sociolinguistics, Zhang Tianwei (2019) conducts a literature survey within the CNKI and finds that there are more introductory and review articles on cognitive sociolinguistics, while empirical research articles are scarce. Therefore, he proposes that there are still many gaps in domestic sociolinguistic studies at this stage. According to the viewpoint put forward by Fang Na and Zhang Weiwei (2015) that "language variants and language contact are the most widely studied topics in cognitive sociolinguistics", Zhang Tianwei (2019) believes that conducting diachronic and synchronic analyses of the contact phenomena between Chinese dialects and foreign languages from the perspective of cognitive sociolinguistics will be new highlights. Similarly, studies on Chinese lexical variants from the perspective of cognitive sociolinguistics is also a new trend in cognitive sociolinguistics and lexical semantics studies.

Sociocognitive linguistics is a combination of social cognitive theory and cognitive linguistics, dedicated to studying "conceptualization in the social domain" by revealing various social interaction processes involved in meaning generation and construction (Harder, 2010: 408). Its aim is to describe social interaction mechanisms, i.e., how language use shapes linguistic knowledge at the speaker and hearer levels (Divjak et al., 2016). These mechanisms are rooted in general social cognitive abilities such as joint action, coordination, and convention (Croft, 2009). Sociocognitive linguistics primarily addresses two questions: first, the representation of sociocognitive functions in language; second, the sociocognitive mechanisms underlying language acquisition, use, and evolution. Its study content mainly encompasses four aspects: conceptualization of sociocognitive functions, language acquisition, language use, and language evolution (Wen Xu, 2019). Sociocognitive linguistics strives to provide new explanations for issues of concern in cognitive linguistics (such as conceptual structure, semantics, and grammar) from a sociocognitive perspective, seeking new breakthroughs for the development of cognitive linguistic theories and offering better insights for the social turn in cognitive linguistics. Currently, compared to sociocognitive linguistics, there is more studies conducted from the perspective of cognitive sociolinguistics, with relatively fewer studies in sociocognitive linguistics. Given sociocognitive linguistics' focus on social factors in the conceptualization process of language and its explanatory power, it is bound to play a significant role in the study of word meaning.

2.4.3 The Empirical and Quantitative Turn in Lexical Semantics Studies

With the widespread application and continuous development of corpus-based methods and experimental methods, there has emerged an empirical turn in lexical semantic research. Given the advantages, disadvantages, and complementarity of these two methods, the future study trend lies in the cross-disciplinary integration of two or more methods, namely the cross-over use of corpus-based methods and experimental methods.

Although corpus-based methods and experimental methods each have their own advantages, they also come with respective disadvantages: corpus-based methods are primarily used to uncover word usage patterns, but the general use of frequency distribution has inherent flaws (Gries & Deshors, 2014) and cannot explain the underlying motivations; experimental methods are mainly used to reveal the motivations behind word usage, but their experimental materials are often based on artificial selections from researchers' personal introspection (Gilquin & Gries, 2009), which raises doubts about the consistency between study findings and actual language use (Fang Yinjie & Liang Maocheng, 2020). Currently, some scholars advocate combining corpus-based methods with psychological experimental methods to compensate for each other's shortcomings and provide converging evidence for cognitive studies on language (e.g., Gilquin & Gries, 2009). Fang Yinjie and Liang Maocheng (2020) summarize that this integration manifests in three types: (1) conducting corpus and experimental analyses on different linguistic materials separately, and then elaborating on their similarities and differences; (2) selecting test materials from high-frequency corpora to conduct experiments, attempting to explain the correlation between frequency information and cognitive entrenchment; (3) extracting typical sentences from large-scale corpora based on multi-factorial statistical models, using them as test materials for experimental tasks, and then conducting comparative analyses of the two approaches. In the study of word meaning, many foreign scholars have integrated corpus-based methods and experimental methods to study vocabulary, such as Arppe and Järvikivi (2007) on synonymous verbs and Liu (2013) on synonymous nouns. Arppe et al. (2012: 3) point out, "In order to seek a comprehensive understanding of language, we need to integrate different study methods to analyze various aspects of language behavior and language knowledge". Therefore, based on the development of corpus-based and experimental methods, the future direction of lexical semantic research is the mutual reference and cross-over use of these two or multiple methods, thereby providing converging evidence for lexical semantic research.

Currently, in China, there are still relatively few study achievements on the cross-over use of corpus-based methods and psychological or neuroscientific experimental methods applied to the study of Chinese word meanings, but an upward trend can be observed. The author conducts an exhaustive search on CNKI for studies that integrate corpus-based and experimental methods, with the following results: Deng Yu et al. (2015) examine the lexicalization patterns of metaphorical motion events in modern Chinese by synthesizing evidence from corpus-based and experimental studies; Lu Jun (2017) employs a combination of corpus data analysis and psychological experiments to explore the implicit and explicit characteristics of second language (L2) collocation knowledge, focusing on typical L2 collocations; Lv Jun and Wu Fuyun (2017) analyze the positional preferences of measure words in Chinese relative clauses by integrating Japanese-Chinese L2 corpora and production experiments; Zhang Di et al. (2020) utilize both corpus-based and experimental methods to investigate the acquisition of modal particles "la" and "ba" at the end of sentences by young children, as well as the relationship between these particles, selective trust, and vocabulary learning; Fang Yinjie and Liang Maocheng (2020) take Chinese students' choices of relative pronouns as the study object, conducts binary logistic regression analysis on large-scale corpora, and carries out experimental studies to explore the prototypical and probabilistic nature of language knowledge in Chinese students' use of relative clauses involving relative pronoun choices.

Empirical quantitative study is a major focus in the field of lexical semantics. Among empirical quantitative study methodologies, the integration of two or more approaches, specifically the cross-disciplinary study combining corpus-based methods with psychological or neuroscientific experimental methods, has emerged as a future study trend in lexical semantics. This trend of cross-disciplinary integration among multiple methodologies will inject more vitality into lexical semantics studies.

2.5 Conclusion

The primary task of semantics is to study and analyze the meanings of words and the relationships between these meanings (Xu Yulong, 2010). Cognitive semantics has opened up new avenues for the study of lexical semantics and is currently the most productive study framework in this field (Geeraerts, 2010). In the past decade, lexical semantics studies within the cognitive semantics paradigm have been the mainstream, primarily involving four major topics: the interface study between lexical semantics and syntactic semantics, the study of word meaning relationships, the study on the semantic processing of vocabulary, and the cross-linguistic comparative study of lexical semantics. In addition to the traditional introspective method, corpus research methods and experimental methods have gradually become new trends in lexical semantics studies. Based on a review of previous study findings, this chapter points out the future directions of lexical semantics studies: the interdisciplinary shift, the social shift, and the empirical quantitative shift in lexical semantics studies.

Chinese possesses unique characteristics in terms of linguistics and culture, and its diachronic textual accumulation spans thousands of years, with a richness unmatched by Western languages. Therefore, Chinese scholars are fully capable of making unique and irreplaceable contributions in the field of lexical studies (Shao Bin, 2014).

In view of this, this chapter reviews and summarizes the disciplinary status, study content, and study methods of domestic lexical semantics over the past decade, and predicts its study trends, with the aim of providing certain inspiration and reference for future lexical semantics studies and related semantics studies.

Chapter 3
Sentence Semantics Studies

3.1 Introduction

Semantics is a significant branch of linguistics and it primarily studies the meaning of linguistic expressions. Linguistic expressions include vocabulary and sentences. According to the categories of linguistic expressions, phrases can be classified as vocabulary. And semantics can be divided into lexical semantics and sentence semantics. Sentence semantics is closely related with lexical semantics but they are different. Lexical semantics primarily studies the meaning of a single word and the semantic relations among words. While sentence semantics studies the semantic structure of a sentence on the basis of single word's meaning and the syntactic roles these words play in sentences. Sentence semantics serves as the transitional study developing from lexical semantics and initiating super sentence semantics or discourse semantics. Therefore, sentence semantics is fundamental to studying well discourse semantics. The relationship between sentence meaning and word meaning has been an essential issue in semantics. One of their distinctions lies in productivity. Specifically, very few new words are created while new sentences can be created frequently. Sentence meaning cannot be listed into the dictionary just as word meaning. Sentence meaning is usually described as having the characteristic of compositionality. Namely, the meaning of an expression depends on the meaning of its components and the ways these expressions combine together. In the grammatical model, meaning exists in two forms: relatively stable word meaning in a word bank and countless compositional meanings of sentences. Chomsky proposes that syntactic structure is responsible for the interaction between word meaning in a word bank and compositional meanings of sentences.

X. Wen and R. Tang, *New Perspectives and Developments in Chinese Semantics*,
https://doi.org/10.1007/978-981-95-1730-5_3

3.2 Current Conditions of Sentence Semantics Studies at Home and Abroad

Studies of lexical semantics have a long history and have achieved fruitful accomplishments. But studies of sentence semantics began rather late. Until the 1980s, there was a specialized monograph on sentence semantics, *German Sentence Semantics* (1988) authored by German linguist Von· Polenz. In China, the monograph titled *Sentence Semantics* was published by Si Lianhe in 2010. Sentence has been a focal topic in modern semantic studies. Meanwhile, though it is phrases that people utter or receive when they engage in social interactions, they understand each other through the unit medium of sentence. That is to say, sentence is the basic unit of interpersonal interactions. It is of significant theoretical value and practical use to study sentence semantics. It not only enriches the content of disciplines such as semantics, pragmatics, text linguistics, and communication studies, but also be significantly meaningful for studies of language teaching, literature, computer understanding linguistics, and artificial intelligence.

Sentence meaning is currently a focal issue of studies of semantics, especially studies of sentence semantics at home and abroad. Leech (1983) proposes predication analysis methodology to analyze sentence meaning. Lyons (1995) analyzes both meaningful and meaningless sentences, the content of sentence meaning and propositions as well as the grammaticalization of sentence meaning. He employs positivism and truth-conditional theory to explain the relations between sentence meaning and propositions, and explains Katz·Fodor theory and Montague theory concerning sentence meaning grammaticalization. Hudson (2005) discusses the compositional and non-compositional meanings, semantic roles, grammatical relations in sentence meaning in a quite general way, which therefore calls for further studies.

Jia Yande (1999) expounds on sentence meaning's structure, categories, formation and performance, analytical basis and procedures, as well as the sememe collocation of sentence meanings, and relations between various sentence meanings. Considering inherent relations between langue-level sentences and parole-level sentences, Guo Yukai (1996) defines the structure of sentence meaning as two major parts: abstract meaning and communicative meaning. Peng Yuhai (1997) defines the meaning structure of utterances embodying three levels: objective meaning, pragmatics, and language subject. The organic combination of semantic knowledge and practices forms the meaning unity of utterances. From perspectives of langue and parole, static and dynamic, their studies uncover the multiple-level system of sentence meanings and elucidate the generative mechanism of sentences' indirect meanings. Qiu Zhenqiang (2003) proposes that semantic clauses can be categorized into static and dynamic types. Lu Jianming (2004) posits that the syntactic structures certain lexical sequence can form and specific meanings they embody primarily depend on the meaning of certain words, namely the concept specific words represent and the interactive restrictions between each other.

Zhang Zhenhua and Yin Xianglin (1992) primarily review the linguistic schools that have significantly influenced the generation of sentence semantics. He Yingyu

(2003) recalls and reviews the accomplishments our country's foreign language scholars had attained in sentence semantics studies since 1978. He points out several defaults in the previous studies. Si Lianhe (2004) holds the view that the generation of sentence meaning is the blending of the meaning of sentence category format and the meaning of its constituents-semantic chunks. Si Lianhe and Zhang Weiping (2005) propose that studies of sentence meaning should not only become formal but also integrate with natural language well, therefore discovering solutions to resolving ambiguity. Lin Yi and Si Lianhe (2005) put forward the modularization theory of semantic competence, elucidate the primary content of sentence semantic competence, and propose approaches to measuring semantic competence. Si Lianhe (2007) posits that sentence meaning is the function composition of lexical meaning and structural meaning. Si Lianhe (2010) studies semantic categories of simple sentences and complex sentences from the perspective of hierarchical network of concepts.

3.3 General Overview of Sentence Semantics Studies over the Past Decade

3.3.1 Core Theories of Sentence Semantics Studies

John Lyons (1995) elucidates sentence meaning in a rather detailed way. He uses three chapters to discuss sentence meaning. The chapter "Meaningful Sentences and Meaningless Sentences" discusses relations between sentence meaning and propositions, arguing that positivism and truth-conditional theory are helpful for explaining such relations. He proposes to accurately distinguish between concepts such as grammatically suitable, meaningful or meaningless, and acceptable or unacceptable. The relations between sentences and propositions depend on the adopted meaning theory. Sentence meaning is the typical usage of this sentence and sentences represent propositions in a sense. He also talks about unreal meaning and sentimental theory, arguing that though the sentimental theory has been abandoned very early, Austin's speech act theory then arises. In terms of truth-conditional theory, he employs the concept of logic to discuss it and thinks that this theory has certain limitations. This is because some aspects of sentence meaning cannot be properly illustrated with standardized propositional logic.

He analyzes truth-functional conjunction and disjunction, implication, and negation and discusses thematic meaning. Artificial thematic meaning is utterance meaning and sentences with the same propositional content might have different thematic meanings. As to simple sentences and complicated sentences, he conducts certain analysis of sentence categories and moods, the meaning of some sentences. In formal semantics, he attaches focal attention to analyzing and discussing Katz-Fodor theory and Montague theory.

Katz-Fodor's sentence semantic theory is a little bit outdated in some sense. But this theory is the first one to elucidate sentence meaning, thereby deserving our attention. We have not yet found the way to determine the number of projection rules and the differences among them. Meanwhile, semantic expressions have also faced criticism from the fields of logic and philosophy. Semantic expression in this theory is actually a formal language and lexical units of this formal language need explanation. Additionally, some people think of semantic expressions as quite unnecessary. Because things can be done in a satisfying way through using interference rules related with meaning postulates instead of using semantic expressions.

Montague Grammar is a campaign of linguistic theory triggered by Montague's thoughts and it happened in the mid-1970s. This grammar employs semantic studies' conceptual equipment in the formal language to analyze natural language. In the domain of semantics, it is more appealing than Chomsky's transformational-generative grammar. And Montague grammar includes syntax and semantics, which have the one-to-one correspondence relation. Syntax is introduced by categorization rules defining syntactic categories to establish phrasal structure grammar. Relevant semantic rules employ truth-conditional predicative logic to form these sentences' propositional explanation. This methodology has conducted the work of revisions and expansions in several aspects. Distinctions between Montague Grammar and Katz-Fodor theory lie in the fact that Montague's monographs are deeply rooted in logic semantics. Montague's books seldom consider numerous pioneering themes that linguists concern and phonological expressions or inflections.

Leech's sentence semantic structure theory involves arguments and predicative. And predicative consists of different valencies. This theory discusses sememe analysis theory, predication analysis and subordinate predication's structural expression, and analyzes the phenomenon of degraded sentence. In conclusion, predication analysis provides meaning relations such as hyponymy and hypernym, and incompatibility as well as relations between basic statements such as implication, inconsistency, synonymous repetition and contradiction. However, predication analysis lacks logic elements and these logic elements involve predication that conducts statements to the real world. Predication isn't concerned with truth or falsehood just like propositions.

Jackendoff's conceptual semantics is a theory of meaning decomposition and its primary idea is that descriptive meaning deals with mental representation. This mental representation is called by Jackendoff as mentalism postulates and sentence meaning is conceptual construction. In his conceptual construction theory, meaning is the more abstract conceptual primitive, which is of great significance to analyzing semantic reasoning rules. Semantic decomposition can be employed to study the correspondence relation between semantics and syntax. Jackendoff has ensured several common categories of meaning: case, situation, agent, approach, location, and characteristics. He posits that as to hierarchical structure of concepts, sentence is composed of these semantic categories. Jackendoff's semantic theory is more powerful in explanation than Katz's because his theory explains the combination and insertion of meaning components not only in the level of words but also in the level of sentences.

Fillmore's Case Grammar and the subsequent development of Frame Semantics all deal with sentence meanings. From Case Grammar that developed in the end of the 1960s to Frame Semantics that developed in the post era of the 1970s, Fillmore's linguistic theory underwent quite substantial changes during the process of development. Case Grammar theory can be divided into "The First Phase of Case Grammar" and "The Second Phase of Case Grammar". Frame Semantics, developing from Case Grammar and inheriting fundamental ideas of Case Grammar, is a kind of systematic and specified Case Grammar Theory. Therefore, Frame Semantics can be seen as "The Third Phase of Case Grammar". There exist potential coherence and leapfrogging turning points permeating three phases of Case Grammar, which can be summarized as the pattern of "three one one two": one main line (verb-priority theory), one concept (frame), one breakthrough (from "case roles" to "situation participants"), and the two-story platform ("situation", "perspective domain"). This theory of the first phase expounds on the infeasibility of its core concept "deep case" from five levels: the uncertainty of deep case's total amount, the ambiguity of the definition, the overlapping parts between cases, the interference of context and difficulties of typology. This theory of the second phase proposes drawbacks and self-contradictory points of this theory from four different aspects: core components, the cognitive process of describing scenes (≠the process of utterance segments activating cognitive scenes during listening), aspects of noticeable different levels, and lexical characters. The third phase of frame semantics theory has its transcendence and deficiencies. In terms of transcendence, with "philosophy of experience" as its basis and "knowledge experience" as its driving force, frame semantics brings shock to traditional grammatical explanation and makes compensation for it. In terms of deficiencies, the framework is over-reliant on "cognition" to elucidate language, therefore exposing it to over-generalized risks and dangers whose similarities nearly cannot be summarized in aspects of human activities embodying cultural characteristics.

Huang Zengyang (1998) puts forward Hierarchical Network of Concepts (HNC). This theory attempts to understand natural language through instructing computers to mimic human brain's perceptive patterns of handling language. Sentence category analysis technology is this theory's application. One core concept in his theory is action-effect chain, namely the agent primitive concept. Its concept category symbol is Φ which is neglected in the mapping symbol. The first-level hierarchy symbol is 0–5 and high hierarchy number is 2. And the number-prefix symbol is 6 m = 0–5; 9; c. There are six links in the action-effect chain: 0, function; 1, process; 2, transference; 3, effect; 4, relation; 5, situation. He also adopts the concept of "semantic chunks", a subordinate semantic unit of sentences. Similarly, phrases belong to the subordinate semantic unit of sentences. Semantic chunks include primary chunks and subordinate ones. Based on six links and analytical concepts in the action-effect chain, he proposes simple sentences of basic categories and argues that complicated sentences are the parallel or combination of these simple sentences. With respect to every category of simple sentences, he distinguishes between common patterns and variant ones. Besides, he produces pattern expressions. However, these expressions are a little bit difficult to operate because of some concepts' ambiguity and the overlap between them.

3.3.2 Study Topics

We first find out study topics from National Social Science Fund (NSSF) projects concerning sentence semantics studies over the past decade and conduct discussions of several focal issues in sentence semantics.

3.3.2.1 Subjects from NSSF Projects Concerning Sentence Semantics over the Past Decade

In the past decade, subjects from NSSF Projects in Linguistics concerning sentence semantics studies can be summarized as follows.

There were altogether 16 subjects in 2010. The principal investigators of these subjects were: Li Jinglian, Zhang Keding, Liu Xiaolin, Wang Yong, Wang Zhenlai, Li Jinxia, Han Jingquan, Huang Jie, Li Xue, Fu Yu, Cao Jin, Song Zuoyan, Yu Guangwu, Luo Jinjun, Huang Caiyu, Li Jinman. This project investigated key subjects in Chinese linguistics, including hierarchical relations in marked complex sentences, ambiguous structures, relative clauses, control structures, spatial relation constructions, word order typology, syntactic functional features, preposition-marked sentence formation mechanism, similar complex sentence relational markers, unaccusative verbs, noun-noun compounds, lexicalization patterns of motion events, elliptical constructions, causative constructions, syntax-semantics interface, semantics of modal verbs, pragmatics-syntax interaction.

There were altogether 9 subjects in 2011. The principal investigators of the these subjects were: Li Jiongying, Xi Jianguo, He Wei, Deng Yunhua, Lu Weizhong, Ma Qinghua, Cheng Qilong, Qiu Wei, and Chang Hui. This project investigated key subjects in Chinese linguistics, including the Polish school of semantics and semantic metalanguage theory, word order, the representation of temporal systems, typology of sentence patterns, lexical comparison, sentence complexification, argument realization constructions, delexical constructions, and syntactic development patterns.

There were altogether 28 subjects in 2012. The principal investigators were Wu Yaqing, Guo Chunjie, Zhang Yan, Cheng Jie, Li Manliang, Jia Guanjie, Xiong Xueliang, Yang Chenghu, He Wenzhong, Lu Zhongyi, Gao Yuhua, Ye Jianjun, Zhou Changyin, Wu Yicheng, Zhang Bojiang, Zhang Guoxian, Song Xuan, Liang Ruiqing, Yu Jianping, Liu Guohui, Zhang Hong, Zhang Ding, Sun Tianqi, Zhang Jian, Si Luohong, Sun Daogong, Qiu Qingshan, and Xu Jiajin. The project encompassed multiple dimensions of linguistic inquiry, including generative typology, the syntax-semantics interface, and syntax-semantics interaction. They investigated parataxis-hypotaxis typological differences, noun phrase structures, and mental representation models of formulaic language. The study further examined compound structures, syntax-semantics interface, middle constructions, and the comprehension of negative sentences, equal comparison and simile patterns, construction blending, and resultative constructions constituted key analytical foci. The research explored the tripartite interaction between syntax, semantics, and pragmatics, along with morphosyntactic phenomena. Specific attention was given to the semantic information of modifiers, semantic transparency in compounds, and cognitive semantics of sensory vocabulary. The project incorporated intelligent disambiguation of polysemous words and dynamic lexicon-sentence-discourse integration. Core grammatical components under investigation included verb semantics-syntax mapping, indefinite pronouns, modal words with instrumental-comitative prepositions, and non-core arguments. The work analyzed complex sentence linkage patterns, sentence generation mechanisms, and advanced theoretical understanding in the syntax-semantics paradigm. Additional components involved lexical semantic research and the analysis of complex verb constructions.

There were altogether 33 subjects in 2013. The principal investigators were Peng Jiafa, Man Zaijiang, Gao Xiuxue, Li Fuyin, Zhou Shihong, Zhang Ren, Kuang Fangtao, Liu Wei, Wang Tianhua, Luo Siming, Wang Zhijun, Fan Li, Wang Huili, Liu Wenzheng, Zhang Xueping, Wu Yilan, Gao Zengxia, Liao Guangrong, Yu Shanzhi, Wu Fuyun, Zhang Tianwei, Wu Huaicheng, Li Wenhao, Ma Junjun, He Wenguang, Hu Quan, Chen Guohua, Lu Rong, Dong Zhengcun, Xuan Yue, Yan Litao, Xie Weiwei, and Liu Haiyan. The research encompassed a wide range of linguistic topics, including syntax-semantics interaction, clausal arguments, topic structures, typological studies of macro-event semantics, sentence information structure, dynamic argument structure, assertive constructions, cleft constructions, grammatical structures encoding evaluative meaning, nominal-adjectival quantificational constructions, verb-object collocations, the acquisition of argument structure, processing of relative clauses, causative pivotal verbs, irrealis modality in sentence grammar, word order typology and constructional patterns, serial verb constructions, deviations from normative linguistic patterns, form-meaning interactions in asymmetrical phenomena, demonstrative-quantifier structures, constraints on ellipsis, typological variations of event nominals, cognitively salient constructions, relative clauses and their semantic functions, mechanisms of semantic operation, correlative conjunctions in complex sentences, causative constructions, reversible sentence structures, constructional ellipsis, the verbal completive category, passive constructions (Bei-sentences), tonal modification in word formation, and logical semantics in sentential systems.

There were altogether 15 subjects in 2014. The principal investigators were Zhang Yan, Liu Jin, Wang Yiguang, Xiong Zhongru, Peng Lizhen, Zhang Shaojie, Li Ying, Du Yi, Wu Fengwen, Zheng Juanman, Li An, Wang Chong, Lu Shuo, Zhao Yanzhi, and Wang Hongming. Their research covered a broad spectrum of linguistic topics including causative usage, complex passive constructions (Bei-sentences), directional verb-complement structures, the syntax-semantics interface of adjectives, the syntactic and semantic dimensions of modality, grammar-pragmatics interactions, non-linear syntactic categories, perfective aspect particles, the syntax-semantics of complex sentences, pejorative idiomatic constructions, semantic composition, the categorical system of verb meaning, syntactic-semantic interaction models in noun phrases, as well as comparative studies on imperative sentences and constructions.

There were altogether 24 subjects in 2015. The principal investigators were Li Xuping, Li Wenchao, Chen Qi, Yang Shu, Tian Zhen, Zhao Linxiao, Zhao Yaqing, Wang Qian, Jia Yue, Guo Lijun, Liu Hui, Kan Zhehua, Shi Chunhong, Guo Yin, Cheng Lixia, Yang Ling, Si Lianhe, Yang Bingjun, Zhang Guohua, Xu Hai, Zhong Shuneng, Wang Honggang, Ma Zhigang, Tong Guobin, Liu Haiping, Lin Yan, Liu Xiaochuan, Wang Yanbin, Zuo Shuangju, Xue Hongwu, Zhang Yichun, Ma Hongcheng, Yan Hongju, Hu Deming, Zhao Jiangmin, Zhang Ping, Yu Xiujin, Liu Shili, Yu Xin, and Zhu Qingxiang. The project covered topics such as the syntax-semantics interface of numerals, resultative constructions, projective constructions, modality, automatic discrimination models of constructions, verb-copying sentences, condensed sentences, quantity-related constructions, morphological structures of static words, the Moscow Semantic School, the history of Western semantics, argument structure, construction grammar theory, ergative semantics and syntax, motion constructions, aspectual features of verbs, sentence meaning of simple sentences, non-finite clauses, the constructionalization and semantic expression of double-object structures, paradoxical constructions, fictive motion constructions, construction-centered pedagogical grammar models, distinctive sentence patterns, the V-Ding-N construction (Verb-Attributive-Noun Construction?), Chinese word order, the syntax-semantics interface of double-object constructions, directional categories, verb-quantifier pairings, transitivity changes of verbs, studies on the categories of "yǒu/shì/zài", patient-fronted structures, full-sentence functional categories, lexicalization patterns of compound words, the rhetorical question construction with "shén me", types of sentence meaning, syntax-semantics coupling, typology of tense-aspect categories, the interaction between syntax and semantics, sentence pattern comparisons, and clause dependency.

There were altogether 35 subjects in 2016. The principal investigators were Jia Yuan, Cheng Qilong, Liu Li, Zhou Tongquan, Zhou Junxun, Wu Zhenyu, Sui Na, Zhang Keding, Zhang Lifei, Li Yongzhong, Wen Weiping, Deng Yunhua, Ma Honghai, Chen Lianjun, Liu Shun, Wu Chang'an, Zhao Qian, Yang Chaojun, He Chuansheng, Luo Yixue, Feng Yuli, Luo Tianhua, Fu Yan, Bai Lan, Zhang Yuan, Zhu Minwen, Wang Liling, Cai Shumei, Zhong Ruiyi, Zhang Jinquan, Lu Chengfa, Li Rong, Lu Ping, Wang Yuan, and Zhao Xu. The project covered topics such as: interaction between syntax, semantics, and prosody, quantitative analysis of syntax-semantics interaction, complex sentences, special modifier-head constructions, verb evolution, verb semantic systems, syntax, semantics, and morphology of noun phrases, metaphorical spatial relation constructions, ditransitive constructions, quantifier structures, semantics of multiple negation, syntax and semantics of causal complex sentences, sentence pattern systems, compound words, syntax-semantics interface of noun decategorization features, embedded constructions, semantic relation types in compound word formation, impersonal constructions, syntax-semantics interface of numeral systems, explanation-effect sentences, quantification phenomena, yes–no questions, middle constructions, cleft sentences, antonym co-occurrence constructions, bonded complement constructions, psychological verbs, emergence of constructions, argument structure cartography, structure, function, and prosodic features of quotations, redundant negation, interaction between discourse and syntax, "Noun + Verb" modifier-head constructions, grammatical aspect, and serial verb constructions.

There were altogether 29 subjects in 2017. The principal investigators were He Xiaowei, Chang Hui, Liu Wenzheng, Qu Yunhua, Lu Junyu, Kong Lei, Xi Jianguo, Tang Jing'an, Mo Qiyang, Zhang Ling, Yu Shanzhi, Wang Li, Lu Qian, Lin Haiyun, Wu Ying, Si Luohong, Zhou Hong, Piao Zhenyu, Ding Jiayong, Li Yong, Cao Daogen, Zhang Zhanshan, Zhang Zeshun, Wang Changsong, Huangfu Sufei, Xiong Jianguo, Huang Xiaoxue, Wang Yong, and Liu Xiaolin. The project covered topics such as: grammatical competence, eye-tracking studies on syntactic structures, coercion and anti-coercion in constructions, sentence structure, event/entity mismatches, lexicalization of pragmatic markers in event semantics, word order universals and harmony, patient-fronted sentences, clause linkage, generic constructions, counter-factual structures, verb-object collocations, quantitative dependency syntax, semantic encoding of change-of-state events, subjectivization of qualitative adjectives, functional sentence centers, potential complement constructions, discourse report, word order typology, syntax and semantics of cleft structures, reference of semantic roles, predication of quantifier elements, deconstructions, "dé" structure, contracted construction clusters, denominalized verbs, word order in "Verb (+ Object) + Complement" structures, typology of existential sentences, evolution of syntactic types.

The year 2018 saw the completion of 30 significant research subjects led by distinguished scholars including Han Jingquan, Wang Wenbin, Niu Baoyi, Li Jiachun, Lü Guoying, Li Jinman, Xu Chunshan, Xu Xiaoqiong, Zhang Yi, Yang Liexiang, Rao Ping, Hu Xuhui, Hu Shen'ai, Liu Hongyu, Lei Dongping, Wang Jianjun, Deng Fei, Li Fuyin, Xu Shijing, Xiao Zhiye, Zhang Chengjin, Tian Yu, Xuan Yue, Li Yuan, Li Mingjing, Li Jinrong, Huang Aijun, Wu Yicheng, Wu Junming, and Zhi Xiaomin. The project covered topics such as syntax-semantics interface, spatiotemporal characteristics, verb-noun collocations, caused state change events, FrameNet semantics database, typologically distinctive constructions, covert syntactic patterns, left-dislocation structures of personal pronouns, the semantics-syntax interface, quantificational structures, incremental interpretation, neo-construction grammar theories, relative clauses, characteristics of "aspectual categories", constructionalization in Chinese, evolution of sentence types, syntactic systems, event integration principles of directional verbs, motivations for the diachronic evolution of conditional sentences, semantic shifts from discourse to description, lexicalization of non-morphological structural words, comparative constructions, basic semantic features of verbs, hierarchical structures of three-clause complex sentences, lexical aspect of verbs, "form-meaning mismatch" constructions, semantic studies of classifiers, non-compositional expressions, non-compositional expressions, complement clause structures and passive voice.

There were altogether 24 subjects in 2019. The principal investigators were Liu Zhengguang, Liu Yun, Xu Xinyuan, Wang Gang, Wang Honglei, Lü Mingchen,

Zeng Tao, Zhan Likan, Chen Songsong, Xing Fukun, Yang Jincai, Ma Zhigang, Zhou Xianwu, Zhang Hongxin, Tan Yilan, Lu Ying, Eerdunchaolu, Zhang Xuhong, Wu Yong, Sun Chongfei, Wang Xiaopei, Su Jing, Jiao Yihe, and Zhang Ping. The topics covered include syntactic-semantic relations, complex sentences and discourse types, unconventional sentence patterns, quantitative constructions, structural symmetry, relational semantics, syntax-semantics interface structures, unrealistic sentences, mismatch constructions, clauses, marked complex sentence relations, non-argument structures, entity category concepts, syntactic coordination models, word order contrast, emphatic expressions, verb semantic role pairing patterns, lexical-constructional integration and the mass conservation of transitive constructions, covert comparative constructions, form-meaning relation types, non-concatenative word formation, oblique object-verb structures, aspectual information expression methods, and the semantic-syntactic analysis of problematic sentences.

There were altogether 23 subjects in 2020. The principal investigators were Li Yanzhi, Yang Yanning, Yang Chenghu, Gao Hang, Wang Yina, Ma Shudong, Wu Jidong, Tong Helong, Zhao Wenchao, Deng Yunhua, Du Shihong, Wu Bingzhang, Zhang Xiaopeng, Chen Zhongyi, Zhu Xiujie, Cao Zhiguo, Wang Lulu, Li Xinliang, Zhang Xiaotao, Sun Daogong, Tang Xuri, Zhou Guanglei, and Zhang Huiping. The research topics involved semantic evolution and syntactic conventions, constructional change, argument structure reorganization, verbal quantity categories, modality of event delimitation, schematic convention patterns of force dynamics, the syntax-semantics interface of complex sentences, noun phrases, semantic representation of property-denoting phrases, unconventional verb-object constructions, the entrenchment effect of expressive assertion sentences, situated cognition, second language constructions, dependency structures, argument structure, multi-layered topic sentences, complex predicate structures, propositional attitude verbs, the integration of "interrogative-negative" constructions, pragmatic constraints at the syntax-semantics interface, constructional mapping of verbal semantic change, argument realization in compound words, and the acquisition of syntax-pragmatics interface structures.

These subjects are heterogeneous and complicated, which generally can be classified into the following aspects.

In terms of the comparison between Chinese and other languages, comparative or contrastive studies, particularly that of English and Chinese, constitute a great proposition of these issues. There are 41 projects dealing with comparative studies of English-Chinese, with 23 projects covering comparative studies of Chinese-English. Certainly, there are comparative studies of Chinese with other main languages like Japanese, Russian and German, and comparative studies of Chinese with minority languages such as Tibetan. Besides, comparative studies of Chinese with foreign ethnic languages such as Hebrew and Bantu languages are involved.

From the perspective that the object of study is words or sentences, since studies of words can be incorporated into the category of lexical semantics, studies of sentences can also be classified into the category of sentence semantics. Sentences are divided into simple sentences (clauses, subordinate clauses, minor clauses) and complex sentences. There are 11 topics studying complex sentences, 6 topics studying subordinate clauses, 5 topics studying clauses, 7 topics studying sentences, and 1 topic studying minor clauses.

From the perspectives of different branches of linguistics, such as phonetics, morphology, syntax, pragmatics, and discourse analysis, the research distribution is as follows: only 1 study involves phonetics; 6 involve morphology; the majority, totaling 75 studies, focus on syntax, among which 27 specifically examine syntax-semantics or the relationship between syntax and semantics; 8 studies explore semantics from a pragmatic angle; and 5 involve discourse analysis.

From the perspective of interactions, interfaces and connections between different branches of linguistics, the research distribution is as follows: 26 studies examine interactions; 11 studies focus on interfaces; another 11 explore connections.

From the perspective of primary components constituting sentences such as verbs and nouns, nouns are arguments from the perspective of semantics. Representation is the embodiment of these lexical classes. Research in this direction can be classified as follows: 23 studies deal with verbs; 33 studies are concerned with nouns; 12 studies examine arguments; 2 studies focus on prepositions; another 5 studies explore representations.

In terms of structures, constructions, patterns or models of sentences, 58 studies focus on structures; 50 studies examine issues of constructions; 8 studies explore sentence patterns; 12 studies deal with models.

From the perspective of structure's irregular forms, 3 studies examine parallelism; 3 studies focus on ellipsis; 2 studies explore compression; two studies deal with serial verb construction; 1 study explores ergative structure.

In terms of structure's features, 17 studies explore mechanisms; 6 studies examine development; 14 studies focus on events.

From the perspective of scenario types, only 1 study deals with situation.

From the perspective of tense, aspect and voice which not only belong to verbs, but also belong to sentences as well as word sequence in sentences, there are 2 studies dealing with tense; there are 6 studies dealing with aspect; there are 2 studies dealing with middle voice; there are 2 studies dealing with passive voice; there is one study dealing with mood; besides, there are 7 studies dealing with word order.

In terms of the diversity of research methods, 38 studies conduct research from cognitive perspective; 16 studies use functional linguistics or involve the concept of function; 7 studies deal with information; 17 studies adopt corpus to carry out research; 13 studies conduct research from the diachronic perspective; only 1 study carries out research from the synchronic perspective.

In terms of the theoretical frameworks employed in the research, 23 studies employ typology as the theoretical framework; 38 studies are based on cognitive science and 16 studies follow functional linguistics; 10 studies use frame semantics or involve the concept of frames; 3 studies apply the semantic map theory.

In terms of the application of semantics, 11 studies deal with the issue of acquisition.

3.3.2.2 Sentence Meaning and Utterance Implication

With studies of sentence meaning proceeding further, it is insufficient to study meaning just at the level of static linguistics. It is essential to expand the research into the level of pragmatics. And only through having an overall depiction of these two levels can the general picture of language serving as the tool of thinking and communication be clearly painted. Before 2010, Guo Yukai and Hua Shao conducted relevant studies. With internal relations between sentences at the linguistics level and sentences at the speech level thoroughly taken into consideration, Guo Yukai (1996) then determines the hierarchical structure of sentence meaning: abstract meaning (including proposition, structural meaning, signifier meaning, abstract communicative meaning) and communicative meaning (including proposition, structural meaning, signified meaning, specific communicative meaning). Hua Shao (1998) divides utterance meaning, the smallest constituent unit in the speech, into several component modules: propositional content, meaning produced by actual divisions, moods of utterances, referential meaning, and covert meaning probably contained in utterances. Each basic module can be further divided. Such kind of meticulous hierarchical division of sentence meaning deepens our knowledge of sentence's semantic structure.

In the last decade since 2010, there have been 3 articles concerning this issue published, and 1 paper published respectively in 2017 and 2018. The four papers exhibit different perspectives. Jin Nan (2010) expounds on sentence meaning and utterance implication from the perspective of context.

Zhang Xin and Zhang Feng (2011) give a brief analysis of relations between sentence meaning and utterance implication while focusing on studying semantic immanency and meaning.

Yao Mingjun and Song Bei (2012) study from the perspective of linguistics' different branches, arguing that sentence meaning and utterance implication respectively belong to the research domain of semantics and pragmatics. Sentence meaning is abstract, static, and independent of context while utterance implication is concrete, dynamic, and it is the combination of sentence meaning and context.

Lin Xiaqing (2017) analyzes distinctions between proposition, sentence meaning and utterance meaning while attaching focal attention to philosophical research methodologies. He posits that in studies of semantics, it is essential to elucidate and classify certain fundamental concepts. Liu Jibing and Fan Chunyu (2018) discuss the relations between sentence patterns and meaning from the perspective of semantic structure. Their papers' quality has improved substantially but still calls for perfection.

Another relevant issue is the boundary between semantics and pragmatics.

Kang Canhui (2007) expounds on the complementarism between semantics and pragmatics. His paper first elucidates relevant theoretical basis and research tasks shared by pragmatics and semantics. Taking Grice's theory of conversational implicature as example, his paper then explains the complementarism between semantics and pragmatics in specific linguistic analysis.

Zhao Mi and Chen Lianfeng (2011) propose that context is the boundary existing between semantics and pragmatics. The paper distinguishes between the meaning of semantics and pragmatics from the perspective of vocabulary and sentences. It proposes that context was the dividing line between semantics and pragmatics and concludes that there are not only distinctions but also relevance between them.

Hou Guojin (2012) analyzes the complementarism between semantics and pragmatics. His paper clarifies the classical semantics-pragmatics interface conundrum by retrospection and comment of cross-century debate over interface, from Gazda's equation and Levinson's seven types of communicational content/meaning to the disputes over "what is said" and "what is implicated". The paper displays a list of classical topics of study in semantics and pragmatics, and a panorama of their respective research interfaces. Thus, the paper positions the author on the stand of "radical pragmaticism" of "complementarism", maintaining that the twenty-first century is an epoch of meaning studies.

Zhang Ren (2012) studies semantics-pragmatics interface and layers of meaning. On the basis of comparison between several concepts including truth-conditional meaning and non-truth-conditional meaning, what is said and what is implicated, decoded meaning and inferred meaning, his article outlines the category of meanings each concept covers, further divides meaning into several concrete layers, and introduces several different solutions to differentiating semantic and pragmatic meaning.

Wu Sijing and Liu Longgen (2012) expound on semantics/pragmatics "interface" research from the perspective of misleading or enlightening. The article reviews and analyzes various schools' discussions and opinions of this issue in recent years. It finds that semantics/pragmatics "interface" inquiry caused fiercer debates, generating three primary approaches and six primary schools in studies of this area, which has currently become one of the most pioneering topics in present linguistics and philosophy. Up to now, disputes over semantics/pragmatics interface have not reached an agreement. But different schools' researches into issues such as semantics, context, and contextual dependency still progress on.

Chen Xinren (2015) provides an alternative account of the boundary between semantics and pragmatics. Based on a critical review of several competing solutions, his article proposes an alternative account of the semantics-pragmatics boundary by further differentiating various processes of pragmatic enrichment with varying degrees of defaultness, expanding the notion of "slot" on the strength of cognitive frame theory, broadening the scope of semantics to include all sorts of enrichments, and restricting the scope of what is implicated. It was aimed to provide a new solution that is both intuitively plausible and descriptively adequate and concise.

Liu Wenshuo and Pang Yue (2017) expound on the boundary between semantics and pragmatics. Semantics is closely related with pragmatics and also they distinguish from each other. Speaking explicitly, semantics studies the literal meaning of words, phrases and sentences in a language while pragmatics deals with relations between languages and speakers as well as relations between conversation contexts. The issue of boundary between semantics and pragmatics involves numerous aspects such as meaning and usage, language's conventional and unconventional meaning, truth-conditional and non-truth-conditional meaning. Discussions of this issue is beneficial to our better knowledge of the boundary between semantics and pragmatics.

Xia Yang and Li Jia (2017) briefly introduce studies of semantics and pragmatics interface. This paper recalls and reviews concrete research content and directions of lexical-pragmatics theory at home and abroad, enlightening scholars in their future research and broadening their horizons.

Tan Can (2018) publishes *Trial Discussion of Relations between Semantics and Pragmatics*. This paper focuses on conducting further discussion of the complementarity and distinctions between semantics and pragmatics.

Studies of Hou Guojin, Zhang Ren and Chen Xinren are more inspirational. Studies of other scholars mentioned above can provide entry-level references.

3.3.2.3 Sentences with Semantic Plausibility and Semantic Anomaly

What kind of sentences are accurate? How to determine an effective filtering mechanism to ensure the accuracy of generated utterances during the formation of sentences? It is of substantial significance for studies of linguistic theories, language teaching, and even computer processing of natural language to solve these problems. The issue of accurate utterances not only involves sentences' truth-condition, but also acts as a multifaceted one involving grammatical accuracy, semantic accuracy, and pragmatic accuracy. The currently urgent thing that waits to be solved is the issue of semantic accuracy.

Before 2010, there was an article written by Ding Xin (1994). The article primarily studies how to exclude sentences with improper semantic collocations to ensure the appropriateness of sentence semantics. Starting from analyzing relations between word meaning and syntactic functions, semantic relations between predicate and object, predicate and subject, the author discusses the general law concerning how to avoid violating semantic identity law and generate accurate utterances. He elucidates the law of semantic collocations in utterances. Besides, the author proposes a set of approaches to classifying argument's semantic subcategory, which is of certain instructive meaning for us to further probe into the issue of accurate utterances.

Over the past decade, papers specialized in studying unusual phenomena of sentence semantics have increased. Research in this field has been augmented but the number of papers published is small and perspectives of studies are scattered. Such situation still calls for improvement.

Zhuo Ru (2010) studies semantic anomaly in topsy-turvy songs. Such kind of semantic anomaly differs from the rhetoric of common literary language. It alters the internal law of semantic fields and overturns the normal concept, judgment and inference in people's minds, therefore producing an unexpected aesthetic effect.

Li Cuiying (2011) studies different approaches to elucidating semantic anomaly. Through conducting an overall review of different opinions of various semantics schools, the article summarizes analysis of semantic anomaly as adopting three approaches: formal, pragmatic, and cognitive. Meanwhile, it points out features and deficiencies of these different approaches.

Li Qingqing (2013) explores combination words of semantic anomaly in the master dissertation. Taking the 208 Unusual Semantic Combination Words included in *Modern Chinese Dictionary* (6th Edition) as linguistic data, with combination of related theories such as componential description and word motivation for integrated survey, the thesis will systematically analyze such words from three aspects in terms of type division, causes, and features and functions.

3.3.2.4 Logico-Semantic Relations Among Sentences

Among sentence semantics there exist certain logical relations which include synonymy, implication and contradiction. The exploration of these logical relations in natural language is an essential constituent of sentence semantic research. Synonymous relations of sentences have a significant position in relations of sentence meanings. China's scholars attach great importance to it, with numerous dissertations and monographs studying synonymous sentences released and published. Before 2010, there were Ni Bo (1983), He Ziran (1979), Guo Yukai (1998), and Wang Mingyu (1996a) who were linguists paying attention this issue rather early. Wang Mingyu has plentiful monographs and articles studying issues such as the definition of synonymous sentences, the principle of classification as well as the explanation of synonymous sentences' internal mechanisms.

Wang Mingyu (1996a) gives a relatively scientific definition of synonymous sentences based on the semantics-structure theory. The author conducts a specific explanation of standards of defining synonymous sentences from three aspects: the semantic principle of synonymous sentences, the structural principle, relations between synonymous sentences and general forms. Wang Mingyu (1996b) also conducts a valuable attempt at the classification of synonymous sentences. He divides relations between synonymous sentences' predicates into embodiment, derivation, equivalence, and suppletion. Then he conducts a relatively comprehensive and classified description of synonymous sentences from these four aspects respectively.

Guo Yukai (1998: 3–5) discusses the entailment relation between sentences, defining it as "an inclusive semantic relation formed due to the hyponymy and hypernym relation between correspondent components of two sentences". The author questions the entailment formula put forward by Leech and proposes that the factors influencing entailment relation and direction are various. These factors includes referential features, quantifiers, negation, logical stress.

After 2010, there are several articles concerning this issue. Their study objects and bases are different and all have achieved certain accomplishments. But obviously in this field there are still many things that deserve studying. Li Dan and Lai Wei (2011) study logical-semantic relations in conditional clauses of unconditional compound sentences of "many enumerates" type. This article primarily examines the "many enumerates" type of unconditional compound sentences linked by “regardless”, combines syntactic features, and grasps linking words to discuss internal logical-semantic relations in conditional clauses.

Based on Chomsky’s transformational-generative grammar, Zhao Yushan and Yang Jie (2012) briefly discuss sentences’ equivalence of deep logical-semantic relations while translating scientific and technological texts. The article posits that it is essential to employ methods of logical reasoning to display a strong chain of logical reasoning and clarify the original text’s logical-semantic relations. It is necessary to look into relevant professional books in certain conditions so as to ensure logical relations, therefore achieving equivalence of deep logical-semantic relations between target text and source text.

Wang Kun (2014) compares the transitivity and logico-semantic relations of Chinese and English clauses. Based on conceptual metafunction theory of systemic functional linguistics, this article conducts a comparative analysis of Mo Yan’s Nobel Prize Lecture in Chinese and Howard Goldblatt’s English translation from aspects of transitivity and logico-semantic relations, thereby summarizing numerous rules of clauses’ transformation during the process of Chinese-English translation. These rules influence Chinese and English’s different choices of environmental components and participants in clauses and logico-semantic relations between clauses.

Huang He (2017) studies the logico-semantic relations of the “longest sentence in English literature” from the perspective of Functional Stylistics. The last episode in Joyce’s Ulysses is a transcriptive presentation of Molly’s monologue in an over-3000-sentence text characterized by a lack of punctuation and known as the first “longest sentence in English literature”. This article analyzes the complex logico-semantic relations in this episode from the perspective of Functional Stylistics, with special focus on an excerpt in which the most common connective “and” is frequently used. The analysis of the logico-semantic relations explicitizes the multi-level flow of consciousness in the linear textual progression, in the hope of shedding light on stylistics, discourse analysis and the study of the stream-of-consciousness fiction.

He Wei and Liu Jiahuan (2019) contrasts the logico-semantic relations between English and Chinese clauses and the representations. The article conducts a contrastive study of the logico-semantic relations between English and Chinese clauses from the functional perspective. Emphasis is put upon displaying types and occurrence probability of the logico-semantic relations between English and Chinese clauses, and differences between lexical grammar and logical order representations in order to reveal the differences between English and Chinese in terms of cognition. It summarizes the research findings and gives some explanations.

From the perspective of multimodality, based on the model for images—texts relations proposed by Martinec and Salway, Zhong Weiwei (2020) analyzes the logical-semantic relations between images and texts in narratives picture books in English and points out that there exist three logico-semantic relations between images and texts: elaboration, extension, and enhancement. This article studies the handling of logico-semantic relations between images and texts in the translation of narratives picture books. Picture books have two basic attributes: images and texts, so they own multimodal features. She points out that while translating picture books, translators need to focus on the logico-semantic relations between images and texts and shouldn't separate images from texts.

3.3.2.5 Sentence's Semantic Structure: Presupposition

In studies of sentence semantics, "presupposition" has been an enduring focal issue. China's scholars also attach substantial attention to the issue of "presupposition". The initial focal attention was placed on introducing the concept of presupposition, the method of distinguishing between presuppositions and assertions, as well as differentiating between semantic and pragmatic presuppositions. With studies proceeding further, research in this field has achieved plenty of new accomplishments. For example, Xu Shenghuan (1993) discusses some theoretical issues concerning semantic presupposition, puts forward new categories as well as some new characteristics and features, reference methods and application presuppositions, which are of benefit for us to have a deeper understanding of such semantic phenomenon as presupposition.

Jiang Hong and Xu Yin (1997) studies the issue of negation of presupposition (metalinguistic negation). Zhang Keding (1997) analyses the phenomenon of presupposition in English cleft sentences. All these work significantly promote studies of the issue of presupposition.

Over the last decade after 2010, studies of presupposition are still progressing on and becoming increasingly concrete and functional. Scholars such as Wei Zaijiang have published a set of articles in terms of presupposition. Han Li and Yang Yangkai (2010) analyses the formal studies of presupposition theory. They discuss issues concerning presupposition which have generally attracted scholars' attention. Besides, in this article, the focal point of discussion is Gazdar's presupposition theory, involving its formal definition and systematic definition. And the development of presupposition theory is re-surveyed from the formal perspective.

Wei Zaijiang (2010a) argues that studies of presupposition in aspects like the receptions and understandings, the representation, reception, and the interaction between the two are insufficient. Presupposition is the behavior of mutual communication between two subjects carried out from three perspectives. Discussion should be conducted in terms of presupposition discourse power and expression strategy, presupposition explanatory power and reception strategy, as well as the operating mechanism of mutual interaction between the two. He proposes a general framework on the study of presupposition, i.e., three perspectives on presuppositions: Representation, Reception, and Interaction. He then gives a brief discussion on the three perspective.

Wei Zaijiang (2010b) conducts studies on cognition of the object ellipsis, arguing that it is a question of pragmatic presupposition. Pragmatic supposition is one of the important mechanisms of the generation and understanding of such structures. The question of object ellipsis is closely related to the aspect of meaning, syntax, and function. Only from the holistic ways can the more pervasive explanation be achieved.

Wei Zaijiang (2011a) argues that in the concrete context and discourse, the features of pragmatic presuppositions are as follows: (1) the agent's engagement function; (2) the activate function of implicit information; (3) the positive or negative evaluative functions to the third person. These reflect the subjectivity of presuppositions and the appraisal functions of presuppositions. These features of pragmatic presuppositions intersect in many ways with the current hot topic in discourse research—the study of discourse evaluation systems.

Wei Zaijiang (2011b), starting from the cognitive psychology of the prototypical structure of pragmatic presupposition and based on the construction theory of cognitive linguistics, conducts a cognitive analysis of pragmatic presuppositions in Chinese real estate advertisements. It helps us to have a better understanding of advertisements' presupposition mechanism through analyzing Chinese real estate advertisements from cognitive perspective.

Wei Zaijiang (2011c) concentrates on the cognitive approach to zeugma in Chinese and English from the perspective of Construction Grammar, and tries to introduce a new view to the study of rhetorical devices. The study finds that pragmatic presupposition exerts a strong limitation on the zeugma. Meanwhile, it is construction that leads to the motivations of form-meaning correspondences of zeugma. Without constructions, there would be no zeugma sentential patterns.

Wei Zaijiang (2012) approaches the study of the recipient's psychology and cognitive expectations regarding presupposition from the perspective of the presupposition recipient, employing the theoretical framework of philosophical hermeneutics. He posits that expression and reception are two inseparable organic components of linguistic dialogue, which together constitute the complete cognitive process of discourse production and comprehension. The subjects of utterance and reception are speaker and listener respectively, jointly constituting the two parties of a discourse activity. As a communicative interaction inevitably involves psychological processes, the psychological state of the listener, as the receiving party, is bound to influence the speaker's expression of presupposition.

Wei Zaijiang (2013) studies the phenomenon of Chinese intransitive verbs taking the objects. The major findings are as follows: (1) the implicit presuppositional meanings of the constructions as a whole lead to the formation and high-level entrenchment of such structures; (2) the implicit presuppositional meanings of verbs themselves are closely related to the place objects; (3) the patient presuppositional meanings of locative nominal objects lead to the shift in role salience. Pragmatic presupposition is one of the basic cognitive mechanisms that generate such grammatical structures. Besides, pragmatic presupposition is a significant and generalized mechanism of linguistic cognition. Actually, the collocations of the sentential elements are the presupposition relationship between them. It is presupposition mechanism that provides the conditions and possibilities for such collocations. Pragmatic presupposition is the fundamental motivation of such structures.

Zhang Yisheng (2011) studies methods, types, motivations, and functions of superimposition for presuppositional negation. There are three types of superimposition for double presuppositional negation in Chinese: entail meaning, overlaying, and mutual. Multi-layered superimposition by adding another overlaying consists of three kinds:

"overlaying + entailment"; "overlaying + collocation"; and "overlaying + cooperation". Impetuses for superimposition include subjective highlighting, semantic wearing, feature consideration, and structure integrating. The primary function is to aggrandize and leads to redundance in negation. These superimpositions satisfy not only different pragmatic needs for presuppositional negation, but also produce other morphological and syntactic consequences such as the lexicalization and idiomatical constructions with negative morphemes.

Zhang Jiahua (2013) tries to explore the issue proposed by Lv Shuxiang through analyzing the impact of the semantic presupposition on double negation in sentences where propositional attitude verbs act as predicates.

Chen Zhenyu and Qianpeng (2015) prove five "formulae of integrating processes", and it is also proposed that the relation P $\rightarrow$ Q between two propositions must be integrated into that Q is P's presupposition, the relation P $\leftrightarrow$ Q must be integrated into equation between Q and P. Truth Value Gaps, Focus-Negation, and other issues about integration have been also studied in this paper for the purpose of revealing the necessity for language expression.

Zhangling (2016) argues that generic sentences result from presuppositions in the fields of semantics, pragmatics, and cognition. The author hopes that the research will help deepen our understanding and the studies of generic sentences' features.

From a new perspective, Cong Rizhen and Qiuwei (2016) achieve the new development and breakthrough, proposing that semantic presupposition stresses linguistic forms in a sentence/proposition while pragmatic presupposition is more concerned with speaker centered meanings outside of a sentence/proposition. The study concludes that it is more practical and dialectical to interpret natural language from the perspectives of both semantic and pragmatic presuppositions rather than a single one.

Based on presupposition theory, Yuan Mengxi (2017) points out that some Chinese modal adverbs denote the meaning of emphasis. These adverbs impose certain requirements on the previous discourse, and are thus more suitable to be analyzed as presupposition triggers. The meaning of "emphasis" is a discourse effect resulting from the combination of the presupposition triggered by the adverbs and the meaning of the sentence type.

3.3.2.6 The Issue of Ambiguity in Sentences

Ambiguity refers to the use of a single linguistic form to express two or more meanings, a universal phenomenon in natural languages. The study of ambiguity in sentences has a long history. Before 2010, foreign language researchers at home and abroad first engaged with this field of sentence semantic research, as it is closely related to grammar teaching. In teaching practice, people naturally reflect on issues such as the types of ambiguous sentences and the causes of their formation, as seen in the works of Shen Jiaxuan (1985), Qiu Shude (1992), and others. Some scholars began to comprehensively evaluate and reflect on domestic and international research on the issue of ambiguity. For example, Li Rongbao (1992) introduced and commented on ambiguity research from three perspectives of philosophy, logic, and linguistics, involving issues such as the generation of ambiguity, its specific manifestations, and its impact on language use. His research is highly helpful for us to clarify the context and evolution of ambiguity issues. Domestic scholars have also conducted in-depth studies of ambiguity from other perspectives. For instance, Ma Bosen (1995) carries out a multi-scale and multifunctional analysis of grammatical ambiguity in English from the perspective of systemic functional linguistics. Zhang Weiding (1996) explores several psychological cognitive models for analyzing ambiguity from the perspective of cognitive linguistics. Cheng Gong (1998) compares the analyses of ambiguity from three sources by structuralist grammar and generative grammar, arguing that generative grammar surpasses previous approaches in ambiguity analysis due to its increased analytical levels, richer analytical tools, and more rigorous analytical framework.

After 2010, the number of scholars studying ambiguity has increased. Some scholars have adopted experimental methods and drawn convincing conclusions that provide insights for our teaching. Some have explored semantic and pragmatic ambiguity, as well as ambiguity in certain constructions, indicating that the study of ambiguity has become more in-depth. However, many issues still warrant further investigation. Zhao Chen (2010) uses experimental methods to explore the psychological representation of homographic ambiguous words, metaphorical polysemous words, and metonymic polysemous words among Chinese English learners. Both Zhang Caiyun and Zhou Mingqiang have consecutively published two papers on ambiguity.

Zhang Caiyun (2010) argues that pragmatic ambiguity and pragmatic perspective are two pragmatic strategies. Pragmatic ambiguity refers to the phenomenon of ambiguity where appropriate interpretations are made through inferring the implied pragmatic meaning of an utterance. As an external factor related to experience that constrains the formation of linguistic meaning, pragmatic perspective can be used to summarize and explain the causes of pragmatic ambiguity. Analyzing pragmatic ambiguity through this perspective allows for a reasonable interpretation of certain linguistic phenomena. These two pragmatic strategies are often employed to depict characters' personality traits and advance the orderly development of story lines. Zhang Caiyun (2011) examines pragmatic vagueness, pragmatic ambiguity, and their pragmatic values from the perspective of viewpoint. In specific discussions, there are frequent instances of confusing pragmatic vagueness with pragmatic ambiguity. By examining these two strategies through an external factor of linguistic structure—viewpoint—their generative causes and distinctions become clearer. The differences are manifested in: (1) distinct semantic boundaries; (2) the subjectivity versus objectivity in semantic establishment; and (3) different modes of semantic comprehension. In speech, they reflect pragmatic values such as the pragmatic adaptability of the "politeness principle", the tendency toward positive values and aesthetic appreciation in human values, and the artistry of the law of verbal contradiction.

Zhou Mingqiang (2011a) argues that the resolution of lexical ambiguity can be achieved through cognitive models such as semantic hierarchical networks, activation-inhibition, lexical access, and feature comparison; the formation of cognitive models relies on verbal interaction. For word meanings, verbal interaction facilitates the formation of implicit-explicit semantic structures; for cognitive agents, verbal interaction enhances their cognitive competence. Zhou Mingqiang (2011b) states that syntactic structural ambiguity is primarily caused by differences in sentence structure hierarchy, structural relations, semantic orientation, semantic features, semantic relations, and semantic focus. Ambiguities arising from different causes require different processing methods for comprehension. Commonly used processing methods for ambiguity comprehension include the "chunking method", "directional method", "conversion method", and "projection method". Individuals with different language proficiencies exhibit variations in their mastery of these methods, thereby creating differences in the understanding of syntactic ambiguity.

Zhang Wenpeng and Tang Chen (2011) use behavioral experiments and ERP (Event-Related Potentials) experiments as methods to investigate the cognitive processing mechanisms by which Chinese-English bilinguals resolve ambiguities in English nouns within sentence contexts.

Chang Haichao (2012) takes 502 non-English major college students as test subjects and explores the mediating effect of learning strategies between ambiguity tolerance and English proficiency through a questionnaire survey. Xu Zhilin (2012) argues that at the synchronic level, strategies for semantic differentiation in ambiguous ditransitive constructions exhibit differences between northern and southern dialects: northern dialects and Mandarin mostly use the "V + gěi" structure to express the "giving" meaning, while the "V + le" structure denotes the "obtaining" meaning; southern dialects mostly adopt syntactic strategies, using two sentence patterns with different word orders to express the "giving" and "obtaining" meanings, respectively. The causes of this differentiation can be understood as the result of the historical development of Chinese ditransitive constructions.

Han Baijing and Xue Fen (2012) investigates the morphological representation and ambiguity interpretation characteristics of Chinese English learners regarding structurally ambiguous words in the "un-V-a-ble" format. The branching directions of English morphological structures are complex and chaotic, while structurally ambiguous words clearly demonstrate the correspondence between the internal morphological hierarchical structure of vocabulary and lexical semantics. Zhao Chunli and Shi Dingxu (2012) argue that the sentence pattern "NP1 + zài NP2 + V + NP3" is a typical ambiguous sentence, but the ambiguity does not originate from the structure itself; rather, it is based on multiple interpretations of real-world relationships. Its ambiguity is mainly manifested in: (1) the ambiguity of spatial relationships between NP2 and NP1, and between NP2 and NP3; (2) the diversity of NP2's semantic functions when there is a spatial relationship between NP2 and NP3; (3) the ambiguity of NP2's semantic functions when there is no spatial relationship between NP2 and NP3. This sentence pattern can be semantically decomposed into 10 unambiguous sentence patterns, and different types of ambiguity can be resolved using distinct disambiguation strategies.

Hu Yang (2013) notes that there is significant academic divergence in interpreting and determining ambiguity arising from the combination of English manner-of-motion verbs with spatial prepositions like under/behind and in/on. One school of scholars argues that the former type of verb-preposition combinations (with under/behind) are semantically ambiguous, while the latter type (with in/on) are not; another school maintains that both types are analogous and exhibit semantic ambiguity. By examining the essential properties of ambiguity in these two types of combinations, providing justifications, and distinguishing between pragmatic and syntactic ambiguity, it is argued that the ambiguity of the former type belongs to the syntactic category, while that of the latter type is pragmatic. This perspective resolves and unifies the disputes between the two schools to a certain extent.

Liu Juan et al. (2013) classifies ambiguous phenomena in English from a semantic perspective, analyzes various factors causing ambiguity, and proposes some means to eliminate ambiguity, hoping to contribute to the further study of English ambiguity.

Hu Yang and Chen Jingli (2014) distinguish between the lexical and syntactic nature of VPP (Verb-Particle Phrase) semantics, hypothesizing that the uninterpretable feature [uV] is the source of ambiguity in English VPPs. They used an animation selection task to investigate how adult English learners with Chinese or Spanish as their mother tongue master the ambiguity of target VPPs, combining insights from ambiguity acquisition and the influence of mother tongue tense. Zhao Chen and Hong Aichun (2015) employ a priming experiment to explore the cognitive mechanisms by which Chinese English learners at different proficiency levels interpret ambiguous noun-noun combinations.

Based on a comparison between typical game processes and the generation and resolution of ambiguous structures, Yang Quan and Feng Zhiwei (2015) proposes a game-theoretical model for structural ambiguity. This model uses the concepts and methods of game theory to describe the process of structural ambiguity generation and resolution, providing a new approach and method for ambiguity resolution. Examples of ambiguity resolution demonstrate that this perspective offers useful insights for understanding and analyzing the process of resolving ambiguity.

Wang Yu and Sui Mingcai (2015) use masked priming experiments to investigate the effects of meaning relatedness and relative meaning frequency on the early recognition of lexical ambiguity among Chinese English learners at different proficiency levels in the absence of context. To gain in-depth insight into the disambiguation strategies of Chinese learners regarding relative clause attachment ambiguity in English as a second language (e.g., Someone shot [the servant] NP1 of [the actress] NP2 [who was standing on the balcony] RC), Dai Yuncai (2016) conducts three experiments with 27 Chinese college freshmen. The participants showed a significant tendency for relative clauses to attach to NP1, indicating that syntactic factors play a significant role in resolving relative clause attachment ambiguity. The results of two questionnaire surveys revealed that under the influence of post-syntactic factors such as lexical types and semantic pragmatics, the participants' preferences for relative clause attachment changed significantly, thus also having a significant impact on the resolution of relative clause attachment ambiguity. Additionally, Chinese learners' processing strategies for English relative clause attachment are constrained by their own learning experiences and syntactic competence.

Yang Zi (2017) proposes using the factor of "expectation"—related to but independent of "anticipation"—to analyze the dual interpretations of the structure "chà diǎn er méi VP". Based on the pragmatic constraint of non-expectation for VP in the Nn-type "chà diǎn er méi VP", it is argued that "méi" in the Nn-type interpretation serves a pragmatic function of emphasizing unexpectedness, rather than being a redundant negative marker attached to "chà diǎn er". Instead, "méi" is an interjectory element embedded within the "chà diǎn er + VP" structure, with a compositional function similar to that of a discourse marker. This view is supported by multiple lines of evidence: the co-occurrence of "méi" with the aspect marker "le" in this structure, the position of "méi" when the object is proposed, its stress pattern, and a comparative analysis of the features of "méi" and discourse markers.

Wang Yue and Zhang Jijia (2017) investigate the cross-linguistic recognition process of different types of translation ambiguous words among Chinese English learners through psycholinguistic experiments, aiming to reveal the impact of the asymmetry in form-meaning mapping between the two language systems on lexical access.

Liu Bin and Yuan Yulin (2018) summarize the distributional characteristics of the two senses of the Chinese word "huái yí" by examining real text corpora. They point out that "huái yí" reflects a psychological game based on expectation, probability, and possibility, and further propose a more universal and abstract semantic construal principle of "yí shí xìn xū". This principle helps us more accurately construe the two different meanings of "huái yí" while also resolving issues left over from previous studies.

In response to the shortcomings of structural and functional approaches, Jia Guangmao (2020) proposes a new framework for analyzing quantifier scope ambiguity based on cognitive grammar, attempting to conduct core syntactic research beyond generative grammar. Through the analysis of related linguistic phenomena in English and Chinese, this study finds that quantifier scope ambiguities in simple sentences, ditransitive structures, topicalization, and relativization in both languages can be explained by the mechanism of establishing conceptual reference points. This approach addresses issues such as the lack of theoretical justification in the expert system voting mechanism and its failure to account for both scope and binding relationships.

Wang Hongqi (2020) discusses the existence of ambiguous grammatical patterns. Through analysis of what academia refer to as "ambiguous patterns", it is argued that when such patterns are given two semantic interpretations, some do not belong to the same overt grammatical structure pattern, while others are merely grammatical structure patterns with the same overt grammatical meaning but different covert grammatical meanings. In a strict sense, an ambiguous pattern should be a grammatical structure pattern with both identical overt and covert grammatical meanings. However, such ambiguous patterns do not exist. Instead, two grammatical structures with the same word-class sequence but different overt grammatical meanings, or two grammatical structure patterns with the same overt grammatical meaning but different covert grammatical meanings, cannot be generalized into a single ambiguous (grammatical structure) pattern.

3.3.2.7 Valence Theory and Arguments

In logic, propositions are analyzed as combinations of predicates and arguments, a method that has been borrowed in linguistics to analyze the semantic components of sentences. Valence grammar, case grammar, and other approaches all analyze sentences along these lines, and the principles and parameters theory of generative grammar has also introduced "theta theory" to handle the interface between syntax and semantics.

"Valence" and "arguments" have become core concepts in the study of sentence semantics, attracting significant attention. Chinese scholars have achieved fruitful results in this field, with some notable achievements dating back to before 2010. For example, scholars such as Jin Lixin (1997) and Xu Liehong & Shen Yang (1998) conduct research on the semantic structure of propositions from different perspectives. Inspired by Fillmore's case grammar theory, Li Xiyin (1998) proposes the "event case" theory, which provides a clear and profound interpretation of the semantic structure and semantic changes within sentences. Fu Xingshang (1999) elaborates on this idea in the form of monographs. This theory views the signified of a sentence as an event, which is further divided into "event-core cases" and "event-cause cases". The propositional semantic structure of all sentences can be regarded as variations of the primary event case pattern $V(x,y,z)\langle\alpha\rangle$. When the primary pattern is further specified, secondary and tertiary event case patterns emerge. These patterns can also undergo various expansions, variations, and extensions.

In the decade following 2010, valence theory has seen new developments and applications. Some scholars have approached the study of valence theory from the perspectives of corpus linguistics, foreign semantic schools of thought, dynamic valence, and diachronic analysis. Zhong Jingyao (2010), through analyzing errors in transitive verb patterns and noun/verb and verb/noun collocations in the *Chinese Learner English Corpus*, finds that errors in transitive verb patterns may stem from learners' lack of knowledge about the valence requirements of verbs, while errors in noun/verb and verb/noun collocations may be due to learners' ignorance of the semantic role requirements of verbs. Meanwhile, many errors may also be caused by the influence of Chinese and interference from similar English words.

Zheng Qiuxiu (2011) mainly elaborates on the concepts of valence and argument and their relationships with sentence patterns based on the perspectives of the Moscow Semantic School, aiming to illustrate the status and roles of valence and argument in syntactic and semantic research. Valence and argument are important concepts in syntactic and semantic research: valence is a semantic component of verbs, belonging to the concept at the lexical semantic level; while argument is participant elements of propositions, belonging to the concept at the sentence level. When verbs rise to the sentence level, valence is manifested as argument through the filling of governance patterns, and the quantity and combination of argument are always constrained by lexical semantics, syntax, and especially sentence pattern meanings.

Zhou Tongquan (2011) provides a new research perspective for the study of Chinese verb valence from the aspect of dynamic valence, which can also serve as a reference for cross-linguistic valence research. The verb valence continuum is a pragmatic-level continuum, reflecting the variation patterns of verb valence in different contexts in modern Chinese. Structurally, the valence continuum consists of three sub-systems with hierarchical priorities: valence quality continuum > valence quantity continuum > valence position continuum (> indicates the left subsystem dominates the right). Valence variation is constrained by limited conditions—there are more conditions for valence increase than decrease, though statistics show valence decrease occurs more frequently than increase.

Liu Bingli and Liu Haitao (2011) aim to study the evolutionary process of verb syntactic valence from a diachronic perspective. They construct three types of corpora—classical Chinese, ancient vernacular, and modern vernacular—select ten major verbs as research objects, provide methods for example sentence selection and analysis, and statistically analyze the complements and specifiers of these verbs. Zhen Fengchao and Yang Feng (2015) primarily aim to explore a corpus-data-driven descriptive system for verb valence structures and apply it to the analysis of learner English corpora. In phraseological research within the corpus linguistics framework, pattern grammar is a relatively systematic grammar for describing structures. However, as it only retains specific words and part-of-speech categories in its descriptive system, it may lead to the emergence of some ambiguous patterns. Additionally, its emphasis on the meaning of patterns somewhat overlooks the importance of vocabulary in language.

Zhen Fengchao and Yang Feng (2016) first summarize the impact of corpus linguistics research on English teaching, emphasizing that vocabulary instruction should prioritize phrase teaching and pointing out existing issues in current phrase teaching—particularly collocation instruction. They then explore the main linguistic ideas of valence structures and collocation valence, as well as their application value in English vocabulary teaching, highlighting the co-selection relationship among vocabulary, structures, and meanings. Finally, they introduce teaching approaches and methods for valence structures and collocation valence.

Zhen Fengchao (2017) adopts a corpus-driven approach focusing on valence patterns, using the verb consider as a case study to explore the identity between word meanings and structures. Data analysis shows that valence patterns provide syntactic-level contexts for establishing word meanings, and different valence patterns can distinguish between different senses of a word. However, the relationship between word meanings and valence patterns is not always one-to-one; instead, they form a complex, interconnected whole.

Other scholars have based their research on mathematical probability theory, while some have adopted cognitive perspectives. For example, to better explain the difficulty in understanding garden-path sentences, Gao Song (2013) analyzes the comprehension process of Chinese garden-path sentences from qualitative and quantitative angles using probability valence pattern theory, elucidating their understanding mechanisms. Shi Chunhong (2013) revisits the valence hierarchy and valence ambiguity of verb-resultative constructions from aspects such as the construction mechanism of basic sentence patterns in argument structure integration, the necessity and effectiveness of valence hierarchy analysis, the generality of ambiguity analysis for homomorphic verb-resultative constructions, and the impact of the dual semantic relations of resultative complements on structure integration. This sparks new reflections on issues such as the fundamental goals of valence research, identity and diversity in linguistic phenomena, the descriptive and explanatory power of syntactic analysis models, and exceptional/counterexample phenomena in linguistic research.

Wang Lin (2014) examines syntactic variation in Chinese-English code-switching from both syntactic and cognitive perspectives, revealing the syntactic and cognitive functions of verbs in authentic Chinese-English mixed discourse. Using a dependency grammar-annotated Chinese-English code-switching corpus (dependency treebank), the study measures verb syntactic valence and the dependency distances of the syntactic relations they govern. It finds differences in the distribution and dependency distances of subject, object, and adverbial relations governed by Chinese and English verbs across two types of dependencies (monolingual and mixed). The study indicates that verb-governed primary dependency relations exhibit syntactic variation in code-switching, with mixed dependencies being more cognitively demanding than corresponding monolingual dependencies.

Wang Honglei (2015) introduces international neuropsycholinguistic research progress on verb valence processing and proposes adapting these approaches to investigate theoretical issues in Chinese verb valence. Against this backdrop, the study examines Broca's aphasia patients' processing of typical one-valent, two-valent, and three-valent verbs. Accuracy and reaction time data show that verbs with higher valency suffer more severe impairment. This confirms that Broca's area is the neural basis for verb valence processing, implying the syntactic nature of verb valence and that the three verb types belong to distinct entities in the language representation system. The paper also outlines future research directions, noting that neuropsycholinguistic perspectives can help resolve theoretical controversies in Chinese valence grammar research.

Du Guizhi (2018), taking Russian verbs as examples, analyzes the characteristics, transformation forms, and correspondences among semantic valence, governance patterns, and theta structures to reveal the deep linguistic mechanisms of lexicogrammatical research and provide a multi-dimensional perspective for integrative language description.

Sun Haiyan and Qi Jianxiao (2020) explore the usage characteristics of valence structures by Chinese learners from the valence grammar perspective. Using the verb prevent as a case study, they compare the types, distributions, and accuracy of valence structure usage between native speaker corpora and learner corpora. The study finds significant differences in the types of typical valence structures used by Chinese learners versus native speakers, along with various misuse patterns in accuracy. Learners' semantic features of collocation words also differed from those of native speakers, indicating incomplete mastery of valence variations in verb forms and their correlation with meanings. The paper discusses factors influencing learners' valence knowledge, such as language input and contrastive analysis, and recommends data-driven learning methods for valence structure acquisition.

Sentence semantics studies in this field are closely linked to syntax, offering crucial insights into sentence generation rules. There are two fundamental approaches to studying propositional semantic structures: one is a model-based method that summarizes a set of comprehensive sentence semantic structure models; the other is a rule-based method that uses a minimal set of semantic constraint rules to ensure the semantic correctness of generated sentences. It should be said that both approaches contribute to propositional structure research and can achieve their respective objectives.

3.3.2.8 Empirical or Computational Studies

The study of sentence semantics has been closely integrated with computational linguistics, and there are increasingly more cross-disciplinary studies in this field, which have achieved certain results and revealed that many more areas are waiting to be explored.

Cai Yuehong et al. (2009) discuss the calculation of Chinese sentence similarity based on a three-dimensional model of sentence meaning. Through in-depth analysis of sentence semantic representation, they propose a three-dimensional representation model for Chinese sentence meaning and develop a sentence similarity calculation method based on this model. This method comprehensively describes sentence semantics from three dimensions: semantic facets, semantic primes, and semantic contexts, and optimizes calculation results by iteratively solving the weights of each dimension. Compared with traditional methods, it more comprehensively and accurately measures sentence similarity, achieving better experimental results.

Wang Qian et al. (2014) explore the identification of Chinese sentence meaning types based on predicates and sentence meaning type blocks. From the perspective of modern Chinese semantics, sentence meaning types can be divided into four categories: simple sentence meanings, complex sentence meanings, compound sentence meanings, and multiple sentence meanings. As a way to describe sentence meaning structures holistically, sentence meaning type identification is a critical step in comprehensive semantic structure analysis of Chinese sentences. The paper proposes a method for identifying Chinese sentence meaning types based on predicates and sentence meaning type blocks, achieving recognition of the four types. The method first preliminarily identifies some simple sentences by the number of predicates, then uses the C4.5 machine learning algorithm to determine the maximum number of sentence meaning type blocks passed by predicates in remaining sentences, then combines top-level sentence nodes in syntactic structures for judgment, and finally we can get the semantic type determination results of the remaining sentences. Tests on 10,221 sentences from the BFS-CTC Chinese annotated corpus achieve an overall identification accuracy of 97.6%, laying a technical foundation for research based on modern Chinese semantics.

Zhang Han et al. (2015) study cross-document personal name disambiguation integrating sentence meaning analysis. Based on constructing a text feature space, they propose a three-stage name disambiguation method combining sentence meaning analysis. Aiming at the characteristic that query words often appear as common words, the method uses heuristic rule post-processing after text preprocessing to determine whether a query word refers to a personal name, extracts local named entity features and occupations using feature templates, conducts sentence meaning analysis via a sentence structure model to extract semantic features, statistically analyzes word frequency using a bag-of-words model, constructs a three-layer feature space, and achieves name disambiguation through rule-based classification and two-stage hierarchical clustering. Introducing an overlap coefficient to calculate semantic feature similarity, experiments on the CLP2012 Chinese name disambiguation corpus achieve an F of 88.79%, demonstrating the effectiveness of applying sentence meaning analysis to cross-document name disambiguation.

Yuan Yujiao et al. (2015) discuss a short text recommendation algorithm integrating sentence meaning structure models to address privacy concerns in traditional collaborative filtering recommendation systems that require collecting user preference data. To a certain extent, the algorithm involves users' personal privacy, and current information security and privacy protection are one of the hotspots in the field of data mining. To avoid security issues caused by user information leakage effectively, a short text recommendation method integrating a semantic structure model of sentences emerged. The method takes sentences as research objects, first constructs document-topic matrices using LDA topic models to divide subtopics, then extracts semantic cases of sentences via sentence meaning structure models to obtain semantic features, calculates semantic similarity between sentences using LDA and sentence semantic structures to build similarity matrices, comprehensively weights sentences by fusing semantic and associative features, measures document weights by the highest single-sentence weight within documents, sorts documents by weight, and recommends texts after redundancy removal. Under a compression ratio of 0.5%, the method achieved a ROUGE-1 score of 31.388% and ROUGE-SU* of 15.701%. Experimental results show that the sentence-level short text recommendation algorithm enriches feature information of context, deepens the level of semantic analysis, and avoids user information leakage by not collecting user data during processing, thus providing safer and faster text recommendations.

Xiong Liyan et al. (2016) study Chinese personal name disambiguation based on sentence meaning structure analysis. Aiming at the problem that many existing name disambiguation methods based on person attribute features are ineffective for texts with sparse features, they propose a method using sentence meaning structure analysis to extract person relationship feature words, construct social relationship graphs based on these features, use occupation and organization as auxiliary attributes, and perform relationship clustering combined with entity features, mapping clustering results to texts for disambiguation. Sentence meaning structure analysis improves the accuracy of person relationship and attribute features, and experimental results show the method effectively enhances Chinese name disambiguation accuracy.

Lin Meng et al. (2015) study a microblog topic summarization algorithm integrating sentence meaning structure models. To quickly extract core content from massive microblogs, they propose a method that uses sentence meaning structure models to extract semantic case features, calculates sentence similarity via LDA and sentence structures to build similarity matrices, divides subtopics, and fuses semantic and associative features to select the most informative sentences within subtopics as summaries. At compression ratios of 0.5%, 1.0%, and 1.5%, ROUGE scores significantly outperforms comparison systems; at 1.5%, ROUGE-1 reaches 51.30% and ROUGE-SU* 25.27%. The results show that integrating sentence meaning structure analysis deepens semantic analysis, enhances semantic expression through extracted features, enriches sentence representations via comprehensive weight calculation, reduces semantic loss, strengthens intra-class semantic relevance, mitigates noise, and improves summary-topic relevance. The method also demonstrates strong generalization ability across different topics.

Luo Senlin et al. (2016) study multi-document automatic summarization algorithms integrating sentence meaning features. The research is a key problem in natural language processing. To ensure that the extracted summaries can better reflect the themes of multiple documents, this paper, based on the division of sub-themes, proposes a sentence optimization method combining sentence meaning features based on subtopic division. The method extracts topic and predicate features from sentence meaning structures, fuses statistical features to construct feature vectors for sentence weight calculation, and extracts summaries using a combination of comprehensive weighted selection and maximum marginal relevance. Experiments on text sets of different topics show that at a 15% compression ratio, the system achieves an average precision of 66.7% and recall of 65.5%. The results indicate that introducing sentence meaning features effectively improves multi-document summarization performance.

3.3.3 Study Methods

There are actually three approaches to semantic studies:

(1) The language-world approach, where meaning is viewed as the relationship between linguistic words and entities in the external world.
(2) The intra-linguistic approach, where meaning is studied as the relationship between words within the language system.
(3) The conceptual approach, where the meaning of linguistic words is regarded as the conceptualization methods in language users' minds (Taylor, 2002).

In studies on language-world relations, the question to answer is: for this word, what kind of situation is expressed through it? In research on world-language relations, the question to answer is: for such a state of affairs, what linguistic words can be used to describe it? Key issues with the language-world approach include:

(1) This approach is limited to words expressing concrete entities; the meanings of words like "soul" or "ghost" cannot be reasonably explained through this method.
(2) Linguistic words do not directly refer to the external world; they refer to entities in mental spaces, which can include imaginary entities. Additionally, mental spaces themselves can be hypothetical, imaginary, or virtual.
(3) Even for words with concrete referents, this approach has limitations, as word meanings are not confined to the word-referent relationship. For example, the distinction between stingy and thrifty.

The intra-linguistic approach focuses on structural relations within the language system, primarily paradigmatic and syntagmatic relations between linguistic components. Lyons (1968) notes that the meaning of a lexeme can be defined as depending on—and equivalent to—the set of relations between that lexeme and other lexemes in the same system. However, the problem lies in how these words acquire meaning in the first place? Knowing only the relationship between buy and sell does not help us understand their conceptual content.

The third approach to semantic research is the conceptual approach, which defines word meanings based on the processes and characteristics of concept formation. Examples include the "profile/ground" theory, concepts of "domain", frames, scripts, scenarios, and idealized cognitive models (ICMs). Cognitive linguistics adopts the third approach.

There are three methods for studying sentence meaning: the formal method, the psychological method, and the conceptual method.

The formal method focuses on structural patterns manifested in the explicit forms of language, which are abstracted from meaning and considered self-contained systems. Formal semantics within the generative grammar framework primarily addresses meaning corresponding to formal categories and their operations—the core concerns of this tradition. Generative linguistics connects with psychology mainly to explain the cognitive structures and processes underlying formal categories and operations.

The psychological method examines language from the perspective of general cognitive systems. Therefore, psychology has long studied language through perception, memory, attention, and reasoning, partially involving the other two approaches to linguistic meaning. It thus examines language from both formal and conceptual features, including analyses of semantic memory, conceptual associations, category structures, and contextual knowledge. However, the psychological method tends to overlook the structural categories central to the conceptual method, as well as the overall system of schematic structures—the tools through which language organizes its conceptual content.

The conceptual method focuses on the laws and processes by which conceptual content in language is organized. It studies fundamental categories in language such as space and time, scenes and events, objects and processes, motion and location, and force and propulsion. It also explores linguistic structures for basic conceptual and emotional categories in cognizers, such as attention, perspective, volition, intention, and syntactic structures, as well as relationships between conceptual structures (e.g., metaphorical mapping, within the same semantic frame, context, and combining conceptual categories into larger structural systems). In short, cognitive linguistics seeks to identify the overall structural system of conceptual structures in language.

Cognitive approaches to sentence meaning include introspection, analysis of others' introspective content, discourse and corpus analysis, examination of contextual and cultural structures, psycholinguistic observation and experimentation, neuro-psychological study of language pathology, and neuroscientific instrumental observation.

The main goal of introspection and analyzing others' introspective content is to study mental phenomena accessible to consciousness.

Discourse and corpus analysis are common methods in semantics, but the discovery of new corpora or examining familiar corpora from new perspectives can help better explain semantic phenomena.

Examining contextual and cultural structures. Allwood (1999) proposes an "operational approach to semantics" in semantics and meaning determination, which is cognitive, dynamic, and context-integrated. The author argues that discourse meaning in context arises from the combination of words' semantic potential, constrained by semantic operations and various contextual information.

Psychological observation and experimentation. Recent years, with the development of computers and imaging technologies, human brain activities can now be simulated, observed, and studied through computer experiments. Holmqvist (1999) titled his paper *Conceptual Engineering*, providing a computational model for Langacker's cognitive grammar. The model's first part consists of a semantic composition process that views semantic construction as "image imposition", which grows incrementally and relates to "semantic expectations". This model is significant because it demonstrates the possibility of understanding the mechanisms of the superimposition process through experiments, thus enabling revisions to the overall model.

Zlatev (1999) uses computational models to discuss how linguistic words are experience-based, adopting a "situated embodied semantics" model where meaning emerges from the pairing of words with situations. The author uses connectionist models to test the feasibility of this approach and understand how to acquire categories without relying on necessary and sufficient conditions, the context dependence of meaning, and the ability to say and understand novel expressions.

Neuropsychological methods. Engberg-Pedersen (1999) discusses sign languages used by the deaf and mute from the perspective of cognitive semantics in her paper *Space and Time*. She first analyzes space–time words in verbal communication, then describes how Danish sign language uses space to represent time. The author finds systematic connections between linguistic means for expressing temporal relations and words for spatial relations. Based on Gibson's psychology, she notes that while time and space are not entirely distinct perceptual domains, conceptual distinctions between them are possible at certain cognitive levels. However, neither time nor space can necessarily be seen as a metaphorical extension of the other; what constitutes a metaphorical extension depends on language users' understanding of a word's basic meaning.

The comparative method. The comparative method is crucial in sentence semantics research, involving both cross-linguistic comparisons and diachronic analyses of different stages of the same language. Sometimes sentence meaning research requires combining diachronic and synchronic perspectives.

Theories underlying our current research include typology, cognitive science, functional linguistics, frame semantics, and semantic maps. Of course, traditional semantic models such as general semantics, Whorfian semantics, semantic taxonomies, logical-mathematical semantics, interpretive semantics, and generative semantics, as well as contemporary semantic theories like collocation theory, structural semantics, semantic component analysis, and semantic field theory, still play roles in research.

Some social science projects study semantics from an information perspective. For example, Si Lianhe's 2015 project "*A Comparative Study of Sentence Meanings in Chinese and English Simple Sentences from the Trinitarian Perspective of Lexicon, Semantics, and Syntax under the Theory of Semantic Information Conservation*" adopts this approach, based on the principle of semantic information conservation. Guided by this theory, the project starts with a comparative study of sentence meanings in Chinese and English simple sentences, systematically examining similarities and differences in semantic expressions across syntactic, lexical, and constructional levels. It integrates the three branches of semantics into a unified theoretical framework, holding significant theoretical and practical value. Grammatical information, semantic information, and pragmatic information correspond to the formal, content, and utility levels of information, respectively. Grammatical information is the most basic level, involving only the structure of things' movement; semantic information relates to meaning; pragmatic information relates to utility. The organic whole of grammatical, semantic, and pragmatic information is called full information. Concepts linked to grammatical information include grammaticality, those linked to semantic information include meaningfulness, and those linked to pragmatic information include acceptability. Semantic information remains conserved. This project focuses on comparative research of sentence meanings in Chinese and English simple sentences, excluding complex sentences, as complex sentences are composed of simple sentences through coordination and embedding, and can be studied based on simple sentences. Research on simple sentences mainly focuses on lexical items, syntactic structures, semantic structures, and the interaction between lexical and structural meanings.

We can sort out similarities and differences in syntactic structures and word order between Chinese and English simple sentences, and analyze the rationale behind these similarities and differences. Starting from the five major sentence patterns in English and Chinese—SV, SVC, SVO, SVOO, and SVOC—we explore in detail the sub-classifications of each pattern in both languages, their similarities and differences, and the corresponding causes.

Si Lianhe's project analyzes five sentence structures in English: (1) intransitive construction (SV), (2) neuter construction (SVC), (3) transitive construction

(SVO), (4) dative construction (SVOiOd), and (5) factitive construction (SVOC). Chinese sentences can all be subsumed under these five basic patterns, corresponding to: (1) subject-predicate (SV), (2) subject-predicate-complement (SVC), (3) subject-predicate-object (SVO), (4) subject-predicate-double object (SVOO), and (5) subject-predicate-object-complement (SVOC).

Si conducts a comparative analysis of variants of these five structures in Chinese and English. For the SV pattern, Chinese has only one variant: VS. English has three main variants: VS, ModalVSV, and VSModalV, with overall low usage frequency.

For SVC, Chinese has two variants: CVS and SC. English has six main variants: VSC, ModalVsVC, CVS, CSV, CModalVSV, and VCModalVS, with varying usage patterns.

For SVO, Chinese has seven variant patterns: SOV, OSV, OSV + pron., S + prep. + O + V, prep. + OSV, prep. + OSV + pron., and the emerging variant VOSModalV. English has nine variants: OSV, OSV + pron., prep. + OSV + pron., VSO, OVs, ModalVsVO, VOSModalV, OModalVSV, and ModalVS(V + O), but all have limited or low usage frequency.

For SVOiOd, Chinese has 13 variant patterns: the extinct SVOd + Oi and OiSVOd; the general SVOd + prep. + Oi; the common S + prep. + OiVOd; emerging variants prep. + OiSVOd, prep. + OiSVOiOd, and prep. + OdSVOiOd; the common but weakened SVOi + prep. + Od; the common S + prep. + Od + VOi; the low-frequency S + prep. + Od + V + pron. + prep. + Oi and Ods + prep. + OiV; the general S + prep. + Od + prep. + Oi + V; and the rare OiSV + pron. + Od. English has six variants: the low-frequency SVOi + prep. + Od and SV + prep. + OiOd; the common SVOd + prep. + Oi; and the very low-frequency prep. + OiSVOd, prep. + OiSVOiOd, and prep. + OdSVOiOd.

For SVOC, Chinese has nine variant patterns: the common S + prep. + OVC; the low-frequency SOVC, prep. + O + SVC, OSVC, and SVC + prep. + O; the general SVCO; and several new variants in modern Chinese influenced by translated language: prep. + O + SV + pron. + C, SV + pron. + CO, and OSV + pron. + C. English has four main variants: the general CSVO and SVCO; the common SV + pron. + CO; and the low-frequency OSV + pron. + C.

Guided by the principle of semantic information conservation, this comparative study of simple sentences in Chinese and English analyzes the five sentence patterns and their variants in English, as well as their corresponding Chinese translations, from linguistic, lexical, syntactic, semantic, and rhetorical levels, identifying similarities and differences between the two languages. For example, consider the structure S + V + noun (pron.) + adj.:

Example 1 Mary's words made the woman (her) angry. mǎ lì de huà ràng zhè wèi fù rén hěn(tā) shēng qì

Correspondences between the English and Chinese sentences include:

Chinese English
mǎ lì de huà Mary's words
ràng made

zhè wèi fù rén the woman
hěn shēng qì angry

At the phonological level, neither sentence has distinctive phonological-semantic features. At the syntactic level, "mǎ lì de huà" and "Mary's words" are both third-person plural nominative nouns denoting entities outside the speaker and hearer, serving as subjects. "ràng" and "make" are both transitive verbs, specifically complex-transitive verbs taking a compound object. Chinese "ràng" has no morphological changes and does not take the past marker "le", while English "make" undergoes complex inflections for person, tense, gender, number, and case. Here, "make" should take the past tense form with the inflectional suffix -ed. But "make" is an irregular verb, specifically a strong verb, it indicates the past tense through a change in the root vowel, resulting in the final form "made". Chinese "zhè wèi fù rén" is a noun phrase in the structure "number + classifier + noun", while English uses the definite article "the + noun", losing the semantic information of "quantity". Chinese "hěn shēng qì" (very angry) uses the adverb of degree "hěn" + adjective "shēng qì", while English uses the adjective alone, with Chinese conveying more degree-related semantic information. At the morphological level, there are no compound or derived words, meaning no special morphological-semantic information in these sentences. Syntactically, both "mǎ lì de huà" and "Mary's words" function as subjects equivalent to "they" (third-person plural nominative). "Ràng" and "make" are both complex-transitive verbs involving an object O denoting a person or thing ("zhè wèi fù rén"/ "the woman") and a complement C for that object ("hěn shēng qì"/"angry"). Both sentences have the syntactic structure:

S + V + noun + adj.

This is a typical complex-transitive structure, semantically describing the subject's causative action—causing someone or something to be in a certain state. More specifically, the syntactic structure is:

S → NP + VP
NP → DET + N
VP → V + NP + ADJP
NP → DET + N
ADJP → ADJ

At the semantic level, "mǎ lì de huà" and "Mary's words" are both agents and themes, the action initiators. "Ràng" and "make" are complex-transitive verbs expressing incomplete actions with typical causative meanings, involving an agent subject, a patient object expressing person/thing, and a complement describing the object's state, a ternary verb. The semantic structure of both sentences is:

Mary's words made the woman angry.
mǎ lì de huà ràng zhè wèi fù rén hěn shēng qì
Agent – Action – Patient – Attribute

Both describe the agent's causative action on the patient.

At the logical level, since these are simple sentences without conjunctions or other function words, there is no logical-semantic information.

According to the HNC (Hierarchical Network of Concepts) theory, correspondences can be established between the semantic formats of simple sentences and their syntactic types:

- If E is an action X, XJ = A + X + B (B = XB + YB + YC); corresponds to SVO or SVC.
- If E is a process P, PJ = PB + P; corresponds to SV.
- If E is a transfer T, TJ = TA + T + TB + TC; corresponds to SVOO or SVOC.
- If E is an effect Y, YJ = YB + Y; corresponds to SV.
- If E is a relation R, RJ = RB + R (RB = RB1RB2; RB1 + RB2); corresponds to SV.
- If E is a state S, SJ = SB + S; corresponds to SV.
- If E is a judgment D, DJ = DA + D + DB + DC; corresponds to SVC.

Action sentences, process sentences, transfer sentences, effect sentences, relation sentences, state sentences, and judgment sentences each have their different categories, with each categories containing distinct subcategories that own their detailed semantic formats. We have made a detailed exploration. For example, process sentences are divided into general process sentences, basic process sentences, sketch sentences, causal sentences, and effect-cause sentences. The format for general process sentences is:

PJ = PB + P
PmJ = PmB + Pm
P0J = PB + P + PC
Pm0J = PmB + Pm + PmC

Basic process sentences have the format:

P01J = PBC + P
Pm01J = PmBC + Pm

Sketch sentences have the format:

P11J = PB + P11 + P11C

Causal sentences have the format:

P21J = PBC1 + (P21) + PBC2

Here, PBC1 is the cause and PBC2 is the effect, both of which can be clausal downgrading.

Effect-cause sentences have the reverse format:

P22J = PBC2 + P22 + PBC1

The relationship between sentence meaning (Jm), structural meaning (sm), and lexical meaning (lm) can be formalized as: Jm = f1 (sm) + f2 (lm).

This formula states that the meaning of a sentence is a function of its semantic structure meaning and the meanings of its individual words. Both structural meaning and lexical meaning are variables; any change in either will lead to a change in the overall sentence meaning.

The principle of semantic information conservation applies to Chinese-English translation, but whether pragmatic information is also conserved requires further study. If pragmatic information is conserved, what is the relationship between pragmatic information, semantic information, and contextual information in Chinese and English?

3.3.4 Study Limitations

The study limitations pointed out by He Yingyu (2003) still apply to the current status of sentence semantic research.

First, there is unbalanced development across research domains. Domestic scholars often focus on chasing trendy issues while paying insufficient attention to more fundamental questions. In fact, the most basic questions in sentence semantic research should be: how to ensure the semantic correctness of generated sentences? How to filter out sentences that are syntactically correct but semantically invalid? Researchers should focus more on these questions and integrate syntactic and semantic research to make sentence semantic research serve sentence generation.

Second, there is unbalanced development of research methods. In terms of methodology, research on formal semantics in domestic linguistics circles is notably weak. Researchers often lack systematic logical knowledge, making it difficult to formally express and reason about semantics. This is inconsistent with the development trend of global semantics.

Finally, the application of the research needs improving. While theoretical exploration is undoubtedly necessary, the application of theories in practice is also important. The application mainly refers to language teaching and the computer processing of language. Sentence semantic theory will not only directly turn theory into "productivity", but also test and promote the development of the theory itself, if it can better combine language teaching and the computer processing of language.

3.4 Future Directions of Sentence Semantics Studies

3.4.1 Interdisciplinary Studies of Sentence Semantics

Future studies of sentence semantics is likely to progress toward interdisciplinary and cross-disciplinary studies. Lexical semantics and sentence semantics are two major branches of semantics, and they will intersect. Lexical meaning influences sentence meaning. In sentence meaning, lexical meaning and structural meaning exhibit an interactive relationship.

Semantics is a branch of linguistics, which also includes other sub-fields such as phonetics, morphology, syntax, pragmatics, and discourse analysis. Studies of sentence semantics has already developed close interdisciplinary connections with morphology, syntax, and pragmatics, with a growing number of interface-focused projects and publications. In the future, sentence semantics is also expected to intersect with phonetics, leading to further research in this area. This trend is reflected in the projects funded by the National Social Science Fund of China over the past decade. Studies of syntax-semantics far outnumber those of phonetics-semantics, morphology-semantics, and semantics-pragmatics.

We can now explore several key issues in sentence semantics studies, including compositional meaning, semantic roles, grammatical relations, and paraphrasing. By proposing common challenges and sharing different ideas, we aim to advance a more systematic and in-depth understanding of sentence meaning.

Question 1: Is sentence meaning compositional in the same way as word meaning?

In terms of compositional principle, the most well-known is Frege's Compositional Principle, proposed by the German scholar Gottlob Frege. It holds that the meaning of an expression (a word, phrase, or sentence) is a function of the meanings of its constituent parts and the way they are combined. In other words, compositional meaning arises from the summation of morphemes and lexical meanings within a phrase, and further, from the combination of phrase meanings. This can be formally represented as:

$$S = (P1 = W1 + W2 + W3) + (P2 = W4 + W5 + W6) + (Pn = Wm + \ldots + Wn)$$

Example 2 S = [[boys + [in [the swimming pool]] + [by [the hotel]]]] + [are discussing [about [their swimming skills]] + [in [a happy manner]] + [with [their friends]]]].

In this sentence, "the hotel" is a noun phrase, with "hotel" as its headword; "by the hotel" is a prepositional phrase, with "by" as its headword; "the swimming pool by the hotel" is a noun phrase, with "swimming pool" as its headword; "in the swimming pool by the hotel" is a prepositional phrase, with "in" as its headword; "boys" is a plural noun, formed by adding the plural suffix "-s" to the noun "boy"; "boys in the swimming pool by the hotel" is a noun phrase, with "boys" as its headword, functioning as the subject of the sentence; "their swimming skills" is a noun phrase, with "skills" as its headword; "about their swimming skills" is a prepositional phrase, with "about" as its headword; "are discussing" is the progressive aspect of a verb, formed by the auxiliary verb "be" plus the present participle of the verb; "are discussing about their swimming skills" is a verb phrase, with "discuss" as its headword; "a happy manner" is a noun phrase, with "manner" as its headword; "in a happy manner" is a prepositional phrase, with "in" as its headword; "their friends" is a noun phrase, with "friends" as its headword; "with their friends" is a prepositional phrase, with "with" as its headword; "are discussing about their swimming skills in a happy manner with their friends" is a verb phrase, with "discuss" as its verbal head, functioning as the predicate of the sentence. The noun phrase "boys in the swimming pool by the hotel" and the verb phrase "are discussing about their swimming skills in a happy manner with their friends" combine to form the sentence. We employ parallel processing to handle different components simultaneously. For instance, when dealing with the prepositional phrases "in the swimming pool", "by the hotel", "about their swimming skills", "in a happy manner", and "with their friends" in the above sentence, although the sentence has a hierarchical structure, our brains process it linearly—adding the meaning of each component one by one.

This principle is widely applied in linguistics and can be viewed as the reverse application of sememe analysis. Because the latter involves decomposing a word into its constituent sememes. Conversely, the compositional principle actually operates by combining these different sememes to form words. For example, the word man can be decomposed into the sememes [+MALE], [+ADULT], and [+HUMAN]. Reversing this process, these sememes can be recombined to form a word. For instance, [+MALE], [+ADULT], and [+HUMAN] together constitute man. If we alter one of these sememe features, we derive different words: changing [+MALE] to [-MALE] yields woman. Changing [+ADULT] to [-ADULT] yields boy. Changing [+HUMAN] to [-HUMAN] yields animal. These three words, woman, boy and animal, are all antonyms of man, though they differ in hierarchical scope: animal represents the broadest opposition. Woman opposes man at the level of gender. Boy opposes man at the level of age. If we simultaneously alter two semantic features—for example, changing [+MALE] to [-MALE] and [+ADULT] to [-ADULT], we derive girl. However, girl is not an antonym of man.

Compositionality can be categorized into linear and non-linear types. In linear compositionality, each phrase combines with adjacent phrases to form higher-level constituents. However, linear compositionality is not the only way to account for sentence formation. If it were the sole mechanism, we could easily derive algorithmic rules to compute sentence meaning such as through first-order predicate calculus representation and assume both lexical and structural meanings were unambiguous. Yet reality proves otherwise. Not all meaning is compositional, and not all compositional meaning is linear. Sentences often contain discontinuous constituents, where elements are separated by intervening words or phrases. In English grammar, two prominent examples of discontinuous constructions are extraposition and Wh-fronting. Extraposition is the discontinuous construction where a clause becomes separated from the nominal phrase it modifies and appears at sentence-final position. Look at example 3:

Example 3 A girl is in the conference room who wants to engage with you.

The relative clause "[who wants to engage with you]" demonstrably does not modify its immediately adjacent noun phrase "the conference room", but rather qualifies "a girl", forming the complete attributive clause "a girl who wants to engage with you". While "girl" serves as the headword of this construction, the constituent elements "a girl" and "who wants to engage with you" are separated due to the intervening verb phrase "is in the conference room". In summary, the attributive clause "[who wants to engage with you]" has been extraposed, being separated from the noun (a girl) it modifies.

In English, wh-words such as who, when, what, how, and where are typically fronted to the beginning of interrogative sentences, even when they form part of a verb phrase in terms of compositional meaning. This fronting separates them from the subject, auxiliary verb, and main verb. For example: when are you going? What do they want? We can compare the linear sentence "Who told you that?" with the non-linear sentence "Who did you tell that?".

Noncompositional meaning cannot be constructed as the sum of the meanings of its parts. This occurs in idioms, where the meaning of idioms is derived from metaphor and other types of semantic extension. For instance, "to get up on the wrong side of the bed" is a verb phrase with the structure "[vp[v pav up pp [p on np [Det the Adj wrong N side pp [p of NP[Det the N bed]]]]". The idiomatic meaning, "to be in a bad mood", bears little relation to its compositional meaning. Other idioms, such as "a snake in the grass" ("a hidden enemy") and "kick the bucket" ("to die"), also cannot be inferred from the combination of their parts. Idioms are stored in the lexicon store as inseparable units, much like other lexical items.

In summary, when analyzing sentence meaning: idioms require retrieval of their stored meanings from the lexicon rather than compositional construction. Non-continuous elements (e.g., extraposition and wh-fronting) necessitate non-linear composition. Linear composition remains applicable in most other cases.

Question 2: How many semantic roles exist in language?

Semantic roles, also called semantic cases or thematic roles, are a method of representing sentence meaning using logical terms. These roles are assigned to nouns and noun phrases based on their relationship with the verb. It is widely held that all languages employ semantic roles, which are utilized in both formal and functional analyses of language. At least 10 distinct semantic roles can be identified. They are agent, the doer or actor of an action; patient, the entity affected by the action of an agent or cause; location, the place where an action or event occurs; instrument, the entity used by an agent to perform an action; time, the temporal point or duration of an action or event; recipient, the receiver of the result of an agent's action; experiencer, the perceiver of a stimulus; stimulus, the entity perceived or experienced by an experiencer; cause, a non-agentive reason or motivator (involuntary and unintentional); goal, the target location, also referred to purpose or finality.

Example 4 Farmers (Ag) raise crops (Pa) for city folk (Re).

Example 5 Rain (St) pleases the farmers (Ex) but too much rain (Ca) harms the crops(Pa).

Example 6 In the summer (Ti), the farmers (Ag) use trucks (Ins) to bring crops (Pa) from the fields (Lo).

Example 7 The farmers (Ag) may send their crops (Pa) to market (Go) through cooperatives (Ins).

The crops (Pa) are sent by train and truck (Ins) to distribution centers (Go) in large cities and towns (Lo).

Market value (Ca) determines which crops (Pa) farmers (Ag) will plant the next spring (Ti).

From this, we can observe that the semantic properties of a verb largely determine the semantic roles of its complements. The same noun or noun phrase have different semantic roles in different sentences. For example:

Example 8 The worker (Ag) listened to the wind whistle.

Example 9 The worker (Ex) heard the wind whistle.

Example 10 The worker (Ag) watched the wind whistle.

Example 11 The worker (Ex) saw the wind whistle.

The verbs "see" and "hear" exhibit involuntary properties, meaning their subjects function as experiencers rather than as agents. This distinction can serve as a basis for syntactic/semantic classification of verbs.

Jia Yande (1999) argues that sentence meaning can be divided into topic and comment, and that sentence meaning consists of predicates, arguments, descriptive components, and connective components. Jia considers predicates the most crucial, categorizing them into zero-valent, monovalent, bivalent, and trivalent types. We believe these roughly correspond to verbs in sentence-final clauses (without explicit subjects), intransitive verbs, mono-transitive verbs (taking one object), and ditransitive verbs (taking two objects), respectively. Arguments in sentence meaning represent objects or participants, corresponding to nouns and personal pronouns in grammar. They exhibit various semantic types, known as semantic cases. Jia analyzes basic cases (including agentive case, objective case, and dative case) and general cases (including environmental case, instrumental case, causal case, and modifying case). There are 9 sub-types under the three basic cases and 13 sub-types under the four general cases, totaling 22 semantic cases. Descriptive components correspond to modifiers and complement in grammar, divided into argument-modifying components, predicate-modifying components, and predicate-complementing components. Connective components express relations such as causality, hypothesis, concession, condition, coordination, alternative, progression, and contrast. We acknowledge that some semantic cases are well-defined, while others are more ambiguous. The use of semantic cases opens a window for studying sentences at the semantic level, adding a new dimension to the analysis of sentence meaning. However, some of Jia's case labels borrow grammatical terms like "dative", which might be clearer if renamed "recipient case". More importantly, the exact number of semantic cases in a language remains indeterminate, unlike the consensus on grammatical cases. This ambiguity led C. Fillmore to ultimately abandon his Case Grammar framework.

Question 3: How can verbs be classified from the perspective of semantic roles?

Verbs play a central role in sentences. Many scholars consider them the nucleus of clauses, as verb categories determine sentence types. Syntactically, verbs can be classified into linking verbs, intransitive verbs, mono-transitive verbs, ditransitive verbs, complex verbs, and other categories, each corresponding to distinct syntactic sentence patterns. While verbal items themselves carry meaning, verb semantics also partially reside in the semantic roles of their nominal complements that co-occur with them in clauses. Regarding the aforementioned ten common semantic roles, we could add source as an additional category. These roles cannot all coexist in a single sentence. Some are obligatory while others optional. Generally, Agent and patient are indispensable; verbs requiring both agent and patient roughly correspond to mono-transitive verbs and align with SVO structures. Some verbs take only an agent without a patient, approximating intransitive verbs and correlating with SV structures. Others require agent, patient, and recipient, approximating ditransitive verbs and corresponding to SVOO structures. Certain verbs take agent and goal, maintaining SV syntax but adding a prepositional phrase indicating goal. Some verbs take recipient and patient while maintaining SVO syntax, but with the recipient becoming the formal subject, suggesting passive voice.

Based on required semantic roles, English verbs can be classified into five categories with corresponding expression patterns and deep case frames. Deep case frames of verbs are enclosed in "[]", with "+" indicating simultaneous occurrence of listed semantic cases and "____" representing the verb (phrase) in case frames. No connectors are used between semantic cases.

Verbs requiring agent and patient, such as, open, eat, fill, expressed as S (Ag) V O (Pa). Example: Mom (Ag) opened a box of cornflakes (Pa). Its deep case frame is [+_Ag Pa].

Verbs requiring only agent and no patent, such as, resign, smile, wake up, expressed as S (Ag) V. Example: Nixon (Ag) resigned. Its deep case frame is [+_Ag].

Verbs requiring agent, patient, and recipient, such as give, award, send, expressed as S (Ag) V O (Pa) <-> O(Rec). Example: She (Ag) gave money (Pa) to the United Fund (Rec). Its deep case frame is [+_Ag Pa Rec].

Verbs requiring agent and goal, such as walk, go, travel, expressed as S (Ag)V A (Go). Example: They (Ag) went into the bar (Go). Its deep case frame is [+_Ag Go].

Verbs denoting a recipient (non-agent) and a patient, such as win, get, and receive, take the form of S (Rec) V O (Pa). For example 12:

Example 12 Five people (Rec) won a magazine subscription (Pa).

Its deep case frame is [+ Rec Pa]. Many scholars take the in-depth study of syntax and semantics based on semantic roles as their goal.

Question 4: What are the similarities and differences between semantic roles and grammatical relations?

Grammatical relations include subject, object, and prepositional object. Unlike semantic roles, these are formal or grammatical relations based on sentence structure rather than the meanings of nouns and verbs. In English, the agent is typically the subject, the patient is a typical object, and other semantic roles are expressed as objects of prepositions. For example, the recipient as the object of "for" or "to", the instrument as the object of "with", and the location as the object of "on, at, near, beside", etc.

Similarities:

Both grammatical relations and semantic roles are related to verbs, and there is a strong correspondence between them. Therefore, sometimes we study grammatical relations from the perspective of meaning rather than form. For example, the subject is considered the performer of an action. However, this is incorrect because there is no one-to-one correspondence between meaning components (or semantics) and formal components.

Differences:

Grammatical relations and semantic roles differ in three aspects: (1) their formal or structural nature; (2) their permanent invariance in paraphrasing; (3) their expressions in language.

Regarding formal nature, grammatical relations reflect the formal relationships between sentence components, while semantic roles reflect the meaning relationships between sentence components.

Regarding the permanence of semantic roles in paraphrasing, we know that although the grammatical relations of components change in paraphrasing, the meaning remains constant across different forms. For example:

Example 13 Dogs eat meat <-> Meat is eaten by dogs.
S (Ag) O (Pa) S (Pa) O (Ag)

Regarding the formal expressions of grammatical relations, grammatical analysis has certain regular and specific formal properties, but semantic roles do not (e.g., dogs and meat differ formally in the examples above). For instance, in English, subjects as grammatical relations have the following properties: generally positioned before the verb; when the subject is third-person singular, the present-tense verb takes a special suffix -s; can be replaced by nominative pronouns; in yes/no questions, auxiliary verbs typically precede the subject; In tag questions within special questions, personal pronouns and the number of the subject are included (Hudson, 2005). Objects as grammatical relations in English have these properties: generally positioned after the verb in both declarative and yes/no questions; can be replaced by accusative pronouns; in declarative sentences with the formal subject there, they agree with the verb in singular/plural form according to the principle of notional concord. Different languages have different ways of marking subjects and objects. For example, in Japanese, the subject is marked by the nominative particle ga, and the object by the accusative particle o. In Latin, nouns have six cases indicated by suffixes with nominative for subjects and accusative for objects, etc.

Question 5: What is the role of semantic roles in paraphrasing?

As noted above, semantic roles are permanently invariant in paraphrasing, while grammatical relations change. For sentences containing some types of verbs classified by the semantic roles of their associated nouns or noun phrases, systematic paraphrasing is possible, where semantic roles remain constant but grammatical relations may alter.

Verbs with cause/agent and patient. This type of verb is the so-called transitive verb, where the cause or agent serves as the subject, and the patient serves as the object. Active sentences with such verbs can be paraphrased as passive sentences, in which the patient becomes the subject, and the agent becomes the object of the preposition by. For example: the sentence of Dogs eat meat can be paraphrased as Meat is eaten by dogs.

Verbs of state change. Verbs where the patient undergoes a state change may take the patient as the subject of the active verb, while the agent does not express, and requires the presence of manner adverbs such as easily, quickly, etc. For example:

Example 14 These boxes light easily.

It can be paraphrased as Someone lights these boxes easily. For verbs that do not obviously involve a patient, there are exceptions to this usage, such as This magazine reads easily. These sentences are formally active but express passive meanings, and we can call them pseudo-active sentences.

Verbs with agent, patient, and recipient. These verbs take the patient as the direct object and the recipient as the object of indirect object, beneficiary object), or omit to and treat the patient and recipient as double objects. In paraphrasing, the to-phrase form can be converted to a double-object structure, and passive constructions can also be used. For example:

Example 15 He hasn't sent the book to her.

It can be paraphrased as He hasn't sent her the book or She hasn't been sent the book (by him).

Verbs with sources and targets. The source also belongs to semantic roles. If the source is the subject, then the target is the object of into. If the target is the subject, then the source is the object of from. For example:

Example 16 Little boys grow into men.

It can be paraphrased as Men grow from little boys. The target seems like a recipient, but such a paraphrase is not allowed: I sent my little sister to the store; * I sent the store my little sister.

Verbs with the agent and patient as one. These verbs take the agent as the subject, and the same noun phrase agent can optionally be expressed as an accusative reflexive pronoun. For example:

Example 17 Smith shaved.

It can be paraphrased as Smith shaved himself. This is roughly equivalent to the middle voice in Greek, referring to the action in the sentence involving himself, or the action being performed for his own benefit. The middle voice is used by some grammarians to describe structures in English like I am getting shaved, which means either I am shaving or I am being shaved.

3.4.2 Empirical Quantitative Studies of Sentence Semantics

According to Zhou Shaoxuan (1978), the distributive-statistic analysis method in semantics, which was employed by the American Descriptive Linguistics School for content-independent analysis of linguistic forms as early as the 1950s, was later adopted by linguists in Britain, America, and the Soviet Union for semantic studies starting in the 1960s, primarily for pragmatic purposes. With the advancement of computing technology, the application of distributive-statistic analysis has become increasingly widespread. This method involves conducting statistical analyses on the distribution and frequency of words within sentences, enabling precise identification of semantic features and mitigating subjectivity in semantic studies. For instance, taking Shakespearean dramas as corpus, we analyze the distribution and frequency of the indefinite articles a and an in character dialogues. Our findings reveal a higher occurrence of these articles in the speech of clowns, servants, and villagers compare to solemn figures like monks and judges. This distributional pattern is considered a significant semantic-rhetorical feature of the indefinite articles.

Lexical distributional information falls into two categories: the distribution of words across different positions within sentences and the co-occurrence distribution between words. The latter type of information holds greater significance for semantic analysis. For instance, by conducting a co-occurrence frequency analysis of the words burn, fire, hot, and light in Shakespearean dramas, we observe that burn most frequently co-occurs with fire, while its co-occurrences with hot and light are comparatively less frequent. Therefore, this enables us to gauge the semantic closeness of burn to these associated terms.

While the advancements in distributional statistical analysis remain modest, this methodology constitutes a significant stride toward achieving objective semantic description, and its future evolution is certain to unfold further.

3.4.3 Studies of the Application of Sentence Semantics

Sentential semantics has broad applications. Firstly, it can be applied to language teaching. Secondly, it can be used in translation. Furthermore, it can also be employed for natural language processing and artificial intelligence.

3.4.3.1 Employing Theories of Sentence Semantics to Instruct English Teaching

We can employ collocational theory to guide English teaching. The juxtaposition, the collocation of words, is conventionalized. Mastering such conventional usage requires dedicated efforts. We are apt to produce Chinglish sentences and ungramatical sentences that are grammatically well-formed but collocationally deviant. Some words collocate naturally, while others do not. Words that are correlated in semantics do not necessarily collocate in practical applications. We should focus on collocational patterns such as noun-verb collocation, noun-adjective collocation, verb-preposition collocation, adjective-preposition collocation among others. Meanwhile, we should also pay attention to the unconventional collocations occurring in specific contexts and habitual usages.

We can also employ structural semantic theory to guide English teaching. Implicit semantic relations incorporate the hyponymy and hypernym relation, antonymy and relative relation. The hyponymy-hypernym relation can be understood by using hypernyms to summarize and through expanding hyponyms. Mastering the antonym enhances contrasts, highlights things' characteristics, and helps semantic explanation. It is essential for us to work out the distinctions between contradictory terms and contrary terms, as well as to enrich students' vocabulary. Learning relative relations helps to broaden vocabulary, enabling students to flexibly employ various sentence types.

We can also employ semantic componential analysis theory to instruct English teaching. Semantic componential analysis can be employed to interpret word meaning, distinguish synonyms, explain figures of speech, elucidate objective things and semantic changes.

We can also employ case grammar and frame semantics to instruct English teaching. Deep case frame is closely correlated with Hornby's verb pattern.

We can also apply the theory of synonymy and synonymous transformation to English teaching, aiming to effectively enhance students' expressive abilities. For instance, we can design various exercises such as word order transformation drills, simplification transformation drills, deletion transformation drills, synonym contrast drills, and conversion drills for antonyms and relational words.

Frame Semantics can guide the teaching of English reading comprehension. Adopting a framework-based approach significantly enhances reading effectiveness. Event Semantics facilitates comparative linguistic studies between Chinese and foreign languages, encompassing areas such as verb comparison, sentence structure analysis, and others.

3.4.3.2 Employing Sentence Semantic Theory to Instruct Translation Teaching

Semantics and translation are closely interconnected. The application of semantic field theory, componential analysis, semantic categorization, contrastive Sino-English semantics, and semantic translation methodologies draws upon insights from both semantics and translation studies, enabling the practical integration of semantic theories into translation practice. For instance, semantic field theory encompasses three core tenets: firstly, lexical items in a language form an integrated system where word meanings are interrelated; secondly, vocabulary should be studied as a holistic system rather than isolated semantic shifts of individual words; thirdly, the precise meaning of a term can only be determined through comparative analysis of its relationships with other lexical items. Taking English and Chinese as examples, the relevance of semantic field theory to translation lies in comparative studies of lexical groups under shared conceptual frameworks, thereby ascertaining precise denotations. Furthermore, componential analysis serves as a methodology for dissecting word and phrase meanings, operating on the premise that lexical semantics can be derived through analyzing sets of broader, more generalized semantic features. With regard to its application in translation, this analytical framework holds significant practical value for translators.

3.4.3.3 Employing Sentence Semantic Theory to Instruct the Processing of Artificial Intelligence and Natural Languages

One major bottleneck in natural language processing is semantics. Only by solving semantic issues can we achieve better performance in natural language processing and machine translation. Computer programs can be employed to process semantic information, extract semantic features, and so on.

3.4.4 Contrastive Studies on Sentence Semantics: Chinese vs. Foreign Languages

A significant number of projects funded by the National Social Science Fund over the past decade have focused on Chinese-foreign language contrastive or comparative studies. These include studies comparing Chinese with major languages such as English, German, Japanese, and French, as well as less commonly studied languages like Hebrew and Bantu Languages. Additionally, there are comparative studies between Chinese and domestic minority languages, such as Mongolian and Tibetan.

The field of lexical semantics has a long-established history, and contrastive studies of lexical units between Chinese and foreign languages have yielded abundant results. In contrast, comparative studies of sentence semantics between Chinese and foreign languages remain relatively limited. However, with advancements in the development of sentence semantics and improved methodologies for contrastive analysis, such studies are expected to increase.

For instance, we can conduct contrastive studies of English and Chinese simple perfect sentences. Previous studies on situation types were confined to lexical aspect, which traditionally categorized under tense and considered as a grammatical unit, and often conflated with tense. In contrast to tense, a purely grammatical category, aspect is now recognized as a grammatical-semantic unit. Studies of aspect encompasses viewpoint aspect and situation aspect, with the former providing the perspective of observation and the latter determining whether a situation is an event or state, a category at the sentence-semantic level. The application of the compositional principle has bridged studies of lexical and sentence semantics, thereby expanding the scope of sentence meaning studies.

3.5 Conclusion

Based on the above discussion, we can draw the following conclusions about domestic studies of sentence semantics in China over the past decade:

(1) Substantial progress has been made in sentence-semantic studies within China's foreign language academia. Over these ten years, scholars have advanced nearly all previously explored study areas, achieving considerable depth in their investigations.
(2) Chinese scholars have demonstrated timely assimilation and application of new theories and perspectives. While the 1970s and 1980s primarily involved learning Western theories, the 1990s saw scholars actively applying Western sentence-semantic theories to concrete problems—critically adapting and innovating upon them. Original frameworks with strong explanatory power, such as Event-Case Grammar and Implicature Ontology, were proposed by Chinese researchers.
(3) In general, the study of sentence semantics in China's foreign language academia shows the following developmental trends: analysis of sentence semantics is continuously developing toward a more microscopic and granular direction. For example, analyses of sentence semantic structures have become increasingly specific and classifications of arguments have become more detailed. The communicative dimension of sentences is increasingly coming to the focal attention, exhibiting the transition from isolated studies of static sentence meaning to dynamic discourse meaning. Study scope is continuously broadening, moving beyond single-sentence analysis to investigate meaning in larger discourse contexts. Theories of cognitive linguistics have been increasingly integrated to study sentence meaning, showing a clearer trend toward combining highly explanatory cognitive frameworks with sentence semantic studies.

Chapter 4
Discourse Semantics Studies

4.1 Introduction

Since pragmatics branched off from the language philosophy matrix and gradually became an independent branch of linguistics, and Grice's theory of conversational implicature rose to prominence, contextualists represented by Recanati, Levinson, Jaszczolt, Sperber & Wilson, Carston and Parikh and semantic minimalists represented by Borg, Bach, Cappelen & Lepore, Stanley, Predelli, MacFarlane and Kölbel, these two opposing post-Grice theory[1] and its various variants have been focusing on the criticism and development of the classical Grice's theory of conversational implicature. In their fierce confrontations and debates, the Multiple Gradient Meaning Interpretation Model (Borg, 2012; Recanati, 2005a, 2012; Liu & Wu, 2013) eventually emerged, and thus joint efforts were made to promote the in-depth growth of studies of utterance meaning.

The classic Grice's theory of conversational implicature (Grice, 1975, 1978) involves three levels of binary divisions: natural meaning and non-natural meaning; what is said and what is implicated; conventional implication and conversational implicature. The non-natural meaning contains what is said and what is implicated. What is said refers to the conventional meaning of a sentence, which is the propositional content of truth-conditions, within the semantic research. What is implicated, on the other hand, is the meaning inferred on the basis of what is said in combination with specific pragmatic factors. It is the propositional content of non-truth-conditions and belongs to the pragmatic research. Therefore, the boundary between them is clear.

However, Grice (1989) also acknowledges that the understanding of what is said contains reference resolution, deixis fixing, and disambiguation, or "pragmatic intrusion" (Borg, 2004, 2010). That is, the output of the pragmatic process serves as the input of the semantic process, thus giving rise to the "Gricean Circle" (Levinson,

[1] It refers to after Gricean, based on the principle of parsimony, which aim to reduce the number of conversational principles to enhance the explanatory power of pragmatic theories and enable psychological interpretations. The main representatives include Horn, Levinson, Sperber & Wilson.

X. Wen and R. Tang, *New Perspectives and Developments in Chinese Semantics*,
https://doi.org/10.1007/978-981-95-1730-5_4

2000b). And Grice distinguishes what is implicated into conventional implicature and conversational implicature. Then, according to the degree of context involvement, conversational implicature is further divided into generalized conversational implicature and particularized conversational implicature, forming the "semantics-pragmatics continuum" (Huang, 2014). Conventional implicature is triggered by the conventional features of certain words, but it is different from the conventional meaning of words. It is the meaning of non-truth-conditional inference (Levinson, 1983). Generalized conversational implicature refers to the default meaning that the use of some certain language structures can be given a preferential interpretation without relying on contextual derivation (Bach, 2007; Jaszczolt, 2007; Levinson, 2000a; Recanati, 2004a). Like conventional implicature, generalized conversational implicature is associated with both semantic content and pragmatic elements, and possesses characteristics of both conventional meaning and conversational implicature (Zhang, 2008). Particularized conversational implicature refers to utterance meaning that relies on the specific context and has nothing to do with semantic content.

It is easy to know that Grice draws a tremendous gulf between semantics and pragmatics to sustain truth-conditional theory and the principle of semantic composition. In this way, truth-conditional theory and the principle of semantic composition can be strictly confined within semantics without pragmatic interference. However, confronted with linguistic facts, Grice has to allow some pragmatic factors to intrude into the propositional content of truth-conditions. As a result, what is said encompasses both conventional meaning and the speaker's intention (Carston, 2009). Moreover, he creates two concepts of vague extensions, conventional implicature and generalized conversational implicature, to explain the pragmatic intrusion in what is said. It is the situation that triggered intense confrontations between contextualism and semantic minimalism about the semantics-pragmatics interface.

In response to the limitations of the classical Gricean theory of meaning, contextualism, semantic minimalism, and their numerous variants focus on revising their definition of what is said, the handling of generalized conversational implicature, and interpretation of the pragmatic process, there is relatively little relevant research in China currently. Thus, in this chapter, we will first introduce and comment on the latest foreign research from the above three aspects. Then, we will focus on discussing the future development trends of relevant domestic research. Our aims are to comprehensively sort out and carefully evaluate the diverse and complex interpretive models of the two camps, and strive to clarify the ideological threads and theoretical differences of the major schools in the current arena of meaning research. This will provide researchers in this field with a feasible perspective for observing and analyzing the new progress of the theory of utterance meaning, and also drew a clear sketch for beginners in utterance meaning research to overview the development of meaning theories.

1 Contextualism can be traced back to the use theory of meaning in the Ordinary Language School, emphasizing language use and focusing on informal and contextualized studies of meaning. Its representative views include: moderate contextualism scholars such as Recanati (2001, 2010), Levinson (2000b), Travis (1985, 2008),

and Jaszczolt (2010, 2011) argue that some utterances in language exhibit contextual sensitivity and cannot express complete propositions. They must undergo pragmatic enrichment based on contextual factors to form complete propositions that can be judged true or false; radical contextualism scholars like Sperber and Wilson (1986, 1995), Wilson and Sperber (2002, 2004), Carston (2010), and Parikh (2010) contend that all utterances are context-sensitive in explicit or implicit ways, with incomplete semantic contents expressing propositional fragments. Only by relating to the context of speech acts can complete propositional contents be determined; while semantic minimalism is rooted in the logical positivism of the Ideal Language School, assuming an isomorphism between language and the world and focusing on formalized and conventionalized studies of meaning (Huang, 2013a, 2014). Representative views include minimal semantics (Borg, 2012), radical semantic minimalism (Bach, 2010, 2012), insensitive semantics (Cappelen & Lepore, 2005), indexicalism (King & Stanley, 2005; Stanley, 2007; Stanley & Szabó, 2000), semantic relativism (Garcia-Carpintero & Kölbel, 2008; Kölbel, 2008; MacFarlane, 2009; Predelli, 2005).

4.2 The Definition of "What Is Said"

In response to Grice's "what is said", moderate contextualist Recanati believes that it is from pragmatic enrichment, Levinson advocates that it is generated through the expansion of conversational implicature, and Jaszczolt holds that it is obtained from the combined calculation of semantic and pragmatic information. While, radical contextualists insist that it is determined by the explicit meaning based on pragmatic inference, or propose that it is generated by the dynamic game between semantics and pragmatics. Thus, they all adopt an expansive perspective, incorporating pragmatic factors either partially or wholly into what is said, which expands the connotative components of Grice's classical what is said. While semantic minimalists take an opposite and narrowing perspective, eradicating the influence of pragmatic factors on semantics to ensure the independence and integrity of semantics, and reconstructing the conceptual connotation and triggering factors of what is said.

Recanati (2005b) adopts the term "what is said" from classical Grice's theory, but in content, he abandoned Grice's semantic view of "what is said". He believes that most sentences contain unarticulated constituents (Bach, 2012; Huang, 2013b; Perry, 1986, 1998; Recanati, 1993, 2002b, 2004b). The semantic interpretation of these sentences produces a conceptual schema but not a complete truth-value proposition. To form a complete uttered proposition, it is necessary to consider the specific context, the speaker's intention, and pragmatic expansion. Recanati adheres to the pragmatic view of "what is said". Although Levinson (1995, 2000b) denies the semantic view of "what is said" and adheres to the semantics-pragmatics interface view, he believes that pragmatic content would intrude into "what is said". But, unlike Recanati, he put the extended meaning into the "conversational implicature", trying to simplify the levels of meaning representation and the understanding mechanism. Different from the above two, based on the "parsimony of levels principle" (POL), Jaszczolt (2005, 2007) proposes the "merger representation model". This model integrates semantics and pragmatics into one meaning level and replaces Grice's "what is said" with the primary meaning obtained from the merger representation. He holds that the primary meaning is the "primary, intuitive, and prominent intentional meaning" generated by the combined calculation of semantic and pragmatic information, and it is "the main information recognized by the hearer" (Jaszczolt, 2010: 196–197). Similar to Jaszczolt's merger representation, Parikh (2010) incorporates semantic and pragmatic factors into his "contextualized game of partial information". Through the dynamic game of four constraints: syntax, convention, information, and fluid, linguistic meaning achieves a balance between the grammatical system and the information context (Jiang, 2015), and generates individual contextualized meaning. And it means that "what is said" and "conversational implicature" are generated simultaneously. Relevance theorists such as Sperber and Wilson (1986), Wilson and Sperber (2004), and Carston (2002, 2010) insist on the comprehensive intrusion of pragmatic factors into semantic content. That is, "what is said" in the Gricean does not exist. Instead, they propose "semantic representation + explicature", which refers to semantic content and "the inferential expansion of incomplete conceptual representations or logical forms in discourse" (Huang, 2014: 275).

In contrast to the above interface perspective, moderate semantic minimalists such as Borg (2012), Cappelen and Lepore (2006), Stanley (2005), Stanley and Szabó (2000), and MacFarlane (2007) strictly limit the boundary between semantics and pragmatics. And they attempt to completely remove the classical Gricean concept of "what is said" from semantics and treat "what is said" as an implicature within the pragmatics. However, in order to preserve the truth-conditional theory and to limit the scope of pragmatic operations, they assert that the proposition expressed by a sentence and its truth-value are determined by the sentence components and syntactic combination. Furthermore, they reconstruct the triggering factors of the speaker's meaning in "what is said", and postulate "hidden arguments" (Borg, 2004: 110–131; King & Stanley, 2005), or "basic sets of context sensitive expressions" (Cappelen & Lepore, 2005: 1–2), or "circumstances of evaluation" (MacFarlane, 2007), etc. Thus, in line with the spirit of contextualism, they expanded the distance between sentence meaning and propositional content (Shen, 2011). They transform the strict principle of semantic composition into a relative truth-conditional composition principle, fully demonstrating the tension and contradiction between the truth-conditional semantic theory and the principle of semantic composition under the influence of context-sensitive components. Different from moderate semantic minimalists, Bach (2004, 2007) dismisses the semantics-pragmatics interface view as "a misguidance". He advocates a purely semantic view of "what is said", and believes that "what is said" is entirely composed of syntactic projections independent of context (Liu, 2011). It often has propositional "incompleteness" and merely provides a semantic pattern or conceptual configuration for the propositional content the speaker intends to express (Bach, 2002). As a result, he excludes the truth-value semantic view from formal semantics (Bach, 2006). But we hold that "what is said" without truth-conditions corresponding entirely to linguistically encoded meaning is a redundant concept and should be eliminated with Occam's Razor.

4.3 The Processing of Generalized Conversational Implicature

Regarding the processing of generalized conversational implicature, post-Gricean pragmatists did not reach an agreement on the nature of its pragmatic process. Generally, three opposing theories were formed: the default inference of moderate contextualism, the contextual inference of relevance theorists, and the coordinated inference of radical semantic minimalism.

Recanati (2010) distinguishes meaning into "sentence meaning—what is said—what is implicated", and includes generalized conversational implicature in "what is said", which is processed by a pre-propositional and local primary pragmatic process to yield default meaning. However, unlike Grice, Recanati (2002a) argues that it was not due to the nature of the language structure type, but rather a default expansion established in a specific context. Levinson (1995, 2000b) also divides the research on meaning into three levels: sentence meaning—utterance-type meaning—utterance-token meaning. According to his explanation, utterance-type meaning is independent of context. It is "based on general expectations about the normal use of language" (Levinson, 1995: 93) and "conveyed by the conventional use of language structure" (Levinson, 2000b: 22). It is the default meaning generated by the processing of the pre-semantic pragmatics interpretation model, which basically corresponds to Grice's generalized conversational implicature. However, the classical Gricean generalized conversational implicature, as a member of "what is implicated", has the integrity of propositional processing. While Levinson's utterance-type meaning is automatically activated by the conventional use of language structure without relying on the complete processing of a proposition and is local (Zhang, 2012). If it conflicts with the subsequent utterance processing output, it will be cancelled. The holistic view emphasizes the integrity of the sentence proposition. Since the proposition is complete and is known to all discourse participants, re-processing the proposition not only reduces the timeliness of discourse understanding but also goes against the original intention of Grice's the conversational implicature theory. The local view of Recanati and Levinson also raises the issue of canceling local implicatures. Because when components of sentences are being processed, they can potentially trigger default meaning. During subsequent discourse processing, it is necessary to cancel one by one many local triggered meanings that were generated earlier, which also makes discourse understanding time- and effort-consuming. As Jaszczolt (2008: 24) points out, "In the theory of meaning, we not only need to retain our intuitions about those more salient and common understandings, but also avoid those extended meanings with a high rate of cancellation". Therefore, Jaszczolt

(2011) integrates the above two models and argued that default meanings independent of context and constrained by context could coexist in the merger representation model. These default meanings can be either logical judgments based on language-culture conventions or default expansions relying on context and conversational principles. But Jaszczolt (2010), adhering to the "post-semantic pragmatic interpretation model", holds that the processing of default meaning can only be carried out on the basis of a complete proposition. And the processing of default meaning is post-propositional and holistic, and is difficult to cancel in a specific context. Because they have different understandings of factors such as context, pragmatic inference, and propositional integrity in the identification of default meanings, default theories have been strongly criticized by radical contextualists (Noveck & Sperber, 2007; Noveck & Reboul, 2008; Wilson & Carston, 2007). Carston (2004b: 72) considers that default meanings did not exist at all. "No implicature is a default inference. Contextual relevance is fully sufficient to guarantee the derivation of implicatures". Generalized conversational implicatures are explicatures generated by pragmatically expanding or conceptually contracting the logical form of a sentence in a relevant context.

Radical semantic minimalist Bach (1994, 2010) distinguishes meaning into "what is said—impliciture—what is implicated1". Meanwhile, Bach (1984, 2007) synthesizes the opposing viewpoints within contextualism, and considered that implicit meaning is the default meaning generated by the synergistic effect of default inference and contextual inference. The implicit meaning is dominated by the taking-for-granted principle and the not-worth-considering principle, and generalized conversational implicature falls into this category. In addition, similar to Bach's comprehensive perspective, Parikh (2010) incorporates semantic and pragmatic factors into his "equilibrium semantics". But he does not emphasize the holistic-local issue generated by propositional content of truth-conditions and conversational implicature. Situational information reaches equilibrium simultaneously in the communicative game among conversationalists. Propositional content and conversational implicature are generated in parallel, thus avoiding the redundant processing of meaning in the holistic view and the issue of implicature cancellation in the local view.

1 Bach's three-tiered meaning division differs from Levinson's three-layer meaning model in that Levinson's "utterance-type meaning" is neither purely semantic nor purely pragmatic; instead, it encompasses both semantic content and pragmatic components. In contrast, Bach's impliciture falls entirely within pragmatics and contains no semantic elements. Additionally, Bach's impliciture diverges from Relevance Theory's explicature: according to Bach, impliciture refers to the default meaning hidden within what is said rather than conventional meaning, lacking the "explicitness" claimed by Relevance Theory.

4.4 The Explanation of Pragmatic Processes

Contextualism and semantic minimalism advocate different methods of complementation regarding pragmatic intrusion in what is said. That is free enrichment with strong contextual effects and logical expansion of syntactic constraints. However, both approaches are like trying to fathom the ocean with a ladle, making it difficult to see the whole picture.

Recanati (2004a, 2010) points out that there are three ways for primary pragmatic processes to be realized: (1) saturation; (2) free enrichment; (3) semantic transfer. Saturation is a bottom-up process of compulsory pragmatic intervention, which is often triggered by the linguistic lexical-syntactic system. And it aims to complement the "unarticulated constituents", fill in the "slots", and determine the values of "free variables" for context-sensitive sentences with "incomplete logical forms", thus forming a complete utterance proposition that can be judged as true or false. Free enrichment and semantic transfer are based on pragmatic requirements such as relevance and informativeness. They are optional pragmatic processes that are top-down and context-driven and aim to make pragmatic adjustments to the "logically complete" semantic content and generate propositional forms that can be judged as true or false in an appropriate context. These two types of pragmatic intervention processes seem clearly distinct, but in fact, they are not (Chen, 2015). For example, the optional pragmatic intervention process also involves assigning values to the parameters of the index component. Relevance theorist Carston (2004a, 2010) points out that, apart from the three ways mentioned above, there are also disambiguation, reference resolution, and ad hoc concept construction. Disambiguation and reference resolution are "preconditions" derived from the classical Gricean theory. The former refers to selecting the "immediate meaning" from the multiple meaning potentials of words or structures in relation to a specific context. The latter means determining the contextual value assignment of the "free variables" in relevant referential expressions. Ad hoc concept construction refers to the pragmatic modulation, such as narrowing, broadening, generalizing, or weakening, of the lexical concepts in the logical form of sentence in light of the context. Although this pragmatic modulation is relevant to semantics, they are limited by language use. The modulated lexical concepts directly affect truth-conditions and form components of the sentence proposition. While relevance theorists emphasize the universality of context-sensitivity, their free enrichment is not restricted by syntactic or semantic features. Due to individual differences in background knowledge, contextual assumptions, etc., the enriched propositions that we have may vary widely, or may even not be the propositions the speaker intends to convey. Therefore, pragmatic modulation not only fails to take into account the systematicity of linguistic meaning, but may also lead to over-generation, which has been widely criticized by semantic minimalism (Stanley, 2002). In light of such doubts, relevance theorists propose that "expectations of relevance" (Carston, 2010; Hall, 2008, 2014; Wilson & Sperber, 2002) determines the direction and termination of free enrichment, aiming to rationally constrain the mechanism of pragmatic enrichment. However, "expectations of relevance" is an extremely abstract and vague concept, without transparency and regularity. There is an urgent need to make it more concrete in order to better restrict the operational mechanism of free enrichment. Bach (2010), a radical semantic minimalist, expels truth-conditions from semantics and includes implicit meaning within pragmatics. Consequently, in terms of the proposition-completion mechanism, he leaned toward contextualism and proposed completion and expansion. But both the "completion" pragmatic process of filling in the propositional radical and the "expansion" pragmatic process of extending the minimal proposition are forms of pragmatic enrichment of what is said without syntactic constraints.

Comparing with above view of pragmatic expansion, moderate semantic minimalists such as Borg (2007, 2012), Stanley (2005), Stanley and Szabó (2000), and King and Stanley (2005) deny the top-down optional pragmatic process imagined by contextualism——"free enrichment". They postulate hidden argument (Borg, 2007) or hidden or covert indexical (Stanley, 2005) as the only completion strategy. In other words, "hidden unarticulated constituents are posited in a sentence if and only if the hearer is forced to do so by syntactic evidence" (Sennet, 2011: 416). Although hidden components are psychological entities without directly perceivable external manifestations, they still leave traces. Their identification requires hypothesis and verification, and "depends on certain presuppositions" (Xu, 2001: 6). Regrettably, they have not provided a clear and reliable explanation for the definition of hidden components. As a result, the generation of hidden components is arbitrary, lacking the rigor and rigidity required for scientific research. In addition, in order to explain the universality of semantic indeterminacy, they have to postulate countless covert syntactic variables. They even force some unarticulated constituents with strong contextual effects to fit into the framework, regarding them as products of the syntactic constraint mechanism. This leads to inefficiencies in syntactic representation and renders their theoretical assumptions unreasonable.

4.5 Enlightenment and Prospect of Theoretical Contention

4.5.1 Enlightenment of Theoretical Contention

This debate in post-Gricean pragmatics is less a dispute over the semantics-pragmatics interface and more a progress to meaning research. It has led to a fundamental change in people's understanding of meaning, evolving from a single-dimensional to a multi-dimensional, and from a shallow to a profound perspective. Various theories of meaning are interconnected in a coherent lineage, all dedicated to addressing the limitations of the classical Gricean theory. Looking at this debate as a whole, we can draw the following enlightenments:

First, the definition and reconstruction of "what is said". In classical Gricean theory, "what is said" encompasses both the conventional meaning of language and the speaker's intention, thus becoming a vague concept straddling semantics and pragmatics. To define "what is said", contextualism and semantic minimalism generally adopt three methods: (1) "What is said" only contains the conventional meaning of language without the speaker's intention (such as the radical semantic minimalist, Bach); (2) "What is said" is the carrier of the speaker's meaning rather than the conventional meaning (such as contextualists); (3) Reconstruct the triggering factors of the conventional meaning and the speaker's meaning in "what is said" (such as moderate semantic minimalists). But it is a pity that although minimalists expand the unarticulated components in "what is said" through explicit or implicit syntactic constraint mechanisms, they fail to account for the influence of strong contextual effects. On the other hand, contextualists attribute the completeness of a sentence in what is said entirely to pragmatic intrusion, overlooking syntactic restrictive. Therefore, in the construction of the proposition of what is said, neither syntactic constraints nor free enrichment can be neglected and both of them are indispensable.

Second, new interpretations of the "pragmatic enrichment" approach. Generally, both contextualism and semantic minimalism acknowledge the existence of two types of communicative propositions, namely the utterance proposition and the speaker's proposition. However, they differ significantly in defining these two concepts and label them with different terms, such as "primary—secondary", "what is said—what is implicated", and "explicit—implicit". Although there is a growing consensus regarding the speaker's proposition, that is, the particularized conversational implicature in the Gricean, significant disagreements exist within and between the two camps concerning the utterance proposition, which refers to the speaker's meaning incorporating pragmatic enrichment. Since this proposition is connected to both semantic content and pragmatic elements, bearing characteristics of both conventional meaning and conversational implicature, different scholars, driven by diverse research aims and tasks, have provided various theoretical definitions. Examples include Recanati and Levinson's pre-semantic pragmatic interpretation models, Bach and Jaszczolt's post-semantic pragmatic interpretation models, and the semantic-to-pragmatic inferential interpretation model of Relevance Theory. It is this divergence that has changed the traditional view that semantics and pragmatics are relatively independent and semantic output serves as pragmatic input. Instead, the two are now regarded as intertwined, interdependent, interactive, integrated, and permeating research fields, jointly participating in the construction of utterance meaning.

Third, the abandonment of the truth-value semantic view by contextualism and the reflection on the truth-value semantic view by semantic minimalism. When confronted with the issue of context-sensitivity, contextualists expand the bearer of truth-conditions from sentences to utterances, abandon traditional truth-conditional semantics or objectivist truth-conditional theories, and establish truth-conditional pragmatics. That is, the truth-conditions of an utterance are influenced by various pragmatic factors, the factors include free variables and indexical elements triggered by the lexical-syntactic system, as well as unarticulated constituents triggered by non-linguistic systems. In essence, they are the product of pragmatic enrichment. On the one hand, semantic minimalists uphold the principle of semantic composition and strive to avoid introducing context-sensitivity that is not syntactically constrained into semantic content. On the other hand, they offer explanations for the fact that truth-values vary with context, attempting to clearly define "the function of contextual factors in the mechanism of obtaining propositional truth-values" (Sullivan, 2015: 23). They allow for context-sensitivity constrained by syntax, thus, in line with the spirit of contextualism, extending the distance between sentence meaning and propositional content. This evolves the objectivist truth-conditional theory into a relative truth-conditional theory.

Fourth, the leap from monotonic logic to non-monotonic logic. Semantic minimalism adheres strictly to the principle of semantic composition. It contends that semantic content is determined by the meanings of its components and syntactic projection, emphasizing monotonic logical reasoning, which cannot be canceled. In contrast, contextualism insists on semantic indeterminacy, emphasizing the cancellability and non-monotonicity of reasoning. "People always reason under conditions of incomplete knowledge. When new facts are recognized and new conditions are added, the original conclusion can be overturned, thus demonstrating the non-monotonicity of reasoning. And that is a core idea of so called non-monotonic logic" (Yuan, 2000). Obviously, the understanding of meaning in contextualism, especially in the local processing of generalized conversational implicatures or default meanings, demonstrates the non-monotonicity and cancellability of reasoning.

Fifth, the leap from the modular theory of language to holism. Based on the modular view of language, semantic minimalism demarcates the disciplinary boundaries between semantics and pragmatics, confines the impact of pragmatics on semantics to the minimum extent, and overlooks the multi-dimensional complementary between them. While contextualism adheres to holism, and they advocates an integral and holographic approach to utterance interpretation that combines semantics and pragmatics. Meaning is internalized in the overall perception of the subject and externalized in the form of local symbolic language. Due to the information asymmetry, the understanding or "restoration" of meaning can only be achieved through a holistic semantic pragmatic holographic approach, aiming to approximate and identify the speaker's intention. The semantic pragmatic interface view of contextualism integrates various meaning components in parallel, making the construction of utterance meaning more in line with the actual situation of discourse. Moreover, the holism it advocates is becoming the future development direction of scientific research and is being put into practice by the rapidly advancing linguistic theories. Examples include the cognitive, social, and cultural orientations of macro-pragmatics, as well as construction grammar and cognitive grammar in cognitive linguistics.

4.5.2 *The Prospect of Utterance Meaning Studies*

Based on the above review, we believe that there are the following development trends in the domestic research on utterance meaning:

First, both contextualism and semantic minimalism have reached a consensus on context-sensitivity triggered by the lexical-syntactic system, namely free variables and indexical elements in the logical form of sentences, and have explained them through different methods. However, they consist divergent views and engage in intense disputes regarding unarticulated constituents triggered by non-linguistic systems. Does the unarticulated constituent, a product of strong contextual effects not restricted by syntax, exist or not? If it exists, how can it be retrieved and reconstructed and what is the pragmatic mechanism of retrieval and reapplication? Is it Recanati's pragmatic enrichment, Levinson's conversational implicature, the explicature of relevance theory, or Bach's implicit implicature? Since it is not limited by syntax, how can its over-generation be restricted? These disputes and mysteries are what post-Gricean pragmatic scholars, whether they hold the stance of contextualism or semantic minimalism, should work together to resolve (Cao & Xiang, 2017).

Second, regarding the ontological status of generalized conversational implicature, post-Gricean pragmatic scholars have employed research methods such as corpora, optimality theory, and psychological cognitive experiments, providing new data support for revealing its essence (Zhou & Ran, 2007). But they do not obtain a consensus on the nature of its pragmatic process. Is it Levinson's default inference, the contextual inference of relevance theory proponents, or Chierchia's (2013) structural inference? Although experimental data tend to support relevance theory and deny the existence of default inference, Garrett & Harnish (2007, 2009), Gronder et al. (2007) and Panizza & Chierchia (2008) have respectively counter-evidenced the existence of default inference and structural inference through experiments. If all implicatures are derived in specific contexts relying on the principle of relevance, that is, all implicatures are token-based meanings and there is no type-based meaning, then humans' deductive and inductive ability to extract relatively stable meanings from recurring language structures and social activities would be greatly weakened. Moreover, the existence of default inference and structural inference allows listeners to directly draw judgments by skipping intermediate inferential steps, providing a shortcut for utterance comprehension, which is also consistent with the "least effort" principle of information processing in relevance theory. Therefore, it cannot be simply denied. Post-Gricean scholars should further objectify their experimental designs, free from the influence of pre-existing theoretical biases. By integrating interdisciplinary evidence from psychology, brain science, information science, big data, etc., they can make a fair and objective theoretical interpretation of the ontological status and pragmatic process of generalized conversational implicature.

Third, post-Gricean pragmatists have reconstructed the classic Gricean binary meaning representation levels of "what is said-what is implicated" through multiple levels and strategies, forming such as Recanati's "sentence meaning—what is said—what is implicated", Levinson's "sentence meaning—utterance-type meaning—utterance-token meaning", and Bach's "what is said—implicit implicature—what is implicated". Then there is the binary contrast of "explicature and implicature" in relevance theory. Furthermore, there are unitary integration models like Jaszczolt's "merged representation" and Parikh's "contextualized game". Each scholar presents a different view, and no consensus has been reached. Semantic minimalists like Bach and contextualists like Recanati and Levinson adopt two totally different approaches to defining "what is said". The former holds that "what is said" only contains the conventional meaning of language without the speaker's intention, while the latter contends that "what is said" is the carrier of the speaker's meaning rather than the conventional meaning. In addition, both them generally acknowledge the existence of two communicative propositions, the utterance proposition and the speaker's proposition. However, they define these two propositions differently. For example, "primary—secondary" of Recanati, "type—token" of Levinson, and "implicit—implicated" of Bach. Although about the speaker's proposition, that is, the particularized conversational implicature in the Gricean sense, the two camps tend to agree that it is "guided by pragmatic principles". Nevertheless, they have serious disagreements with the utterance proposition. Due to different research purposes and tasks, they provide different theoretical definitions. For instance, Recanati and Levinson uphold a local view of meaning processing and affirm a pre-semantic pragmatic interpretation model, while Bach adheres to a holistic view of meaning processing and affirms a post-semantic pragmatic interpretation model. In fact, the debate exaggerates the differences among various theoretical models and obscures their common features and shared flaws. The above-mentioned theories all adopt the basic framework of "representation mechanism" and "inference mechanism". They focus on exploring the inference mechanism but neglect to reflect on the representation mechanism. As a result, each theory holds its own ground and the views diverge. This not only threatens the overall self-consistency of the theories but also gives rise to their own problems (Cao & Xiang, 2019). Therefore, it is really difficult to give a simple and straightforward answer for the number of meaning representation levels. Because different representation models come from researchers' diverse philosophies of language and serve different research purposes and tasks. No single theoretical model can be accepted and recognized by all scholars. To solve this problem, it is necessary to integrate related achievements in cognitive and psychological fields and explore a theoretical model——representation—inference mechanisms mutually compatible.

Fourth, meaning studies show a trend of diversification in theoretical frameworks and research methods, as well as an interdisciplinary. Disputes over the interface/demarcation between semantics and pragmatics all stem from researchers' different philosophies of language perspective and serve different research purposes and tasks. In fact, after a long-lasting border war, people have come to realize that it is difficult to get a clear demarcation between the disciplines. Over-emphasizing the independence of semantics/pragmatics is likely to be excessive and overly absolute. Only by grasping the relationship between the two from a perspective of integration, interdependence, and interaction can we uncover the process of utterance comprehension and the path of meaning generation. If domestic scholars combine the "pragmatic enrichment" characteristics of Chinese (Shen, 2014) and explore new corpus facts, they will surely promote the research on the meaning interface from a typological perspective. This will also deepen our understanding of the allocation of semantic and pragmatic information in the Chinese.

4.6 Conclusion

The intense debates between the contextualism and semantic minimalism groups, as well as within each group, clearly demonstrate that it is extremely difficult to provide a simple and straightforward answer regarding the semantic pragmatic interface/demarcation relationship. There is no one theoretical model can be accepted and recognized by all scholars. The theoretical disputes surrounding the semantic pragmatic relationship will go on as a common phenomenon in the academic community, accompanied by the sublation of traditional theoretical concepts and the reconstruction of new ones. The current trend of diversification in theoretical frameworks and research methods, as well as the interdisciplinary approach in the study of utterance meaning, is precisely the inevitable outcome of this debate. "Debates are benefit to generating new ideas, distinguishing right from wrong, and promoting the development of disciplines" (Zhang, 2010). Post-Gricean pragmatic scholars will surely work together to promote the in-depth development of the utterance meaning research in the fierce exchanges and debates.

Chapter 5
Formal Semantics Studies

5.1 Introduction

Formal semantics is also called Montague Grammar, model-theoretic semantics, truth-conditional semantics, logical semantics, logical grammar, possible world semantics. (Fang, 2000; Jiang & Pan, 1998; Partee, 2011; Zou, 1995). Formal semantics adopts mathematical logic, including the syntax-semantics interface and the semantics-pragmatics interface, to study the semantics of natural languages. And it aims to help machines understand natural languages. (Li & Zou, 2013). Formal semantics originated from three academic papers published by Richard Montague in the early 1970s: *English a Formal Language*, *Universal Grammar*, and *The Proper Treatment of Quantification in Ordinary English* (Montague, 1974). These three papers establish the basic framework, research methods, and main topics of formal semantics, and pioneer new paths to the semantic study of natural languages (Partee, 1975, 2011). In the early 1980s, with the deeper study of Montague Grammar, scholars such as Kamp (1981) discovered that simply relying on mathematical methods that are independent of context could not describe phenomena such as indefinite noun phrases, quantifier scopes, and anaphors. And they held that it is almost impossible to analyze the meaning of natural languages without incorporating context into the research (Kamp & Partee, 2004). In 1981, Kamp proposed the Discourse Representation Theory, which marked the shift of formal semantics research from a static to a dynamic approach, and other dynamic semantics theories also emerged one by one. For example, Heim's (1982) "file change semantics", Barwise and Perry's (1983) "situation semantics", Groenendijk and Stokhof's (1990, 1991) "dynamic Montague grammar" and "dynamic predicate logic", and Asher's (1993) and Asher and Lascarides' (2003) "Segmented Discourse Representation Theory" (Gao, 2013; Peng, 2007; Xia, 2006, 2010).

However, both static and dynamic formal semantics adhere to the basic research hypotheses proposed by Montague (Abbott, 1999; Partee, 2011). These hypotheses

X. Wen and R. Tang, *New Perspectives and Developments in Chinese Semantics*,
https://doi.org/10.1007/978-981-95-1730-5_5

mainly include: (1) Language analysis is highly dependent on abstract mathematical logic methods. This is because formal semantics originated from the critique of the study of formal language in the 1950s and 1960s. Logical positivists believed that natural language was imperfect, unsystematic, full of ambiguity, vagueness, and irrelevant syntactic components. Therefore, natural language could not be formally analyzed. Montague creatively proposed that natural language is also a formal language, an interpreted formal system (Bach, 1989). Natural language and formal language are essentially the same and theoretically no difference (Montague, 1974). Both of them have "universal grammar" which is a grammatically possible in logic, a syntactic-semantic algebraic grammar, and essentially an intermediate language. (2) Truth conditions and entailment relations play vital roles in semantics. Lewis (1972: 169) advances that "semantics without truth conditions is not semantics", thus we can see that formal semantics is also known as "truth-conditional semantics". Truth conditions and entailment relations are fundamental semantic data. And these two principles constitute important guiding principles within the framework of Montague's universal grammar. (3) The semantics of natural language is compositional. Another important guiding principle of Montague's universal grammar framework is the principle of semantic composition: the meaning of a complex expression is a function of the meanings of its components and the meaning of the way the components are combined (Partee, 2011). Formal semanticists rewrite the principle of semantic composition into two recursion principles: syntactic rule n and semantic rule n. They also put forward the syntactic-semantic correspondence rule, the "rule-to-rule hypothesis". Syntactic rules not only provide the structure for expressions but also serve as the structural basis for semantic interpretation; semantic rules are responsible for giving a semantic interpretation of these expressions. Formal semantics inherited the formalization of philosophers and logicians, as well as their semantic views, such as truth conditions, model theory, and combinational principle. They used mathematical logic to study the syntax and semantics of natural languages with concise methods and clear expressions. However, there were many difficulties in promoting it to linguists. For example, formalized languages do not belong to human natural languages, and formalized research does not concern with the psychological reality that linguists focus on (Partee, 2011).

Three important academic papers form Montague not only established the basic framework and assumptions, but also defined the topics, scope, and methods for formal semantic. One of the characteristics of Montague grammar is adopting the method of fragments, aiming to provide a complete syntactic and semantic analysis specific fragments of a language. Instead of setting syntactic and semantic rules for sentences such as relative clauses or other structures, it is even less about establishing a complete syntactic and semantic system for a particular language. Based on such a research methodology, there are common topics in Montague grammar: (1) Semantic research related to noun phrases, including noun phrases, especially quantified noun phrases, negative polarity items, determiners, pronouns/anaphors, discourse deictic words, plural features of nouns, collective nouns, etc.; (2) Semantic research related to verb phrases, including tense logic, modal logic, temporality, etc.; (3) Semantic research related to sentences, including coordinating conjunctions "and" and "or", relative clauses, verb phrase ellipsis/anaphora, control, etc.; (4) Research related to quantification and scope, including scope, scope ambiguity, binding and variables, etc.; (5) Semantic research related to adverbs and adjectives, such as quantification of temporal adverbs, scope of adverbs, etc. With the proposal of the segmented discourse representation theory, formal semantics studies have expanded to complex sentences, sentence groups, and discourse fields.

Formal semantics is an interdisciplinary field of logic and linguistics and has also drawn significant attention from computer science (including information science and artificial intelligence). Therefore, research in formal semantics shows biases towards logic, linguistics, and computer science (Dai & Sun, 2014; Li, 2009; Zou, 2001). Specifically, the logic-biased formal semantics research aims to construct a logical deduction system with the characteristics of natural language. A typical example is the Logic and Scientific Methodology column in the Journal of Chongqing University of Technology (Social Science Edition), led by Zou Chongli, who is the president of Chinese Association of Logic. Each issue of this journal publishes several research articles on formal semantics, covers lots of aspects of formal semantics research. The computer-science biased to formal semantics research aims to construct a partial sentence system of natural language, emphasizing computer processing of natural language. The linguistics-biased formal semantics research focuses on the logical analysis of natural language, and the issues it concerns are consistent with those of theoretical linguistics (Jin, 2011; Zou, 2001).

With linguistic-biased study of formal semantics at its core, the book has a review of relevant domestic academic achievements over the past decade, revealing the following characteristics in formal semantics research: (1) There is a focus on the introduction, translation, and interpretation of the development history, basic theories, and fundamental content of formal semantics. Most of these introductory and interpretive achievements are about various theories of formal semantics, are of marginal significance. Therefore, apart from reviewing some cutting edge of achievements, this book will not separately reiterate the domestic introduction and interpretation of various theories over the past decade. (2) Conduct research on the syntax and semantics of Chinese discourses from the aspects of description, analysis, comparison, and experimentation. The research topics are relatively concentrated, mainly focusing on the syntactic and semantic features of quantifiers. Pan Haihua and his collaborators' series of studies on "dōu" are typical examples. Most of these studies are static formal semantics. (3) Focus on the application of the Discourse Representation Theory and the Segmented Discourse Representation Theory in Chinese, such as research on the rhetorical patterns of Chinese discourse structures, Chinese complex sentences, Chinese sentence groups, and dialogue relationships (Gao, 2011, 2013), research on Chinese donkey sentences (Chen, 2013), research on conditional sentences (Zou, 2014), etc. All are dynamic formal semantics. This book selects representative literature, including journal papers and dissertations. Taking the research on typical Chinese topics as the main material, it reviews the achievements of formal semantics over the past decade.

5.2 Theories and Methods of Formal Semantics Studies

5.2.1 Context Dependence

In the 1980s, "contextualism" was advocated in philosophy. In this context, formal semantics gradually shifted from static to dynamic research. The status of context became prominent, and context became as one of the core topics in formal semantics research (Guo, 2009; Xia, 2006). What' more, context plays a vital role in determining reference and explaining the definite and indefinite features of nouns. Over the past decade, the focus of context research has been on the issue of context dependence, that is, to what extent the determination of truth-value semantics depends on the context. There are two different answers to this question: contextual determinism and semantic minimalism. Shen (2011) figures out the origin of the divergence between the them, analyzes the essence of their disagreement, and explores the challenges this debate poses to formal semantics. He finds that contextual determinism and semantic minimalism originates from different philosophical traditions. The former originates from the Ordinary Language School, emphasizing that meaning lies in use. It holds that all sentences are sensitive to context. At the semantic level, sentences only express "propositional fragments". Context has intruded into the semantic level, and it only expresses a complete proposition by introducing context. The latter comes from the Ideal Language School, following the tradition of formal semantics. It holds that sentences express complete propositions at the semantic level, and semantics can be abstracted from language use. Only a small number of expressions such as personal pronouns, demonstrative pronouns, and temporal adverbs are sensitive to context. These expressions form "the basic set of context-sensitive expressions" (Cappelan & Lepore, 2005: 1–2). Shen Yuan believes that contextual determinism poses a huge challenge to the basic methods and assumptions (the principle of compositionality and truth-value semantics) advocated by formal semantics. In the face of these challenges, on one hand, formal semantics adheres to the principle of semantic compositionality, avoiding the introduction of extra-syntactic driving factors into the process of determining semantic content. On the other hand, it acknowledges the role of context and clearly defines the intervening role of context in the process of assigning truth values. The question that follows is: what are the levels, paths and ways of context intervention?

Shen (2015) then provides elaborate answers to these questions by comparing contextual determinism and semantic minimalism. About the ways in which context affects truth-values, contextual determinism holds that context influences truth-values by affecting semantic content. In contrast, semantic minimalism contends that context affects truth-values by providing an evaluation environment. And regarding the relationship between semantic composition and context dependence, the principle of semantic composition emphasizes the relative independence of the meanings of words that make up a sentence, while the context principle emphasizes that the determination of the meaning of words needs to rely on the context. Taking the semantic interpretation of adjectives as an example, Shen Yuan demonstrates that these two principles, despite appearing contradictory, are actually not. The changes in lexical semantics within the context are precisely the result driven by the combinational principle. In addition, regarding the inference of discourse relations and the relationship with context, the derivation of discourse relations is dependent on context. And without discourse and context, the unresolved information in logical forms and determining ambiguous expressions cannot be achieved.

5.2.2 Semantic Experimental Method and Semantic Diagnostic Method

In addition to the main methods of mathematical logic, formal semantics has also introduced research methods employed in other branches of linguistics, such as the experimental method and semantic diagnostic testing. Shen (2017, 2020) provides a detailed introduction to the applications of these two research methods abroad. Experiments are one of the common methods in theoretical linguistic research, such as experimental phonetics, experimental syntax, experimental pragmatics, and so on. Shen (2017) explores the special significance of experiments for semantic research from many aspects. For example, research on scalar implicatures through self-paced reading time experiments, reaction time experiments, etc., provides evidence for scientifically distinguishing semantics from pragmatics. Semantic processing experiments on complement coercion are used to explore the differences between complement coercion sentences and simple transitive verb sentences, thus providing evidence for determining the nature of implicit semantics. Experimental research on expressions with the same monotonic truth conditions and quantifiers helps us find semantically relevant properties or forms of semantic representation that have psychological reality.

Fortunately, experimental semantics has also started to be employed in foreign language learning and Chinese information processing. For example, Liu et al. (2011) study the process of children's acquisition of Chinese additive operators (such as "hái", "yě", "yòu") through game experiments; Wu and Li (2015) examine the understanding of scope relations by Chinese speakers from the perspective of online processing (reaction time); Tang and Chen (2018) conduct experiments and studies on the surface/inverse scope of English active and passive sentences among Chinese learners. They used the self-paced reading method to complete 64 picture-based truth-value judgment tasks; Lv and Lu (2018) explore the acquisition process of the semantic scope of English quantifiers by Chinese native speakers. The experiment adopts picture-sentence matching experiments and records the reaction time of the subjects from the presentation of the pictures to their first judgment. Zhou et al. (2018) explore the influence of complex sentence features such as Chinese hypothetical conjunctions, compound sentence patterns, and the propositional content of conditional clauses on the generation of counter-factual meanings through psycholinguistic experimental methods.

In addition to experimental research, diagnostic testing methods are mostly adopted in various branches of linguistics, and formal semantics is no exception. Shen (2020) introduces the commonly used semantic diagnostic testing methods in semantics over the past few decades and the ways to handle exceptions and counterexamples. The specific methods include: the semantic minimal pair test, which is used to study the usage or meaning of specific expression forms in specific contexts; the non-deniability test or contradiction test, and the S-sentence group test, mainly for implications, presuppositions, conventional implicatures, illocutionary meanings at the speech act level, and subjective meanings, etc.; the challengeability test, which is used to distinguish illocutionary acts, locutionary contents, and non-locutionary contents; the faultless disagreement method and the verb (find) non-finite complement method, which are mainly for the identification of subjective meanings. Shen Yuan reminds that in semantic tests; attention should be paid to the clarity of the testing criteria and the pertinence of the testing methods. Meanwhile, it is necessary to have a correct understanding of exceptions and counterexamples. Because these exceptions will prompt linguists to reflect on the existing testing methods, and trigger new methodological considerations and theoretical innovations. In addition, we should also treat seriously the issue of the cross-linguistic applicability of various semantic testing methods.

5.3 Typical Topics in Chinese Studies

Formal semantics has undergone a shift from static to dynamic research. However, we have found that the existing explorations in China still tend to static research, and the research on Chinese quantifiers is a typical example. Although dynamic semantics has also been touched upon, it is only limited to several types of complex sentences, such as conditional sentences, counter-factual sentences, donkey sentences, and so on. This chapter provides a detailed introduction to the research achievements on these topics over the past decade.

5.3.1 Quantifiers Studies

Quantification is one of the topics that have been most thoroughly studied in formal semantics. Quantification includes universal quantification and existential quantification, and it is often expressed by quantifiers. Universal quantification expresses the meaning of "set/quantification domain". Typical universal quantifiers include "suǒ yǒu", "quán bù", "fán", "měi, "rèn hé in Chinese, and "all", "every", "any" in English. Existential quantification expresses the meaning of "there is at least one within the set/ there is at least one within quantification domain". Typical existential quantifiers include "yǒu/ mǒu + unit word" in Chinese, such as "yǒu rén" and "mǒu gāo xiào", and "some" in English. Judging from the results of the literature search, Chinese quantifiers studies are also one of the most remarkable topics in formal semantics research. Among them, the studies on the universal quantifiers "dōu" and "měi" are the most comprehensive and thorough, while there is relatively less research on other types of quantifiers, especially existential quantifiers.

1. Universal Quantifiers: Dōu

The 800 Modern Chinese Words (Lv, 1999: 177–178) distinguishes three types of "dōu". Among them, "$dōu_1$" is the meaning of "summarization", "$dōu_2$" is the meaning of "even", and "$dōu_3$" is the meaning of "once". However, most scholars expect to summarize the various specific usages of "dōu" with a unified semantics, proposing that "dōu" can express "universal quantification" (Jiang Yan, 1998, 2009; Pan, 2006), express "combination" (Yuan, 2005, 2012), express "distribution" (Lin, 1998), and express "maximization" (Cheng & Giannakidou, 2013; Xiang, 2008). Correspondingly, "dōu" has also been defined as a universal quantifier/universal quantification operator, a combination operator, a distribution operator, and a maximization operator. Among them, most scholars agree that "dōu" expresses the meaning of universal quantification, and they are nearly based on the research of Cheng (1995), Pan (2006) and others.

Cheng (1995) proposes that "dōu" expressing the meaning of universal quantification has three semantic features: plurality, distributivity and exhaustivity. And Pan (2006) puts forward that the universal quantification operator "dōu" always restricts the free variables in the restricted part, and quantification consists of three parts: the universal quantification operator "dōu", the restricted part, and the core part. The ternary structure can be determined by two mapping rules, the topic rule and the focus rule. The topic rule is that if there is a phrase in a sentence on the left side of "dōu" that can serve as the quantification domain, it will be mapped to the quantification domain, and at the same time, the remainder of the sentence will be mapped to the core domain. The focus rule is that if there is a focus constituent in the predicate, it will be mapped to the core domain, and at the same time, the remainder of the sentence will be mapped to the quantification domain. Therefore, the topic rule is also known as the left vectorization rule, and the focus rule is also named the right vectorization rule. The order of precedence for the two rules is that the left vectorization rule takes precedence over the right vectorization rule. Hence, the ternary structure proposed by Pan Haihua has had profound influence on the Chinese universal quantifier studies.

Zhang et al. (2012), based on the research of the predecessors, makes a detailed comparison of the similarities and differences in semantic features when "dōu" is vectorized left or right: (1) Plurality. Regardless of whether "dōu" expresses the meaning of "summarization", "even" or "once", and whether it is vectorized left or right, the quantification domain of "dōu" is a semantically plural component, and the cardinal number of the core domain is bigger than "one". (2) Focus Variable. The focus variable is different from the variable introduced by the focus itself. The focus variable is outwardly compatible, while the variable introduced by the focus itself is inwardly directed. Different from Xiong (2008), the author believes that what "dōu" restricts is the focus variable rather than the variable introduced by the focus itself.

(3) Exhaustivity. When "dōu" is vectorized left, the exhaustivity of the quantified component can be unrestricted or not restricted by pragmatic factors; while, when it is vectorized right, the exhaustivity of the quantified component is completely restricted.

Based on the study of Pan (2006), Jiang and Pan (2013) further divide the universal quantification "dōu" into two major categories: "$dōu_1$" and "$dōu_2$", and each category was further divided into two subcategories. The basis for classification is the features of the quantification domain of "dōu", which includes two specific criteria: (1) The sequence of the quantification domain, that is, whether the members in the quantification domain are ordered and whether there are hierarchical differences? (2) The direction of quantification, that is, whether the quantification domain is provided by the component on the left side of "dōu"? According to different answers to these two questions, the author distinguished four types of "dōu" (see the table below). In addition, the author also further distinguished these four categories according to the two semantic interpretation rules proposed by Pan (2006)—the "topic rule" and the "focus rule": "dōu $_{1a}$" and "dōu $_{2a}$" are applicable to the "topic rule" of left vectorization and are not exclusivity; while "dōu $_{1b}$" and "dōu $_{2b}$" are applicable to the "focus rule" of right vectorization and are exclusivity. Table 5.1 demonstrates that the classification by Jiang Jingzhong and Pan Haihua is more refined, has stronger explanatory power, and is more in line with people's intuitive judgments of language facts.

However, Shen (2015) believes that distinguishing between left vectorization and right vectorization will lead people into the "quantification dilemma". This is because there is a lack of coordination between the "topic rule" and the "focus rule", leading to contradictions. Specifically, when it comes to left vectorization, for sentences that are applicable to the topic rule, a focus can almost always be found on the right side of "dōu", and the focus is subject to the "focus rule". Instead, when it comes to right vectorization, for sentences that are applicable to the focus rule, a topic can almost always be supplemented on the left side of "dōu". So as long as topics exist, the "topic rule" should be applied. It follows that each of these two rules considers the other to be redundant. In response to this confusion, Shen Jiaxuan abandons left vectorization and proposes the "Rightward Government Rule", that is, according to

Table 5.1 The Category of "dōu"

		Orderly quantification domain	Left vectorization	Exhaustivity	Examples
$Dōu_1$	**$Dōu_{1a}$**	–	+	–	Everyone agrees
	$Dōu_{1b}$	–	–	+	Where has he been?
$Dōu_2$	**$Dōu_{2a}$**	+	+	–	Even such a serious illness was cured
	$Dōu_{2b}$	+	–	+	It's already twelve o'clock, but you still haven't gone to bed!

the topic-focus structure of the sentence, the focus syntactically governed by the operator "dōu" (always on the right side) is mapped to the restrictive part, and at the same time, the remainder of the sentence is mapped to the core part. The innovation of Shen Jiaxuan's work lies in corresponding the semantic governing domain of "dōu" with its syntactic governing domain, and establishing a one-to-one correspondence between semantics and syntax.

Is the Chinese word "dōu" a universal quantifier? Scholars have doubted this view, contending that the universal quantification theory is an oversimplified analogy to the English universal quantifier all. Xu (2014) demonstrates, from the perspectives of double quantification, universal quantification, maximality, exhaustivity, exclusivity, and distributivity, that these semantic properties are sufficient conditions rather than necessary conditions for the use of "dōu". The necessary conditions of "dōu" are "degree" and "subjectivity". Specifically, "dōu" can be added to a sentence as long as the speaker perceives that some aspect of the statement has reached or exceeded the expected degree. The author re-examines various types of sentences containing "dōu", as well as the example sentences provided by Jiang Jingzhong and Pan (2013), and finds that these examples invariably demonstrate that some aspect has reached a certain degree. The so-called "certain degree" is subjectively determined by the speaker, rather than being an objective standard. Thus, even syntactic elements expressing a small amount can be used with "dōu" if the speaker feels the amount meets or surpasses their own standard. For these reasons, the author categorizes "dōu" as an adverb, a modal adjunct.

Zhou and Wu (2018, 2020) and Wu and Zhou (2019), based on universal quantification—"true if all are true, false if any is false"—compare "dōu" with typical universal quantifiers in Chinese and English, such as "suǒ yǒu", "měi", "all," and "every." They find that "dōu" does not carry a constant universal meaning and allows for exceptions, as in the sentence "tóng xué men dōu zhǎo dào gōng zuò le, zhǐ yǒu liǎng sān gè méi zhǎo dào" (All the classmates have found jobs, except for two or three who haven't). The universal quantification is merely an illusion. Starting from the diachronic evolution of the "dōu", the author discovers that "dōu" has gone through the original meaning of "convergence" and extended to the meaning indicating "degree". However, regardless of the syntactic context, it can express the scope of relevant components. Therefore, this word is defined as a scope adverb by the author (Zhou & Wu, 2020). It can be used in either explicit sentence structures or implicit temporal or modal elements. Meanwhile based on the semantic and pragmatic functions of "dōu", the author defines it as an adverb that strengthens the degree. From the perspective of semantic function, "dōu" is an intensifier, and pragmatically, it plays a role in enhancing the force of the sentence (Wu & Zhou, 2019; Zhou and Wu, 2018).

Yuan (2012) not only critiques the "universal quantification theory" but also casts doubt on the "generalization theory," the "distributive operator hypothesis," and the "summation operator hypothesis". Some scholars have adopted a mediating approach, synthesizing and interrelating the diverse semantics or theories associated with "dōu". For example, based on the "universal quantification" and "sum operator", Shang (2011) proposes the "Two-level Quantification Theory", aiming to resolve semantic issues of subject plural noun in sentences with "dōu". The double quantification includes primary quantification and universal quantification. Primary quantification refers to the process where the individuals denoted by a plural noun in the subject form a background set, and the event type quantifies each element of this set into distinct types and quantities of covers. Based on this, "dōu" re-quantifies the covers, resulting in the standardization and equalization of these covers. Shang Xin's two-level quantification theory fully explains the semantic features such as plurality, collectivity, and distributivity of noun phrases in sentences with "dōu". However, Feng and Pan (2017) reject the necessity of the cover-based theory, arguing that it might permit interpretations that do not actually exist in practice and fails to precisely characterize all possible understanding of a sentence.

Li (2013) simplifies the three-part semantics of "dōu" (that is, "summarization", "even", and "once") into two categories: "dōu 1" and "dōu 2". He believes that "dōu 1" is a distributive operator, but "dōu 1" does not simply represent the "distributivity". Instead, it includes two semantic elements: "distribution" and "relatively large quantity". The object associated with "dōu 1" is always on the left side of "dōu". The semantic core of "dōu 2" only contains "relatively large quantity". Its associated object can be on the left side of "dōu" (that is, "dōu 2" with the meaning of "even"), or on the right side of "dōu" (that is, "dōu 3" with the meaning of "already"). Feng Yuli and Pan (2018) sorts out various meanings of the "dōu". They propose that the universal quantification meaning is the semantic core of "dōu", which has two characteristics, exhaustiveness and exclusivity. Other semantics, such as distributivity, exceeding expectations, and high degree, all belong to accompanying meanings. These accompanying meanings stem from different mapping methods of the universal quantification structure and the different compositions of the restricted domain. Specifically, distributivity is an accompanying meaning presented when "dōu" is mapped in the topic-comment structure. It is endowed by the exhaustive semantic feature of universal quantification. The sense of exceeding expectations is a semantic effect brought about by the order of scalar options within the restricted domain during the mapping of the topic-comment structure or the background-focus structure. The high-degree meaning and exhaustiveness are two sides of one thing. They are caused by different perspectives of restricted domain, so they also belong to accompanying meanings.

Regarding the "maximization operation" of "dōu", Feng (2018) first distinguishes the differences and connections among the concepts of maximization operation, summation operation, maximization effect, and universal quantification. He criticizes that the existing analyses of the maximization operation of "dōu" has confused these concepts. Thus, he concludes that the maximization operation was not suitable for precisely describing the semantics of "dōu", and confirms that "dōu" is a universal quantification operator but not a maximization operation operator.

2. "měi"

Same to "dōu", there are also controversies in the academic circle regarding the semantic attributes of "měi". There are many theories such as the universal quantification theory (Feng, 2019; Huang, 1996, 2005; Huang & Shi, 2013), the summation operator theory (Lin, 1998; Zhang & Pan, 2019), the variable theory (Yang, 2002), the dual function theory (Pan et al., 2009), the partitioning operator theory (Yuan, 2012), and so on. And most of scholars hold the view of the universal quantification theory.

For example, Huang and Shi Ding Hong (2013) explore the structure of the universal quantifier "měi" and distinguish the "měi" structure of universally quantifies individuals and the "měi" structure of universally quantifies events. The former is "měi + (numeral) quantifier + noun phrase", such as "měi gè xué shēng" (Every student). The latter is "měi + (numeral) cì / huí + event expression component", such as "měi cì huí jiā" (Every time go home). Syntactically speaking, the "event expression component" excludes complex structures, shows selectivity towards tense and aspect components, the forms of objects, and the semantic types of predicate words, and has a preference for conditional components. Semantically speaking, the "event expression component" shows event categories. Having compared the two types of "měi", the author finds that these two types of structures have parallel internal structures. Both of them refer to categories and map plural components into singular countable components. Also, the author compares "měi" structures with the structure of "every + countable noun" for quantifying individuals and the structure of "every time + clause" for quantifying events. And then he the two have the same structure. However, whether "měi" is equivalent to "every" in English? Feng (2019) compares the semantic differences between the English universal quantifier "every" and the Chinese universal quantifier "měi". He finds that the logic of universal quantification can better describe the semantic features of the English universal quantifier "every", but it is unable to accurately describe the meaning of the Chinese universal quantifier "měi". This is because "měi" has multiple meanings. It can express universal quantification, perform a summation operation on a single set, or merely introduce a variable. From the above, the author concludes that it is not feasible to directly study the quantification logic of natural languages, especially the meanings of quantificational components in Chinese.

Zhang and Pan (2019) raise doubts about the theory of universal quantification of "měi". In line with Lin (1998), they prove that "měi" is sum operator. In the structure of "měi" + numeral-measure noun, "měi" performs a summation operation on its associated object "numeral-measure-noun", thus obtaining a maximized plural set. This set includes a summation operator "měi", a summation unit "numeral-measure", and the object of summation "noun". The summative unit feature of "měi" endows the "měi + NP" structure with distributivity. When "měi NP" functions as the subject, its distributivity requires that the predicate should be distributivity. When "měi NP" functions as the object, there is no specific requirement for the predicate in semantic. Hence, the author proposes that probably there is no restrictive universal quantifiers in Chinese. While the author doubts the universal quantification theory, he also claims that "měi NP has a "universal interpretation" (Zhang, Pan, 2019: 513). Zhang et al. (2009) also hold that "měi" as subject is a universal quantification operator.

3. Other Universal Quantifiers

Apart from "dōu" and "měi", there are other universal quantifiers in Chinese, such as "suǒ yǒu", "quán" and "zǒng" in modern Chinese, "qún", "zhòng" and "fán" in ancient Chinese, and "shài" in Cantonese.

Zhang et al. (2009) compare "suǒ yǒu NP", "měi NP" and "quán NP", and conclude that when these expressions are used alone and functioned as the subject, "suǒ yǒu" and "quán" are sum operator, while "měi" is a quantification operator. From semantic view, "měi" emphasizes individuality; "suǒ yǒu" and "quán" emphasize integrity. The difference between them are that "suǒ yǒu" only emphasizes the whole without considering exceptions, while "quán" emphasizes that there are no exceptions in the whole.

Huang (2013) and Xiong (2016) compare the universal quantifiers "dōu" and "zǒng". Huang Zanhui argues that the difference between the two lies in the direction of quantification: "dōu" is left vectorization, and the quantification object is on the left side of "dōu"; "zǒng" is global quantification, and the quantification object is not in a certain position on the left or right side of the quantification operator, but involves the whole sentence in which the quantification operator is located. Obviously, Huang Zanhui denies the right vectorization of "dōu". Both Huang Zanhui and Xiong Zhongru consider that "zǒng" can only quantify events and cannot quantify individuals, while "dōu" can only quantify individuals. Different quantification objects can also help explain the different syntactic manifestations of "zǒng" and "dōu" as well as the word order when they occur at the same time.

Huang (2016) analyzes the common universal quantifiers "qún", "zhòng" and "fán" in pre-Qin Chinese. Those universal quantifiers have semantic feature of collectivity and totality. When "qún" appears before a noun phrase that represents human, "qún + (person)NP" is formed, which can only be right vectorization. "zhòng" often appears after a noun, forming "NP + zhòng", and it can only be left vectorization. "fán" is placed before a noun phrase and is right vectorization.

Li Baolun (2012) discusses the modifier universal quantifier "shài" in Cantonese. As a universal quantifier affix, "shài" attaches to a verb, gives the associated component a universal meaning, and requires that the associated component must meet the plural condition. For example, "wǒ jiě jué shài dī wèn tí lā (I have solved all the problems)." The author proposes the accessibility hierarchy for quantification of "shài": direct object > post-verbal prepositional phrase/indirect object > pre-verbal prepositional phrase > subject > predicate, and proves that regardless of whether there is a focus in the sentence, the quantification object selected by "shài" will be determined by the accessibility hierarchy for quantification. Partee (1991, 1995) makes a distinction between determiner quantification and modifier quantification. The determiner quantification is highly syntacticized and represents a kind of quantification that is insensitive to focus. The modifier quantification, on the other hand, is sensitive to focus and can override syntactic factors. Li Baolun challenges Partee's binary perspective. He argues that the universal quantifier "shài" in its modifier use is insensitive to focus, but its component association is determined by the accessibility hierarchy for quantification, which is clearly syntactic factors.

Not only do scholars explore the syntax and semantics of individual universal quantifiers, but they conduct research on the co-occurrence of multiple universal quantifiers. For example, Li et al. (2009) explore the co-occurrence of "dōu", "gè", and "quán", Niu and Pan (2015), as well as Zhang and Pan (2019), discuss the co-occurrence in "měi", "dōu" and "gè". Does the co-occurrence of these words belong to the co-occurrence of words with similar semantics or different categories? If it is the former, will it cause semantic redundancy? If they are all quantifiers, why can one component be subject to double quantification? If it is the latter, what categories do these co-occurring words belong to respectively? For example, Li et al. (2009) believe that "dōu" is both a quantifier operator and a distributive operator, "gè" is a distributive operator, and "quán" is a dual-functional operator, which can be used both as a scope determiner and as a quantifier adverb. Zhang and Pan (2019) hold that "měi" is a sum operator, while "dōu" is a universal quantifier adverb.

5.3.2 Complex Sentences Studies

Studies on quantifiers lean more towards static formal semantics, focusing on the syntactic and semantic perspective of these words within single-sentence fragments. Instead, complex sentences studies are not only limited in individual sentences. It explores semantics at the discourse/text level and is the dynamic semantics research. In the late 1980s, various theories of dynamic semantics emerged, among which the Discourse Representation Theory (Kamp, 1981) and the Segmented Discourse Representation Theory are the most influent. (Asher, 1993; Asher & Lascarides, 2003). Reviewing the domestic research over the past decade, whether it is the phenomenon of Chinese anaphora, donkey sentences or counter-factual sentences, most of the research has been carried out within the framework of the DRT. To process these extra-single-sentence linguistic segments, one first needs to process the clause S_1 to obtain its Discourse Representation Structure DRS_1. Then, add the clause S_2 to DRS_1 to get a new Discourse Representation Structure DRS_2. Proceed in this way until the last clause S_n is processed. In this manner, the final Discourse Representation Structure of the sentence sequence S_1, S_2, …, S_n can be obtained. DRT has its inherent theoretical modules and operation steps, mainly including syntactic rules, the construction rules of Discourse Representation Structures, and the semantic interpretation of Discourse Representation Structures. For detailed introductions, you can refer to Pan (1996), Zou (1998), Gao (2013), etc. In this section, only a few types of sentence patterns that have drawn considerable attention in the academic community over the past decade are selected to introduce the application of the DRT to relevant Chinese sentences.

1. Donkey Sentences Studies

Donkey sentences are also a hot topic in formal semantics studies. This kind of sentence was first proposed by the Stoic philosopher Chrysippos in the fifth century AD and came into the view of linguists in the 1980s.

Example 1 If a farmer owns a donkey, he beats it.

Example 2 Every farmer who owns a donkey beats it.

Taking Example 1 as an example, the typical feature of this sentence type is that the two indefinite noun phrases, "a farmer" and "a donkey," carry universal quantification, while the pronouns "he" and "it" refer to "a farmer" and "a donkey," respectively. According to Russell's Analytic Theories, this type of indefinite noun phrase is an existential quantifier. However, the indefinite noun phrases in Example 1 have obtained the meaning of universal quantification and thus are universal quantifiers. The pronouns "he" and "it" have an anaphoric relationship with the two indefinite noun phrases and are bound variables constrained by the quantifier. But from a syntactic perspective, the pronouns "he" and "it" are not constrained within the clause and it is impossible for them to be used as bound variables (Wen, 1997). Traditional logical semantics cannot explain how indefinite noun phrases can have the meaning of universal quantification and how indefinite noun phrases can form an anaphoric relationship with pronouns. There are two typical types of English donkey sentences: conditional donkey sentences (such as Example 1) and quantificational relational sentences (such as Example 2) (For a detailed introduction to the characteristics of English donkey sentences, please refer to Wen Weiping's (2006) doctoral dissertation A Study of English and Chinese Donkey Sentences). In order to explain this contradictory phenomenon, Evans (1980) puts forward the "E-type Pronoun Theory", Kamp (1981) and Heim (1990) propose the Theory of Unselective Binding based on the "Discourse Representation Theory", and Chierchia (1992, 1995, 2000) puts forward the Dynamic Binding Theory (For detailed introductions of each theory, please refer to Wang and Wu, 2012; Wen Binli, 1997; Wen, 2006; Wen & Fang, 2008). Cheng and Huang (1996) introduce the concept of donkey sentences into Chinese and distinguish bare conditional sentences and "if/ dōu conditional sentences". Since then, donkey sentences have become a hot topic in the study of Chinese syntax and semantics. Scholars have described, classified and explained donkey sentences in English and Chinese from perspectives such as generative grammar (Wen, 1997, 1998) and the generic theory (Wen, 2006; Wen and Fang, 2008).

Within the framework of the DRT, Chen (2013) discusses three types of Chinese donkey sentences: conditional donkey sentences, relative clause donkey sentences, and generic implicit donkey sentences, and explains the cases of ellipsis in each type of donkey sentence. First, the author revises the DRT: (1) The author modifies the syntactic rules of the DRT and integrating the special syntactic forms of Chinese into the rule system of DRT. For example, there are no relative pronouns in Chinese, but there is structure "de". The author incorporates it into the syntactic rules and refines the lexical insertion rules at the same time. (2) The author modifies the discourse representation structure and incorporated the structure of the indefinite noun phrase "yī + (quantifier) noun" in Chinese donkey sentences and the "wh…wh" structure of interrogative words expressing "non-interrogative". Among them, the indefinite noun phrase can indicate existence or generic reference. However, the interrogative words in the "wh…wh" structure do not indicate existence but rather indicate generic reference. The semantics of these two types of structures differ, and as a result, the methods used to process them are also different. At the same time, syntactic construction rules related to the "de" construction, construction rules for the pronoun PRO, rules for negation, conditionals, and universal quantifiers, etc. were also added. Finally, the author explains the discourse representation structure with reference to the model M. The conditional donkey sentences were illustrated within the model interpretation of conditional sentences, and the relative donkey sentences and generic implicit donkey sentences are explained within the model interpretation of universal quantifiers. Chen (2013) incorporates all kinds of donkey sentences that had been discussed in the academic community, including the controversial ones. Therefore, this is a formal semantics study that, up to now, is the most comprehensive and profound.

2. Conditional Sentence

As one of the common sentence patterns in Chinese, conditional sentences have received extensive attention from both logic and linguistics. The research on logic-oriented studies has provided meaningful explorations into the logical nature of conditional sentences and their syntactic order characteristics (Chen & Shi, 2019; Lou, 2012; Zou, 1996, 2000). Linguistic approaches have converged on several features of these complex sentences, classifying conditional sentences as causal relations including hypothetical, sufficient, necessary and unconditional types, though their deeper logical-semantic structures require further elaboration [see Tong, 2012].

In his 2012 doctoral dissertation Linguistic Expressions of Conditional Relations, Tong Fuqi takes theories such as logical theory, discourse meaning construction theory, relevance theory, discourse representation theory, and situational semantics as the background. With the category of conditional relations as the research object, he sorts out four types of logical reasoning structures of the category of conditional relations: the category of hypothetical reasoning, the category of disjunctive reasoning, the category of negative proposition reasoning, and the category of reasoning related to modality. And based on the partial sentence system Cp proposed by Jiang and Pan (1998), he constructs the sentence system CCpo for the category of conditional relations. The system includes four syntactic rules, four translation rules, and a semantic interpretation based on truth conditions. The author examines the holistic meaning of linguistic expression patterns in conditional categories. He argues that these meanings could not be sufficiently explained through traditional, simple conditional relations such as implication, inverse implication, or necessary and sufficient conditions. Rather, a comprehensive perspective must be adopted, because these meanings emerge through a process of pragmaticalization—ascending from fundamental logical-semantic foundations to the level of linguistic expression. For example, the holistic meaning of the "yīn wèi (because)… suǒ yǐ (so)…" construction—which expresses the category of sufficient conditional hypotheticals. It is causal narration, negation of certain situational or factual possibilities, and emphasis on specific connections. Based on the holistic meanings of different linguistic expression patterns, Tong (2012: 115) constructs a semantic map of conditional categories, which clearly delineates the proximity relationships between different semantic items. Finally, the author analyzes the communicative intentions of conditional sentences and constructed a semantic generation model for relational categories. Obviously, the study of Tong brakes limitations of the single-dimensional logical analysis and purely grammatical description in conditional sentences; instead, it integrated logic, syntax, semantics, pragmatics and cognition and constructed a systematic analytical framework that presents a comprehensive panorama of conditional sentences.

In contrast to Tong's adoption of classical logical theory to analyze the connection between antecedents and consequents in conditional sentences, Zou (2014) instead employs DRT to explicate their connection. This shift stems from the observation that classical logic (truth-functional logic) inevitably gives rise to "paradoxes of material implication" when applied to natural language conditionals—where the antecedent and consequent may in fact express entirely unrelated or irrelevant propositions. However, conditional sentences rely not merely on the truth-value combination of their antecedents and consequents, but more on the conditional connection. Because under the connection, antecedents can be turned into truth-valuable proposition, with the transformation of consequent following. This exemplifies the analytical approach of dynamic semantics: first generating a DRS for the antecedent, then incrementally projecting this structure onto the consequent, whereby the embedding verification function in the DRT model undergoes dynamic expansion (Zou, 2014). Taking "Ruò mǎ shì bǔ rǔ dòng wù, zé tā shì jǐ zhuī dòng wù." (If a horse is a mammal, then it is a vertebrate.) "If Jones owns a book, then he uses it" as example, Zou describes the syntactic rules and DRS in conditional sentences. When interpreting semantics through the embedding verification function, the author proposes that cognitive factors need to be added in the DRT. For instance, we provide the extension of the embedding verification function cognitive grounding. Only those extensions with cognitive grounding are permissible, while those lacking are not be expanded. Like, the sentence "Rú guǒ yī shì zhěng shù, nà me xuě shì bái de." (If 1 is an integer, then snow is white) is lack of cognitive evidence. The book focuses (on natural language conditional sentences within the framework of dynamic semantics, yet its analysis remains limited in scope, so that it cannot comprehensively account for the diverse conditional relational patterns observed in such constructions.

3. Counter-Factual Sentences

Since Bloom (1981) proposes that Chinese grammatical categories lacking counter-factual semantic, the research on counter-factual constructions and the counter-factual category has emerged as a central research focus in linguistic research. Through the study of psychological reality, linguistic ontology and linguistic typology, counter-factual category was proved to existed in Chinese. But the category is semantic, not grammatical. (Jiang, 2000; Yong, 2014, 2015; Yuan, 2015; Zhou & Zhang, 2019). Counter-factual makers in traditional and modern Chinese can be classified into specific counter-factual marker and non-specific counter-factual marker. The specific counter-factual marker contains conjunctions, verbs, adverbs, particles, clitics and affixes; the non-specific counter-factual marker contains verbs, tense, aspect, modality and mood. (Wang, 2013; Yong, 2017, 2019; Yuan, 2015).

Yong (2014: 62–63) establishes, via a pragmatic approach, three types of truth values for propositions in counter-factual conditionals: (1) Given $p \rightarrow q$, where p is false, it is needed proving that q is false. For example, "If one plus one equaled three, I would go meet her." The pragmatic purpose of this conditional sentence is to use an established false fact p to negate another fact q whose truth value is uncertain. The determination of the established fact's truth value relies on contextual factors. (2) Given $p \rightarrow q$, where q is false, it is needed proving that p must be false. For example, "If you could get admitted to a PhD program, the sun would rise from the west." The pragmatic purpose of this conditional sentence is to use an established false proposition q to negate a proposition p whose truth value is uncertain. (3) Given $p \rightarrow q$ where p is false, it follows that $\neg q$ holds. For example, "If I hadn't been here just now, I wouldn't have heard you cursing at me." The pragmatic purpose of the conditional sentence is not to establish the truth values of propositions p and q, but rather to construct a causal connection between $\neg p$ and $\neg q$. In the three kinds of counter-factual conditional sentences, the determination of truth values for propositions p and q is inherently dependent on contextual or utterance-based factors.

Lin (2016), building upon Chen (2015)'s framework within modal semantics, investigates three types of counter-factual interpretations in deontic modal constructions of the form "yīng gāi Ø de" (such as "Nǐ yīng gāi tōng zhī tā de") (You should agree with her): counter-to-past-fact interpretation, counter-to-present-fact interpretation and counter-to-future-possibility interpretation. "yīng gāi Ø de" can also express counter-to-future-possibility interpretation. The interpretation of temporal reference and event type exhibits a systematic correlation: bounded verb phrases tend to yield a counter-to-past-fact reading, whereas unbounded verb phrases typically generate a counter-to-present-fact interpretation. The author attributes the counter-factual and non-counter-factual interpretations of the "yīng gāi Ø" construction to the grammatical meaning of "de": it introduces a non-future time interval, confirming that the modified proposition holds true within this non-future period, while presupposing that the referent of the verb phrase constitutes given information in the discourse context. The emergence of counter-factual meaning stems from the fact that the authenticity strength of the events described in modal propositions is weaker than that of directly asserting a past or present event. Based on Grice's pragmatic principles, the inference is drawn that the event did not hold in reality the counter-factual meanings cannot be canceled because "de" carries a generalized commitment function that confirms the truth of both the assertion and its entailments within its syntactic domain.

Therefore, Zhu (2019) raises a doubt about Lin Ruowang's (2016) analysis. Through corpus-based retrieval, Zhu (2019) finds that the "yīng gāi Ø de" construction can convey not only counter-factual meanings but also past/current factual meanings. Crucially, the construction itself is shown to possess dual temporal-directional capacity while prototypically expressing factual obligation, it can also target past events to generate counter-factual meanings. This observation suggests that the expression of counter-factual meanings is not strictly dependent on the presence of "de", thereby calling into question Lin Ruowang's claim that "de" exclusively introduces a non-future time interval. Based on Palmer's (2001) analysis on deontic modality, Zhu (2019) proposes that the usage of the deontic modality "yīng gāi Ø de" is influenced by two semantic-pragmatic features: [permanence] and [obligatoriness]. The construction "yīng gāi Ø de" does not involve counter-factual meanings when expressing permanent deontic situations. This is because what we are talking about does not refer to specific one-time events or particular individuals, but rather articulate enduring deontic norms that maintain relative constancy within a given temporal scope, possessing universal applicability to all members within that domain. In contrast, when the "yīng gāi Ø de" refers to specific events and particular individuals, it exhibits a three-way semantic distinction: counter-factual, non-counter-factual, and factual. The author has carefully divided it into four scenarios: when one ought to perform an action but fails to do so or performs it incorrectly, and the event either does not occur or contradicts the facts, it is considered counter-factual; when one ought to perform an action, and there is an opportunity for its performance, which can be carried out immediately or in the future, it belongs to non-counter-factual in the future; When an action conforms to morality, one ought to perform it and has actually done so, and the event has truly occurred, which can be morally affirmed, it is factual rather than counter-factual; when one does something that one should not do and it goes against morality, and the event has already taken place, and it deserves moral condemnation, it is also factual rather than counter-factual.

The determination of truth values for both the antecedent p and consequent q propositions in counter-factual conditionals relies not only on the linguistic form of the utterance itself but also depends on contextual information for proper interpretation. Therefore, context serves as the pivotal determinant in establishing the semantic interpretation of counter-factual conditionals. Wang (2013) constructs a three-layer context system to explain counterfactual sentences: (1) In the local context, the counter-factual elements contribute to the factual meaning and negative meaning of the sentence; (2) The composite sentence context is responsible for the semantic interpretation of the antecedent and the consequent. Among them, the semantics of the counter-factual elements in the antecedent play a decisive role in the semantic interpretation of the whole sentence; (3) The macro context/discourse context includes the context, encyclopedic knowledge, communicative situations and so on. These three layers interact with each other, and two reasoning patterns are formed: (1) Bottom-up reasoning from the counter-factual elements to the composite sentence. The counter-factual elements in the antecedent provide sufficient counterfactual information, triggering a counterfactual interpretation of the consequent. In this case, there is no need to rely on the macro/discourse context; (2) Top-down reasoning from the macro context/discourse context to the composite sentence. When the macro context/discourse context contradicts the counterfactual information in the antecedent, or when the antecedent lacks the information to express counter-factuality, it is necessary to resort to the macro context/discourse context. Wang (2016) also constructs a composite system for the realization of counter-factual meanings in Chinese conditional sentences, mainly including five key factors: encyclopedic knowledge, context, past-time markers, negation and result-clause final "le". Among these factors, context and negation exhibit the highest frequency of occurrence, while encyclopedic knowledge and context constitute the most cognitively accessible elements for achieving counterfactual interpretation.

5.4 The Studies and Prospect of Formal Semantics

The formal study of language is a defining characteristic of modern linguistics, with diverse schools of thought and theoretical frameworks continually emerging. Formal syntax, championed by Noam Chomsky, and Formal semantics, pioneered by Richard Montague are the most influential. As an interdisciplinary field bridging logic and linguistics, formal semantics has evolved over five decades into a predominant research methodology in international philosophy, mathematical logic, linguistic theory, information science, and natural language processing. However, as Shen Yuan pointed out ten years ago, formal semantics has yet to attain mainstream status within China's linguistic academia (Shen, 2011). Perhaps we can discern the profound underlying reasons from Partee's analysis a decade ago. Partee (2011) points out that logicians have created formal languages and used formal methods to study the syntax and semantics of such languages. However, the structure of formal languages is different from that of natural languages. Naturally, linguists exclude formal languages from the scope of possible human languages. Taking model-theoretic semantics as an example, logicians have grown accustomed to designing formal languages replete with uninterpreted non-logical terms. While these theoretical frameworks offer alternative approaches to interpreting formal languages, semantically oriented researchers grounded in linguistic tradition view natural language as an autonomous empirical phenomenon, regarding the alternative explanations provided by model-theoretic semantics as profoundly unnatural. Moreover, although logicians avoided the psychological reality of language, the psychological reality remains crucial for linguists.

However, a decade later, we see that these disciplinary barriers and boundaries still exist. Formal semantics, as a group of disciplines that take natural languages as their research objects, encompasses Montague Grammar, generalized quantifier theory, dynamic semantics, situation semantics, game-theoretic semantics, type-logical grammar, categorical combinatory grammar, dynamic syntax, and so on. A review of domestic research literature on formal semantics reveals that formal semantics research with a logical bias covers a wide range of topics and touches on many of the aforementioned issues. For example, Gao (2011, 2013) applies the Segmented Discourse Representation Theory to study Chinese complex sentences and sentence groups. Besides, she introduces rhetorical structures into the logical forms of discourse, aiming to solve more semantic problems and promote the integration of Chinese semantic research with international standards. Conversely, an analysis of linguistics journals reveals that linguistically-oriented formal semantics research still presents vast uncharted territories waiting for our exploration and development.

(1) While paying attention to typical topics, we should extend to broader topics. Existing research focuses on quantification and scope, donkey sentences, counterfactual sentences. There are also studies on polarity items (e.g., Chen, Pan, 2020a, 2020b; Wen, 2013), tense logic (e.g., Wang, 2011a, 2011b; Yu, 2013; Yu & Zhang, 2017), Chinese function words (e.g., Wang, 2012), interrogative words (e.g., Liu,

2018), adverbs (e.g., Jiang & Liao, 2012; Shi & Sun, 2016; Yao & Shi, 2015), focus and scope (Li, 2016; Liu, 2014), etc. However, compared with the rich achievements in universal quantification, these topics are less discussed.

(2) While paying attention to the research of static semantics, we should also move forward in the research of dynamic semantics. Existing topics mainly focus on quantification. For example, studies on universal quantifiers or on polarity-sensitive words related to quantification (the numerous studies conducted by Pan Haihua and his collaborators are the most representative). Quantification research is one of the core topics of Montague grammar. But there are also big limitations in Montague grammar. For example, it cannot properly handle indefinite noun phrases and cannot depict the anaphoric relationships of pronouns in a discourse. Therefore, Dynamic semantics, represented by the Discourse Representation Theory and the Segmented Discourse Representation Theory, emerged in response to this situation. These theories can not only clearly depict the semantic structure of discourse, but also handle the coherence of discourse based on rhetorical structures, presenting and characterizing the semantics of natural language texts in a formalized way. Therefore, they have strong descriptive and explanatory power. These new theories have long been introduced and translated in the field of linguistics, for example, by Pan (1996). However, they have not yet become the main research topics. Few studies have applied them to the semantic research of Chinese or used Chinese language facts to modify or challenge these theoretical models.

(3) While paying attention to the theoretical exploration of formal semantics, we should conduct experimental semantics research. Shen (2017) explores the significance of experiments in formal semantics research. We can also see that domestic scholars such as Liu et al. (2011), Wu and Li (2015), Zhou et al. (2018) have adopted positivist methods to study semantics such as quantifiers, scope, and counterfactual meanings. But an analysis of linguistics journals reveals that linguistically-oriented formal semantics research still presents vast uncharted territories need our exploration and development. Conducting empirical research has important practical significance for deeply understanding formal semantics itself, constructing the psychological reality of formal semantics, and understanding the laws of language acquisition.

(4) While paying attention to formal semantics, we should actively conduct research on formal pragmatics. In his 1974 collected papers under the title *Pragmatics and Intensional Logic*, Montague pioneers the formal study of indexical expressions, thereby establishing a rigorous formalization path for pragmatic research. Later, the File Change Semantics, Situation Semantics, Discourse Representation Theory and other theories proposed by scholars have all incorporated contextual factors into semantic research. The aim is to conduct formal operations on pragmatic phenomena and mechanisms such as context, deictic information, explicit meaning, implicit meaning, presupposition, and propositional attitudes (Ran, 2005). The first decade of the twenty-first century witnessed the process of the introduction of domestic formal pragmatics and its combination with Chinese language facts. Examples include "A Brief Introduction to Formal Pragmatics" of Lv Gongli (2003), "Formal Pragmatics and the Doctrine of Explicature" of Jiang (2005), "A Comprehensive Review of

Formal Pragmatics Research" of Liu (2005), the monograph "An Introduction to Formal Pragmatics" of Zhang (2008), "An Outline of the Development of Formal Pragmatics" of Zeng and Mao (2010), "The Strengthening of Conditional Sentences and the Doctrine of Explicature" of Huang (2010), "The Issue of Meaning Comprehension in Formal Pragmatics" of Yu (2010), and the monograph "Approaching Formal Pragmatics" of Jiang (2011), etc. However, in the past decade, international research in formal pragmatics has enjoyed great enthusiasm. In contrast, domestic research has barely touched on this topic.

5.5 Conclusion

Formalization, as a major means of exploring natural languages, has become the core method and concept in research fields such as syntax, semantics, pragmatics, artificial intelligence, and computer language processing. However, generally speaking, we can say that the development of formalized research in our country lags behind, on the whole, the development of other branches of linguistics, research paradigms, or research approaches. Thus, we expect that domestic language learners and researchers will be less resistant to formalized research and have a better understanding of it. Only in this way, formalized research can attain a steady development.

Chapter 6
Cognitive Semantics Studies

6.1 Introduction

Emerging in the 1970s as a transformative movement, cognitive linguistics represents a groundbreaking approach that has reoriented linguistic research over the past four decades. Grounded in experientialist philosophy, this theoretical framework offers innovative conceptual perspectives for systematically describing, analyzing, and explaining diverse linguistic phenomena. As a part of the cognitive linguistics movement, cognitive semantics has abandoned the tradition of purely formal language research. It has incorporated the issue of semantics (meaning) into the core topics of linguistic research, with a particular focus on the problems of meaning construction and knowledge representation. Moreover, it has unified the two traditionally separate fields of pragmatics and semantics. The cognitive semantics is not a single semantic theory, but a new language view or meaning view. The cognitive semantics theory usually takes "meaning is conceptual" as its basic theoretical claim. In terms of vocabulary, its meaning is not the entity or relationship in the "real world" that the word refers to, but rather a concept formed in the mind based on the experience related to that entity or relationship. This means that semantics is not objective and semantic knowledge is not isolated either. Instead, they processed the attribute of encyclopedic knowledge. Therefore, cognitive semantics theory generally establishes a semantic analysis framework of "cognitive modes, conceptual structures, and semantic systems" based on interactive experiences and cognitive processing. This framework is used to study and describe the formation, comprehension, and mental representation of the meanings of words and sentences.

The cognitive semantics is another key research in semantics following formal semantics. Although both of them pay attention to the issue of meaning, there are significant differences between them in terms of the understanding of meaning and the specific issues they concern. Formal semantics constructs the research on meaning of natural languages within the framework of logic and structural linguistics, spanning multiple disciplinary fields such as logic, formal linguistics, and linguistic typology.

X. Wen and R. Tang, *New Perspectives and Developments in Chinese Semantics*,
https://doi.org/10.1007/978-981-95-1730-5_6

Classical formal semantics studies natural languages by means of logical and mathematical formalization, and explores the corresponding relationship between syntax and semantics. When the syntactic rules are fixed, it studies the laws of semantic operations. It focuses on the truth conditions of linguistic forms and emphasizes the principle of compositionality of meaning.

Cognitive semantics explains the conceptual basis of semantic structures from the perspective of human cognitive abilities and ways, and it has the following differences from formal semantics: first, it emphasizes the role of context in the generation and understanding of semantics. Due to the influence of the minimalist theory, formal semantics tries to minimize the influence of context on semantics (Shen Yuan, 2011), which has been greatly challenged by context determinism. Cognitive semantics posits a fundamental theoretical tenet: the nature of semantic structure is inherently encyclopedic, where lexical meaning depends on contextual information. Second, cognitive semantics emphasizes the role of conceptual metaphor and conceptual metonymy as fundamental cognitive tools in language, whereas formal semantics overlooks these pervasive phenomena in natural language, without enough theoretical explanations for them. Third, formal semantics operates in theoretical alignment with formal linguistics' conception of language, particularly its foundational commitment to the modularity of language faculty, while cognitive semantics categorically rejects linguistic modularity and dismisses purely formal logical operations that are detached from authentic language usage.

Over the past decade, cognitive semantics in China has evolved from initial theoretical introductions to progressively engage with substantive semantic issues in Chinese, continually expanding its research scope. This trajectory has yielded dual contributions: empirically validating core tenets of cognitive semantics through Chinese linguistic phenomena while simultaneously enriching semantic theory by illuminating language-specific particularities. Therefore, it is of great benefit to sort out through the development of cognitive semantics in China over the past decade, summarize the contributions of Chinese scholars to the research of cognitive semantics, identify the shortcomings of domestic research, and look forward to the future research trends of cognitive semantics.

6.2 The Basic Theories and Claims of Cognitive Semantics

6.2.1 The Guiding Principle of Cognitive Semantics

In cognitive semantics, although scholars have different research focuses and interests, they all follow some basic guiding principles. And these principles are derived from the two "commitments" adhered to by cognitive linguistics. First, we should simply talk about two "commitments". The two "commitments" refer to the commitment to generalization and the commitment to cognition. The commitment to generalization means that one should seek the general principles that can generalize all aspects of human language. There is a common structure in all aspects among human languages, and the function of linguistics is to identify these common principles. The commitment to cognition, on the other hand, means that when describing linguistic theories, knowledge and theories from other disciplines should be borrowed, and language description should also reflect the principles of human cognition that have been proven in other disciplines. According to the two "commitments", there are four fundamental principles in cognitive semantics: conceptual structure is embodied, semantic structure is conceptual structure, meaning representation is encyclopedic knowledge, and meaning construction is conceptualization. For better understanding cognitive semantics, domestic scholars have held active discussions on these four guiding principles.

1. Conceptual Structure Is Embodied

Cognitive semanticists are most concerned about the relationship between conceptual structure and the perceptual experience of the external world. The Embodied Cognition Hypothesis holds that the essence of conceptual organization comes from our bodily experience, and the conceptual structure also derives its meaning from the bodily experiences associated with it. In order to better understand this fundamental principle, we will take the image schema as an example to explain the Embodied Cognition Hypothesis. Johnson (1987) explains the essence of image schema. He argues that bodily experiences generate image schemas within the conceptual system, with these schemas originating from sensory and perceptual experiences acquired through human interaction with the physical world. Johnson (1987) defines the image schema as a dynamic pattern that repeatedly emerges in perceptual interactions and motor activities. This structure imparts coherence and structure to our experiences. The image schema serves as the foundation of conceptual structure. It is also a very abstract and special kind of concept, yet it can produce more specific concepts. For instance, let's take the "container" as an example. A container is composed of a boundary, an interior, and an exterior. We often say, "I came out of the house". "Woke up from a dream". and "Walked into the supermarket". In these three sentences, "home", "dream", and "supermarket" are all regarded as a container. We "enter and exit" different containers every day, repeating this activity, and thus the concept of "container" is formed in our minds.

2. Semantic Structure Is Conceptual Structure

Semantic structure is the meanings associated with words and other linguistic units. The guiding principle holds that language represents the concepts in the human brain, rather than directly representing the objects in the external world. That is to say, the semantic structure is equivalent to the concept, but this does not mean that the two are completely identical. The meaning of language only constitutes a part of the concept and fails to reflect all the concepts in the brain. For example, in English, there is no specific word to describe the area between the nose and the mouth where a mustache grows. Therefore, the lexical concept is just a small part of the concepts in our brain thinking. Moreover, semantic structure is not only related to vocabulary but also to all language units, such as bound morphemes, the active and passive voices of sentences.

For example:

Example 1
William Shakespeare wrote Romeo and Juliet.

Example 2
Romeo and Juliet was written by Shakespeare.

Example 1 is an active sentence, emphasizing that our focus is on the doer of the action; whereas Example 2 is a passive sentence, meaning the emphasis of the sentence lies on the receiver. Cognitive semanticists argue that linguistic units, ranging from entire sentences down to morphemes and even articles, are inherently meaningful in themselves. One defining characteristic of cognitive semantics is its commitment to providing a unified account of both lexical items and grammatical structures, rather than studying them in isolation.

3. **Meaning Representation Is Encyclopedic Knowledge**

Influenced by frame semantics, cognitive semantics rejects the dictionary view of lexical concepts and instead adopts the encyclopedic view of meaning, maintaining that the essence of semantic structure resides in encyclopedic knowledge. Words are not mere containers of meaning, but rather serve as access points to vast stores of knowledge associated with particular concepts or conceptual domains. For example, the word "bachelor" in English has a dictionary definition of "a man who has never been married". However, people's cognitive frameworks also contain cultural knowledge associated with the term "bachelor", frequently linking this word with specific behavioral patterns. For example, "a man who doesn't love hygiene", "a man whose emotion is causal", and so on. The encyclopedic meaning does not negate the existence of conventionalized meanings. But these conventionalized meanings serve merely as cues for meaning construction, while the true comprehension of lexical meaning ultimately relies on contextual information in discourse. For example:

Example 3
The child is safe.

Example 4
The beach is safe.

We can image a child playing in the beach. Example 3 indicates that the child is safe, meaning the child is free from any dangers; Example 4 suggests that the beach is safe, implying that the environment poses no danger to the child. The two examples demonstrate that the word "safe" does not have a fixed, uniform attribute when collocated with "child" or "beach". To comprehend the meaning of "safe", we must integrate encyclopedic knowledge with the concepts of "child" and "beach" constructing its significance within the specific context.

4. **Meaning Construction Is Conceptualization**

Cognitive semantics holds that language itself does not encode meaning. Instead, words or other structural units are merely "cues" for meaning construction, and the semantic structure is identical to the conceptual structure. Hence, meaning construction is conceptualization, a dynamic process. In this process, linguistic units function merely as entry points triggering conceptual operations and activating background knowledge. Fauconnier (1994) argues that the most crucial element in meaning construction is mapping, that is, the localized connections between mental spaces and the conceptual blending of information during the online process of meaning building. Then, we will introduce the new concept integration theory in cognitive linguistics regarding meaning construction.

Conceptual blending theory, a highly influential framework in cognitive linguistics for explaining meaning construction, was originally proposed and developed by Fauconnier (1994, 1997). Its initial formulation was termed mental space theory. Fauconnier posits that meaning construction involves two processes: the construction of mental spaces, and the establishment of mappings across different mental spaces. Crucially, mapping relations are constrained by local discourse contexts, rendering meaning construction usually localized and context-dependent. Mental spaces are the fundamental category in mental space theory. They are neither linguistic forms per se nor semantic structures per se, but rather temporary containers for relevant information in linguistic structures' conceptual packets constructed for achieving local comprehension and action during thinking and communication (Sun Ya, 2001). Mental spaces are constructed by space builders within which various semantic elements, generally noun phrases, are interconnected through mappings. Space builders clarify the properties and relations among elements within a mental space. With the development of the discourse, more constructed space structure forms a mental space lattice. Within such a network, elements across different mental spaces become interlinked through counterparts and connectors, and relative elements will map cross space.

Conceptual blending theory represents an advanced development of mental space theory. It explains how certain elements from the two input spaces in the mental space theory are compressed into the blending space. Conceptual blending theory's most crucial viewpoint is that meaning construction generally involves the integration of structures, and manifests more content than the sum of its individual components. Fauconnier & Turner (2002) holds that a complete conceptual blending network contains at least four mental spaces: two separate input spaces, a generic space, and a blending space. The shared abstract information and structure in two input spaces can be projected into the generic space, while through partial mappings, counterpart elements from both inputs are selectively projected into the blending space, where emergent structure is formed. Finally, the four spaces are connected through mapping, forming a complete conceptual blending network.

6.2.2 *The Usage-Based View of Language*

The "usage-based theory" posted in the later Wittgenstein's thought puts forward the idea that "meaning is usage". The theory holds that words and even a whole language are a tool to some degree. According to different purposes, they have different uses, and its meaning lies in their specific uses (Liu Longgen, 2001). "Theory of Meaning and Usage" underscores the primacy of context, asserting that linguistic meaning is conferred through practice. This view coincides with the "usage-based" view of language in cognitive linguistics. Cognitive linguistics believes that linguistic knowledge is from the usage patterns of language, which refers to how language is used. It is impossible to study the linguistic structure without considering the usage of language. Langacker (1987) first puts forward the concept of "usage-based". On this context, various theories and models have been derived, such as abstraction, schematization, and so on. The "usage-based" view of language has also become a core concept in cognitive grammar and construction grammar (Wang Tianyi, Wang Yin, 2010).

The core idea of the usage-based view of language is the specific language usage event. A language usage event is similar to a unit, which uses the conventionality of language to express a coherent and consistent idea. A specific language usage event is a discourse, which is the entity of language use, reflecting cultural characteristics and contextual features, and it is also a part of the speech acts of language users.

The usage-based view of language also has its own unique perspectives in the study of language acquisition, which is opposite to the view of generative grammar. That is to say, the usage-based view of language holds that linguistic knowledge originates from language use. Human beings do not acquire language through activating an existing language system. Instead, in the process of using language, they rely on their cognitive abilities to extract language units and language structures.

The usage-based view of language also emphasizes the role of context, holding that context has a significant impact on the meaning of words. Although a word itself has a conventional meaning, which is its typical meaning, a certain word can be endowed with local pragmatic meanings in different contexts. The context is divided into the discourse context and the background context: the discourse context is related to other elements in the sentence, while the background context is related to the background knowledge which the discourse generates. Due to the effect of context, the ambiguity and vagueness in discourse are enhanced. In real language phenomena, the context combines with the typical meaning of words, endowing words with pragmatic meanings. In the usage-based view of language, pragmatic meaning is the real meaning, and this view is also in line with the encyclopedic view in cognitive semantics.

6.2.3 Conceptual Metaphor and Conceptual Metonymy

1. Conceptual Metaphor

Metaphor has always been regarded merely as rhetorical language. But Lakoff & Johnson (1980) holds that metaphorical language is based on a metaphorical system. We not only communicate with metaphorical language, but our thinking is also metaphorical. Therefore, the concepts in our thinking are also metaphorical. Hence, we call metaphors conceptual metaphors in cognitive linguistics. Conceptual metaphor is built in the process of human interaction with the external world and has an experiential basis. A conceptual metaphor contains a source domain and a target domain. Through mapping, we can understand the target domain by using the source domain. Because the target domain is more abstract, we use relatively concrete concepts as the source domain to help us understand abstract things. This is the theory of conceptual metaphor, which is different from the traditional rhetorical view of metaphor. Since then, the research on metaphor has been entrusted with the new task of revealing human cognitive thinking. In the view of cognitive linguists, metaphor is not merely a modification at the linguistic level. Instead, it is a cognitive means or tool, and its application occurs subconsciously. The essence of metaphor is conceptual, representing a mapping across conceptual domains that follows constant principles. Here we take a classic conceptual metaphor as an example:

Example 5
Love Is a Journey.

We have to go our separate ways.
It has been a long road.
They are at a crossroads in their relationships.
We can't turn back now.
They are in a dead-end relationship.

We take the first sentence as the object of analysis. In this conceptual metaphor, we use journey to represent the abstract noun love. Two people who are together because of love will walk to same direction and destination. The first sentence, its literal translation is "We're going to take different roads", but its real mean is "We will part ways".

Subsequently, Grady (1997a) puts forward the Primary Metaphor Theory. According to the theory, metaphors are divided into primary metaphor and compound metaphor. Primary metaphors originate from our initial bodily experiences. Since almost everyone has a body and a brain and the living environment is also largely similar, most of the primary metaphors that directly stem from our initial bodily experiences are inevitably universal. They only involve two simple concepts from two domains, possess cross-linguistic commonalities, and the basic target concepts reflect subjectivity, presenting concepts related to judgment, evaluation, speculation, and other aspects. Here we give an example of a primary metaphor:

Example 6
Similarity Is Nearness.

That color is quite close to the one on our dining-room wall.

Here, a primary metaphor is to use the distance (near or far) to represent the degree of similarity. When the similarity is high, it is represented by a short distance; when the similarity is low, it is represented by a long distance. The literal translation of this example is "That color is very close in distance to the color of the walls in our living room", but what it actually means is "That color is very similar to the color of the walls in our living room".

A compound metaphor is a unified entity composed of several primary metaphors without characteristics of primary metaphors. Compound metaphors do not come from experience but owns cultural characteristics. Moreover, complex metaphors are not simple single mappings, and the elements in the source domain cannot be directly mapped onto the target domain. For example, Grady (1997b) believes that "Theories Are Buildings" is a complex metaphor. A building is composed of many components, such as windows and doors. But there is no mapping relationship between these components and the source domain. Therefore, we cannot say, "This theory has French windows".

2. **Conceptual Metonymy**

Just like conceptual metaphor, conceptual metonymy is also a conceptual mechanism that reflects human thinking and human language. The essence of metonymy is also conceptual. In the past, metonymy was merely regarded as a rhetorical device. Lakoff & Johnson (1980) first proposes a method for studying conceptual metonymy in cognitive semantics. Different from the cross-domain mapping of conceptual metaphor, the mapping of metonymy occurs within the same domain, emphasizing the highlighting of a less prominent aspect within a single domain. Due to contiguity, the vehicle can be used to represent the target. That is to say, in conceptual metonymy, people use thing A to represent thing B to help understand. There are many tendencies and principles in the selection of the vehicle. Generally, two principles are followed when choosing a vehicle: humans are preferred over non-humans, and the concrete is preferred over the abstract. That is to say, people are more inclined to use human vehicles and concrete vehicles. There are also various types of metonymies, such as the part standing for the whole, the whole standing for the part, and so on. Here is an example of conceptual metonymy:

Example 7
Place for Institution

Buckingham Palace denied the rumors.

In Example 7, "Buckingham Palace" serves as the vehicle and is used to represent "the British royal family". Therefore, the literal translation is "Buckingham Palace denies these rumors", but what it actually means is "The British royal family denies these rumors".

There are both similarities and differences between conceptual metonymy and conceptual metaphor. First, both of them are a conceptual mechanism, reflecting human cognitive thinking. But they have different cognitive structure. Conceptual metonymy helps people understand thing B by means of thing A, while conceptual metaphor uses thing A to represent thing B. Because they have different mapping bases. The mapping basis of conceptual metaphor is the similarity between two domains, while conceptual metonymy is the contiguity between the vehicle and the target.

6.2.4 *Prototype Theory and Typicality Effects*

The emergence of the theory of family resemblance put forth by Wittgenstein inspires a group of linguists in their understanding of linguistic categories. Psychologists believe that categorization is the most basic cognitive behavior of human beings. Humans classify cognitive objects according to the similarities and differences among things, so as to form a systematic understanding of the external world. Categorization is the core of the conceptual system. And the prototype theory of categorization is adopted in cognitive semantics, which was put forward by Eleaor Rosch and her colleagues on the basis of experiments, refuting Aristotle's classical theory. From the view of this theory:

> Categories are not defined by the important features shared among entities, but by their family resemblances;
> The boundaries between categories are fuzzy;
> The status of entities within a category are not equal, and their status is determined by typicality;
> Categories are established around the prototype, in a radial pattern.

Firstly, the prototype theory adopts Wittgenstein's idea of family resemblance. It reveals that semantic categories have an internal structure with a "center" (typical members) and a "periphery" (atypical members). The center of a category is the typical member of the category, which is the prototype. Members with low similarity to the prototype belong to the atypical members (Wu Shixiong, Chen Weizhen, 2004). The prototype category also refutes the idea in the classical categorization theory that human beings categorize things through necessary and sufficient conditions. Instead, it incorporates things similar to a prototype into a category.

The theory has provided cognitive linguists with a great many inspirations. Inspired by Rosch's experiments and the prototype theory, Lakoff further puts forward the Idealized Cognitive Model, which explains the source as well as the internal structure of the typicality effect. Lakoff (1987) holds that categories are related to Idealized Cognitive Models. The ICM is a relatively stable mental representation that reveals the abstract structure of the external world and is abstracted from human experiences in the world. First, the ICM posts the origination of the typicality effects, arguing that stems from the mismatch between the ICM and certain concepts in people's thinking. For instance, in people's thinking, the ICM of the word "bachelor" will incorporate information such as a monogamous society, the concept of marriage that people have, and the criteria for the marriageable age. However, "the Pope" is not considered a typical "bachelor" within ICM. Although the Pope is single and falls within the "bachelor" model, people generally understand the concept of the word "Pope" based on the ICM of religion. That is to say, the Pope is not allowed to get married. Therefore, the Pope cannot be regarded as a typical "bachelor". What's more, Lakoff also put forward all kinds of models that can give rise to the typicality effect, such as the cluster model and so on. In addition, metonymy, radial categories, and the like can all constitute the typicality effect.

6.3 The Studies Status of Cognitive Semantics in the Decade at Home

In the past ten years, the research on cognitive semantics in China has caught more and more attentions. In this chapter, we first explore the traditional research topics (conceptual metaphor, conceptual metonymy, categorization theory, mental spaces, and conceptual blending). In the past decade, conceptual metaphor and conceptual metonymy remained hot topics of discussion among scholars. Most scholars took use of the conceptual metaphor theory to explore linguistic phenomena in either English or Chinese, or applied it into translation and teaching. At the same time, the categorization theory, as well as the theories of mental space and conceptual blending, began to arouse the interest of scholars. The categorization theory is widely used to explain the polysemy, while the theories of mental space and conceptual blending were applied to the analysis of translation, pragmatics, and other aspects. Besides, we also notice that domestic scholars have explored some other topics and came up with their own understandings and theories, such as the cognitive analysis of synecdoche, the semantic research under Embodied Linguistics, and the semantic construction of multimodal metaphors. In addition, using cognitive semantics to solve certain semantic issues in Chinese has also become a key point of concern for scholars. Typical research includes the comparison of cognitive mechanisms between Chinese and other languages, as well as the evolution of word meanings in Chinese itself and the issues regarding the new "bèi" construction sentences. All these studies enable us to have a more profound understanding of the Chinese language.

6.3.1 Traditional Topic Studies

In order to explore the hot research areas in cognitive semantics by domestic scholars over the past decade, following the statistical method in the "Review of Domestic Research on Cognitive Semantics" (Zhang Minghui, Cui Xiangning, 2017), we took

Table 6.1 The statistics of papers on cognitive semantics in core journals from 2010 to 2020

Metonymy	375
Metaphor	819
Category	395
Conceptual blending and mental space	184

the scope of "Chinese Languages and Characters" and "Foreign Languages and Literatures" under the category of "Philosophy and Humanities" on CNKI as the search range. We respectively took "metaphor", "metonymy", "category", "conceptual blending", and "mental space" as the themes, and took "cognition" as the parallel theme, and searched for the number of CSSCI papers published in core journals during the period from 2010 to 2020. The results are as follows (see Table 6.1):

According to the search results, we can see that cognitive semantics has received great attention from the linguistics community in recent years, and enjoys high enthusiasm in research. Compared with the situation from 2000 to 2008 (Zhang Minghui and Cui Xiangning, 2017), the number of research papers in cognitive semantics on conceptual metonymy, metaphor, and categorization theory has increased significantly. Among them, the research on the direction of conceptual metaphor has been the focus of attention of domestic scholars in the past decade. And the number of published papers in this area far exceeds that of other directions, up to 819. The research enthusiasm for conceptual metonymy has also increased greatly compared with that before 2010. Moreover, research on categories is also an area that scholars focus on. Although the number of papers on the search direction of conceptual blending and mental spaces is relatively small, many linguists have already started to pay attention to the research in this regard. Next, we will analyze the hot research areas and vital topics one by one from theoretical research and theoretical application.

1. **Conceptual Metaphor**

In the past decade, conceptual metaphor has been the most important topic in the domestic research of cognitive semantics. Starting from the definition of conceptual metaphor and theory, scholars have not only explored their own insights into conceptual metaphor and theory, but also applied it to aspects such as teaching and translation. We will roughly divide the discussions on conceptual metaphor by domestic scholars into three parts: semantic cognitive mechanism, language teaching, and translation.

(1) **Semantic Cognitive Mechanism**

Many domestic scholars, when exploring the semantic mechanisms of various words, such as the evolution of word meanings and semantic derivation, mention conceptual metaphor as the main cognitive mechanism. Zhang Shaoquan (2010) discusses the motivation behind the evolution of words and their cognitive mechanisms, and puts forward three motivations for speakers to innovate word meanings: objective motivations, subjective motivations, and linguistic motivations. He argues that the cognitive mechanisms mainly include metaphor, metonymy, and subjectification. Comparing the lexical sources in English and Chinese during the twentieth century and the semantic cognitive mechanism, Bai Jiehong and Chen Zhongping (2011a) realize that conceptual blending and conceptual metaphor were the main player in cognitive mechanisms, for a convergence between English and Chinese new words from morphological formation to semantic cognitive mechanisms.

(2) **Language Teaching Applications of Conceptual Metaphor**

In teaching aspect, most of domestic scholars applied metaphor theory to English teaching or second language acquisition. Some scholars, such as Chen Lang (2010), who focus on the research of the application of conceptual metaphor in second language teaching, hold that teachers should not only paid attention to the explanation of metaphors, but also develop students' ability to analyze metaphors independently. Also, some scholars, such as Liu Yan and Chen Haiyan, demonstrate the feasibility of applying conceptual metaphor to foreign language vocabulary instruction through experiments. Experiments have confirmed that conceptual metaphor-based vocabulary instruction enhances students' long-term retention of words and solved some issues like polysemy to some degree (Chen Haiyan & Wang Lirong, 2013). Besides, some scholars focus on the impact of conceptual metaphor on the comprehension of English idioms. By experiments, Tang Ling and Wang Weiqian (2014) prove that an explicit conceptual metaphor teaching approach significantly enhances learners' comprehension and short-term retention of English idioms; meanwhile the way learners transfer their metaphorical ability in their mother tongue appropriately to that in a second (foreign) language is also an important factor influencing their comprehension and intention of metaphorical expressions.

(3) **Translation Studies from the Perspective of Conceptual Metaphor**

In translation studies, some scholars adopt the conceptual metaphor theory perspective to discuss detailed analyses of translation strategies for specific literary works, including books and poetry. For example, Sun Fenglan (2016) demonstrates how three types of conceptual metaphors manifest in different English translations of *Huangdi Neijing (The Yellow Emperor's Inner Canon)*, analyzing the factors underlying translational variations and proposing metaphor-specific translation strategies. Cao Lingmei and Liu Chaojian (2018) conduct a cognitive analysis of "grass" metaphors across four English versions of *Shui Huzhuan* (*The Water Margin*), identifying four translation approaches: literal metaphor transfer, metaphor substitution, literal metaphor transfer + explanation, metaphor + substitution with explanation. Also, some scholars explore translation strategies from a macro perspective through the concept of cognitive metaphor. For example, Yu Gaofeng (2011) holds that translators should use different translation methods according to different metaphorical cognitive patterns for the best effect of cultural transmittance.

2. **Conceptual Metonymy**

The metonymy studies have also garnered more and more attention from scholars in China over the past decade. Same to the conceptual metaphor studies, when domestic scholars examine metonymy, they focus both on its theoretical foundations and cognitive basis, as well as it applied the groundwork of conceptual metonymy to teach or translate. Additionally, when discussing metonymy, scholars often compare conceptual metonymy with conceptual metaphor. The book will categorize and review the work of domestic scholars on conceptual metaphor from three perspectives: ontological research, translation applications, and comparative studies between conceptual metonymy and conceptual metaphor.

(1) **The Ontological Studies on Conceptual Metonymy**

In the ontological research on conceptual metonymy and exploring the theoretical dimensions of metonymy, Cheng Qilong (2010) classifies metonymy from different views, such as, symbolic ontology, conceptual structure, domain relations, speech acts, and conceptual blending. Wei Zaijiang (2010) integrates conceptual metonymy with functional linguistics to explore its function at the discourse level. He finds that conceptual metonymy played a significant role in discourse cohesion. Later, Wei Zaijiang (2016) explores the embodied philosophical foundations of conceptual metonymy, revealing that it is based on embodied experience and is an unconscious and automatic thinking pattern. As a result, metonymic reasoning makes most abstract thinking possible.

(2) **Research on the Relationship Between Metonymy and Metaphor**

Usually, conceptual metaphor and conceptual metonymy are intertwined. Therefore, a large number of scholars will compare their similarities and differences or apply them to a specific area of research. Zhu Jianxin and Zuo Guangming (2012) systematically elucidate the distinctions and connections between metaphor and metonymy from a cognitive perspective, including cognitive structure, mapping bases, cognitive functions, cognitive mechanisms, cognitive motivations, and thinking patterns. What they have done has further revealed the cognitive essence of metaphor and metonymy. From the perspective of embodied philosophy, Gong Pengcheng and Wang Wenbin (2014) endeavor to analyze the differences between metonymy and metaphor, their continuum relationship, and the nature of their interface. They find that, under embodied philosophy, there is relativity in human cognition, allowing for the mutual transformation between metaphor and metonymy. This transformation results in a continuum relationship due to the cognitive interface between metaphor and metonymy.

(3) **Research on Translation from the Perspective of Conceptual Metonymy**

In translation studies, scholars represented by Lu Weizhong have proposed effective methods for the translation of metonymy and explored the metonymic mechanisms of linguistic transformation during the translation. Lu Weizhong (2011) holds that "target language equivalent vehicle translation", "target language-specific vehicle translation", "source vehicle + literal explanation", "source vehicle + annotation or gloss", and "source vehicle omission" are effective methods for the translation of metonymy. The adoption of the methods depends on the specific contexts. Li Ke and Lu Weizhong (2017) test that the ability of translation of metonymy influenced the capacity of translation to some extent. The factors include capabilities for identifying and creating translation of metonymy and frequency that transforms translation of metonymy. Also, they produce that teachers should adopt interventional mechanisms in translation teaching to improve student's abilities of translation. Meanwhile Wang Yin (2019) constructs metonymic and metaphoric dimensions of translation based on translation of titles of English films. He argues that translation does not operate solely via metaphor or metonymy in isolation; rather, the two function synergistically. With the help of metaphor, words can be selected vertically, and with the help of metonymy, words can be combined horizontally to form sentences. By combining the two, a neighboring relationship between the original text and the translated text can be constructed, as well as a connection among literature, culture, ethnicity, customs, etc. Moreover, as a cognitive mechanism, both metaphor and metonymy control the entire translation process.

3. **Categorization Theory**

Domestic scholars mainly focused on categorization theory in implications for foreign language teaching, polysemy and word classed. Therefore, this book will also concentrate on the three aspects.

(1) **Applications of Category Theory in Language Teaching**

Domestic scholars often applied category theory to vocabulary teaching. There is general consensus among researchers about crucial importance of basic-level category vocabulary in foreign language teaching. For example, Yang Jichun, and Qi Shuling hold that teaching Chinese as a foreign language should prioritize vocabulary at the basic level of category. Some scholars also conduct experiments in an attempt to explore students' acquisition of different levels of words. Ma Shuhong (2010) experimentally tests that the core meanings of prepositions are more easily acquired by learners. Li Yanping and Zhu Yushan (2011), based on prototype theory, explore the necessity and operational principles of English grammar teaching through research.

(2) **Categorization Theory and Polysemy**

The thriving of categorization theory has strongly aroused the interest of a large number of scholars in word meaning and word classes. Based on prototype category, most scholars discuss the polysemy with the mechanisms of metaphor and metonymy. For instance, Zhang Jianli (2010) investigates the dual-level polysemy model of "over", and thinks that "over" has a superordinate conceptual layer and a subordinate contextual layer. The superordinate layer reflects Lakoff's radial set principle, and the subordinate layer incorporate Rosch's earlier overlapping set theory. Scholars pay attention not only to the explanation of polysemy in Chinese and English, but also to the exploration of the mechanisms of polysemy in Japanese, Russian, and even ethnic minority languages. Based on the categorization theory and prototype theory in cognitive linguistics, Zhang Peng (2011) explores the polysemous structure of Japanese passive auxiliary verbs "RERU/RARERU" and its semantic extension mechanism.

(3) **Category Theory and Word Classes Studies**

Research on word classes based on category theory has been a key that scholars have focused on in recent years. Zong Shouyun (2011, 2014) proposes the categorization research of quantifier twice. He believes that the main function of quantifier is categorization, and he ranks the intensity of the categorization functions of various quantifiers. Ma Yongtian (2014) has also made use of categorization theory to understand the phenomenon of "one entity with multiple quantifiers" and "one quantifier applying to multiple entities" in Chinese and English quantifiers. He believes quantifiers serve a categorizing function for the nouns they quantify, leading to "one quantifier applying to multiple entities". According to family resemblances, Liu Yuelian (2010) explores the categorization of euphemisms and taboo words. And she holds euphemisms are a superordinate category of taboo words and a polysemous category. Some scholars also use categorization theory to discuss the motivation and phenomena of the syntactic functions of word classes. Huangfu Sufei (2010) attributes the generation mechanism of the structure "adverb of degree + noun" to category conversion. She also specifically analyzes and explains the categories, methods, and motivation of the category conversion. Wang Renqiang and Yang Xu (2017) analyze the question of word classes related to "publication" and the categorization of double-tiered word classes. They recognize that the theory of categorization of double-tiered word classes that coordinates classical and vague logic is effective in resolving the questions related to word classes of an analytical language such as modern Chinese language. Although most scholars firmly argue that prototype theory was deeply meaningful to categorization studies, some scholars doubt it, believing that prototypes exist, yet they cannot be used as a basis for category division (Zhao Yanchun 2010).

4. **Mental Spaces and Conceptual Blending**

The mental spaces and concept integration theory have gradually started to attract the attention of domestic scholars in the past decade. Although its research popularity is not as high as that of metaphor and categorization studies, there have been some remarkable breakthroughs and innovations. Since the concept integration theory originates from the mental space theory and both of them elaborately explain the process of meaning construction. Besides, domestic research is at the initial stage and lacks research on mental spaces. Therefore, we will discuss them together. We will summarize the research of the two theories from three aspects: translation, application, and language structure.

(1) **Translation Studies Under the Theory of Mental Space and Conceptual Blending**

Firstly, some domestic scholars tend to link the concept integration theory with translation. Miao Ju and Huang Shaoshuang (2014) interpret the translation criteria from the perspective of concept integration, aiming to explain the translation process with cognitive mechanisms, vividly demonstrating the complexity, integrity, and creativity of the cognitive thinking process in translation, revealing the connections between different disciplines, inspiring the multi-disciplinary thinking mode and research methods in translation studies. Jin Shengxin and Lin Zhengjun (2016) discuss the cognitive mechanism of translator's subjectivity based on the conceptual blending theory.

1 After Grice, scholars based on parsimony theory have tried to reduce the number of conversational principles to enhance the explanatory power of pragmatic theories and enable psychological interpretations. Main representatives include Horn, Levinson, and Sperber & Wilson.

They hold that the construction progress of translator's subjectivity mainly includes two rounds of conceptual blending that are carried out when deconstructing the original work and constructing the translated work. There are also scholars who analyze specific translation cases from the perspective of conceptual blending, such as Wang Wei[1] and others.

(2) **Applications of the Theory of Mental Space and/Concept Integration**

Some scholars tend to explain some specific language application issues through conceptual blending and mental space. Wang Shaohua and Wang Peng (2011) use conceptual blending theory to analyze Chinese allegorical sayings. Moreover, they believe that conceptual blending theory could better explain the cognitive motivation, reason logic, and meaning construction of allegorical sayings. Tang Xianqing and Li Hongqian (2016) study the conceptual blending mode in the generalization of military terms. They consider that in the generalization process of modern Chinese military terms, 76% of them adopt the single-domain network conceptual blending mode, and the rest adopt the double-domain network conceptual blending mode. What's more, scholars like Zhan Liwen and Li Rui analyze and discuss euphemisms and vague language on account of mental space and conceptual blending.

(3) **Construction Analysis from the Perspective of Mental Space/Conceptual Blending Theory**

The theory of mental space and conceptual blending is also widely used in the semantic cognitive interpretations of various constructions. By the two theories, Wang Zhiying (2014) analyze the theoretical mechanism of formation of "xiǎo xīn bié VP"; from the perspective of conceptual blending, Li Sixu and Shen Caiyun (2016) explore "ài V bù V", and analyze its syntactic function and the semantic features of V. Finally, the structure "ài V bù V" is divided into three levels of low, medium, and high, according to the degree of integration. In addition, scholars such as Chen Wenbo and Dai Lingling explore the cognitive semantics or the hierarchy of conceptual blending of various types of constructions from the perspectives of the two theories.

6.3.2 *Other Topics Studies*

1. **The Cognitive Exploration of Synecdoche**

Synecdoche was generally regarded as a rhetorical device by linguists. In cognitive semantics, most scholars focus on two important cognitive mechanisms, metonymy and metaphor, and consider synecdoche as a branch of metonymy, with few scholars paying attention to synecdoche studies. Li Yini (2011), when exploring the cognitive research on the semantic extension of Japanese word "hand", puts synecdoche, metaphor and metonymy together, examining their role in semantic extension. Therefore, she holds that the understanding of synecdoche requires the cognitive ability to grasp the same object from different perspectives. The key lies in finding out the differences on the basis of acknowledging the variations in the detailed parts of the same object. However, this book has relatively few cognitive analyses of synecdoche and the research is not in-dept. Chen Xinren and Cai Yiming (2011) propose that, from the perspectives of rhetoric and cognition, synecdoche and metonymy are not merely a relationship of superordinate and subordinate categories, and their natures differ significantly. From a cognitive perspective, the cognitive bases of the two are similar, both using adjacency, where the name of thing is used to refer to the name of another thing that is in an adjacent relation with it. However, synecdoche is based on the understanding of the thing itself, while metonymy is based on the understanding of the connections between things. Synecdoche inherently involves a relationship where the vehicle and tenor intrinsically belong to the same entity. Judging whether there is a relationship of whole and part or a connection between the two reflects people's basic cognitive ability.

2. **Semantic Studies Based on Embodied-Cognitive Linguistics**

Wang Yin (2014) proposes embodied-cognitive linguistics, aiming to localize the research on cognitive linguistics. Its core elements are reality—cognition—language, that is, both the mind and language come from the "embodiment" (interactive experience) and "recognition" (cognitive processing). He believes that the terminology cognitive linguistics was ambiguous and cannot highlight the main issues and main perspectives of cognitive linguistic research. If we change the terminology cognitive linguistics into embodied-cognitive linguistics, the experiential nature of the mind and language can be emphasized. And the core principles can be more clearly understood. The term "embodiment" represents the objectivity of language and the language comes from life practices; the term "cognition" indicates that language is largely objective and diverse. Based on embodied-cognitive linguistics, Wang Yin (2017) proposes the "Metonymic View of Nomenclature", arguing that when people perceive a characteristic of something through "embodiment and cognition", they name it accordingly, thus giving rise to the metonymic phenomenon of "using part for whole". The proposal of embodied-cognitive linguistics has gained support from domestic scholars, who have conducted studies on linguistic phenomena based on embodied-cognitive linguistics. For example, based on embodied-cognitive linguistics, Wei Zaijiang (2019) explores the mechanism by which the coordinate structure in Chinese idioms forms total reference meanings from aspects such as holistic meaning and salience meaning; Zhao Yongfeng (2019), based on social embodiment, focuses on the evolution of Chinese first-person pronouns to analyze linguistic intersubjectivity and the underlying cognitive mechanisms.

3. **Multimodal Metaphor and Meaning Construction**

Over the past decade, rapid development in IT have enabled people to access diverse resources such as advertisements, news, and TV series via smartphones and online media. With various information flooding in through different ways, "visualized" information era arrived, and it started to attract the attention from linguists. Thus, part of domestic scholars began to focus on metaphorical phenomena from a multimodal perspective. Multimodal metaphor research emerged as a new research paradigm in the humanities academia during the "multimodal" turn: specifically, it refers to a metaphor in which the source domain and the target domain are embodied through different modalities or primarily through different modalities. A modality is a symbolic system, which can be interpreted by a specific perceptual process. People could perceive symbolic system from different modalities, such as visual symbols, written symbols, spoken symbols, gestures, sounds, music, smells, tastes, tactile sensations, and so on. Li Yi and Shi Lei (2010) propose that multimodal metaphors in teaching constitute a new research model with important theoretical and practical value. Zhao Xiufeng (2011) referencing *Multimodal Metaphor Studies* written by Forcevill & Urios-Aparisi simply reviews the origins, development, research key, contributions, challenges, and prospects of multimodal metaphor research. She holds that multimodal metaphor research put conceptual metaphor theory to a new stage, expanding research scope and refining its framework. Zhang Hui and Zhan Weiwei (2011) explore multimodal metaphors and metonymies in advertisements, whose views align with those of Li Yi and others. They argue that multimodal metaphors and metonymies can further reveal the essence and mechanisms of metaphor and metonymy, thus providing a significant supplement to linguistic research on these concepts. Scholars like Feng Dezheng, Xing Chunyan, Lan Chun, and Cai Ying explore multimodal metaphors and metonymy according to ads. Multimodal metaphors in political cartoons have drawn attention from part of scholars. Through studying the metaphorical phenomena in cartoons, they can find the underlying ideology. Based on multimodal metaphor, Pan Yanyan and Zhang Hui (2011) analyze cultural connotations of metaphor and metonyms in two cartoons, further highlighting their role in identity construction. Zhao Fengxiu & Feng Dezheng (2017) summarize eight source domains representing China in *The Economists*, revealing Western negative stereotypes on China.

6.3.3 Chinese Cognitive Semantics Studies

1. **Cognitive Semantic Research on Vocabulary**

(1) **The Semantic Change and Cognitive Mechanism of Chinese Words**

When studying Chinese words, some domestic scholars use basic theories of cognitive semantics to explore the semantic change and cognitive mechanism of some certain words. Sun Chongfei and Zhong Shouman (2013) investigate prototypical meanings and polysemous evolution mechanism of Chinese verb "ná" through cognitive mechanisms. In word classes studies, scholars have also employed the prototype theory to explore various word classes. Bai Jinhong and Wang Shasha (2014) analyze the semantic change process of the word "méng" from its Japanese form to its Chinese usage by utilizing the mechanisms of conceptual metonymy and metaphor. Wang Wenbin (2015) discusses the causes of polysemy in the Chinese verb "chī" and the English verb "make" from the perspective of the reversibility of figure and ground. He argues that not only conceptual metonymy and metaphor could give rise to polysemy, but also the mutual conversion of figure and ground was one of the mechanisms underlying semantic change. Comprehensively speaking, scholars have primarily explored the causes of semantic change in certain Chinese words through the cognitive mechanisms of conceptual metaphor and metonymy. The research objects are relatively random and unstandardized, lacking clear criteria or limitations, and the research results remain scattered, failing to form systematic research outcomes.

(2) **A Comparison of Word Meanings and Cognitive Mechanisms Between Chinese and Other Languages**

When studying semantic change and cognitive mechanisms of Chinese, domestic scholars often conduct comparative analyses of English and Chinese words to explore whether there are commonalities in the semantic change and cognitive mechanisms between Chinese word meanings and their corresponding words in other languages. Most of scholars analyze and compare the cognitive mechanisms of word meanings between English and Chinese. Jia Dongmei and Lan Chun (2010) compare and analyze the cognitive meanings of the Chinese word "shuǐ" and the English word "water". They find that their prototype meanings are identical, and numerous extended meanings in both languages involve many metaphors. However, the metaphorically extended meanings are not entirely consistent between English and Chinese, indicating both differences and universality in how English and Chinese speakers use the word water. Scholars such as Qin Xiugui and Huang Xingyun have conducted similar research and hold same views. Bai Jinhong and Chen Zhongping (2011b) compare the sources and semantic change mechanisms of neologisms in English and Chinese, revealing that the primary mechanisms for semantic change in both languages are conceptual metaphor and metonymy. Using the English word "cold" and Chinese word "lěng" as examples, Deng Qi and Yang Zhong (2014, 2019) explore the cognitive word meanings and functional analysis of sensory adjectives in English and Chinese, discovering a close connection between the linguistic representation of metaphorical meanings and their semantic functions. What's more, the semantic change paths of the two words are not the same. The "descriptive" function of "cold" has become increasingly prominent, gradually becoming its primary semantic function, while the "attributive" function of "lěng" has become more prominent, gradually becoming the main semantic function. In addition to comparing cognitive mechanisms of word meanings with English, some scholars have also compared and analyzed semantic change between Chinese and languages such as Japanese and Russian, including Xu Lian, Zong Shouyun, Yang Hua, and others. Through analysis of semantic change and comparison of cognitive mechanisms between Chinese and other languages, we can better know the universality and differences in human cognitive thinking, which is of great significance for cross-cultural research. However, similar to the cognitive research on Chinese vocabulary, domestic-related studies still fail to produce systematic research achievements, with the word classes and objects of study being rather arbitrary.

(3) **Research on Chinese Quantifier**

The Chinese quantifiers are highly unique words, usually expressing the quantity of people, objects, or actions. But it cannot function as sentence components alone and can only be flexibly applied when combined with nouns to form numerical noun phrases. In recent years, the studies of Chinese quantifiers have remained hot. Domestic scholars conduct the characteristics, attributes, or grammatical features of quantifiers from different views. And Zong Shouyun has gained great achievements. Zong Shouyun (2011) studies the categorization paths and motivations of Chinese quantifiers, aiming to promote the whole research of quantifiers. He holds that quantifiers take the function of categorization whose meaning is to classify various words into a category. The categorization of quantifiers follows prototype theory, extending from central members to marginal members through absolute and relative approaches. While the motivations for quantifier categorization contain metaphor, metonymy, schema transformation, and conventional imagery. And later Zong Shouyun (2013) also studies the hierarchical sequence of quantifier categorization and finds that the hierarchical sequence is related to the typicality of quantifier categories. The more typical a quantifier is, the stronger its categorization function. In major categories, nominal quantifiers have the strongest categorization function, followed by verbal quantifiers, while temporal quantifiers do not have this function. In smaller categories, individual quantifiers have the strongest categorization function, followed by collective quantifiers, but measurement quantifiers do not have categorization function. In addition, other scholars like Li Jiwei and Feng Xuefang have conducted some quantifiers in Chinese.

2. **Cognitive Semantic of Syntax Studies**

In recent years, the cognitive semantic studies on Chinese syntax have made some breakthroughs. Most scholars have focused on the cognitive semantics of one specific structure or word class, with a wide range of research. Some scholars not only pay attention to the semantic change of Chinese words and their cognitive mechanisms, but also explore the semantics and grammatical functions of some Chinese structures from a cognitive perspective. For example, phenomena in traditional grammar such as "bèi" construction and the "bǎ" construction have been interpreted from cognitive semantic perspective. And some achievements have been made.

Take the study of "bèi" construction as an example. The construction has emerged new usages and meanings in the new era. And with development of new media, it has caught more and more people's interest. While the linguistic research has focused more on its semantic change and cognitive mechanisms. For example, Chen Wenbo (2010) studies the semantic cognitive interpretation of the "bèi X" structure, analyzing its cognitive mechanism from the perspective of conceptual blending. He argues that the semantic features of "bèi" and the information contained in "X" are the result of conceptual composition and reasoning through conceptual blending. Deng Yunhua and Zeng Qingan (2011) also investigate the integration patterns of special passive sentences in English and Chinese, proposing that the cognitive mechanisms of such sentences involve cross-space conceptual metaphors and metonymies during conceptual blending. They further compare the similarities and differences in the cognitive models of special passive sentences between English and Chinese. Scholars like Yuan Hongmei have also analyzed the new construction within the framework of concept integration theory. However, Shi Chunhong (2010) argues that the new "bèi" construction is formed and functioned under multiple interactive relations (such as those between the linguistic system and real-life communication, between constructional structure, and meaning and between lexical items and constructions). And its fundamental generative mechanism is conceptual metonymy.

6.4 The Development Trends in Cognitive Semantics Studies

6.4.1 Data-Driven Cognitive Semantics Studies

Although cognitive semantics has yielded numerous theoretical achievements, many theories remain highly controversial. To demonstrate the validity of hypotheses, empirical research is essential. Scholars also start to realize that studies based on linguistic phenomena should be grounded in language use. In the empirical research of cognitive semantics, authentic linguistic materials can be widely used (Shao Bin et al., 2012). According to Wang Hongwei (2020), cognitive semantics has recently undergone an empirical version, with various studies confirming the feasibility of using quantitative and empirical research methods to investigate meaning. This section primarily introduces corpus-based cognitive research on semantic prosody and cognitive research on conceptual metaphor and metonymy.

1. **Corpus-Driven Cognitive Research on Semantic Prosody**

Semantic prosody is the sematic selection tendency revealed by the collection of lexical items. Certain lexical items tend to attract collocates sharing similar semantic features. When these semantically related terms co-occur with the keyword at high frequency in texts, the latter consequently acquires corresponding semantic characteristics, thereby creating a distinctive semantic ambiance throughout the context (Wei Naixing, 2002). The semantic prosody can be divided into three parts: positive, neutral, and negative. The main research on semantic prosody includes the "corpus data-based" approach, the "corpus data-driven" approach, and the "corpus data-based and corpus data-driven" approach. Semantic prosody studies are based on a large number of data analysis. Both corpus linguistics and cognitive linguistics advocate the integrity of vocabulary and grammar. Hence, the studies of semantic prosody in cognitive perspective are also important. However, currently, there is a lack of studies on semantic prosody under the cognitive dimension, with few scholars focusing on it. Through semantic prosody, we can know the collocational preferences of key terms, thereby exploring their underlying cognitive mechanisms. Furthermore, by conducting contrastive studies of semantic prosody patterns across languages, we may examine the similarities and differences in cognitive mechanisms, thus advancing cross-linguistic comparative research. In addition, the analysis of linguistic collocations through cognition can positively contribute to language teaching.

2. **Corpus-Based Cognitive Research of Metaphor and Metonymy**

The parallel growth of corpus linguistics and cognitive linguistics provides new entry points for conceptual metaphor and metonymy. Through corpus studies on metaphor and metonymy, we could compare the patterns of metaphor and metonymy in reality to identify their similarities and differences, and analyze the concepts in different languages as well as their underlying thinking patterns and cultural disparities. Corpus-based cognitive studies on conceptual metaphor and metonymy grounds cognitive linguistics in empirical studies, providing evidence for cognitive linguistics. Nowadays, corpus-based studies on conceptual metaphor and metonymy remain an emerging field. And the automatic recognition of conceptual metaphor and metonymy in natural language remains a big challenge. Now scholars who focus on the studier of corpus conceptual metaphor and metonymy conduct research through data analysis of one specific word. Therefore, it is difficult to generate deep-seated theoretical achievements. In addition, domestic scholars pay more attention to synchronic studies of conceptual metaphor and metonymy, while they neglect the significance of diachronic studies. It is crucial to emphasize the dynamic development of cognition and thinking behind conceptual metaphor and metonymy. Furthermore, corpus-based research on conceptual metaphor and metonymy in Chinese is in its initial stage. There are still many steps for ontological studies on Chinese metaphors to walk by fully using Chinese corpus. It remains an issue for domestic linguists to ponder how to identify and annotate potential metaphorical and metonymical expressions in Chinese.

6.4.2 Cognitive Semantics Research Based on Language Typology

Currently, the studies of cognitive semantics mainly focus on cognitive semantic phenomena in one language, especially Chinese or English, or compare them to explore the differences and similarities of cognitive mechanisms. The comparability of human languages reveals the cognitive patterns behind language and explores the universal characteristics of humanity. Cognitive typology integrates cognitive linguistics and linguistic typology, conducting typological comparative analyses across diverse languages to reveal the universality and particularity of human language. Therefore, cognitive semantics can also explore research from a typological perspective or within the framework of linguistic typology. According to linguistic typology, languages around the world can be classified into many language families such as Sino-Tibetan, Indo-European, Altaic, Afroasiatic, Uralic, Iberian-Caucasian, Austroasiatic, and Dravidian. Each language family contains several language branches, and each language branch includes many languages. We put forward two studies based on linguistic typology: cognitive semantic research within language families and cross-linguistic typology research.

1. **Cognitive Semantics Studies Within Language Families**

In this section, we will focus on cognitive semantics research within Sino-Tibetan language family including Chinese. Sino-Tibetan language family contains Chinese and the Tibeto-Burman language branch. Some Chinese scholars also consider Miao-Yao language branch and Zhuang-Dong language branch belong to it. Firstly, cross-language branch cognitive semantics research in the Sino-Tibetan language family, such as word classes, basic category terms, conceptual metaphor, and metonymy, can explore the commonalities of cognitive thinking behind different language branches through analyzing the differences and similarities from a cognitive perspective. However, this kind of studies are very few, and systematic comparisons and universal analysis have not been formed. Moreover, there is nearly no cognitive semantics research between the Chinese language branch and other language branches. Secondly, some languages within language branches are worth of thinking and further exploration. For example, Chinese contains languages such as Cantonese, Xiang language and Mandarin. What are the similarities and differences in the universal analysis of cognitive semantics across these languages? We need to carefully study it. As Chen Shumei (2015) proposes that previous studies on the category of quantity only notice short term category, while there are rich expressions of long-term category in Yingshan dialect in Hubei. In Yingshan dialect, the duration of actions in time is the main form for expressing long-term category.

2. **Cross-Language Family Cognitive Semantics Studies**

Cross-language family cognitive semantics studies can involve both synchronic and diachronic comparisons. We hold that synchronic cognitive semantics studies across language families should be based on the universals already proven within language families, thereby enabling cross-language family cognitive comparisons. Diachronic cross-linguist family allow us to contrast the cognitive origins of various language families and differences in cognitive pattern changes during their development. Existing cross-family research still remains at verifying genetic relationships between language families, lacking exploration of the underlying cognitive mechanisms. Therefore, some scholars have proposed cross-family historical comparative etymology, attempting to prove commonalities between non-related language families and thereby explore similarities and differences in human language development. However, this discipline has shown no progress in recent years. In 2014, Wang Yin put forward the concept of cognitive contrastive linguistics, which uses the basic principles of cognitive linguistics and "cognitive styles" advocated by cognitive linguistics. The concept uses a new perspective to analyze and compare English and Chinese. But the discipline remains in the hypothetical stage, and is only limited to studying differences between English and Chinese. Therefore, there are still many steps that cross-linguistic family cognitive semantic research needs to take.

6.5 Conclusion

Through the above introduction to cognitive semantics in China over the past decade, we can observe that research in cognitive semantics domestically is on the increase. And some achievements already were made, particularly in the study of cognitive semantics of Chinese. More and more domestic scholars start to pay attention to cognitive semantics research, and the research enthusiasm is growing in recent years. However, the current situation remains that most domestic scholars still use existing theoretical frameworks from abroad to study Chinese, lacking their own thinking and innovation, with few critical achievements to theoretical development. There is more cognitive research incorporating English corpora, while studies focusing on Chinese grammar itself remain relatively scarce. What's more, the most research focus of scholars is still on typical cognitive issues such as "metonymy" and "metaphor", ignoring other aspects of cognitive semantics. In the future, we can utilize corpus data for analysis, particularly since the study of cognitive mechanisms behind semantic prosody and similar phenomena remains relatively underdeveloped. For semantic research on linguistic typology, we can consider studying the cognitive universals of languages within the same language family, and on this basis conduct synchronic or diachronic cross-family research to analyze the commonalities of cognitive thinking. In conclusion, the combined study of cognitive semantics and Chinese, as well as research on cognitive semantics based on linguistic typology, are worth of our further exploration.

Chapter 7
Semantic Change Studies

7.1 Introduction

Cognitive linguistics posits that language serves to express various concepts closely related to human experience, as this experience evolves across time and cultures, language naturally adapts in tandem. From a diachronic perspective, language changes are obvious, exemplified by shifts like that from classical Chinese to vernacular, and from old English to standard English (Freeborn, 2009). However, a purely synchronic view renders such changes difficult to detect and explain, as Hudson (2000: 392) points out:

> "Within a single generation, language changes are rarely noticed. However, we commonly observe distinct speech patterns across generations—both preceding and following our own. Their preferences for language forms and usage rules are different from ours, and there are even some completely different forms and rules. This change becomes evident when comparing a language from one period with its form centuries later."

Language evolution naturally encompasses the change of meaning, a phenomenon termed semantic change in historical linguistics. While linguists seem to be able to describe instances of language change in considerable detail, they have yet to establish a comprehensive theoretical framework for its diverse changes. This limitation applies especially to the description of semantic change. Because, compared with the changes of other aspects of language (such as phonology, spelling, etc.), semantic change is often closely related to the changes of social and cultural factors with strong arbitrariness. Consequently, many linguists argue that predicting the direction, scope, and depth of semantic changes remains highly challenging. For this reason, semantic change was once regarded as arbitrary. Saussure (1974:107) argued that "diachronic events are accidental and particular in character", illustrating this with the French word "*poutre*". The word originally referred to "mare", but later acquired the meaning of "rafter". The change of its meaning is related to the contextual transformation, but it has nothing to do with the evolution of other contemporary languages. This

X. Wen and R. Tang, *New Perspectives and Developments in Chinese Semantics*,
https://doi.org/10.1007/978-981-95-1730-5_7

perspective elucidates the contemporary linguists' consensus that words in isolation lack inherent meaning; rather, meaning is assigned by speakers within concrete communicative contexts. Therefore, semantic change occurs when language users assign or confer new meanings to linguistic expressions. Another example is that the English word "cart" has undergone great semantic changes with the rise and development of modern automobile industry.

Since the early twentieth century, research on semantic change in the international linguistic community has developed from the initial focus on the results of semantic change to the research on the ways of semantic change, such as metaphorization, metonymization, pejoration, amelioration, narrowing, generalization, and now to a usage-based view of language that investigates the semantic change regularity, as well as the cognitive factors, meaning-making processes, and evolutionary mechanisms driving it such as metaphorization, metonymization, invited inference, subjectification, and inter-subjectification (Hilpert, 2012; Traugott & Dasher, 2002; Traugott, 2010; Traugott, 2012 et al.), with fruitful results. Over the past decades, substantial progress has been made in the research on semantic change in China, which has further enhanced scholarly understanding of this phenomenon. This chapter begins by tracing the disciplinary development of semantic change research, then synthesizes domestic research achievements over the past decades, drawing on representative academic works and journal articles to summarize progress in terms of research languages, contents, and methodologies, and thereby forecasts new trends in this field.

7.2 Changes in Disciplinary Status of Semantic Change Research

Before summarizing studies of semantic change in China over the past decade, it is necessary to induct the current disciplinary status of semantic change studies, particularly its research origins and the shifts in disciplinary status. Semantic change was a core component of the philological tradition that emerged in nineteenth-century continental Europe (Allan & Robinson, 2012). In the first stage of the history of lexical semantics (1830–1930), scholars primarily focused on semantic change, including its identification, classification, and explanation (Geeraerts, 2010). Although the studies of semantic change at this stage were the mainstream, it lacked a unified name, either "traditional diachronic semantics" or "prestructuralist semantics". Geeraerts (2010) called it "historical-philological semantics", and this name has gradually been accepted by many scholars. Over the past half century, while the semantics research has gradually revived (Allan & Robinson, 2012), semantic change studies have not regained the same prominence. The main reasons include (but are not limited to) the scarcity of historical corpus, the lack of representativeness of limited historical textual materials, and the irregularity and unpredictability of semantic change, which made the research of semantic change increasingly ignored by linguists at that time. Durkin

(2009: 222–223) summarized and explained the challenges brought to semantics researchers by semantic change at that time as follows:

> "As we all know, it is difficult to classify or systematize semantic change because we do not yet have tools like historical grammar to help us judge what kind of changes are possible or credible. In addition, although some semantic changes occur in the form of clusters, such as a change in one word triggering a corresponding change in another word, we have not yet found a regularity comparable to phonetic changes... Semantic change is more similar to some occasional phonetic changes, but the difference is that the former is more variable and easily influenced by other factors. Moreover, semantic changes are more closely related to external non-verbal factors, especially the development of culture and technology."

However, over the past two decades, with advancements in computer science, various large-scale corpus resources have continuously emerged, and corpus-based linguistic research has gradually become mainstream. Large-scale processing and analysis of linguistic data have now become feasible, enabling linguists to identify abstract linguistic structures and trace their evolution in usage accordingly. Against this backdrop, an increasing number of historical linguistic studies represented by semantic change and grammaticalization have begun to emerge. Representative works include those by Traugott & Dasher (2002), Hopper & Traugott (2003), Allan & Robinson (2010), Glynn (2010), Glynn & Fisher (2010), Kerremans, Stegmayr & Schmidt (2010), Hilpert (2012, 2013), Traugott & Trousdale (2013), Glynn & Robinson (2014), and Perek & Hilpert (2017). Linguists represented by Traugott et al. combine semantic change research with morphosyntax, situating it within the frameworks of grammaticalization (Hopper & Traugott, 2003) or constructional change and constructionalization (Noel, 2007; Trousdale & Nord, 2012; Traugott & Trousdale, 2013; Hilpert, 2013; Trousdale, 2013), yielding fruitful results. Different from previous views that semantic change is arbitrary and unpredictable, Traugott & Dasher (2001) insisted that semantic change has unidirectionality, such as semantic bleaching, which is common in grammaticalization (Hopper & Traugott, 2003). As grammaticalization research deepens, the regularity of semantic change has been discovered and accepted by more and more linguists.

7.3 Overview of Domestic Studies of Semantic Change in the Past Decade

7.3.1 Quantity of Published Papers and Research Languages

Undoubtedly, compared with grammatical and phonological change, semantic change has long been a notably underdeveloped area in domestic diachronic linguistic research (Wu Fuxiang, 2015). This makes it particularly significant to review the past decade's domestic research on semantic change and explore the future trends in this field. Based on CNKI (China National Knowledge Infrastructure), we conducted a partial statistical analysis using "semantic change" and "lexical change" as title keywords, with the publication period set from January 2010 to February 2020. The search covered journals in Chinese linguistics & literature, foreign linguistics & literature, and the database of outstanding master's/doctoral theses. A total of 477 relevant documents were initially retrieved. After manually excluding irrelevant materials, primarily publications by foreign scholars affiliated with non-domestic institutions (e.g., Brigandt, Ingo (Department of Philosophy, University of Alberta), *The Epistemic Goal of a Concept: Accounting for the Rationality of Semantic Change and Variation.* 460 valid documents were actually obtained. The overall trend of publication is as follows:

As can be seen from Fig. 7.1, domestic research on "semantic change" has shown an overall upward trend over the past decade. The top three most published authors are Wu Fuxiang (13 articles), Jin Xiaodong (6 articles), Chen Manjun (4 articles), and Zhou Hong (4 articles). It should be noted that we did not use "grammaticalization", a central topic in the study of Chinese semantic change history, as a title keyword for the following reasons. The grammaticalization of content words in Chinese historical linguistics is largely equivalent to "lexical grammaticalization", a phenomenon universally observed in human language development (Liu Jian et al., 1995; Ma Qinghua, 2003, etc.). Shen Jiaxuan (1998: 41) also posits that "grammaticalization is the process by which content words evolve into grammatical markers". While acknowledging the commonalities between grammaticalization and bleaching, Yang Yonglong (2017) points out that these two concepts discuss linguistic phenomena from different angles: they are interconnected and sometimes refer to the same diachronic change process.

In terms of the languages studied, according to current statistics, domestic research on semantic change over the past decade has involved seven languages: Chinese, English, Japanese, Uyghur, Manchu, Russian, and Turkic. Among these, publications focusing on semantic change in Chinese as the primary research subject constitute

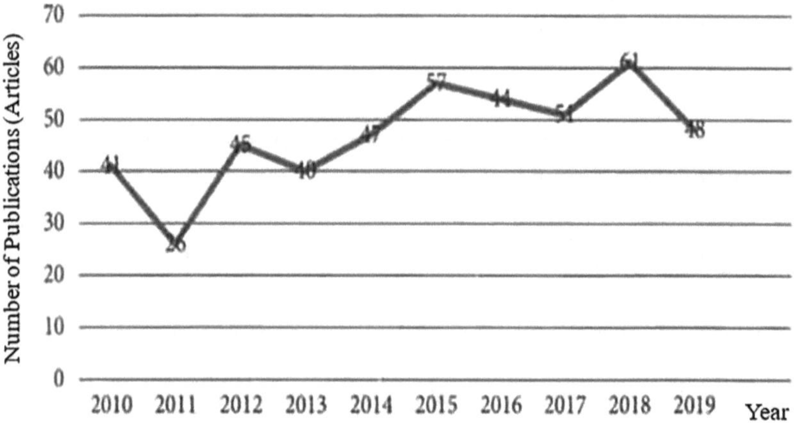

Fig. 7.1 Trend analysis of domestic "Semantic Change" Research Publications (CNKI: 2010–2020)

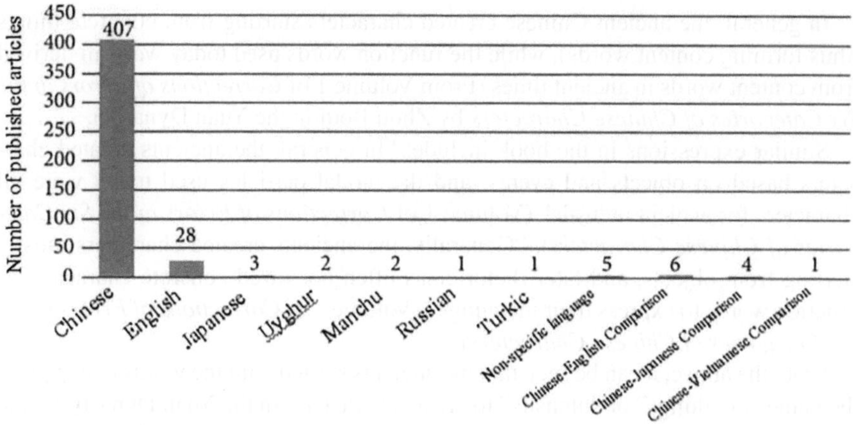

Fig. 7.2 Distribution of languages in Domestic "Semantic Change" Studies in the Past Decade (CNKI: 2010—2020)

the vast majority, totaling 407 articles (88.48%). Excluding five papers that do not specify any target language, 37 studies address semantic change in foreign languages, while another 11 involve comparative research on semantic change between Chinese and other languages. The specific distribution across languages is shown in Fig. 7.2.

As shown in Fig. 7.2, Chinese has been the primary research focus in domestic semantic change studies over the past decade. In foreign language research, English remains the dominant subject of investigation, a trend that aligns with English's status in domestic foreign language education research landscape. Additionally, among studies on Chinese semantic change, 17 focus on dialects, accounting for about 7.5%.

7.3.2 Research on Semantic Change of Content Words

1. **The Grammaticalization of Content Words**

Chinese lacks morphological changes, and function words have become one of the most important grammatical means in Chinese (Wu Fuxiang, 2015; Yang Yonglong, 2017). Therefore, their origins and the process of grammaticalization have naturally attracted extensive attention in the study of Chinese historical grammar. The grammaticalization of content words is an important means of the emergence of function words, and there have been abundant research results in this regard. Many scholars agree that the concept of the grammaticalization of content words in China can be traced back to Zhou Boqi's *Corrections of Errors in the Six Categories of Chinese Characters* in the Yuan Dynasty (Shen Jiaxuan, 1994; Sun, 1996; Wen Xu, 1998; Wang Shiyuan, 2011). Zhou Boqi proposed in the book:

In general, the ancient Chinese created characters starting from concrete things (thus forming content words), while the function words used today were all derived from content words in ancient times (From Volume 1 of *Corrections of Errors in the Six Categories of Chinese Characters* by Zhou Boqi in the Yuan Dynasty).

Similar expressions in the book include: "In general, the ancients created characters based on objects and events, and the modal particles used today were all characters for ancient utensils" (Volume 1 of *Corrections of Errors in the Six Categories of Chinese Characters*), "Generally, the ancients created characters mostly starting from objects, and later rhetoricians often borrowed concrete characters as function words to express their meanings" (Volume 5 of *Corrections of Errors in the Six Categories of Chinese Characters*).

From the above, it can be seen that the ancients started with the words that express the names of "things" or "utensils" to create characters. In the Yuan Dynasty, China saw the emergence of *Annotations on Auxiliary Words* written by Lu Yiwei, which is the first specialized work on function words. In the Qing Dynasty, works such as Yuan Renlin's *Explanation of Function Words*, Wang Yinzhi's *Explanations of Function Words in Classics and Commentaries*, and Liu Qi's *Discrimination of Auxiliary Words* were also monographs on the study of concrete characters' grammaticalization in Chinese traditional philology. Among them, Yuan Renlin has a similar view:

Function words serve as the supportive elements in language, which are what we call "verbal particles". In the Six Categories of Characters (Liù Shū), characters are classified into "content words" and "function words", and further into "semi-content and semi-function words", all distinguished by whether they denote the existence/non-existence or dynamic/static nature of things (From the Preface to *Explanation of Function Words* by Yuan Renlin, Qing Dynasty).

The renowned Polish historical linguist Kurylowicz (1965) points out that grammaticalization refers to a process in which a morpheme gradually incorporates more abstract components into its scope of use, evolves into a more abstract morpheme, or transforms from a less abstract morpheme into a more abstract one. Xie Huiquan (1987) believes that the grammaticalization of content words is the transformation of some words from content words to function words. However, the "grammaticalization" research reviewed in this article mainly refers to the semantic change process in grammaticalization, in which a linguistic unit gradually develops from having a more concrete meaning to a more abstract one. That is, semantic grammaticalization, namely the loss of contentful meaning (Traugott, 2017; Sweetser, 1988). For example, in English, "pretty" originally meant "good - looking", but later acquired the adverbial meaning of "fairly, to some extent".

The sources of Chinese function words mainly include verbs (which are grammaticalized into prepositions, adverbs, conjunctions, auxiliaries, etc.), adjectives (which are grammaticalized into adverbs), nouns (which are grammaticalized into adverbs, pronouns, etc.), and pronouns (which are grammaticalized into adverbs, conjunctions, etc.). In recent years, research on the semantic grammaticalization of content words has mainly been reflected in the following three aspects: research on the grammaticalization of verbs, research on the grammaticalization of adjectives, and research on the grammaticalization of nouns.

(1) **Research on the Grammaticalization of Verbs**

Diachronic research shows that the grammaticalization of many content words often starts from verbs, mainly due to the flexibility of verb syntactic positions and the large number of associated syntactic components (Meng Kai, 2018). Wu Zhenyu and Liang Hao (2013) take unearthed documents as the research object and explores the phenomenon of content words grammaticalization in Yin and Zhou bronze inscriptions in *Research on the Grammaticalization of Content Words in Yin and Zhou Bronze Inscriptions*. It points out that the more obvious routes of content word meaning grammaticalization are "verb → preposition → conjunction" and "verb → adverb", which are also common grammaticalization routes in handed-down documents. This provides excellent reference corpus for exploring the grammaticalization of content words in ancient Chinese. Zhang Hongguo (2016), based on the concept of "three domains" of "action domain, cognition domain, and speech domain" (Shen Jiaxuan, 2003), explores the process of semantic grammaticalization of the Chinese phrase "zāo le (oh no)" in *Semantic Change and Grammaticalization of "zāo le"*. In the "three domains" of "action domain, cognition domain, and speech domain": "action" refers to behavior and conduct; "cognition" refers to knowledge and perception; "speech" refers to language and utterance. Thus, from "action" to "cognition" and then to "speech", the degree of abstraction of the three concept domains increases step by step. The phrase "zāo le" evolved from an initial loose structure (the verb "zāo" + the dynamic marker "le"), with its meaning generalized to "the meaning of spoiling", thus entering the category of the "action domain". Finally, it developed to express "the meaning of being bad", with an evaluative function, belonging to the category of the "cognition domain". Meng Kai (2018) selects 104 disyllabic verbs, such as "bù lùn(regardless)", "jū zhōng(center)", and "bǐ jiào(compare)", which are included in the 7th edition of *Modern Chinese Dictionary* as the research objects. Based on synchronic corpus of modern Chinese, he analyzes the verb meanings and function word meanings of these words and comprehensively examines the directions of semantic grammaticalization for different verbs, the semantic foundations of grammaticalization, the constraints of grammatical components within words on the grammaticalization of disyllabic verbs, and the influence of semantic relationships between intra-word components or inter-word appositive components on the grammaticalization of disyllabic verbs in *The Semantic Conditions for the Grammaticalization of Disyllabic Verbs in Modern Chinese*. The study finds that the grammaticalization of disyllabic verbs in Modern Chinese exhibits unidirectionality: evolving from major lexical categories (verbs) to intermediate categories (adverbs) or minor categories (conjunctions, prepositions, etc.). Semantics develops from concrete to abstract and from objective to subjective, which also confirms the viewpoints of Traugott & Dasher (2002) and Hopper & Traugott (2003). The research also points out that the component meanings of disyllabic verbs (mainly function word meanings), and semantic relations such as synonymy and antonymy between components within the word or between coordinate components of different words may affect the semantic change or grammaticalization direction of the entire word; negative components may be a factor promoting the grammaticalization of disyllabic verbs.

(2) **Research on the Grammaticalization of Adjectives**

The main syntactic functions of adjectives are to modify nouns (such as premodifiers or postmodifiers) and serve as predicates. Adjectives in Chinese naturally possess these functions as well. However, the difference is that Chinese adjectives can also appear in adverbial positions to modify verbs. For example:

Example 1

a. Smile happily
b. Run freely
c. Cry sadly

Su Ying and Wu Fuxiang (2016) argue that the use of adjectives in the adverbial position to modify verbs was very common in ancient Chinese in *The Usage and Grammaticalization of Adjectives in the Adverbial Position in Ancient Chinese.* This should provide the syntactic environment and semantic basis for the grammaticalization of adjectives into adverbs in Chinese. The paper examines the usage of adjectives in the adverbial position in ancient Chinese and their process of semantic grammaticalization. It holds that after some adjectives in ancient Chinese entered the adverbial position, some of their usages would diverge toward adverbial usages. Meanwhile, based on the analysis of historical corpora, the authors propose that adjectives in the adverbial position with different semantic bases have different directions of grammaticalization. Ornament-modifying adjectives, after transforming into action-modifying adjectives and entering the adverbial position, are prone to being grammaticalized into adverbs.

(3) **Research on the Grammaticalization of Nouns**

In the process of grammaticalization, although the proportion of noun participation is far lower than that of verbs and adjectives, it also attracts the attention of many scholars. *The Grammaticalization of "Dàlì" and "Sǐlì"* by Kuang Pengfei and Hu Qian (2013), taking "Dàlì" and "Sǐlì" as examples, explore a type of semantic grammaticalization of nouns into adverbs. Through historical textual research, the authors believe that the semantic grammaticalization of these two nouns was achieved by frequently serving as adverbials, thus acquiring the syntactic and semantic features of adverbs. They were respectively grammaticalized into adverbs in the mid-late Qing Dynasty and the Ming Dynasty. The process can be summarized as: noun → noun directly as adverbial → adverb. The paper also points out that such a way of semantic grammaticalization is somewhat universal in the grammaticalization of nouns. Certainly, there are other ways. For example, nouns lead to part-of-speech transformation through the extension of word meanings, thus generating adjectival or verbal meanings, and then this meaning is bleached into an adverb. Shi Huimin (2016) takes the disyllabic compound word "shēn qiǎn" with the meaning of measurement, a unique language phenomenon in modern Chinese, as the research object in *The*

Semantic Change and Pragmatic Motivation of the Disyllabic Compound Word "shēn qiǎn" with the Meaning of Measurement. From a diachronic perspective, the semantic extension and grammaticalization of this word were explored during its evolution from a coordinate phrase to a nominal component and then to a typical compound noun, with its meaning changing from "the degree of depth and shallowness" to "the meaning of propriety". In addition, the semantic grammaticalization of quantitative nouns has also attracted attention. Dong Zhengcun (2017), through exploring the semantic change of the Chinese word "Duō bàn" in *The Semantic Change from Approximate Quantity to Epistemic Modality in Chinese: Taking "Duō bàn" as an Example*, believes that there is a semantic change sequence of "approximate quantity > epistemic modality" in Chinese:

Example 2

a. Outside the city, palaces and pavilions are connected in a row. In the market, most things are made of gold and silver (Poem by Zhang Ji).
b. There are more fairy flowers and spiritual birds. I'm afraid you don't know most of them (Poem by Fang Gan).

Example 3

a. It's so stuffy. It will probably rain later (Thunderstorm by Cao Yu).
b. If we go to court over this matter, the evidence may not be sufficient, but this matter probably exists. It depends on whether you admit it or not (Phoenix TV / Talk Show / August 12, 2009).

Related research also includes *The Actual Reference of the Character 'Wéi' in Western Zhou Poems and Related Material and Phenomenon-Highlights of the Tendency of Content Word Grammaticalization in the Interpretation of The Book of Songs* by Huang Gang (2014) and *Research on the Grammaticalization of Content Words in Oracle-Bone Inscriptions and Bronze Inscriptions: Taking Common Monosyllabic Function Words in Modern Chinese as Examples* by Zhang Lili (2012).

2. **Non-grammaticalization of Content Words**

Although the grammaticalization of content words is an important field in historical linguistics, especially in the study of semantic change of content words, the phenomenon of non-grammaticalization of content words can not be ignored. Xuan Yue (2010) argues in *Jian Is Not a Resultative Complement of Grammaticalization* that the transitive verb jiàn (see), which originally denoted a resultative visual action (e.g., "rén zhě jiàn zhī wèi zhī rén"(opinions vary from individual to individual)), developed to denote the results of other sensory actions (e.g., "wén jiàn lóu shàng gē shēng liáo liàng" (Hearing and perceiving the loud singing upstairs)) and the completion of general actions (e.g., "nǐ zhǎo jiàn tā ǒu ěr dé dào tā de xiāo xi"(You found him and occasionally got news from him)). This development is not a process of grammaticalization but rather the extension and expansion of word meanings. Kuang Pengfei (2010) in *The Semantic Change and Mutual Influence of "Status" and "Situation"* starts with the semantic change of these synonyms, pointing out that in the history of Chinese, especially in the period of modern Chinese, there was once a phenomenon where the main semantic components of these two words seriously overlapped. Wu Bao'an (2011) argues in *A Brief Discussion on the Semantic Change of "Tóu" and "Shǒu"* that "Shǒu" (head), which originally served as the main linguistic unit denoting the concept of "head", developed to only function as a morpheme in fixed collocations, having been replaced by "Tóu (head)". The primary reasons behind this include the need for semantic clarity and homophonic substitution. Zhang Yanjun (2015) believes that the lexicalization of the time word "later" in Chinese has gone through two stages in *Lexicalization of "Later" and Its Semantic Change*, which shows that the syntactic homograph phrase has solidified into a common noun and then developed into a time word. From the perspective of semantic development, the meaning of the time word "later" has changed from indicating the future time to indicating the past time.

The non-grammaticalization of the semantics of content words can also be reflected in the evolution of nouns such as expressing human body to temporal meanings or square meanings. In Chinese, words representing human body or object parts often acquire usages expressing spatial orientation and time (He Liang, 2016). For example:

Example 4

a. Duan Jiong pursued them, fighting while marching… For more than forty days, he finally reached the source of the Yellow River at Jishi Mountain. (From *Biography of Duan Jiong in Book of the Later Han*) 【Shǒu: denoting the meaning of direction/location】
b. In summer, the Han dynasty revised its calendar, designating the first month of the lunar year as the beginning of the year. From *Biography of Emperor Wu of Han in Records of the Grand Historian* 【Shǒu: meaning "beginning", denoting temporal significance】
c. In the third month, the Tianqiang star appeared, with both ends pointed. From *Book of Heavenly Omens in Records of the Grand Historian* 【Tóu: meaning "the front part", denoting the semantic category of direction/location】
d. To be upfront, sir, even the silver you bestow, this humble woman dare not accept it. I'd rather take your words and relay them to the mistress directly. From *The Plum in the Golden Vase* (Chapter 69) 【Tóu shang: meaning "previously", denoting temporal significance】

He Liang (2016) in *Spatial–Temporal Semantic Change of Chinese Human Body/Object Part Terms* further notes that the semantic change from "human body/object parts > spatial meaning > temporal meaning" is not unique to Chinese but also occurs in many other languages, such as Maasai, Thai, Kikuyu, and Aztec (Heine & Kuteva, 2002). Similar studies on non-grammaticalization of content words include Jiang Lili (2014) *on Semantic Changes of Verbs in the "Arrest" Conceptual Field in Medieval Chinese*, Jiang Lili & Fang Yixin (2014) *on Semantic Evolution of the "Hire-Leasing" Conceptual field Vocabulary System*, and Tao Lei (2015) *on the Earliest Documentary Evidence and Semantic Change of the Verb "yì"*.

7.3.3 Research on Semantic Change from the Perspective of Construction Grammar

Construction grammar adopts a non-modular view and takes construction (form-meaning pairings) as the basic units of language (Goldberg, 1995, 2006). Construction grammar theory breaks the traditional "vocabulary-grammar" view of language knowledge and puts forward the "linguistic construction view": construction is the pairing or connection of form and meaning abstracted from language use through psychological solidification, and the linguistic knowledge of language users is represented by construction. Language can be regarded as constructions from the lowest grammatical unit morphemes to sentence patterns in traditional grammar, while the entire language system is regarded as a hierarchical network of constructions composed of specific morphemes, words, partially schematic constructions, completely abstract schemas, etc., (Hilpert, 2014). In recent years, the theory of construction grammar has gained increasing attention from historical linguists, who employ it to re-examine language change phenomena (e.g., Hilpert, 2013; Israel, 1996; Noël, 2007; Peng, 2017; Traugott, 2008; Traugott & Trousdale, 2013; Wen Xu & Yang Kun, 2015; Wen Xu & Yang Xu, 2016). As an explicit study, construction grammar theory has brought a new perspective to the study of language change, which can be described as the most important development of diachronic morphosyntax research in recent years (Peng Rui, 2016). The study of linguistic change from the perspective of construction grammar theory can not only describe the changes of any dimension within the construction from local and subtle aspects, but also explain the formation of new nodes in the construction network, so as to achieve the unity of whole and local, macro and micro. Precisely because construction grammar takes form-meaning pairings (i.e., constructions) as the basic structural units of language, most research on semantic change within this framework unfolds under the rubric of constructionalization, involving both formal changes to constructions and evolutions in their meanings. Certainly, there are also studies focusing exclusively on constructional meaning change within the construction grammar framework, which belongs to the category of constructional change (Traugott & Trousdale, 2013).

In the field of historical linguistics in China, research on traditional semantic change has primarily been conducted within the framework of lexicology or Chinese exegetics, with the natural focus on word meanings. This perspective has led many scholars to largely equate lexical semantic change with semantic change at large, creating significant research gaps in traditional studies of Chinese semantic change (Wu Fuxiang, 2015). Semantic change research within the construction grammar framework addresses this dilemma effectively. Wang Yagang (2010) notes that

"Thanks to" has evolved into a functional construction through grammaticalization. Through reanalysis, its constructional semantic change has gone through three stages: from "thanks" to "benefit", and finally to denote "cause", with the constructional semantics gradually neutralizing in *Semantic Shifts in the Grammaticalization of "Thanks To"*. Dong Xiufang (2016), taking the evolution of Chinese adverbs expressing suggestions (such as "bù rú (why not)" "hái shì (better)" "qí", etc.) as the research object, points out that such adverbs in Chinese developed from the usages of expressing comparison or selection in *From Comparative Selection to Suggestion: On the Role of Implied Components in Semantic Change*. The paper argues that the mechanism behind the semantic change of "comparison/selection > suggestion" is as follows: some components in the construction are omitted due to clear context, leading to the prominence of other components, which in turn causes changes in the meaning of the construction. Bi Jin and Xiao Xiqiang (2017) examine the "Shuo Hao de X ne" (Where is the promised X?) construction from three aspects: its components, semantic change, and pragmatic value in *The Semantic Change and Pragmatic Value of the "Shuo Hao de X ne" Construction*. The author points out that in practical application, this construction has the rich connotation of superficial negotiation, pragmatic meaning of irony, and the combination of euphemism and irony. The authors point out that in practical use, this construction conveys ostensible negotiation with implicit satire, blending euphemism and irony. In the evolution of construction meaning, its semantic change has gone through three stages in constructional meaning: "others' speech", "social speech", and "self-speech". In this developmental process, the meaning of "shuō hǎo de" (what was agreed upon) gradually becomes grammaticalization, while "X" evolves from concrete to abstract, and the subjectivity of the construction increasingly strengthens. Wu Chunxiang and Cao Chunjing (2018) take the emerging construction "superlative X" as an example, such as "superlative terror", "superlative emotional intelligence", and "superlative love", and explore the semantic function evolution, evolutionary conditions, and driving factors of "superlative" in the constructions of "superlative X" and "the superlative of X" in *The Semantic Change of "Superlative" from Sequence to Degree in Contemporary Chinese*. The paper points out that in the construction of "the superlative X", the component "X" has gradually expanded from prototypical nominal components to verbal phrases, such as "the superlative research", "the superlative treatment", "the superlative autotrophy", and "the superlative public display of affection", and further extended to adjectival phrases, like "the superlative luxury", "the superlative happiness", and "the superlative loneliness". With the expansion of "X" component, the semantic function of the construction is expanded from a single semantic function of representing the first position of the sequence to a dual function of representing the extreme degree and the first position of the sequence. This construction meaning evolution is realized by the interaction between two groups of components "X" and "superlative" in the construction: first, the expansion of component "X", and at the same time, the semantic components of component "superlative" such as "stage/level" and "quality/level" are stripped off, and evolve from the original "highest stage/level" or "highest quality/level" to "highest degree". Similar studies include Xu Shijing (2017) *Constructionalization and Diachronic Change of Chinese*

Conditional Sentences, Li Yanzhi and Wu Yicheng (2018) *Constructional Evolution of [V + Non-subject NP] Expressions*, and Kang Xiaoming and Wu Tingting (2019) *Competitive Change and Stereotype of the Rhetorical "gà (Embarrassment) + X" construction.*

7.3.4 Research Regularities and Pathways of Semantic Change

The main goal of historical semantics is to explain semantic change, and to explain semantic change, the premise is to discover and summarize the pattern of semantic change (Wu Fuxiang, 2015). Therefore, the exploration of semantic change path or pattern is an important cornerstone of semantic change research. Here, "patterns" refer to recurrent evolutionary pathways in semantic change that occur cross-linguistically or within a single language (ibid.). Historically, however, whether semantic change is governed by regularities has been a controversial issue. Many scholars have held skeptical views, a perspective particularly prevalent in the field of diachronic linguistics before the 1980s. Arlotto (1972), for instance, argues that research had not yet established abstract models capable of generalizing semantic change, nor even yielded plausible conjectures comparable to those common in studies of phonological, morphological, and syntactic change. Anttila (1972) also asserts that it is not yet possible to truly generalize the general laws of semantic change. Hock (1986) holds this view, maintaining that semantic change is often vague, irregular, and highly unpredictable. Since the 1990s, however, influenced by functionalism, an increasing number of linguists have come to recognize that semantic change is indeed governed by regularities. Representative researchers are Sweetser (1990), Traugott (1999, 2002, 2003), Traugott & Dasher (2002), Bybee (2006), Bybee et al. (1994), etc. The monograph *Regularity of Semantic Change* by Traugott & Dasher (2002) can be described as a representative work in this research field. In their opening remarks, the authors explicitly state:

"In this book, we demonstrate that semantic change across different conceptual structures and domains of linguistic function exhibits predictable paths for semantic change… In fact, when tracing the historical development of lexemes cross-linguistically, evidence of unidirectional change repeatedly emerges" (Traugott & Dasher, 2002: 1).

Indeed, Traugott & Dasher also contend that the regularities of semantic change observable to us vary by part of speech, particularly noting that "irregular semantic change predominantly occurs with nouns, as these lexemes are highly susceptible to non-linguistic factors, such as changes in the nature of noun referents within social structures" (ibid., pp. 3–4).

The patterns of semantic change primarily refer to non-arbitrary, motivated, and patterned pathways of evolution, i.e., regular changes and evolution paths in the process of semantic change (Wu Fuxiang, 2015, 2017). The semantic grammaticalization discussed earlier can also be viewed as a regular pathway of semantic change from content words meaning to grammatical meaning, which is prevalent in Chinese. Luo Kun (2011) describes and compares the syntactic and semantic features of "Kai" across several Gansu dialects, as well as issues related to its semantic grammaticalization in the article *A Multiple-Perspective Study of "Kai" as an Ingressive Marker in the Dialect of Ningxian, Gansu Province*, summarizing its semantic change pathway as: "original meaning → spatial meaning → temporal meaning". This finding is corroborated by Wang Yiguang's (2015) *Semantic Extension Pathways of the Verb-Directional Construction "V Kai"* and Liu Li's (2016) *Semantic Change Pathways of the Verb "Kai"*. In her two papers, *From Bodily Actions to Speech Acts: The Expansion of Speech Verbs Driven by Rhetorical Motivation* (2010) and *Lexical Change from Bodily Actions to Speech Acts* (2012), Ma Yunxia demonstrates that certain verbs denoting bodily actions in Chinese historical linguistics acquired speech-related semantics, thereby evolving into speech verbs, such as qīng, táo, tí, guà, cāo, qiē, guā, jǔ, and zhǐ.

Subsequent research has also corroborated the existence of this semantic change pathway. For example, Xie Shuying (2013) further refines the developmental trajectory from hand verbs to mouth verbs in *Diachronic Study on the Evolution from Hand Verbs to Mouth Verbs*, categorizing it into five types: hand verbs → mouth verbs (without speech meaning) → mouth verbs (with speech meaning) → speech verbs; hand verbs → mouth verbs (with speech meaning) → speech verbs; hand verbs → speech verbs; hand verbs → mouth verbs (without speech meaning) → mouth verbs (with speech meaning); hand verbs → mouth verbs (without speech meaning). Zhang Hongguo (2016) *Semantic Change and Grammaticalization of "zāo le"* employs the cognitive tripartite framework of "action domain, cognition domain, and speech domain" to investigate the processes and pathways of semantic change in the Chinese phrase "zāo le (Oh no)". The study clearly illustrates that the semantic change of "zāo le" progresses from the "action domain" to the "cognition domain" and finally to the "speech domain". This research aligns with the conclusions of *The Three Domains of "Le*$_2$*": Action, Epistemology, and Speech* written by Xiao Zhiye & Shen Jiaxuan (2009), which characterizes the semantics of "Le$_2$" as denoting "the emergence of new action states", "the emergence of new epistemic states", and "the emergence of new speech states", while "Le$_1$" is categorized under the action domain. Consequently, the semantic change pathway from "Le$_1$" to "Le$_2$" precisely fits the "action-epistemology-speech" tripartite analytical framework.

General Revision Notes: overall, the regularities of semantic change should not be absolute, but should be gradient and flexible. Jin Xiaodong & Wu Fuxiang (2019), while affirming the existence of semantic regularities, draw on historical evidence from ancient Chinese and dialectal data on the evolution of prepositions and adverbs to propose that bidirectional semantic change pathways exist in Chinese in their paper *On Bidirectional Semantic Change Pathways in Chinese*. These pathways are primarily observed in semantic shifts within word classes (e.g., among prepositions or adverbs) and in bidirectional grammaticalization between word classes (e.g., preposition > verb, preposition ↔ conjunction). The study demonstrates that such bidirectional changes are conditioned by specific factors and correlate with the typological features of Chinese. Li & Xiang (2019), in *Semantic Evolution at the Microscopic Level: The Case of suǒ yǐ* offers a novel approach to studying semantic change regularities. The paper argues that previous research has predominantly focused on the macro-level (Traugott & Dasher, 2002), neglecting the micro-level perspective. This is largely because macro-level studies more easily identify recurrent cross-linguistic or intra-linguistic patterns, whereas micro-level regularities are influenced by the inherent properties of lexemes or broader lexical-grammatical systems (Traugott & Dasher, 2002). Grounded in Frame Semantics, the study examines the semantic change of the Chinese word "suǒ yǐ" ("so") and identifies three micro semantic change patterns: frame → frame element, frame element → frame element, and frame element → frame. The authors emphasize that ignoring micro-level regularities hinders a full understanding of the mechanisms driving semantic change.

7.3.5 Research on the Motivation and Mechanism of Semantic Change

As mentioned above, the primary goal of historical semantics is to explain semantic change and identify patterns or pathways of change. To address how these patterns emerge, however, it is essential to investigate the motivation (why changes occur) and mechanism (how changes unfold) of semantic change. The former answers why semantic change occurs, while the latter is about how semantic change occurs. Bréal (1964, quoted from Li & Xiang, 2019) was among the first to propose five types of external motivation for semantic change: avoidance of difficulty, securing of greater clarity, taboo and euphemism, fading and discoloring, and cultural change. Hopper & Traugott (2003: 92) point out that semantic change is driven by problem solving. The problems can be categorized into two types: one is using members of one semantic domain to represent another (involving metaphorical strategies), the other is coordinating speaker-hearer dynamics in communication (involving metonymic strategies) (ibid.).

There are also numerous explorations of semantic change mechanisms. The most widely discussed mechanisms of semantic change involve metaphor and metonymy (e.g., Bréal, 1964; Nerlich & Clarke, 1992). Traugott & Dasher (2002: 27) proposed using the terms "metaphorization" and "metonymization" to denote semantic change mechanisms, distinguishing between synchronic and diachronic concepts. For example: in English *while* "during the time that" > concessive *while* "although", *grasp* "seize" > "understand"; Chinese *wén*, "hear" > "smell", all involve metaphorization; the semantic change mechanism of metonymization includes French *Place de Greve* "square where strikers met" > *greve* "strike", and Fingernail > Finger > Hand in Australian Aboriginal languages. Based on the role of pragmatic factors in semantic change, Traugott (1999) and Traugott & Dasher

(2002) proposes the Invited Theory of Semantic Change to explain semantic change. According to this theory, new meanings originate from invited inferences, which then evolve into Generalized Invited Inferences (GIIN) and finally become the semantic component of linguistic units (Semantic Meaning or SM). IIN and GIIN correspond to Particularized Conversational Implicature (PCI) proposed by Levinson (2000) and Generalized Conversational Implicature (GCI), respectively.

Zhang Shaoquan and Zuo Yafeina (2015) propose that semantic change in legal vocabulary primarily manifests as generalization, narrowing/specialization, and semantic shift in *Ways and Cognitive Mechanisms of Semantic Change of Legal Words*. From a cognitive perspective, the paper further argues that the mechanisms of semantic change in legal vocabulary involve metaphor and metonymy. Shi Huimin (2016) analyzes the formation mechanisms and pragmatic motivations of this compound from the perspectives of semantic basis, cognitive motivations in word formation, rhetorical motivations, cultural influences, and prosody in *Semantic Change and Pragmatic Motivations of the Measure-Related Disyllabic Compound "shēn qiǎn"*. The paper concludes that the grammaticalization of "shēn qiǎn" ("depth and shallowness") not only relies on its inherent semantic foundation but also reflects universal cognitive principles, driven by a combination of cognition, rhetoric, culture, and prosody. Notably, the paper points out that an important mechanism of word formation and semantic change of "shēn qiǎn" is disyllablization. Disylliabization is the tendency that two syllables form the basic prosodic unit (step), and under this prosodic unit, two adjacent monosyllabic words may "compound" into a linguistic unit (Wu Weishan, 2003). Disyllabication can be described as a unique and historically significant phenomenon in the development of Chinese. Wang Li (1980) once asserts that "disyllablization is one of the five most important changes in the history of Chinese", highlighting the crucial role of disyllablization in the development of Chinese. Shi Yuzhi (2002) argues that the trend of disyllablization extends far beyond word formation, playing a pivotal role in transforming the entire grammatical system of Chinese. He identifies disyllablization as a key driver of verb-complement integration. The coordinate phrase composed of antonymous monosyllabic measure adjectives "shēn" and "qiǎn" often co-occurs closely and frequently in use. Their semantic meanings blend, gradually evolving from a coordinate phrase into a concrete compound word, and then further into an abstract compound word "shēn qiǎn" (depth and shallowness). This historical evolution exemplifies the characteristics of disyllablization.

Li Guangyu (2014) argues that the factors driving the semantic change of "bu de" ("must not") involve both internal and external linguistic aspects in *Semantic Change of "bu de" from a Subjectification Perspective*. Internal factors primarily refer to the influence of syntactic distribution, as the semantic change of linguistic units often correlates with changes in the syntactic position of content words. External factors mainly concern cognitive-pragmatic influences, including gestalt, metaphor, and pragmatic reasoning. The shift of "bu de" from "failed to achieve" to "unable to" and further to "not allowed" is primarily governed by mechanisms of subjectification and inter-subjectification. Dong Zhengcun (2015) posits that semantic changes from serial meaning to quantitative restrictive functions in Chinese words like suí, zhú, liè, and pái are primarily driven by Gestalt cognitive factors in *From Sequence to Quantification: A Case Study of Semantic Change in Mandarin*. Dong Zhengcun (2017) argues that the semantic bleaching of duo ban ("most likely"), that is, the semantic change from its approximate quantity usage to epistemic modality usage, is achieved through the important mechanism of metaphor in *Semantic Change from Approximate Quantity to Epistemic Modality in Chinese: The Case of "duo ban"*. The development of approximate to possible cognitive modality belongs to conceptual projection, and it is not gradual. Wu Chunxiang and Cao Chunjing (2018) analyze the driving factors of the semantic functions of the two constructions "the superlative X" and "the superlative of X" in *The Semantic Change of "Superlative" from Sequence to Degree in Contemporary Chinese*. They point out that the evolution is not only driven by subjective factors, that is, the need for the temporary construction of a subjective magnitude sequence, but also influenced by objective factors: the close contact between English and Chinese. The paper boldly proposes the hypothesis: the expression of English adjectival superlatives in Chinese has further stabilized the semantic change of "the superlative X" and "the superlative of X" in specific language communities. Moreover, in the evolution of Chinese, the "X" in "the superlative X" and "the superlative of X" is more diversified, breaking through the restriction in English grammar that X can only be an adjective. Yang Yanning (2019) specifically discusses how the construction meaning is formed, that is, the mechanism of the production of construction meaning in *The Change of Constructions in Old Chinese and Old English: A Study from the Perspective of Non-compositionality*. Based on the theory of functional linguistics, this paper discusses the process of constructive meaning generation of non-constructive constructions. Through the analysis of verbal constructions in ancient Chinese and causal constructions in old English, this paper holds that independent constructive meaning is generated by the organic interaction of the whole constructions (semantic convergence) and internal components (semantic cohesion).

7.3.6 Research Methods of Semantic Change

Since the late twentieth century, the emergence of historical corpora has led to significant transformations in the methods for studying semantic change, particularly in diachronic research on English, but also including other languages such as Chinese and Japanese. Globally, as new research methods are increasingly adopted by historical linguists, there is a growing recognition that semantic change is a both motivated and explainable phenomenon (Allan & Robinson, 2012). Domestic linguists have gradually started to contact and try to adopt these research methods or paradigms.

1. **Diachronic Collostructional Analysis**

The integration of corpus technology and statistical methods makes the study of semantic change research more scientific and operational. Within the framework of construction grammar, Stefanowitsch & Gries (2003) revolutionize traditional collocation analysis and propose collostructional analysis. This method explores constructional meanings by analyzing the usage and distribution of morphemes in (semi-) abstract constructional slots and their collostructional strength with the construction. Collostructional analysis includes three analytical methods: simple collexeme analysis, (multiple) distinctive collexeme analysis, and covarying collexeme analysis (Gries & Stefanowitsch, 2004a, 2004b). Based on collostructional analysis, Hilpert (2006, 2008) innovatively proposes diachronic collostructional analysis, arguing that changes in a construction's collocation patterns across different stages of language evolution in historical balanced corpora can reflect the diachronic evolution of its constructional meaning. Hilpert applied this method to study changes in the verbs collocating with will and be going to across different historical periods.

A few domestic scholars have begun to apply this method to the study of semantic change, but the whole is still in its infancy. Based on the COHA, Sun Xinxin (2015) uses diachronic distinctive collexeme analysis to analyze the collocation changes involved in the evolution of the English way construction in the article *A Corpus-based Diachronic Distinctive Collexeme Analysis on the Way Construction.* Firstly, the paper obtains the historical stage of the development of the way construction through the variability-based neighbor clustering, and then finds that there are significant differences in the distinctive co-occurrence morphemes that appear in the verb slot of the way construction in different historical stages. From 1830 to 1910, the distinctive collocation morpheme of the empty slot of the verb was mainly the verb of "building roads or clearing obstacles", while from 1920 to 1940, it became the verb of "using force", and from 1950 to 2000, the distinctive collocation morpheme mainly expressed the creation of metaphorical paths. By analyzing the diachronic evolution of the distinctive co-occurrence morphemes of the empty slot of the way construction verb, the paper finds that the construction has undergone significant semantic changes in the past two centuries. This research result also further confirms the relevant conclusions of Israel (1996). Based on the English diachronic corpus, Huang Ying (2016) uses diachronic collostructional analysis to investigate the collocation of the word "absolutely" with adjectives and verbs in the article *Intensifier "Absolutely" Collostruction Semantic Preference and Diachrony of Semantic Prosody.* The study finds that the frequency of collocation of absolutely with adjectives and verbs had the same trend: the frequency of collocation was lower in Medieval and early modern English corpora and Contemporary English corpora, but higher in late modern English corpora. The semantic preference of adjectives collocated with absolutely has no obvious diachronic change in the category, while the emotional verbs collocated with them show an upward trend in the category. At the semantic prosody level, the proportion of the collocation of absolutely and positive adjectives increased significantly in the category sign, and the negative verbs collocation with absolutely were still more than the positive verbs in the category sign, but the positive verbs showed an upward trend in the category sign.

2. **Semantic Maps**

A semantic map can be regarded as a geometric representation of a function in a "conceptual/semantic space". These spaces are connected by lines and form a network (Haspelmath, 2003). It serves as a method for describing and explaining models of multifunctional grammatical morphemes. This theory is based on the following assumption: if a grammatical form has multiple meanings and usages, and these meanings or usages repeatedly appear in different languages and are expressed by the same form, it indicates that the correlation among them is by no means accidental. Instead, it should be systematic and universal, which may further reflect some commonalities of human languages at the conceptual level (Zhang Min, 2010). An abstract semantic map can illustrate what meanings a grammatical form has, how these meanings are related, and the degree of similarity between them (Van der Auwera, 2013).

Cross-linguistic comparison is a core feature and advantage of semantic maps. In recent years, semantic maps have also been applied to the study of semantic change, particularly the semantic shifts of content words. Pan Qiuping and Zhang Jiamin (2017) conduct a cross-linguistic comparison of the semantic changes of the five taste terms "sweet", "bitter", "sour", "salty", and "spicy", based on "semantic map model"proposed by Haspelmath (2003), in their paper *Semantic Extension of Words Expressing the Five Cardinal Tastes: A Semantic Map Approach.* The study involves six languages from different language families: modern Chinese (Sino-Tibetan), Malay (Austronesian), Korean (Altaic), Dutch and Norwegian (Germanic within Indo-European), and Czech (Slavic within Indo-European). The paper strictly follows the established operational procedures of semantic maps to identify primitives and arrange them. Then the paper constructs a conceptual space related to the five tastes and validates this space using non-five-taste words. The study confirms that there are regular patterns in the non-grammaticalization semantic changes of content words associated with synesthesia.

7.3.7 *Summary*

From the above review, it is evident that domestic research on semantic change has yielded numerous important achievements and accumulated rich experience over the past decade. Undoubtedly, previous studies still have problems and deficiencies that deserve our in-depth consideration in the future related research. Wu Fuxiang (2015), from the perspective of diachronic semantics, sorting out and reviewing the research on semantic change of Chinese since the Western and Eastern Han Dynasty from the perspective of diachronic semantics, holds that there are some issues in the research on semantic change of Chinese, such as an overly narrow research scope, inappropriate research frameworks, insufficient theoretical exploration, and a lack of cross-linguistic perspectives. We fully concur with this. Five years later, when expanding our focus from Chinese-specific semantic change research to the broader landscape of domestic studies on semantic change over the past decade, we find that the issues outlined by Wu still exist, alongside new concerns such as simple research methods, narrow research perspective, lack of contrast between Chinese and foreign languages, and so on. How to innovate research methods and broaden research horizons on the basis of inheriting the rich achievements and experience of traditional historical research remains a critical issue that all researchers should address.

7.4 Development Trend of Semantic Change Research

Based on the issues and limitations of current domestic semantic change research outlined above, we believe that future research should pay attention to and consider from the following aspects. A brief explanation is given below.

7.4.1 Updating Research Methods of Semantic Change

As previously mentioned, with the development of computer science, the 1990s saw the continuous emergence of corpora, especially diachronic corpora, bringing about significant changes in semantic change research. However, the truly revolutionary turning point came with the integration of computer-aided techniques such as corpora and modern statistics, and got rid of the traditional research idea of over-reliance on "introspection" in semantic change research. Of course, modern research methods such as corpus are only an important means to analyze semantic change. To systematically analyze collected data, propose viable hypotheses, and construct robust theories, introspective analysis remains indispensable. Introspective analysis is more convincing if it can be supported by real corpus and scientific research methods to realize the complementarity of research methods. Specifically, researchers can leverage diachronic language corpora (such as COHA, HCET, ARCHER, BNC, BROWN, and CCL) to extract real, in-use corpus as observation objects, and then carry out corpus processing through computer-aided statistical analysis and other methods. The diachronic collostructional analysis mentioned earlier represents a good attempt. This analysis method uses historical corpora to trace the diachronic evolution of collostructional patterns, through which researchers can detect diachronic changes in constructional meaning (Hilpert, 2012).

However, diachronic collostructional analysis is not universally applicable to semantic change analysis, and it also has limitations. Distributional semantic analysis (Perek, 2016, 2018; Perek & Hilpert, 2017) is a viable alternative. The use of distributional semantic analysis is mainly based on the following considerations. Firstly, linguistic meaning is different from morphosyntactic or phonetic features and cannot be directly observed. Secondly, traditional collostructional analysis encounters challenges with low-frequency corpus or data. At this time, distributional semantic analysis is needed (Perek & Hilpert, 2017). In addition, some linguists have applied the methods of variability-based neighbor clustering analysis and multi-factor analysis to the diachronic language research (Gries & Hilpert, 2008, 2012; Hilpert, 2013). Variability-based neighbor clustering (VNC) mainly uses an iterative process to merge data sets that are adjacent to each other in time and have high similarity in turn until all the data are combined into one, and generating system tree diagrams and steep slope diagrams to identify patterns in diachronic language evolution (Lin, Lu & Wang, Xu, 2016). The application of variability-based neighbor clustering in diachronic linguistics research will enhance linguists' understanding of historical corpora, particularly the stages of quantitative-to-qualitative shifts in semantic change. Historical linguistic research necessarily involves temporal periodization of evolutionary stages in the extracted corpora. The traditional method is to divide the age involved in the corpus equally to observe the distribution and performance of the research objects in various historical stages, so as to analyze the characteristics of semantic changes. For example, in diachronic study of the English modal verb shall by Hilpert (2006), the corpus involved in 1500–1920 was divided into three stages, each stage lasting 140 years: 1500–1640, 1640–1780, and 1780–1920. However, this judgment of linguistic evolution stage is overly subjective, failing to consider the features of the research object, that is, the language unit, and failing to grasp the deep relationship between historical data. The bottom-up VNC avoids the shortcomings of the above traditional eras division methods by emphasizing the maximization of the differences between eras and the minimization of the number of clusters.

However, the application of corpus-based methods represented by diachronic collostructional analysis in Chinese semantic change research remains highly limited. Not only are there few papers, but existing studies are exclusively focused on English. Even in empirical research, data are often merely listed rather than leveraging corpora to provide systematic and comprehensive descriptions of semantic change. We believe that the main reason is that there are relatively few Chinese historical corpora. In addition, a more pressing reason lies in the huge differences in language types between English and Chinese. Chinese lacks morphological changes, so it is more difficult to segment words and part-of-speech tagging. While Chinese certainly has prepositions, conjunctions, auxiliary words, and other grammatical words, many similar grammatical words can be used as content words at the same time, which undoubtedly increases the difficulty of computer processing. However, it is generally infeasible to manually write Chinese corpus suitable for large-scale text processing at present. Accordingly, the accuracy of Chinese corpus in labeling is lower than that of other mainstream language corpus such as English, and labeling is more difficult. In the future research, besides further increasing the application of linguistic research methods, it is necessary to increase the construction of Chinese corpus at the same time. In addition, domestic linguistic theoretical researchers need to strengthen their knowledge reserves in statistical methods and computer programming to keep pace with advancements in corpus linguistics.

7.4.2 Broadening Research Perspectives in Semantic Change

The academic community has recognized that interdisciplinary integration is a powerful way to advance disciplinary development. Some scholars argue that under the current background of great integration of disciplines, linguistic research should adopt a "linguistics+" model. For example, linguistic researches from cultural and anthropological perspectives can deepen our understanding of its nature and changes. Semantic change research should also broaden the research perspective, not only pay attention to the integration of interdisciplinary disciplines, but also pay attention to the cooperation and reference with other branches of linguistics. The semantic change caused by language contact is a good example. Language contact has been a universal objective linguistic fact since ancient times, such as the emergence of pidgin and the transformation of creole. However, the academic understanding of language contact traces back to nineteenth-century inquiries into similarities among Indo-European languages. Language contact has gradually attracted the attention of historical linguists. For instance, the second half of Bynon's (1977) *Historical Linguistics* is dedicated to discussing "language contact", while Hickey (2003) edited volume *Motives for Language Change* includes a dedicated chapter with four papers exploring the role of language contact in promoting linguistic evolution. In 2018, Walter de Gruyter published *Cognitive Contact Linguistics* (co-edited by Zenner et al.), which emphasizes that integrating cognitive linguistics and contact linguistics can offer promising perspectives and insights for linguistic research, especially for studying linguistic variation and evolution caused by language contact.

Previous research on semantic change caused by language contact has primarily focused on phonology, morphology, and lexical (borrowing), with relatively few studies dedicated to semantic change. Take the semantic change of the Chinese word "yǒu" as an example. In Chinese, "yǒu" generally denotes possession, existence, or presentation. Influenced by Minnan dialect and Cantonese, "yǒu" in modern Chinese can also mean "completion" and "affirmation", such as:

Example 5
I have called him.

Example 6
The room is clean.

At present, there are relatively few studies on semantic change caused by language contact in China, and it is still in its infancy. Wu Fuxiang (2014) *Language Contact and Semantic Replication* offers a valuable exploration of language contact as a motivator for semantic change. This paper focuses on the abundant but seldom used facts of minority languages in China as an example, and points out that language contact (mainly including "homophonic replication" and "polysemous replication") is an important factor in the change of grammar and semantics. It further argues that grammaticalization induced by language contact can be regarded as a special a specific subcategory of semantic replication. Wang Feng and Wei Jiuqiao (2017) *Semantic Change, Language Contact and Lexical Transmission* studied the origin and transmission pattern of Yi language words such as "la (tea)" through language comparison, and believed that such words were mainly transmitted from the original Tibeto-Burman "s-la leaves" through the internal transmission of semantic innovation. We believe that the future research on semantic change caused by language contact should focus on the representative semantic change process as the research object, and systematically and deeply summarize the unique influence and promotion of many heterogeneous factors brought by language contact on semantic change, as well as the multi-factor and evolution patterns of semantic change under language contact.

7.4.3 Strengthening Comparative Studies of Semantic Change Between Chinese and Foreign Languages

Comparative method is a logical method for human beings to know the objective world, and language research is no exception. The reason why *Ma Shi Wen Tong* can be regarded as "the foundation work of modern Chinese grammar", and as its author Ma Jianzhong stated in the preface "I will explore the long-concealed mysteries of language since the advent of writing, unraveling their core principles and blazing a trail for subsequent scholars engaged in linguistic research". The foundation of his remarkable achievements stemmed from his profound understanding of both Chinese and foreign languages. As the first scholar in China to systematically compare the grammars of various nations, he immersed himself in classical texts to explore the commonalities and disparities among languages. Through extensive exemplification and copious citations, he accurately apprehended the grammatical rules of the Chinese language. It is helpful to continuously promote the development of linguistics by contrasting and comparing the similarities and differences between two or more languages in phonology, lexicon, phrases, sentences, discourse, and usage and making scientific and reasonable explanations on this basis. Comparative analysis is an important means of linguistic research. As Zhao Yuanren explicitly stated, "Linguistic theory is essentially the comparison of language, which is the scientific conclusions drawn from comprehensive comparative analysis of all ethnologic languages in the world" (Pan, 2003: 381). However, the research field of semantic change in China is not ideal in comparison between Chinese and foreign languages.

As previously summarized, over the past decade, the research on semantic change has been dominated by Chinese studies in China, with only English research showing moderate prominence among foreign languages, while there are even fewer comparative studies on semantic change between Chinese and foreign languages, especially non-identical languages. We concur with Wu Fuxiang (2015) that future research should highlight the attention to the "universals" and "particulars" of Chinese semantic change. These terms refer, respectively, to the universal patterns and laws of semantic change observable across human languages and the specific semantic change laws unique to a certain language (ibid.). Revealing such universals and particulars requires situating Chinese semantic change within the broader context of human linguistic change and exploring shared and distinct features in the paths, mechanisms, and motivations of semantic change between Chinese and other languages. This endeavor will enhance our understanding of Chinese's typological characteristics and principles.

7.5 Conclusion

Semantic change is an important aspect of language development, and it is also one of the crucial topics in historical linguistics. Although it has been unable to have a universal change law like phonetics and grammar among the three elements of language, semantic change has gradually become a shared focus for linguists, philosophers, anthropologists, psychologists, and artificial intelligence researchers. This chapter first reviews and outlines the century-long evolution of the disciplinary status of semantic change research, and then summarizes and prospects the domestic language evolution research in recent ten years through bibliometric methods. Over the past decades, domestic research on semantic change has made great progress in both breadth and depth. This book reviews and reflects on new developments and achievements in several key areas: semantic change in content words, semantic change from the perspective of construction grammar, laws and paths of semantic change, motivations and mechanisms of semantic change, and research methods in this field. Based on acknowledging the achievements and pointing out the shortcomings at present, this chapter proposes three negative issues that should be paid attention to in the future research of meaning evolution in China: updating research methods, broadening research perspectives, and strengthening comparative studies of semantic change between Chinese and foreign languages, so as to provide reference for future research. Although semantic change research in China has a long history and fine traditions, with a wealth of valuable experiences accumulated, it is undeniable that its shortcomings and deficiencies remain prominent, leaving ample room for expansion. We also hope that more scholars can engage in this field, learn from relevant foreign theories and methods, and combine the characteristics of Chinese culture and language types, so as to break through foreign academic barriers and develop semantic change research with Chinese characteristics. This is also the shared responsibility for all scholars.

Chapter 8
Semantics Applied Studies

8.1 Introduction

Semantics has been widely and deeply developed in China since its introduction from the west in the first half of the twentieth century. In recent years, apart from making many new theoretical advancements, applied research in semantics has also shown multi-angle, multi-level, and interdisciplinary development trends, particularly yielding fruitful results in translation studies, foreign language teaching, and dictionary compilation. Over the past decade, among various branches of semantic theory, the applied research of cognitive semantics has been the most active. Many theories in cognitive semantics, such as frame semantics, conceptual metaphor, conceptual metonymy and categorization, have been widely applied to the studies of translation, foreign language teaching and dictionary compilation, facilitating the construction of theoretical models for translation studies, foreign language teaching, and dictionary compilation. Guided by these theoretical models, numerous applied research outcomes have emerged, including new explanations for core issues in translation, foreign language teaching, and dictionary compilation, as well as innovative translation strategies, foreign language teaching models, and dictionary compilation approaches. This chapter primarily reviews the main achievements in the application of semantic theories in China over the past decade from three domains: translation, foreign language teaching, and dictionary compilation, and based on this, forecasts future research trends.

X. Wen and R. Tang, *New Perspectives and Developments in Chinese Semantics*,
https://doi.org/10.1007/978-981-95-1730-5_8

8.2 Semantics and Translation Studies

8.2.1 Translation Studies from the Perspective of Frame Semantics

Frame semantics is an important branch of cognitive semantics. It comprehensively considers context, prototype, perception, individual experience, and other factors, providing a comprehensive and holistic explanation for meaning formation, and has been applied to translation studies by many scholars. The theory of frame semantics was first proposed by Fillmore in the 1970s. At the beginning of the twenty-first century, domestic scholars Zhang Jianli (2000) and Pan Yanyan (2003) introduced this theory to China. Subsequently, more scholars have further developed and innovated Fillmore's frame theory, such as Cheng Qilong (2003, 2007). Based on the literature reviewed by the author, the first scholars in China to apply frame theory to translation studies were Cheng Shanzhen (2003), Wang Lirong (2005), and Yu Jinghe (2008), among others.

Over the past decade, translation studies from the perspective of frame semantics have been recognized by more scholars and further developed. In her 2010 article *Comments on the Perspective of Frame Semantics in Translation Studies*, Deng Jing points out that translation studies should not be confined to the surface linguistic forms of texts but should incorporate cultural, social, political, and translator psychological factors into its scope. As a comprehensive and holistic theory integrating insights from multiple disciplines, frame semantics aligns well with the evolving needs of translation studies, particularly in explaining translator decision-making processes, where it demonstrates significant application value. She further elucidates directions for future development, such as theoretically refining frame theory including clarifying the definition of "frame" and specifying the models of frame composition to meet the demands of translation studies. This article offers an enlightening macro-level forecast for the application of frame semantics in translation studies, providing valuable references for subsequent research.

In addition to the macro-level theoretical discussions on the application value of frame semantics in translation, there have been more focused micro-level studies that delve into basic translation issues such as translation strategies and processes. A representative example is Liu Guohui's (2010) *The Three Steps of Frame Semantics in Translation: Cognitive Schema, Frame, and Construal*, which applies frame theory to explain the translator's translation process and offers a new perspective on exploring the essence of translation processes. Specifically, he discusses the theoretical guiding value of frame semantics in translation studies, emphasizing that the key to translation is to a large extent how to find the optimal correspondence between the cognitive semantic frames of two languages, which lies in how to understand and reconstruct them. Meanwhile, he points out the translator's dominant position is crucial in the translation process, involving three main links: cognitive schema positioning, frame selection, and construal orientation.

In recent years, under the background of the new era, with the promotion of Chinese culture "going global" national strategy, studies on the foreign translation of Chinese literary works, Chinese culture and Chinese classics with the theory of frame semantics have continuously emerged. For example, Chinese martial arts novels contain rich Chinese cultural information, and the English translation of martial arts novels is more difficult because of the multiple cultural information load. Xiao Kairong (2013), in the article *Knowledge System and Cross-Lingual Transmission of Chinese Martial Arts Culture: A Frame Theoretic Approach to the Translation of Louis Cha's Martial Arts Fictions*, taking the classic works of the renowned martial arts novelist Louis Cha (Jin Yong) as specific cases, explores the English translation of martial arts novels based on Frame Theory, aiming to enhance the readability of translated works and spread Chinese knight-errant culture. He argues that translators can achieve alignment between the knowledge systems of source and target readers through frame-based cognitive operations, enabling target readers to activate the cognitive frames necessary for text comprehension and thus construct the meaning of the target. He (2017) further focuses on the English translation of Chinese classical poetry in his book *Frame Operations in Poetry Translation: A Cognitive Study of English Translation of Chinese Classical Poetry*, proposing that translators activate frames to acquire and deploy cognitive resources, and resolve readers' comprehension difficulties caused by differences and gaps in knowledge systems through frame operations. He proposes that visualization serves as the cognitive pathway for frame operations. In addition, there are many studies based on frame theory to discuss English translation of Chinese culture, cultural terms, literary works, and other issues (e.g., Guan Chen, 2019; Lin Haixia, 2015; Liu Wei, 2017; Xin Xianyun, 2010; Wang Zhen et al., 2010). In conclusion, frame semantics offers a new explanatory perspective for fundamental issues in translating Chinese classical poetry and modern literary works, including specific translation operations and strategy, with broad prospects.

8.2.2 Translation Studies from the Perspectives of Conceptual Metaphor and Metonymy Theory

Before 2007, most studies on metaphor in the domestic translation studies community regarded metaphor as a figure of speech. Over the past decade, as cognitive semantics has deepened its exploration of the cognitive essence of metaphor, the translation studies community has increasingly recognized metaphor as a conceptual phenomenon ubiquitous in human language, and one that is indispensable in texts. Against this backdrop, studies integrating conceptual metaphor theory with translation theory and practice have grown steadily. Major research topics include translation strategies of metaphors in different text types, with investigations ranging from macro-level theoretical discussions to micro-level analyses of specific texts.

Macro-level research primarily focuses on exploring translation strategies, principles, and methods for conceptual metaphors in source texts, as well as the translation process. Representative works from this perspective include *A Study of Metaphor Translation from the Perspective of Conceptual Metaphor* by Xiao Jiayan and Li Hengwei (2010), which posits that the metaphor translation is a cognitive process based on translators' cultural embodiment: cultural contexts, literary contexts, and linguistic contexts are the inherent basis on which translators make their choices of translation strategy. Tang Shuhua et al. (2011) propose implicit and explicit translation strategies of concept mapping routes for equivalent functions, based on corpus data in *A Corpus-Based Study on Comparison and Translation Processing of Conventional Metaphor Concept Projection Paths.* Wang Mingshu (2017), in *Cognitive Mechanism in Translation Principles and Strategies/Methods from Perspective of Conceptual Metaphor*, analyzes the interrelationship between "metaphor of translator's identity" and a translator's translation principles, choice of strategies in translation, along with the underlying specific cognitive mechanisms. Xue Mei (2019) argues that for novel metaphors in Chinese in her article *A Study on the Chinese-English Translation of Novel Metaphors*, translators should analyze their psychological foundations and implicit cultural information from a cognitive perspective according to the specific context, authorial intentions, and readers' reactions, and properly choose translation strategies and methods that preserve the cultural image of the source language Chinese as much as possible to achieve the purpose of cultural translation. Wang Yin (2019) combines Tymoczko's "metonymics of translation" with "metaphtonymics" in cognitive linguistics to propose the "metaphtonymics in translation" in the article *Metaphtonymics in Translation: A Case Study of English Movie Title Translation into Chinese*, positing that the translation process is one in which metaphor and metonymy are always operating together.

More micro-level researches focus on metaphors in specific texts to explore their translation strategies. Representative works include *The Translation of Thematic Images in Big Breasts and Wide Hips: On Howard Goldblatt's Translation of Conceptual Metaphors* by Liang Xiaohui (2013), which examines the English translation methods of thematic images through the analysis of abundant breast metaphors in Mo Yan's novel *Big Breasts and Wide Hips.* Gu Yi and Zhang Haoyu (2019) analyze the translation strategy of conceptual metaphor by taking the English translation of human body metaphors in the Chinese classic *Xu shu pu (Sequel to the "Treatise on Calligraphy")* as an example in their article *Translation of Human Body Metaphors in Chinese Calligraphic Classics: Taking the English Translation of Xu Shu Pu as an Example.*

Besides conceptual metaphor, conceptual metonymy is also one of the central concepts and topics of cognitive semantics. Over the past decade, research combining metonymy theory with translation has primarily explored strategies and methods of metonymy translation in texts. Representative works include *Schema-Instantiation of Metonymy and the Cognitive Path of Translation* by Tan Yesheng (2010), which explores the instantiation of metonymy schema based on context and restricted by conventions in the translation process, explains the cognitive creative space it provides for translators, and proposes suggestions for future research on the relationship between metonymy and translation. Lu Weizhong (2011) explores the cognitive foundations and strategies of metonymy translation based on conceptual metonymy theory in his article *Comprehension and Translation of Metonymy*, and further demonstrates that effective methods of metonymy translation including "target language equivalent vehicle translation", "target language specific vehicle translation", "source language vehicle + vehicle marker", "source language vehicle + annotation/note", and "abandonment of source language vehicle". Yang Wenying (2015) explores the cognitive motivation of "Pinglan" (leaning on a balustrade) image in Chinese classical poetry from the perspective of conceptual metonymy in her article *A Study of the Interpretation and English Translation of Chinese Poetry Images from the Perspective of Conceptual Metonymy: Taking "Pinglan" as an Example*, and further proposes specific translation methods. Guan Jialing and Han Mei (2016) first distinguish between the terms "metonymy translation" and "translation metonymy" in their article *Metonymy Translation and Translation Metonymy*, then further argue that whether it is metonymy translation or translation metonymy, translators should flexibly adopt various effective translation methods, such as reproducing source language metonymy, converting them into target language metonymy, abandoning the source language metonymy, or creatively translating to achieve optimal equivalence between source language and target language. Fan Xiangtao (2017) explores strategies for translating chain metonymy in Chinese cultural classics in his article *Research on Chain Metonymy and Its English Translation in Chinese Cultural Classics*, finding that most need to be translated into vehicles to clarify the meaning; when combined with other methods, the ontology of chain metonymy can also be preserved to a higher degree in translation. Jin Shengxi (2017), in his doctoral dissertation *A Study of Metonymy Translation in Classical Tang Poetry from a Cognitive Linguistics Perspective*, takes classical Chinese poetry as the research object and argues that metonymy translation in classical Tang poetry is not merely a transformation between linguistic signs or a rhetorical transformation, but the external manifestation of the translator's cognitive operations. The essence of metonymy translation lies in the translator's conceptual construal of source language metonymy and their exemplification in the target text.

8.2.3 Translation Studies from the Perspective of Other Semantic Theories

In addition to the semantic theories, other theories (such as semantic field theory, etc.) have also been applied to translation studies. The application value of semantic field theory in translation was first explored by scholars as early as the 1990s, with representative works including *Semantic Field Theory and Translation Practice* by Zhang Xinhe and Yang Wanbin (1996). Over the past decade, according to the literature collected by CNKI, translation studies based on semantic field theory mainly focus on lexical translation strategies in different texts, such as *Semantic Field Assimilation Effect and Translation in EST* by Liu Yuanfu (2010). This article highlights the importance of semantic field assimilation effects for translating core terminology in English for Science and Technology (EST). Fu Lihua (2011) demonstrates that the relevance and accessibility of semantic field effects provide a scientific cognitive basis for precise translation in her article *On the Relevance and Accessibility of Semantic Field Effects in Translation.* Wang Bingqin (2008) focuses on fundamental theories of modern semantics, such as the semantic triangle theory, semantic field theory, and basic semantic categories in comparative semantics in his revised edition *Comparative Semantics and Translation.* He mainly uses Russian and Chinese corpus to reveal the internal relationship between semantics, contrastive semantics, and translation theory. As the first systematic exposition of text translation ideas, this book has theoretically advanced translation studies. Additionally, Gao Yanmei (2015) offers a novel perspective for translation theory, practice, and pedagogy through framework analysis methods based on cognitive linguistics and frame semantics in her monograph *The Study of Discourse Semantic Frames,* a new development in discourse semantics.

8.3 Semantics and Foreign Language Teaching Studies

8.3.1 Studies on Translation Teaching from the Perspective of Cognitive Semantics

Cognitive semantics theory is not only widely applied in translation theory but also yield abundant results in translation teaching. First, frame semantics has been extensively used in translation teaching to explore new teaching methods and enhance teaching effectiveness. Research in this area focuses on how the concept of frame can help learners accurately interpret source language meaning and develop innovative teaching practices. Early representative work includes *Semantics, Frames, and Translation Teaching* by Wei Qingguang and Qu Zongde (2008). This paper comprehensively analyzes how to help students accurately determine the specific meaning of source words in translation practice through the framework, and at the same time reduce students' mistranslation through targeted guidance. Over the past decade, on the basis of earlier studies, translation teaching studies guided by frame semantics have deepened. A notable example is *Construction of Frame Semantics and Conceptual Integration of Translation Process: A Study of Translation Teaching Based on Cognitive Corpus "FrameNet"* by Guo Gaopan and Liao Huaying (2016). The study further explores methods to address the challenges of abstract semantic transformation operations in translation teaching. It finds that the frame semantic theory based on the cognitive corpus (FrameNet), combined with the syntactic realization of frame elements in terms of grammatical functions, phrase types, syntactic features, etc., can use the valence relationships between frame elements to achieve logical processing. By demonstrating the construction of information packets, this approach enables translation instructors to analyze the conceptual transformation and integration processes in translation for learners. These new translation teaching methods can show the transformation of abstract semantic concepts more explicitly, so as to reduce the negative impact of translators' subjective judgments in practice on the translated text, thus reducing mistranslation.

Secondly, the core theories of cognitive semantics, such as conceptual metonymy, have also been applied to the research of translation teaching, both in papers and works. Li Ke and Lu Weizhong (2017) investigate learners' metonymic competence, revealing that it exerts a notable impact on translation competence in the article *An Exploration of the Influence of Metonymic Competence of English Majors on Translation Competence.* They further propose enhancing students' translation competence through an intervention mechanism for developing metonymic competence in translation teaching. *Practical Course of Cognitive Metaphor and Translation* by Ye Zinan (2013) is a representative monographic achievement in combining cognitive semantics with translation teaching over the past decade. Taking conceptual metaphor theory as the breakthrough point, the book bridges the gap between cognitive semantics' conceptual metaphor theory and translation practice, systematically addressing a series of translation topics such as text analysis, translation purposes, and literary translation. It not only offers a novel perspective for compiling translation textbooks but also breaks new ground for translation practice studies.

Generally speaking, over the past decade, cognitive semantics theories such as frame semantics, conceptual metaphor, and metonymy have played an important role in translation teaching. Frame semantics is used to solve the problem of semantic transformation in translation teaching, and a new method is found to be more conducive to learners' conceptual transformation of texts, which can reduce mistranslation more effectively. Frame semantics has been applied to address the issue of semantic transformation in translation teaching, and a new method conducive to learners' conceptual transformation of texts has been identified, which can reduce mistranslation more effectively. Conceptual metaphor and metonymy theories have also opened up new topics for translation teaching. Certainly, the implementation of specific teaching methods and the problems that related theories can address require further in-depth research.

8.3.2 Studies on Vocabulary Teaching from the Perspective of Cognitive Semantics

1. **Research on Vocabulary Teaching from the Perspective of Frame Semantics**

Apart from being widely applied in translation teaching practice, frame semantics theory has also exerted its theoretical value in vocabulary teaching and other fields, reflecting its theoretical advantages. In recent years, under the influence of cognitive linguistics, research on vocabulary teaching has garnered increasing attention. Frame semantics offers a unique perspective on interpreting lexical meaning, bringing new insights and advancements to vocabulary instruction. Consequently, its applications in vocabulary teaching have been widely explored, yielding fruitful research outcomes. Representative studies include *Exploring National Cultural Semantic Teaching of Foreign Language Vocabulary from the Perspective of Cognitive Framework* by Li Yueping (2009). Based on the cognitive frame theory, this article proposes practical teaching strategies for national cultural semantics of foreign language vocabulary teaching, aiming to cultivate learners' cultural sensitivity to words and enhance their cross-cultural communicative competence. The study shows that frame theory can improve learners' accurate comprehension of culture-loaded words in vocabulary teaching. Wang Lirong argues that second language vocabulary instruction informed by frame semantics can help learners overcome the "form-meaning dissociation" in the second stage of vocabulary acquisition in the article *The Enlightenment of Frame Semantics on Second Language Vocabulary Teaching.* He embodies it into a teaching method of sorting out, reconstructing, and building a new second language framework, and demonstrates the theoretical and practical advantages of this theory for accurately analyzing and understanding the meaning of second language words. *The Use of Semantic Frames in the Understanding and Teaching of English Word Meanings: With Partial Discussion Devoted to the Use of Corpus in the Teaching of English Word Meanings* was written by Shuang Wenting and Yang Runqing in 2018. The article points out that the appropriate application of frame semantics theory in teaching can, to a certain extent, address the misunderstandings in English word meaning comprehension and the lack of inferential ability among Chinese college students. It further proposes that macro-frames help learners overcome cultural differences between English and Chinese, while micro-frames assist in enhancing word meaning inference ability through syntactic structures themselves. The construction of large framework can be achieved through corpus-assisted methods. Overall, these research outcomes demonstrate that frame semantics plays a pivotal role in improving learners' in-depth and accurate understanding of the meaning of second language vocabulary.

2. **Research on Vocabulary Teaching from the Perspective of Categorization**

Categorization theory is also one of the core components of cognitive semantics, and its main ideas and propositions are widely used in vocabulary teaching to change learners' inherent learning style and improve the breadth and depth of vocabulary learning. Research on vocabulary teaching from the categorization theory perspective encompasses both macro findings concerning vocabulary teaching principles and practical outcomes derived from instructional experiments. Representative works include *Categorization Studies in English Vocabulary Teaching* by Wen Xu and Kuang Fangtao (2016). The article points out that the vocabulary of basic categories is the focus of vocabulary teaching, and the typical theory of categorization plays an important role in the teaching of polysemous words in English vocabulary teaching. This finding aids in helping learners construct lexical semantic networks in practical teaching. Additionally, Kuang Fangtao and Lin Wenzhi (2015) explore the role of categorization theory in vocabulary learning through empirical research in the book *Categorization and English Vocabulary Learning*. Focusing on English major students and combining methods such as experiments and questionnaires, the study reveals that teaching methods based on categorization theory yield positive effects. It also establishes the application mode of categorization theory, offering valuable guidance for English vocabulary teaching practice. Ren Weiya and Long Yan (2012) propose classroom teaching principles grounded in categorization theory, such as emphasizing semantic aggregation, semantic segmentation, and metaphorical meaning instruction in their article *Categorization and English Vocabulary Teaching*. Wang Fen and Chen Xiongxin (2010) use questionnaires and experimental methods to demonstrate that vocabulary instruction guided by prototype theory enhances students' ability to employ vocabulary strategies effectively in their study *An Application study of Prototype Theory in English Vocabulary Teaching*. The above research results theoretically confirm the application value of categorization theory in vocabulary teaching, and also put forward more specific methods and models for vocabulary teaching practice.

3. **Studies on Vocabulary Teaching from the Perspective of Conceptual Metaphor**

Teaching studies based on conceptual metaphor theory have yielded abundant achievements. Earlier works include *Metaphor and Cultural Teaching* by Wang Shouyuan and Liu Zhenqian (2002) and *Metaphor Consciousness and Vocabulary Instruction* by Gong Yumiao (2006). In recent ten years, there have been many research achievements based on conceptual metaphor theory to explore the role of metaphor in English vocabulary teaching, the relationship between metaphorical competence and vocabulary learning effect. Kuang Fangtao (2012) comprehensively discusses metaphor's positive effects on English vocabulary instruction, arguing that it helps students understand the internal mechanisms of lexical meaning extension, enhancing both the depth of vocabulary knowledge and their ability to use words flexibly in the article *A Cognitive Study of Metaphor and English Vocabulary Instruction*. This study has guided the application of metaphor theory in vocabulary teaching. Zhang Linying and Qiu Zhijing (2012) demonstrate that integrating metaphor into English pedagogy represents both a trend and a necessity, particularly in vocabulary teaching and cross-cultural teaching in their article *The Application of Metaphor Theory in English Teaching*. Chen Haiyan and Wang Lirong (2013) use experimental methods to show that the cultivation of metaphorical consciousness in EFL vocabulary teaching is not only beneficial to learners' short-term memory, long-term memory, and autonomous learning of vocabulary, but also can solve the learning problems of polysemous idioms and phrasal verbs to a certain extent in their paper *Cultivating Metaphor Consciousness in College English Vocabulary Teaching*. This study proves the important role of the cultivation of metaphor consciousness in English vocabulary teaching through teaching practice, and further promotes the application of metaphor theory in vocabulary teaching practice. Chen Lang (2017) focuses on teaching components such as basic category words and polysemous terms, advocating for elevating the status of metaphorical competence in foreign language vocabulary teaching and establishing it as an intermediate and advanced objective of vocabulary teaching concept in his article *The Frontiers of Metaphorical Competence in Second Language Vocabulary Teaching*. From these research results, scholars pay more and more attention to learners' metaphorical competence in vocabulary acquisition, and its core value has been confirmed by theoretical reasoning and empirical research. Meanwhile, advancements in conceptual metaphor theory also provides a new perspective for English vocabulary teaching. Domestic scholars have already applied multimodal metaphor theory to vocabulary teaching studies. For example, Zhang Wei et al. (2014) empirically explores the applicability of multimodal metaphor theory in college vocabulary teaching.

In short, over the past decade, the applications of semantic theories in foreign language teaching have encompassed both theoretical, macro discussions and micro, empirical investigations. From the achievements obtained, the cognitive semantics theory, an important branch of semantics, is the most active in foreign language teaching and application research, especially in the fields of translation teaching and vocabulary teaching. The cognitive semantics theories according to them mainly include frame semantics, categorization theory, metaphor theory, etc. Specifically, frame semantics theory effectively addresses learners' inaccurate comprehension of word meanings in translation teaching. In vocabulary teaching, the applications of frame semantics, categorization theory, and metaphor theory stand out prominently. The results show that the effective use of these semantics theories in teaching is conducive to improving the accuracy and breadth and depth of vocabulary comprehension of second language learners. Cultural dimension is regarded as an inseparable part of lexical connotation, and it also highlights the important value of metaphorical competence. Meanwhile, the semantics theory itself is constantly developing, with new theoretical viewpoints gradually being applied to teaching practice.

8.4 Semantics, Dictionary Compilation and Lexicography Studies

8.4.1 Dictionary Compilation from the Perspective of Cognitive Semantics

The relationship among semantics, dictionary compilation and lexicography can be roughly described as the theoretical level, the practical level, and the intermediate level between the two. The corresponding theory of semantics leads the development of lexicography, thus guiding the practice of dictionary compilation practice. The task of dictionary compilation is to describe language vocabulary and analyze the semantic structure of words and their usage characteristics. As the word itself is a complex unit, lexicography also involves many different disciplines. Gu Bolin (1988) believes that among various disciplines, semantics should be most closely related to and have the greatest influence on dictionary compilation. Language is constantly changing with the changes of the times, and the semantics of words are also undergoing different types of changes, such as expansion, narrowing, transfer, etc. This shows that language changes are not only manifested in the increase of new words, but also in the change and expansion of word meaning. As Hu Zhuanglin (2014) says, the expansion of dictionary content depends not only on the increase in the number of words, but also on the increase in the meaning of each entry. It can be said that the change of word meaning is one of the motivations to promote the continuous development of dictionary compilation related studies. In addition, the renewal of semantic theory has changed the perspective of dictionary compilation researchers on the core issues of words such as word meaning relations, which has also promoted the development of lexicographic theory and specific compilation work.

With the development of cognitive semantics, its related theories have also been widely used in dictionary compilation. Firstly, the theory of frame semantics is used to solve the division and interpretation of polysemous words in dictionary compilation. An earlier representative study includes *Cognitive Semantic Frames of Polysemous Words and Cognitive Environments of Dictionary Users* by Tian Bing (2003). Based on the theory of frame semantics, this paper re-examines the thorny problems in the division and definition of polysemous words, and explores the relationship between the cognitive semantic framework of words and the receptive field of dictionary users, so as to realize the optimal interaction between dictionary definition and the perspective of dictionary users' acceptance. It can be seen that the rise of cognitive semantics provides a new perspective for theoretical lexicography and a new way to solve the core problems of word meaning division and interpretation in dictionary compilation practice.

Over the past decades, the studies on the combination of frame semantics and dictionary compilation have been developing continuously, and the representative achievement is *Cognitive Semantics and the Multi-Dimensional Definition for a New Generation of Bilingual/Bilingualized Learner's Dictionaries* by Zhang Yihua (2010). Based on the theory of frame semantics, this paper discusses the definition of bilingual learning dictionaries. In order to address the issue that current mainstream English learning dictionaries lack information relevance and interest, and fail to meet the second language acquisition needs of Chinese users, based on the theories of cognitive semantics, especially frame semantics, he argues that definitions in learning dictionaries for second language learners should selectively highlight semantic components with high cognitive salience. This should be done by considering both the attributes of words and users' linguistic cognitive characteristics, so as to describe semantic structures comprehensively and accurately. From the perspective of dictionary users' learning, this study offers valuable insights for future compilation of learning dictionaries: how to deliver more comprehensive and accurate word definitions that facilitate second language acquisition. At the same time, it also demonstrates that the theoretical frameworks of cognitive semantics can provide solutions to practical challenges in dictionary compilation, enabling definitions to better serve English learners and enhance dictionary utility.

Frame semantics theory is not only applied to address challenges in compiling English-Chinese learner's dictionaries but also guides the compilation of other specialized learner dictionaries. The earlier related studies in this domain includes *Interpretive Meta-Language, Semantic Frameworks, and Comparative Analysis of Semantic Fields* by Liu Xiaomei (2005). She leveraged frame semantics to guide the compilation of advanced extroverted Chinese learning dictionaries, proposing that frame theory can be used to systematically describe lexical usage patterns, while semantic fields can provide synonymous information. Yu Lina and Zeng Dongjing (2007) explore the bilingual online dictionary compilation from the perspective of frame semantics, and holds that the FrameNet based on frame semantics can provide advanced learners with the semantic framework of the required vocabulary and better meet the needs of vocabulary usage in their study *The Application of Frame Semantics in Bilingual Online Dictionary Compilation.* It can be seen that the thought of frame semantics has a good guiding role for various dictionary compilation practices. Over the past decade, influenced by related studies, many dictionary compilation methods have adopted and embodied the thought of frame semantics. A notable example is the *Chinese-French Dictionary* edited by Huang Jianhua (2014). The compilation of this dictionary draws on the research achievements of cognitive semantics, proposing to "regard vocabulary as an organic whole", and also attaches great importance to helping readers establish the psychological lexical semantic network of the target language (Tian Bing, 2016).

Frame semantics has also been applied to the construction of the Chinese lexical semantic database, known as Chinese FrameNet (CFN). Liu Kaiying (2011) reported that his team had constructed 309 frames for 3,151 lemmas and annotated over 20,000 sentences across domains such as cognitive semantics, law, and tourism in his paper *Research on Chinese Frame Net Construction and Application Technologies.* Yang Zonghan et al. (2018) from National Taiwan University leveraged an English-Chinese parallel corpus to transfer machine-annotated English frame elements to corresponding Chinese sentences, enabling the automatic construction of Chinese FrameNet. Previous FrameNet constructions, including those for Japanese (Ohara et al., 2003) and Korean (Park et al., 2014), relied on manual annotation, which was labor-intensive and difficult to achieve large-scale annotation and construction in the short term. The automatic annotation and FrameNet construction method proposed by Yang Zonghan et al. (2018) achieved 779 frames, covering 36,000 lemmas, with an 86% success rate. This achievement demonstrates the feasibility of automating FrameNet construction and corpus annotation.

In addition to the idea of frame semantics, the prototype theory of cognitive semantics is also used to guide dictionary compilation, mainly focusing on the issues of dictionary definition, sense distinction, and sense arrangement. An earlier representative achievement is *On Sufficient and Necessary Condition and the Definition Function of Prototype Theory* by Zhang Yihua (2001). He points out that there were serious defects in the traditional way of interpreting words, and that the Aristotelian approach to word definition would eventually be replaced, while he also noted that prototype definition might have the shortcoming of overly cumbersome semantic definitions. Fang Lu and Chen Conghai (2008) apply prototype theory to solve the problem of meaning arrangement of modal verbs in English-Chinese learning dictionaries in their paper *Assumption of Sense Arrangement Pattern of Modal Verbs in English-Chinese Learning Dictionaries: A Case Study of "Must"*. In the past decade, the application of prototype theory in dictionary compilation has been further expanded, and many research results have been achieved, including *Analysis of the Dictionary Effect of Prototypes and Related Cognitive Theories* by Yang Wei (2011). This paper points out that the dictionary effect of prototype theory can not only operate at the semantic level of language, which enables dictionary compilers to make cognitive sense structure arrangements for words by analyzing the prototype characteristics of semantic categories and category extension mechanisms, but also extend to the pragmatic and syntactic levels of dictionaries, providing editors with more suitable compilation methods for handling the pragmatic functions and grammatical information of lexical prototypes. Jin Yaming (2013) extends this dictionary effect of prototype theory to the compilation of reference books on Chinese grammar in the article *Analysis of the Extension and Application of Dictionary Effect of Prototype Theory*. Furthermore, Li Daguo (2016) reconstructed the definition system of English-Chinese learning dictionaries from the perspective of prototype theory and attempted to provide a unified explanation for its definition in his doctoral thesis *The Construction of the Prototype Definition Model for English-Chinese Learner's Dictionaries*. Yu Xiaomin and Lin Mingjin (2018) argued in *Prototype, Experience, Metaphor: The Enlightenment of Prototype Theory on the Definition of English-Chinese Learner's Dictionaries* that prototype theory offers guiding significance for the division of senses and the arrangement of entries in both monolingual and bilingual dictionaries, providing a new perspective for interpreting polysemous words and demonstrating obvious advantages in the definition of English-Chinese learner's dictionaries. Wang Renqiang (2019), taking the theoretical perspective of categorization theory and regarding the *New Century Chinese-English Dictionary (Second Edition)* as the research object, systematically explores the representation strategies for heterosemy in the New Century Chinese-English Dictionary (Second Edition) in his article *A Study of the Representation Strategies of Heterosemy in A New Century Chinese-English Dictionary*. These research results have promoted the continuous updating of compilation methods for different types of dictionaries, making them more consistent with the essential characteristics of language and better serving dictionary users.

The metaphor theory of cognitive semantics has also been widely applied in dictionary compilation, mainly focusing on the sense presentation, entry arrangement and metaphor representation in dictionaries, with fruitful results. Early research includes *The Arrangement of Single-Word Senses and Multi-Word Entries in Export-Oriented Chinese-English Learner Dictionaries from a Cognitive Metaphor Perspective* by Wang Anmin and Wang Jian (2006). The authors argue that metaphor theory can address the disjointed semantic coherence in the arrangement of single-word senses and multi-word entries in existing Chinese-English dictionaries to a certain extent, and it is more conducive to foreign learners' better construction of vocabulary knowledge system. Liang Qiuhua and Yao Ximing (2006) take Longman Dictionary of Contemporary English as an example, and analyze the microstructure of metaphor theory and dictionaries in detail, pointing out that this can provide a new perspective for future English learning dictionary compilation in their study *The Microstructure of the Longman Dictionary of Contemporary English (4th Edition) from a Metaphor Perspective*. These research results have laid a certain foundation for advancements in this field over the past decade. Wu Jihong (2010) discusses how metaphors are presented in bilingual dictionaries through definitions, examples, usage notes, and etymology, using concrete instances in *On the Representation of Metaphor in Learning Dictionaries*. She emphasizes that the treatment of metaphorical information will get increasing attention from the lexicographical community. Zhong Lanying et al. (2013) propose a sense distinction model based on the interface between metaphor recognition and dictionary sense treatment in *The Interface Between Metaphor Identification and Sense Treatment in Corpus-based Learner's Dictionary Making*. This model aims to describe the development track of potential meaning through this model, so as to help language learners with English as a foreign language develop their metaphorical competence.

With the in-depth development of dictionary compilation research under the guidance of cognitive semantics, the issues in traditional dictionaries have become increasingly apparent such as their definition methods and lexical items arrangement. Under this background, many scholars have begun to further explore the compilation of new dictionaries that are different from the traditional ones. For example, Wang Fufang (2015) advocates the compilation of "meaning dictionaries" as a new member of dictionary typology in the article *Cognitive Arrangement and Compilation Practices of the "Meaning Dictionary"*, and further explains the cognitive arrangement and compilation examples of this type of dictionaries.

8.4.2 Studies of Lexicography from the Perspective of Cognitive Semantics

Cognitive semantics has not only made many achievements in guiding the compilation of different types of dictionaries, but also made outstanding achievements in the theoretical development of lexicography. At present, cognitive lexicography (cognitive lexicography), which is based on cognitive semantics, has developed rapidly at home and abroad, and has become the future development direction of lexicography. Pioneering studies in this field include *Cognitive Lexicography Exploration* by Zhao Yanchun (2003). Based on the cognitive principles of language acquisition, he explores the theoretical characteristics of cognitive lexicography and the treatment of semantic issues from a macro-level perspective. It encompasses a wide range of contents, including meaning theory, the psychological dictionary, semantic networks, etc. Zhang Yihua (2009) systematically discusses the close relationship among semantics, cognition, and dictionary definition in his book *Semantics, Cognition and Definition*.

Over the past decade, studies on cognitive lexicography in Chinese academic circles has been highly active and productive, focusing primarily on the integration of language cognition and lexicography, as well as the theoretical framework, characteristics, and methods of cognitive lexicography. Wang Renqiang (2010) attempts to establish the discipline research system of cognitive lexicography, further explores its discipline orientation, theoretical basis, research tasks and methods, and puts forward a new paradigm of cognitive lexicography in his article *An Introduction to Cognitive Lexicography*. Zhang Yihua (2011) puts forward the meaning-driven multi-dimensional definition theory based on cognitive linguistics in his paper *Research on Dictionary Definition of Chinese as a Foreign Language from the Perspective of User Cognition*. Wang Fufang (2012) explores the reference role of cognitive semantics to lexicography from different aspects and points out that cognitive semantics poses a challenge of cognitive semantics to the classical concept of dictionary meaning in her article *The Challenge of Cognitive Semantics to the Classical Concept of Dictionary Meaning*. Zhang Yihua (2018, 2019) explores the theoretical basis and method and definition basis of cognitive lexicography in his two articles *Theoretical Background and Research Framework of Cognitive Lexicography* and *An Introduction to Cognitive Lexicography*. He argues that cognitive lexicography borrows theoretical methods from cognitive linguistics to study the relationship between language construal and lexical semantic interpretation. As a discipline, it emphasizes researching dictionary compilation and use from the perspectives of linguistic cognition and users. Its theoretical methods include cognitive semantic view, semantic framework and integrity, etc. Dictionary compilers can systematically apply cognitive semantic theories to describe the meaning potential of words in definitional structures, grounded in linguistic examples or events. These theoretical research results have made the theoretical framework of cognitive lexicography as a discipline clearer, the research methods more specific, and the research objects clearer, propelling it steadily toward maturity.

In short, over the past decade, cognitive semantics has been closely integrated with dictionary compilation and lexicography. From a theoretical perspective, the "symbolic meaning" of cognitive semantics has had a great impact on theoretical lexicography. As a new research paradigm, cognitive lexicography has gradually developed from the gestation to the maturity, and scholars have explored a clear theoretical framework, including theoretical basis and methods. From the specific work of dictionary compilation, many theoretical ideas of cognitive semantics, such as frame semantics, categorization theory and metaphor theory, have been proved to be able to address challenges in handling polysemous lexical items, including division, arrangement, and definition. On this basis, these advancements have enriched and optimized the definition and arrangement of traditional dictionaries. At the same time, more new dictionaries that embody cognitive semantics are constantly emerging, such as meaning dictionaries and frame network dictionaries. The continuous development of cognitive lexicography theory is set to enhance both the quality of dictionary compilation and dictionary usability.

8.5 Prospects for Future Research Trends

8.5.1 Future Trends in Translation Study Based on Semantics

The combination of semantics and translation studies has a long history, as the core issue in translation is semantic re-expression, and the development of semantics has offered multiple theoretical models and interpretive tools for translation studies. Therefore, it is not only the combination of the two, but also an important trend in the future to construct translation theories grounded in semantic theory and provide theoretical explanations for semantic and related issues in translation. In particular, the rapid development of cognitive semantics provides many theoretical sources for the construction of theoretical models urgently needed by cognitive translation studies. The construction of translation theories based on semantics especially cognitive semantics will primarily have the following trends:

First, the refinement and further development of existing theoretical models. As previously discussed, theories such as frame semantics, conceptual metaphor, and conceptual metonymy have been applied to translation studies, and theoretical views such as "frame operation theory" of translation, metaphorical process view of translation and cognitive view of metaphor translation, conceptual metonymy process view of translation and cognitive view of metonymy translation have been constructed. It should be said that these theoretical frameworks have indeed offered robust explanations for the translation process and the rendering of specific linguistic phenomena. However, these theoretical models are still in the preliminary stage of exploration and development, and it is necessary to further expand the scope of the targeted objects in order to further enhance the explanatory power of the theoretical models.

The second is to construct new theoretical models for translation based on more semantics theories, particularly cognitive semantics theories. Many theories in cognitive semantics have the possibility of being applied to the construction of translation theory, such as categorization theory, image schema theory, and conceptual blending theory. Based on this idea, Wen Xu and Xiao Kairong (2019) explores and applied some important theories of cognitive semantics to the construction of translation theoretical models. The construction of this aspect needs to be further deepened, especially combined with translation of different types, different subject fields, and different media forms to construct a more specific and targeted theoretical model, and apply it to the interpretation of specific corpus, such as the research of legal translation, financial translation, medical translation, philosophical translation, drama translation, movie subtitle translation, interpretation and machine translation.

The third is to combine semantics with theories in other fields to construct translation theory. Translation studies is an inherently highly interdisciplinary, and current interdisciplinary trends are increasingly obvious. Therefore, the integration of semantic theories with those from related fields represents an essential trend in translation studies. For instance, recent publications in domestic core journals have demonstrated interdisciplinary trends in metaphor translation studies. Wu Guangjun and Wang Ruiyang (2019) explore the translators' cognitive effort in metaphor translation through the empirical method of eye-tracking technology in their article *An Eye-Tracking Study of Cognitive Efforts in Translating English Metaphors into Chinese: With the Translation of Marriage Metaphors in Economic Texts in Focus*; Yang Mingxing and Zhao Yuqian (2020) systematically analyze text features and discourse functions of metaphor and its translation standards from interdisciplinary perspectives such as diplomacy, cognitive metaphors and translation studies, based on real cases, in their article *Strategies for Translating Diplomacy-serving Metaphors with Chinese Characteristics*.

This interdisciplinary trend will have more possibilities in the future. First, cognitive semantic theories and cognitive grammar theories are inherently closely related, and integrating them in translation studies represents a significant trend. For example, combining frame theory based on cognitive semantics with construction theory based on cognitive grammar can address the limitation of separating semantic and grammatical analysis in translation studies, enabling systematic investigations by constructing framework network and construction network. Secondly, semantics can also be combined with other branches of linguistics such as psycholinguistics and sociolinguistics as the foundation for the construction of translation theory. Meanwhile, as Halverson (2013) posits, cognitive semantics can be combined with bilingualism theory and second language acquisition theory to explore cognitive issues of translation, especially to construct cognitive translation theoretical models.

8.5.2 Future Trends of Foreign Language Teaching Studies Based on Semantics

According to the preceding review of semantic in teaching studies achievements, domestic studies over the past decade have mainly focused on theories such as frame theory, categorization theory, and conceptual metaphor theory, as well as translation teaching and vocabulary teaching. These studies predominantly propose teaching ideas, theoretical perspectives, constructed some teaching modes, and are more theoretical explorations based on semantics theory. Future research may have the following trends:

The first is to carry out teaching practice studies based on the existing teaching ideas, viewpoints, and models. This can be reflected in putting forward more specific teaching strategies, teaching methods and implementation process from the existing ideas, views, and models. For instance, the vocabulary teaching model based on categorization can further explore the specific application methods in different levels of learners, including how to design lesson plans, what teaching methods are available, and how to systematically implement teaching. As far as the learner's metaphorical ability is concerned, how to cultivate it, what specific means to be adopted, and to what extent it is related to the vocabulary learning of learners at different levels need to be more practically discussed.

The second is the empirical study of teaching based on semantics theory. Empirical study is an important research method of teaching studies. Students are an important variable in teaching research. The individual differences of students, teaching content and teaching environment all make teaching a complex research object composed of many variables. Therefore, the theoretical explorations discussed earlier require validation and refinement through empirical study. These empirical studies may involve designing experiments based on existing theoretical models or viewpoints to test existing theories, or modify, refine or supplement the proposed theories for different research objects, put forward research hypotheses, and falsify or confirm them through experiments or other empirical studies methods in teaching. These efforts not only advance teaching practices, but also feedback the research findings to the semantic theoretical model, so that it can be continuously improved and revised, and promote the continuous development of language teaching theory, bilingualism theory, translation theory, and linguistic theory.

In addition, the latest and future development of semantics theory can be further applied to the development of language teaching theory and practice, and the research topics can be continuously expanded. For example, continuous developments in discourse semantics, particularly cognitive discourse semantic theory will drive progress in discourse teaching and even translation teaching. The multimodal turn in conceptual metaphor and metonymy research will establish exploring learners' multimodal metaphorical and metonymic competence as a new research focus, such as their ability to interpret multimodal metaphors and metonyms, and teaching methods across diverse discourse genres (e.g., microfilms, advertisements, slogans, sign language, etc.). Meanwhile, cognitive semantic theories will be applied to more teaching fields, including grammar, reading, and writing teaching.

8.5.3 Future Trends of Dictionary Compilation Studies Based on Semantics

In the field of dictionary compilation, the theoretical framework of cognitive lexicography will undergo more detailed and systematic exploration. Current research indicates that while the theoretical frameworks and methodologies of cognitive lexicography have been investigated to some extent, and certain breakthroughs have been made in addressing some key practical issues in dictionary compilation (such as layout patterns) under the guidance of cognitive semantics. There are few studies on the combination of cognitive lexicography and lexicography, that is to say, cognitive lexicography is used as a theoretical perspective to systematically guide dictionary compilation practice. A new theory can only find its value in practical application. How the theoretical development of cognitive lexicography systematically optimizes lexicography depends on the organic combination of the two. Therefore, we can foresee that the study on the interaction between lexicography theory and dictionary compilation practice driven by cognitive semantics theory will become the focus. On the other hand, the purpose of dictionary compilation is to meet the needs of users, and a dictionary that is beneficial to users is a good dictionary. Consequently, the future development trend of lexicography and dictionary compilation will increasingly rely on comprehensive research based on cognitive semantics theory from a user-centric perspective.

In addition, it will be an important trend to update the research methods of dictionary compilation. Traditional dictionary compilation was primarily focused on entries, whereas frame-based dictionary compilation offers a new perspective and dictionary system. This shift indicates that future dictionaries will no longer adhere to a single format; instead, more diverse types of online, dynamic, semantic, and knowledge-based dictionaries will emerge. The method of dictionary compilation will increasingly introduce the participation of machines, including automatic recognition and labeling of machines. Meanwhile, based on large-scale, dynamic and multimodal corpora, building knowledge-based dictionaries for various applications, especially for artificial intelligence, natural language processing, and multimodal applications, is also represents a key future direction in dictionary compilation.

Generally speaking, from the achievements of domestic semantics applied research in recent ten years, cognitive semantics will be the most important branch of semantics theory to promote the development of semantics applied research in the future. Meanwhile, cognitive linguistics research exhibits an obvious development trend: the combination of theory and practice, along with the application of theoretical frameworks to specific linguistic phenomena and related disciplinary fields (Shu Dingfang, 2017: 76). As the core component of cognitive linguistics, cognitive semantics also embodies this development trend. The new development of various branches of cognitive semantics will definitely promote the development of its applied research in depth. Therefore, we can even foresee the possibility of "applied cognitive semantics". Furthermore, interdisciplinary research is bound to be more in-depth, and using neural and cognitive science methods to carry out empirical studies will also be the development trend of research methods.

8.6 Conclusion

Semantics is an important branch of linguistics, and semantics study is the central content of linguistic study. As the study of meaning, semantics has deeply integrated with disciplines closely related to meaning, giving rise to numerous applied research achievements. This chapter focuses on summarizing and looking ahead to the achievements of domestic semantic theory in applied studies within the three fields of translation, teaching, and dictionary compilation over the past decade. From the preceding analysis, it is evident that the applied study achievements of cognitive semantics stand out prominently in the applied research of each field. In the field of translation, the theoretical propositions of cognitive semantics align with the development trends of translation studies. The concept of knowledge framework, conceptual metaphor, and metonymy have become significant topics in translation studies, which provide new perspectives for translation strategies, translation processes, and foreign translation of Chinese classics, thus promoting the development of translation theory and improving the intelligibility of translated texts and reader adaptability. In the field of foreign language teaching, the frame semantics theory, categorization theory, and conceptual metaphor theory of cognitive semantics are widely applied in translation teaching and vocabulary teaching. These applications not only optimize teaching methods and strategies but also drive the in-depth development of teaching research, giving rise to new research focuses, such as lexical metaphorical competence. Cognitive semantics is also closely integrated with dictionary compilation and lexicography. It continuously updates the definition methods and the arrangement of lexical items in dictionary compilation and simultaneously forms cognitive lexicography, a new research paradigm. Despite the remarkable achievements, it is undeniable that there are still deficiencies and flaws, and each application field still has huge development space. For the future applied study of semantics, it is expected that more scholars will join in innovating semantic theories, more extensively and deeply integrating with the development frontier of other disciplines, and jointly opening up a new world of application research of semantics in China.

References

Bai Jiehong, & Chen Zhongping. (2011). Origin of English and Chinese Neologisms since the Mid-20th Century and Their Semantic Cognitive Mechanisms. *Foreign Languages and Literature, 5*, 34–38.

Bai Jiehong, & Wang Shasha. (2014). A Study of the Semantic Change and Cognitive Mechanisms of the Chinese Internet Buzzword "Meng." *Journal of Hubei University, 2*, 139–142.

Bi Jin, & Xiao Xiqiang. (2017). The Semantic Change and Pragmatic Value of the "shuo hao de X ne" Construction. *Linguistic Research, 2*, 44–48.

Cai Yuehong, Zhu Qian, Cheng Xianyi, & Yang Tianming. (2009). The Chinese Sentence Similarity Calculation Based on the Three-Dimensional Model of Sentence Meaning. *Journal of Guangxi Normal University (Natural Science Edition), 1*, 153–156.

Cao Duxin, & Xiang Mingyou. (2017). Chinese Sentence Similarity Calculation Based on the Three-Dimensional Model of Sentence Meaning. *Foreign Languages and Their Teaching, 4*, 78–89.

Cao Duxin, Xiang Mingyou, Yang Guoping, & Guan Bangdi. (2019). The Ternary Representation Models of Meaning. *Linguistic Research, 2*, 39–50.

Cao Meiling, & Liu Chaojian. (2018). A Cognitive Study on the English Translation of "Cao" Metaphors: A Case Study of Four Translations of Water Margin. *Chinese Translators Journal, 6*, 94–99.

Cao Wei. (2011). *Modern Chinese Lexical Semantics.* Academia Press.

Chang Haichao. (2012). Mediating Effect of English Learning Strategies Between Tolerance of Ambiguity and English Proficiency. *Foreign Language World, 2*, 81–88.

Chen Haiyan, & Wang Lirong. (2013). Cultivation of Metaphor Awareness and College English Vocabulary Teaching. *Journal of PLA University of Foreign Languages, 3*, 57–62.

Chen Jingjing, & Shi Yunbao. (2019). Analysis of the Presupposition Projection Problem in Discourse Representation Theory. *Journal of Chongqing University of Technology, 11*, 12–19.

Chen Lang. (2010). On Cultivation of Metaphoric Competence in Second Language Teaching. *Foreign Language Research, 5*, 47–49.

Chen Lang. (2017). The Frontiers of Metaphorical Competence in Second Language Vocabulary Teaching. *Foreign Language Research, 2*, 105–109.

Chen Lixia, & Sun Chongfei. (2015). The Complementation and Fusion of Cognitive Linguistics and Linguistic Typology. *Journal of Jiangxi University of Finance and Economics, 3*, 97–103.

Chen Li, & Pan Haihua. (2020a). The Monotonicity and Polarity Items Licensing of Dou. *Journal of Foreign Languages, 3*, 14–24.

Chen Li, & Pan Haihua. (2020b). Entailment Evaluation in the Theory of Polarity Sensitivity. *Studies of the Chinese Language, 2*, 188–200.

Chen Linlin. (2013). *A Research on Chinese Donkey Sentences Based on the Framework of DRT* (Doctoral Dissertation). Nankai University, Tianjin.

X. Wen and R. Tang, *New Perspectives and Developments in Chinese Semantics*,
https://doi.org/10.1007/978-981-95-1730-5

Chen Shumei. (2006). *Collected Essays on Lexical Semantics*. Chinese Literature and History Press.
Chen Shumei. (2015). On Study from the Perspective of Cognition in the Long Time Category of Hubei Yingshan Dialect. *Studies in Language and Linguistics, 2*, 78–84.
Chen Wenbo. (2010). A Semantic Cognitive Interpretation of the New "Bei + X" Construction in Chinese. *Contemporary Rhetoric, 4*, 80–87.
Chen Xinren. (2015). The Boundary Between Semantics and Pragmatics, An Alternative Account. *Foreign Language Teaching and Research, 6*, 838–849, 959–960.
Chen Xinren, & Cai Yiming. (2011). Let Synecdoche Stand Alone, Its Distinction from Metonymy in Light of Cognitive Semantics. *Linguistic Sciences, 1*, 93–100.
Chen Zhenyu, & Qian Peng. (2015). Entailment, Presupposition, and Integrity. *Contemporary Linguistics, 1*, 998–109, 126.
Cheng Gong. (1998). From the Analysis of Ambiguous Sentences to 20th-Century Syntax. *Journal of PLA University of Foreign Languages, 5*, 3–5.
Cheng Qilong. (2003). Possession Frame and Its Grammatical Realizations. *Foreign Languages and Their Teaching, 4*, 1–4.
Cheng Qilong. (2007). Semantic Frames and Cognitive Operation. *Foreign Language Education, 1*, 1–4.
Cheng Qilong. (2010). Typology of Metonymies. *Foreign Language Education, 3*, 1–6, 12.
Chen Shanzhen. (2003). Frame Semantic Information and Pragmatic Equivalence. *Journal of Soochow University, 10*, 72–74.
Cheng Wenwen, & Zhang Xiancheng. (2018). The Lexicalization of Antonymic Compound Wordsin Chinese. *Journal of Ocean University of China (Social Sciences), 2*, 119–123.
Cong Rizhen, & Qiu Wei. (2016). On the Overlap and Complementarity between Semantic and Pragmatic Presuppositions. *Modern Foreign Languages, 5*, 594–604, 728.
Dai Yuncai. (2016). Ambiguity Resolution of English Relative Clause Attachment by Chinese Learners. *Journal of Foreign Languages, 6*, 65–74.
Dai Zunfeng, & Sun Hongbo. (2014). A Review of the Development of Formal Semantics. *Foreign Languages and Literature, 3*, 85–89.
Deng Jing. (2010). The Frame-Semantic Approach in Translation Studies: A Critical Review. *Foreign Language Teaching and Research, 1*, 66–71.
Deng Qi, & Yang Zhong. (2014). Semantic Cognition and Semantic Function in English and Chinese Sensory Adjectives—A Case Study of "Cold" and "Leng." *Foreign Language Research, 1*, 47–53.
Deng Qi, & Yang Zhong. (2019). A Diachronic Study of Semantic Functions of English and Chinese Sensory Adjectives—A Case Study of English Cold and Chinese Leng. *Journal of xi'an International Studies University, 1*, 12–17.
Deng Yu, Li Fuyin, & Chen Wenfang. (2015). Lexicalization Typology of Mandarin Metaphorical Motion Events, Converging Evidence from Corpus and Experimental Data. *Foreign Languages and Their Teaching, 3*, 73–78.
Deng Yunhua, & Zeng Qingan. (2011). On the Idealized Cognitive Model of English and Chinese Passive Sentences. *Foreign Languages Research, 2*, 1–7, 112.
Ding Xin. (1994). On the Issue of Correct Sentences. *Journal of PLA University of Foreign Languages, 1*, 24–30.
Dong Xiufang. (2016). On the Semantic Change from Comparison and Selection to Suggestion in Some Chinese Words and the Role of the Omission of Some Constituents in the Semantic Evolution. *Journal of Yunnan Minzu University (Philosophy and Social Sciences Edition), 33*(3), 108–113.
Dong Zhengcun. (2015). From Sequence to Quantification, A Case Study of Semantic Change in Mandarin. *Studies of the Chinese Language, 3*, 206–217, 287.
Dong Zhengcun. (2017). From Approximate Quantity to Probable Epistemic Modality, A Case Study of Semantic Shift in Mandarin with Duoban as an Example. *Studies of the Chinese Language, 1*, 63–73, 127.

Du Guizhi. (2018). Re-discussing Verbal Semantic Valence, Government Patterns and Sentence Thematic Structure. *Russian in China, 3*, 8–15, 79.

Fan Xiangtao. (2017). On Chained Metonymies in Chinese Classics and Their Translation into English. *Foreign Language Education, 6*, 84–88.

Fang li. (2000). *Logic Semantics*. Beijing Language and Culture University Press.

Fang Lu, & Chen Congmei. (2008). Conceptions on the Sense Arrangement Patterns of Modal Auxiliaries in English-Chinese Learner's Dictionaries: A Case Study of "Must." *Lexicographical Studies, 6*, 70–76.

Fang Zichun, & Chen Jianlin. (2014). A Corpus-Based Behavioral Profile Study of Six Synonymous Adjectives. *Foreign Language Teaching and Research, 6*, 842–852.

Fang Na, & Zhang Weiwei. (2015). Language Variation Research from a Cognitive Sociolinguistic Perspective: A Statistical Analysis Based on a Survey of Recent Research Papers. *The Journal of Chinese Sociolinguistics, 1*, 69–79.

Fang Yinjie. (2016). Multifactorial Analysis in Linguistic Studies. *Corpus Linguistics, 1*, 82–92.

Fang Yinjie. (2018). Collostructional Analysis: A State of the Art Review. *Modern Foreign Languages, 3*, 426–435.

Fang Yinjie, & Liang Maocheng. (2020). A Study of Relativizer Omission by Chinese EFL Learners, Triangulating Corpus and Experimental Approaches. *Foreign Languages and Their Teaching, 3*, 34–43.

Feng Guoxin. (2016). *Contrastive Study of Chinese Vocabulary*. Tsinghua University Press.

Feng Yuli. (2018). On the Explanatory Power of the Maximality Operation in Semantic Studies and the Problems of Its Application to Chinese Data. *Journal of Foreign Languages, 5*, 38–47.

Feng Yuli. (2019). Universal Quantificational Logic and the Semantic Difference of Universal Determiners in English and Chinese: A Case Study of Every and Mei. *Foreign Language Teaching and Research, 2*, 202–211.

Feng Yuli, & Pan Haihua. (2017). Is the Notion of Cover Necessary, Another Look at the Application of Cover in Semantic Studies and Its Potential Problems. *Contemporary Linguistics, 3*, 379–395.

Feng Yuli, & Pan Haihua. (2018). Revisiting the Semantics of Dou, From the Perspectives of Exhaustivity and Exclusiveness. *Studies of the Chinese Language, 2*, 177–194.

Fu Huanqing. (1996). *An Analysis and Description of Word Meaning*. Language Press.

Fu Lihua. (2011). On Relativity and Accessibility of Semantic Field in Translation. *Foreign Languages and Literature, 5*, 64–66.

Fu Xingshang. (1999). *Modern Russian Case Grammar*. Trident Reference Publishing.

Gao Mingle. (2018). *Modern Semantics-Syntax Interface*. Beijing Language and Culture University Press.

Gao Song. (2013). The Study of Garden-Path Sentences Based on Probabilistic Valency Pattern Theory. *Applied Linguistics, 3*, 126–132.

Gao Yanmei. (2015). *Discourse Semantic Frames Studies*. Peking University Press.

Gao Yun. (2011). *Exploring the Rhetorical Form of Chinese Discourse Structure from the Angle of SDRT* (Doctoral Dissertations). Southwest University, Chongqing.

Gao Yun. (2013). *Formal Semantics Studies*. China Social Sciences Press.

Gong Fang. (1996). Sentence Meaning and Its Study. *Foreign Language Education, 3*, 2–8, 12.

Gong Pengcheng, & Wang Wenbin. (2014). A Study of the Interface between Metaphor and Metonymy from the Perspective of Embodied Philosophy. *Foreign Languages Research, 2*, 1–6, 112.

Gong Yumiao. (2006). Metaphor Awareness and FL Vocabulary Teaching. *Foreign Language World, 1*, 40–45, 76.

Gu Bolin. (1998). Applications of New Semantic Theories in Lexicography. *Russian in China, 4*, 14–19.

Gu Yi, & Zhang Haoyu. (2019). On Translation of Body Metaphor in Calligraphic Theories: A Case Study of Xu Shu Pu. *Chinese Science & Technology Translators Journal, 4*, 44–47.

Gu Yueguo. (1994). John Searle's Speech Act Theory, Critique and Reference. *Foreign Linguistics, 3*, 10–16.

Guan Chen. (2019). Translation Strategies for Culture-Loaded Words in Chinese and English under Frame Semantics. *English Square, 8*, 35–36.

Guan Jialing, & Han Mei. (2016). Translation of Metonymy vs. Metonymic Translation. *Journal of Jiangsu University (Social Science Edition), 5*, 79–85.

Guo Gaopan, & Liao Huaying. (2016). The Construction of Frame Semantics and Conceptual Integration in Translation Process: A Translation Teaching Study Based on the Cognitive Corpus "FrameNet." *Shanghai Journal of Translators, 4*, 33–36.

Guo Guichun. (2009). The Boundaries of the Context and Their Significance. *Philosophical Research, 2*, 94–100.

Guo Yukai. (1996). The Indirect Meaning of Russian Sentences. *Russian in China, 2*, 23–29.

Guo Yukai. (1998). The Entailment Relationship Between Sentences. *Russian in China, 3*, 3–5.

Han Baijing, & Xue Fang. (2012). Branching Directions of Morphological Representation and the Interpretation Bias of Structurally Ambiguous Words. *Foreign Language Teaching and Research, 5*, 728–737, 80.

Han Liyang, & Yang Kai. (2010). On Formalization of Supposition. *Academics, 4*, 85–90, 284.

He Liang. (2016). Semantic Change from Space to Time of Words of the Section of Human Body and Objects. *Research in Ancient Chinese Language, 1*, 63–73.

He Wei, & Liu Jiahuan. (2019). A Contrastive Study of the Logico-Semantic Relations and Their Representations between English and Chinese Clauses. *Journal of University of Science and Technology Beijing (Social Sciences Edition), 2*, 1–17.

He Yingyu. (2003). A Survey of Studies of Sentential Semantics in China. *Journal of PLA University of Foreign Languages, 2*, 43–49.

He Ziran. (1979). A Brief Analysis of Synonymous Interchangeability of English Structures. *Modern Foreign Languages, 4*, 26–30.

Hou Guojin. (2012). Semantics and Pragmatics: Which Dominates Which? Discussion of Complementarism and Interdisciplinary Trend of Pragmatics. *English Studies, 2*, 1–15.

Hou Ruifang. (2015). The Polysemy of "Bu" in Compound Words. *Chinese Language Learning, 6*, 19–27.

Hu Jian, & Zhang Jiayi. (2012). Collostructional Analysis: An Integration of Cognitive Linguistics and Corpus Linguistics. *Journal of Foreign Languages, 4*, 61–69.

Hu Yang. (2013). Ambiguity Attributes and Sources of V-Under/Behind vs. V-in/on Type VPP Structures in English. *Foreign Languages Research, 2*, 33–40.

Hu Yang, & Chen Jingli. (2014). Accessibility Problems of Uninterpretable features in L2 Acquisition: The Case of Ambiguous English VPP Constructions. *Foreign Language Teaching and Research, 5*, 771–782, 801.

Hu Zhuanglin. (2014). Dictionary Compilation and Linguistics. *Contemporary Foreign Language Studies, 8*, 8–13.

Hua Shao. (1998). On the Compositional Modules of Sentence Meaning. *Foreign Language Research, 4*, 3–5.

Huang Fusuifei. (2010). A Cognitive Explanation of the "Degree Adverb + Noun" Structure from Category Shift. *Journal of Southwest Minzu University, 7*, 174–180.

Huang Fang. (2016). Semantic Features and Quantification Functions of Universal Quantifiers "Qun, Zhong, Fan" in Pre-Qin Chinese. *Journal of Hubei Minzu University, 4*, 172–175.

Huang Gang. (2014). The Actual Reference of Wei in Western Zhou Poetry and Related Objects and Phenomena: A Case Study of Substantive Grammaticalization in The Book of Songs Interpretation. *Journal of Soochow University (Philosophy & Social Science Edition), 6*, 146–151.

Huang He. (2017). Logico-Semantic Relations in the Longest Sentence in English Literature: Functional Stylistics Perspective. *Foreign Language Education, 6*, 37–41.

Huang Jianhua. (2014). *A Contemporary Chinese-French Dictionary*. Foreign Language Teaching and Research Press.

Huang Ying. (2016). Diachronic Collostructional Variation of the Intensifier Absolutely in Semantic Preference and Prosody. *Journal of xi'an International Studies University, 2*, 39–43.

Huang Yuehua. (2012). A Cognitive Study on the Polysemy of Guo. *Foreign Language Research, 4*, 67–71.

Huang Zanhui. (2013). A Comparative Analysis of Dou and Zong in Event Quantification. *Studies of the Chinese Language, 3*, 251–264.

Huang Zanhui, & Shi Dinghong. (2013). Event-Quantifying Mei-Constructions. *Chinese Teaching in the World, 3*, 305–318.

Huang Zhenrong. (2010). Conditional Perfection and Explicature. *Contemporary Linguistics, 4*, 326–337.

Jia Dongmei, & Lan Chun. (2010). A Contrastive Cognitive Semantic Analysis of "Water" & "Shui." *Foreign Language Learning Theory and Practice, 3*, 28–35.

Jia Guangmao. (2020). A Cognitive Grammar Account of Quantifier Scope Ambiguities in English and Chinese. *Modern Foreign Languages, 4*, 451–462.

Jia Yande. (1999). *Chinese Semantics*. Peking University Press.

Jiang Hong, & Xu Ying. (1997). The Functions of Presupposition and Negation. *Russian in China, 2*, 3–7.

Jiang Tao. (2015). The Latest Development of Post-Gricean Contextualism—Equilibrium Semantics. *Foreign Language Research, 1*, 85–89.

Jiang Jingzhong, & Pan Haihua. (2013). How Many Dous Do We Really Need? *Studies of the Chinese Language, 1*, 38–50.

Jiang Yan. (1998). Pragmatic Reasoning and Syntactic/Semantic Characterization of Dou. *Modern Foreign Languages, 1*, 10–24.

Jiang Yan, et al. (2000). Counter-Factual Interpretation of Chinese Conditional Sentences. In F. Mei (Ed.), *Grammatical Research and Exploration* (pp. 257–279). The Commercial Press.

Jiang Yan. (2005). Formal Pragmatics and Explicature Theory: With a Discussion on the Relationship Between Explicitation and Valence Studies in Chinese. In L. Danqing (Ed.), *Frontiers of Linguistics and Chinese Studies* (pp. 143–170). Shanghai Education Publishing.

Jiang Yan. (2011). *Approaching Formal Pragmatics*. Shanghai Education Publishing.

Jiang Yan, & Pan Haihua. (1998). *An Introduction to Formal Semantics*. China Social Sciences Press.

Jiang Yong, & Liao Qiaoyun. (2012). The Emergent Polarity Sensitivity and Scalar Logic of Conglai. *Modern Foreign Languages, 2*, 118–124.

Jin Li. (2011). *Logical Analysis of Chinese Sentences*. Zhejiang University Press.

Jin Lixin. (1997). Explanatory Procedures of Functional Explanatory Grammar and Valence Studies. *Journal of Foreign Languages, 3*, 44–49.

Jin Shengxi. (2017). *A Study on Metonymic Translation of Tang Poetry Classics from the Perspective of Cognitive Linguistics* (Doctoral Dissertation). Northeast Normal University.

Jin Shengxi, & Lin Zhengjun. (2016). The Conceptual Blending Mechanism in the Construction of a Translator's Subjectivity. *Foreign Languages and Their Teaching, 1*, 116–121, 149–150.

Jin Xiaodong, & Wu Fuxiang. (2019). Some Paths of Bidirectional Semantic Evolution in Chinese. *Chinese Linguistics, 4*, 40–49, 95–96.

Jin Yaming. (2013). An Analysis of the Extension and Application of Prototype Theory's Lexical Effects. *Language Planning, 14*, 10–11.

Kang Canhui. (2007). On the Complementarity of Semantics and Pragmatics. *Examination Weekly, 43*, 33–34.

Kang Xiaoming, & Wu Tingting. (2019). The Competition Evolution and Finalization of Rhetorical Structure "Ga + X." *Modern Chinese, 12*, 69–73.

Kuang Fangtao. (2012). A Cognitive Study of Metaphor and English Vocabulary Instruction. *Contemporary Foreign Languages Studies, 2*, 13–17.

Kuang Fangtao, & Lin Wenzhi. (2015). *Categorization and English Vocabulary Learning*. Science Press.

Kuang Pengfei. (2010). Semantic Change and Mutual Influence of "Diwei" and "Dibu." *Linguistic Research, 2*, 16–20.

Kuang Pengfei, & Hu Qian. (2013). Two Cases of Nouns Bleaching into Adverbs: The Grammaticalization of Dali and Sili. *Studies in Language and Linguistics, 3*, 84–90.

Li Baolun. (2012). Are all A-quantifiers Sensitive to Focus? *Contemporary Linguistics, 2*, 111–128.

Li Baolun. (2016). Non-uniformity of Chinese Negators Mei (You) and Bu Towards Focus. *Contemporary Linguistics, 3*, 368–386.

Li Baolun, Zhang Lei, & Pan Haihua. (2009). The Co-occurence Constraint and Division of Labor of Adverbial Universal Quantifiers/Distrbutors in Mandarin Chinese. *Chinese Lingusitics, 3*, 59–70.

Li Cuiying. (2011). Different Approaches to Semantic Anomaly. *Journal of Chongqing University of Arts and Sciences (Social Sciences Edition), 5*, 104–108.

Li Daguo. (2016). *The Construction of the Prototype Definition Model for English-Chinese Learner's Dictionaries* (Doctoral Dissertation). Soochow University, Su Zhou.

Li Dan, & Lai Wei. (2011). Logical-Semantic Relations in Conditional Clauses of Unconditional Compound Sentences of "Many Enumerates" Type. *The Guide of Sciences & Education, 8*(208), 223.

Li Fuyin. (2017). Path Elements in the Characterization of Typical Displacement Motion Events. *Foreign Language Education, 4*, 1–6.

Li Guangyu. (2014). The Semantic Evolution of "Bu De" from a Subjective Perspective. *Research in Chinese Language, 4*, 69–76.

Li Kesheng. (2009). Formal Semantics in the Linguistics. *Journal of University of Chinese Academy of Social Sciences, 2*, 112–117.

Li Kesheng, & Zou Chongli. (2013). Axiomatic Formal Deduction: From Formal Syntax to Formal Semantics. *Jiangxi Social Sciences, 8*, 54–58.

Li Ke, & Lu Weizhong. (2017). On the Influence of Metonymic Competence on English Majors' Translation Competence. *Foreign Language World, 1*, 64–71.

Li Meixiang. (2015). The Analysis Methods and Classification of Semantics Correspondence of Homographs in Modern Chinese and Korean. *Chinese Language Learning, 4*, 95–103.

Li Qingqing. (2013). *The Study of Unusual Semantic Combination Words* (Doctoral Dissertation). Ocean University of China, Qingdao.

Li Rongbao. (1992). Review of Ambiguity Research. *Fujian Foreign Language, Z2*, 1–5, 9.

Li Sixu, & Sheng Caiyun. (2015). Cognitive Semantics and Integration Degree of the Construction "ai V bu V." *Chinese Language Learning, 2*, 57–65.

Li Wenshan. (2013). On the Semantic Complexity of Dou in Mandarin: A Partially Unified Account. *Chinese Teaching in the World, 3*, 319–330.

Li Xiyin. (1998). Case and Sentence Meaning. *Foreign Languages and Their Teaching, 7*, 3–5.

Li Xiaojun. (2016). The Semantic Evolution Model of Quantifier "ge" in Chinese. *Linguistic Sciences, 2*, 150–164.

Li Yanping, & Zhu Yushan. (2011). The Prototype Category Theory Perspective in English Grammar Teaching. *Foreign Language Education, 1*, 62–65.

Li Yanzhi, & Wu Yicheng. (2018). On the Evolution of [V + Non-Patient NP] Constructions. *Modern Foreign Languages, 2*, 147–160.

Li Yini. (2011). Cognitive Study on the Semantic Extension of Japanese Body Part Word "Hand"-Focusing on Metaphor, Synecdoche, and Metonymy Expressions. *Journal of Henan Normal University (Philosophy and Social Sciences Edition), 2*, 199–201.

Li Yi, & Shi Lei. (2010). Multimodal Metaphor in Teaching—A New Direction for Applied Metaphor Research. *Technology Enhanced Foreign Language Education, 3*, 47–49, 56.

Li Yueping. (2009). On National Cultural Semantics Teaching of Foreign Language Vocabulary from the Perspective of the Cognitive Frame Theory. *Foreign Language World, 2*, 92–96.

Liang Qiuhua, & Yao Ximing. (2006). A Microscopic Study of the Metaphorical Structure in Longman Contemporary English Dictionary (Fourth Edition). *Lexicographical Studies, 4*, 126–131.

Liang Xiaohui. (2013). The Translation of Thematic Images in Big Breasts and Wide Hips: On Howard Goldblatt's Translation of Conceptual Metaphors. *Foreign Languages and Literature, 5*, 93–99.

Lin Haixia. (2015). Frame Semantics Guidance to the Pragmatic Study of Thunderstorm's English Translation. *Journal of Nantong University (Social Sciences Edition), 31*(5), 82–86.

Lin Lu, & Wang Xu. (2016). Variability-based Neighbor Clustering: An Integration of Diachronic Linguistics and Corpus Linguistics. *Foreign Language Education & Research, 1*, 6–12.

Lin Meng, Luo Senlin, Jia Congfei, Han Lei, Yuan Yujiao, & Pan Limin. (2015). Microblog Topics Summarization Algorithm Merging Sentential Semantic Structure Model. *Journal of Zhejiang University (Engineering Science), 12*, 2316–2325.

Lin Ruowang. (2016). The Structure, Modality, and Counterfactual Reasoning of "De." *Studies of the Chinese Language, 2*, 131–151.

Lin Xiaqing. (2017). The Difference Between Propositional Meaning, Semantic Meaning, and Discourse Meaning. *English on Campus, 26*, 212.

Lin Yi, & Si Lianhe. (2005). The Ability of Interpreting the Analects and Its Cultivation. *Journal of Nanjing Normal University* (Higher Education Research Special Issue), 23–30.

Liu Bin, & Yuan Yulin. (2018). On the Lexical Ambiguity of the Chinese Verb Huái Yíand Its Meaning Construal Strategy. *Foreign Language Teaching and Research, 1*, 15–23, 159.

Liu Bingli, & Liu Haitao. (2011). A Study on the Evolution of the Verbal Syntactic Valence Based on Corpus. *Language Teaching and Linguistic Studies, 6*, 83–89.

Liu Genhui. (2005). A Comprehensive View on Formal Pragmatics-With a Perspective on Chinese Formal Pragmatics. *Studies in Language and Linguistics, 1*, 12–18.

Liu Guohui. (2010). The "Triplet" Process of Frame Semantics for Translation: Cognitive Schemas, Frames and Construal. *Foreign Languages and Literature, 8*, 74–79.

Liu Hui, & Yu Linlong. (2019). A Study on Polysemy of Chinese Noun "Time" Within LCCM Theory. *Foreign Language Research, 3*, 20–25.

Liu Huijuan, Pan Haihua, & Hu Jianhua. (2011). Acquisition of Mandarin Additive Particles. *Contemporary Linguistics, 3*, 20–25.

Liu Jibin, & Fan Chunyu. (2018). The Relationship Between Sentence Form and Meaning from the Perspective of Semantic Structure. *Journal of Harbin University, 6*, 102–105.

Liu Jian, Cao Guangshun, & Wu Fuxiang. (1995). On Several Factors Inducing the Grammaticalization of Chinese Lexicon. *Studies of the Chinese Language, 3*, 12–18.

Liu Juan, Liu Xiaoyan, & Liu Yichun. (2013). On the Ambiguity Phenomenon in English from the Perspective of Semantics. *Journal of xi'an University of Electronic Science and Technology (Social Sciences Edition), 3*, 133–136.

Liu Kaiying. (2011). Research on the Construction and Application Technology of Chinese Frame Semantic Network. *Journal of Chinese Information Processing, 6*, 46–62.

Liu Li. (2016). *The Semantic Evolution Path of the Verb "Kai"* (Master's Thesis). Jiangxi Normal University, Nanchang.

Liu Liping. (2014). Scope of Negation and the Meaning of Focused Negation. *Language Teaching and Linguistic Studies, 5*, 69–78.

Liu Longgen. (2001). On Wittgenstein's Theories of Meaning. *Jilin University Journal of Humanities and Social Sciences, 5*, 101–105.

Liu Longgen. (2011). Unarticulated Constituents: Myth or Reality? *Foreign Languages in China, 2*, 50–56.

Liu Longgen, & Wu Sijing. (2013). Another Masterpiece of Minimal Semantics-Introduction to New Theory of Meaning. *Journal of Foreign Languages, 5*, 87–91.

Liu Mingming. (2018). *Formal Semantics Analysis of Focus Adverbs and Interrogative Words in Chinese*. Peking University Press.

Liu Wei. (2017). Research on Chinese Culture and Translation from the Perspective of Frame Semantics. *Education Modernization, 4*, 87–88.

Liu Wenshuo, & Feng Yue. (2017). The Boundary Between Semantics and Pragmatics. *Journal of Jiamusi Vocational Institute, 2*(374), 376.

Liu Xiaomei. (2005). Interpretation of Meta-Language, Semantic Framework, and Semantic Field Comparison Analysis-Talking about Advanced Outward-Oriented Chinese Learning Several Issues with Dictionaries. *Academic Exchange, 8*, 144–148.

Liu Yuhong. (2010). Three Models of Lexical Semantics and Syntactic Interface Research. *Foreign Languages and Their Teaching, 6*, 1–6.

Liu Yuhong. (2011). From Case Grammar Through Frame Semantics to Construction Grammar. *Journal of PLA Foreign Languages Institute, 1*, 5–9.

Liu Yuqian, & Meng Kai. (2019). Factors Affecting the Comprehension of Antonymic Compound Words by Second Language Learners. *Chinese Language Learning, 3*, 69–77.

Liu Yuanfu. (2010). On Semantic Field Assimilation Effect and Translation of EST. *Chinese Science & Technology Translators Journal, 2*, 1–3.

Liu Yuelian. (2010). On Family Resemblance of Euphemism and Taboos. *Foreign Language Education, 6*, 10–13.

Lou Yongqiang. (2012). A Tentative Study of the Pragmatic Perspective in Situation Semantics. *Journal of Chongqing University of Technology (Social Science), 8*, 6–11.

Lu Weizhong. (2011). Understanding and Translation of Metonymy. *Chinese Translators Journal, 2*, 64–67.

Lu Weizhong. (2015). Cognition-Based English-Chinese Contrastive Studies in Lexical Meanings: Some Thoughts on CCLS. *Journal of Foreign Languages, 3*, 33–40.

Lv Gongli. (2003). A Brief Discussion on Formal Pragmatics. *Journal of Foreign Languages, 4*, 15–23.

Lv Jun, & Lu Dawei. (2018). An Empirical Study on the Acquisition of Quantifier Scopes by Chinese L2-English Learners. *Foreign Language Teaching and Research, 5*, 542–555.

Lv Jun, & Wu Fuyun. (2017). On the Learnability of Asymmetrical Distribution of Demonstrative-classifier Phrases in Chinese Relative Clauses: Evidence from L2 Corpus and Sentence Production Studies. *Journal of PLA Foreign Languages Institute, 4*, 62–70.

Editor-in-Chief: Lv Shuxiang. (1999). *Eight Hundred Words of Modern Chinese* (Rev. ed.). Commercial Press.

Lu Jianming. (2004). The Influence of the Specific Meaning of Words on Sentence Comprehension. *Chinese Language Learning, 2*, 1–5.

Lu Jun. (2017). Implicit and Explicit Knowledge of L2 Collocations: A Case of Integrating Corpus-based Analysis with Psycholinguistic Experiments. *Journal of PLA University of Foreign Languages, 3*, 1–9.

Luo Kun. (2011). *A Multiple-Perspective Study of "Kai" as an Ingressive Marker in the Dialect of Ningxian, Gansu Province* (Master's Thesis). Central Chain Normal University, Wuhan.

Luo Senlin, Bai Jianmin, Pan Limin, Han Lei, & Meng Qiang. (2016). Research on Multi-Document Summarization Merging the Sentential Semantic Features. *Transactions of Beijing Institute of Technology, 10*, 1059–1064.

Ma Bosen. (1995). A Multirankand Metafunctional Interpretation of Grammatical Ambiguity in English. *Journal of Foreign Languages, 6*, 14–18, 80.

Ma Qinghua. (2003). Motivations of the Lexical Grammaticalization. *Chinese Language Learning, 2*, 13–18.

Ma Shuhong. (2010). Classification and Acquisition of English Spatial Prepositions by EFL Learners: The Perspective of Categorization Theory. *Journal of PLA University of Foreign Languages, 4*, 64–69, 127.

Ma Yongtian. (2014). The Cognitive Construe of Chinese and English Quantitative Nouns. *Journal of PLA University of Foreign Languages, 2*, 77–85.

Ma Yunxia. (2010). From Body Action to Linguistic Action: The Extension of Verbal Verbs Under Rhetorical Motivation. *Contemporary Rhetoric, 5*, 63–73.

Ma Yunxia. (2012). The Change of the Lexical Meaning of Verbs: From Body Action to Linguistic Action. *Language Teaching and Linguistic Studies, 4*, 89–96.

Mao Haiyan. (2010). Comparison of English and Chinese Lexical Semantics on the Basis of Frame Net: Taking Emotion Words as an Example. *Foreign Language Research, 4*, 48–51.

Meng Kai. (2018). Semantic Conditions for Delexicalization of Disyllabic Verbs in Modern Chinese. *Linguistic Research, 2*, 26–32.

Miao Ju, & Huang Shaoshuang. (2014). Exploring Translational Norms in Light of Conceptual Integration Theory. *Foreign Languages in China, 1*, 94–99.

Ni Bo. (1983). Lexical Functions and Paraphrasing Techniques. *Journal of Foreign Languages, 6*, 39–44.

Niu Changwei, & Pan Haihua. (2015). On the Numeral Constraint in "Mei + Num+ CL + NP + Dou/Ge." *Chinese Language Learning, 6*, 10–18.

Pan Haihua. (1996). An Overview of Discourse Representation Theory. *Foreign Linguistics, 3*, 17–26.

Pan Haihua. (2006). The Semantic Interpretation of the Focus, Tripartite Structures and Dou (都) in Chinese. Studies of the Chinese Language (Eds.), *Grammatical Studies and Explorations* (Vol. 13, pp. 63–84). The Commercial Press.

Pan Haihua, Hu Jianhua, & Huang Zanhui. (2009). Distributional Constraints and Semantic Interpretation of "Mei (every) NP" in Chinese. In Cheng Gong, & Liu Danqing (Eds.), *Studies on Form and Function in Chinese* (pp. 110–122). The Commercial Press.

Pan Qiuping, & Zhang Jiamin. (2017). Semantic Extension of Words Expressing the Five Cardinal Tastes: A Semantic Map Approach. *Essays on Linguistics, 1*, 318–372.

Pan Wenguo. (1997). *An Outline of Chinese-English Constructive Study*. Beijing Language and Culture University Press.

Pan Yanyan. (2003). Frame Semantics: The Theory and Its Applications. *Foreign Languages Research, 5*, 14–18.

Pan Yanyan, & Zhang Hui. (2013). The Cognitive Mechanism of Multimodal Discourses: a Case Study of the Documentary China's National Image Promotion: Perspectives. *Foreign Languages Research, 1*, 10–19, 112.

Pang Yang. (2016). Online Construction of Lexical Synonymy and Cognitive Similarity. *Foreign Language Education, 1*, 29–32.

Pang Yang, & Zhang Shaojie. (2012). The Cognitive-Relevance Interpretation of Lexical Synonymy. *Foreign Language Research, 4*, 85–89.

Peng Jiafa. (2005). Contemporary Debates and Advances in Formal Semantics. *Foreign Language Research, 3*, 46–50.

Peng Jiafa. (2007). New Developments in the Study of Formal Semantics: The Paradigm Shift from Static to Dynamic Meaning Representation. *Journal of Anhui University (Philosophy and Social Sciences Edition), 4*, 68–72.

Peng Rui. (2016). Grammaticalization, Diachronic Construction Grammar, and Constructionalization: The Evolution of the Approaches to Historical Morphosyntax. *Language Teaching and Linguistic Studies, 2*, 14–29.

Peng Yi, & Bai Jiehong. (2010). An Exploration into Divergent Construals of the Polysemy Issue of Adjectives. *Foreign Languages and Their Teaching, 3*, 12–15.

Peng Yuhai. (1997). A Discussion on the Meaning Construct of Sentences. *Russian in China, 2*, 7–11.

Peng Yuhai. (2001). The Descriptive Function of Semantic Presupposition. *Russian in China, 4*, 2–10.

Peng Yuhai, & Yu Xin. (2013). Metaphor Verb of Thinking Activity and Its Metaphorical Semantic Development: About Verbal Polysemy and Metaphor. *Foreign Language Research, 6*, 25–29.

Qian Jun. (1994). Syntactic-Semantics of the Prague School. *Foreign Language Research, 2*, 1–8, 12.

Qiu Shude. (1992). Ambiguity: A Humble Inquiry. *Foreign Languages and Their Teaching, 3*, 16–21.

Qiu Zhenqiang. (2003). Two States of Sentence Meaning and Their Relations. *Journal of Huaihua University, 4*, 71–75.

Ran Yongping. (2005). Recent Trends in Contemporary Pragmatics. *Modern Foreign Languages, 4*, 403–412.

Ren Weiya, & Long Yan. (2012). Categorization and English Vocabulary Teaching. *Journal of the Chinese Society of Education, 1*, 17–18.

Shang Xin. (2011). Cover, Event Type and Two-level Quantification in Chinese "dou" (都) Sentences. *Foreign Language Teaching and Research, 3*, 363–374.

Shao Bin. (2014). Lexicon·Semantics·Cognition·Corpus-An Interview with Professor Dirk Geeraerts. *Journal of Foreign Languages, 2*, 86–92.

Shao Bin. (2019). *Contrastive Studies of English and Chinese Lexis*. Foreign Language Teaching and Research Press.

Shao Bin, He Lianzhen, & Wang Wenbin. (2012). A Corpus-Based Approach to Cognitive Semantic Analysis of English Neologisms-The Case of "Carbon Compounds." *Foreign Language Learning Theory and Practice, 4*, 21–27.

Shao Bin, & Wang Wenbin. (2014). A Corpus-Based Study of Emerging Affixes: The Case of-friendly in English. *Modern Foreign Languages, 4*, 461–471.

Shao Bin, Wang Wenbin, & Huang Danqing. (2017). A Collostructional Analysis of English Amplifiers and the Visualization of Their Semantic Distances. *Foreign Language Teaching and Research, 3*, 379–391.

Shen Jiaxuan. (1985). Types of Ambiguity in English. *Modern Foreign Languages, 1*, 26–35.

Shen Jiaxuan. (1994). A Survey of Studies on Grammaticalization. *Foreign Language Teaching and Research, 4*, 18–25.

Shen Jiaxuan. (2003). Compound Sentences in Three Conceptual Domains: Acting, Knowing, and Uttering. *Studies of the Chinese Language, 3*, 5–14, 97.

Shen Jiaxuan. (2014). A Review of Yuen Ren Chao's Two Articles on Chinese Grammar and Logic. *Language Teaching and Linguistic Studies, 2*, 1–10.

Shen Jiaxuan. (2015). Leftward or Rightward? The Quantifying Direction of "Dou" (都). *Studies of the Chinese Language, 1*, 3–17, 95.

Shen Yuan. (2011). Formal Semantics Under the Challenge of Contextualism: Issues and Responses. *Modern Foreign Languages, 4*, 413–419.

Shen Yuan. (2015). Contextual Studies in Formal Semantics. *Contemporary Linguistics, 4*, 470–483.

Shen Yuan. (2017). Formal Semantics and the Experimental Approach. *Contemporary Linguistics, 2*, 234–245.

Shen Yuan. (2020). Diagnosing Meaning: Using and Misusing Diagnostic Tests. *Contemporary Linguistics, 1*, 87–97.

Shi Chunhong. (2012). The Cognitive Foundation of the Lexical Meaning Structure and the Principles of Lexicographical Definition. *Studies of the Chinese Language, 2*, 114–127, 191.

Shi Chunhong. (2013a). Generative Mechanisms, Semantic Interpretation, and Pragmatic Effects of New "Bei" (被) Constructions. *Contemporary Rhetoric, 1*, 12–28.

Shi Chunhong. (2013b). More About the Valence Hierarchies of Verb-Resultative Constructions and the Issue of Multivalence. *Language Teaching and Linguistic Studies, 5*, 65–74.

Shi Dingxu, & Sun Jiaming. (2016). Frequency Adverb and Probability Adverb: The Case of Changchang and Wangwang. *Chinese Teaching in the World, 3*, 291–302.

Shi Huimin. (2016). Semantic Evolution and Pragmatic Motivation of the Quantitative Disyllabic Compound "Shen-qian" (深浅). *Contemporary Rhetoric, 3*, 87–94.

Shi Yuzhi. (2002). The Motivation of the Disyllabification for the Emergence of the Resultative Construction-The Effect of Phonological Change on the Evolution of Chinese Grammar. *Studies in Language and Linguistics, 1*, 1–14.

Shu Dingfang. (2017). New Developments in Metaphor Research. *English Studies, 6*, 71–79.

Shu Dingfang, & Tang Shuhua. (2008). *Cognitive Lexical Semantics: A Review*. In Shu Dingfang (Eds.), *Pragmatic and Cognitive Perspectives on Language Studies* (pp. 115–145). Shanghai Foreign Language Education Press.

Shuang Wenting, & Yang Runqing. (2018). The Use of Semantic Frames in the Understanding and Teaching of English Word Meanings:With Partial Discussion Devoted to the Use of Corpus in the Teaching of English Word Meanings. *Foreign Languages and Literature, 6*, 138–145.

Si Lianhe. (2003). On the System of Multiple Sentences in Chinese. *Journal of School of Chinese Language and Culture Nanjing Normal University, 2*, 132–138.
Si Lianhe. (2004). On Generation of Sentence Meaning. *Foreign Languages and Their Teaching, 7*, 1–4.
Si Lianhe. (2007). The Interaction Between Structural Meaning and Lexical Meaning in Sentence Interpretation. *Foreign Languages and Their Teaching, 12*, 12–14.
Si Lianhe, & Zhang Weiping. (2005). On the Study of Sentence Semantics. *Journal of Henan Polytechnic University (Social Sciences), 4*, 304–309.
Su Xinchun. (1992). *Words Meaning of Chinese*. Guangdong Education Publishing House.
Su Ying, & Wu Fuxiang. (2016). Usage and Grammaticalization of Adjectival Adverbials in Archaic Chinese. *Linguistic Research, 4*, 42–46.
Sun Chengjiao. (2015). A Contrastive Study of the Lexicalization Patterns of "Take" Type Hand Verbs in English and Chinese. *Journal of PLA University of Foreign Languages, 38*(4), 22–28, 159.
Sun Chongfei, & Zhong Shouman. (2013). The Meaning of the Hand Verb "Take" and Its Cognitive Mechanism. *Foreign Language Research, 3*, 41–47.
Sun Daogong. (2011). *A Study of Lexical-Syntactic Semantic Cohesion*. World Book Publishing Company.
Sun Fenglan. (2016). Translation of *HuangDi Neijing* from the Perspective of Conceptual Metaphor. *Shanghai Journal of Translators, 2*, 84–88.
Sun Haiyan, & Qi Jianxiao. (2020). An Exploration of Learners' Use Characteristics of English Verb Valence Structure. *Foreign Languages and Their Teaching, 3*, 72–81, 148.
Sun Shufang. (2015). *A Contrastive Study of Russian and Chinese Semantics*. The Commercial Press.
Sun Xinxin. (2015). *A Corpus-Based Diachronic Distinctive Collexeme Analysis on the Way Construction* (Master's Thesis). Jiangnan University, Wuxi.
Sun Ya. (2001). Psychospatial Theory and Translation. *Shanghai Science and Technology Translation, 4*, 12–14.
Tan Can. (2018). On the Relationship Between Semantics and Pragmatics. *Young Writers, 3*, 190.
Tan Yesheng. (2010). Schema-Instantiation of Metonymy and the Cognitive Path of Translation. *Foreign Language Teaching and Research, 6*, 465–471.
Tang Jing, & Lei Rong. (2015). Cognitive Interpretation of the Asymmetry in the Syntax-Semantics Interface: A Case Study of "Rob" and "Steal." *Wuhan University of Technology (Social Science Edition), 3*, 586–590.
Tang Ling, & Wang Weiqian. (2014). A Study of English Idiom Comprehension and Memory Based on Conceptual Metaphor Theory. *Journal of Foreign Languages, 5*, 55–58, 65, 112.
Tang Shuhua, Sun Xu, & Chen Yumei. (2011). A Corpus-Based Study on Comparison and Translation Processing of Conventional Metaphor Concept Projection Paths. *Foreign Language Education, 1*, 108–112.
Tang Xianqing, & Li Hongqian. (2016). A Study on the Conceptual Integration Network of Generalized Military Terms Applied Linguistics. *Applied Linguistics, 4*, 42–51.
Tang Yiwen, & Chen Xiaoxiang. (2018). An Experimental Study on Chinese Learners' Interpretation of Quantitative Jurisdiction in English. *Foreign Language Teaching and Research, 2*, 205–217.
Tian Bing. (2003). Cognitive Semantic Frames of Polysemous Words and Cognitive Environments of Dictionary Users. *Modern Foreign Languages, 4*, 340–350.
Tian Bing. (2016). A Study on the Design Characteristics of Large-Scale Chinese-Foreign dictionary Compilation: Taking the Chinese-French Dictionary as an Example. *Dictionary Research, 5*, 7–16.
Tian Xiaoyu, & Zhang Weiwei. (2020). A Study on the Variation of Analytical Causative Construction in Chinese Variants--Multi-Class Logistic Regression Modeling. *Foreign Languages and Their Teaching, 3*, 22–81, 148.

Tian Zhen. (2012). An Empirical Study on the Relevance of Chinese Existential Constructions and Verbs. *Language Teaching and Research, 3*, 58–65.
Tong Fuqi. (2012). *Linguistic Expression of Conditional Relationship Category* (PhD Thesis). Jilin University, Changchun.
Wang Feng, & Wei Jiuqiao. (2017). Semantic Evolution, Language Contact and Vocabulary Transmission—The Origin and Transmission of * la "tea." *National Languages, 5*, 61–78.
Wang Lirong. (2005). On Translation from the Perspective of Frame Theory. *Chinese Translators Journal, 5*, 2–32.
Wang Lirong. (2006). Implicit-Explicit Translation and Explicit-Implicit Translation and Their Cognitive Interpretation. *Foreign Language Teaching and Research, 5*, 208–214.
Wang Lirong. (2011). The Enlightenment of Frame Semantics on Second Language Vocabulary Teaching. *Foreign Language Research, 3*, 49–56.
Wang Shaohua, & Wang Peng. (2011). An Analysis of the Conceptual Integration of Xiehouyu. *Foreign Language Research, 4*, 40–44.
Wang Xinxiao, Yan Xiuying, Zhang Jijia, & Dong Fanghong. (2017). Spatial Metaphors and Weight Metaphors of Seniority Rules in the Semantic Processing of Kinship Words of the Same Generation: Evidence from Chinese Korean nationality and the Han Nationality. *Acta Psychologica Sinica, 2*, 174–185.
Wang Zhen, Yang Sihui, & Hu Dongping. (2010). A FT-Based Study on Translation Strategies of Luxun's Metaphor—Take English Versions of A Madman's Diary and Medicine as Example. *Journal of Hunan Agricultural University, 1*, 87–94.
Wang Anmin, & Wang Jian. (2006). From the Perspective of Cognitive Metaphor Theory: On the Arrangement of Monosyllabic Word Senses and Compound Entries in Outward-Oriented Chinese-English Learner's Dictionaries. *Lexicographical Studies, 4*, 92–98.
Wang Chunhui. (2016). The Accessible Factors of Counterfactual Meaning of Chinese Conditionals. *Chinese Language Learning, 1*, 12–20.
Wang Fen, & Chen Xiongxin. (2010). Application Research of English Vocabulary Instruction Guided by the Prototype Theory. *Foreign Languages and Literature, 4*, 114–116.
Wang Fufang. (2012). Challenges of Cognitive Semantics to the Classical View of Lexical Meaning. In *Lexicographical Studies (Vol. 2), Compiled by the Secretariat of Shanghai Lexicographical Association* (pp. pp. 115–126). Shanghai Lexicography Publishing House.
Wang Fufang. (2015). Meaning Dictionary: Cognitive Organization and Exemplar of Entry Description. *Lexicographical Studies, 5*, 9–17.
Wang Hongqi. (2020). Is There Any Ambiguous Syntactic Pattern. *Chinese Language Learning, 3*, 3–12.
Wang Hongwei. (2012). Four Guiding Principles of Cognitive Semantics. *Journal of Huaibei Normal University (Philosophy and Social Sciences), 3*, 103–106.
Wang Honglei. (2015). An Empirical Study on Verb Valency in Chinese Based on Aphasic Patients. *Foreign Languages Research, 6*, 42–47.
Wang Juan, & Zhang Jijia. (2016). The effects of category consistency and neighborhood size of the semantic radical on the semantic processing of Chinese character. *Acta Psychologica Sinica, 11*, 1390–1400.
Wang Kun. (2014). A Contrastive Study of Transitivity and Logical-Semantic Relations in Chinese-English Clauses: A Case Study of the English Translation of Mo Yan's Nobel Lecture. *Foreign Language and Literature, 1*, 30–35.
Wang Li. (1980). *A Draft History of the Chinese Language* (Rev. ed.). Zhonghua Book Company.
Wang Lin. (2014). Investigating Syntactic Variation in Chinese-English Code-Switching: A Treebank-Based Analysis of Verbal Syntactic Valency. *Foreign Languages and Their Teaching, 5*, 47–53.
Wang Meng, & Wu Wenbin. (2012). The Unselective Binding Analysis of Chinese Donkey Sentences. *Journal of Hebei University, 2*, 119–122.
Wang Mingshu. (2017). Cognitive Mechanism in Translation Principles and Strategies/Methods from Perspective of Conceptual Metaphor. *Foreign Language and Literature, 2*, 99–103.

Wang Mingyu. (1996a). Criteria for Defining Synonymous Sentences in Modern Russian. *Russian in China, 1*, 1–7.

Wang Mingyu. (1996b). Classification of Synonymous Sentences in Modern Russian. *Russian in China, 2*, 1–5.

Wang Qian, Luo Senlin, Han Lei, & Pan Limin. (2014). Chinese Sentential Semantic Type Recognition Based on Predicate and Sentential Semantic Type Chunk. *Journal of Chinese Information Processing, 2*, 8–16.

Wang Renqiang. (2010). An Introduction to Cognitive Lexicography. *Foreign Language Research, 5*, 36–39.

Wang Renqiang, Huo Zhongzhen, & Deng Jiao. (2019). A Study of the Representation Strategies of Heterosemy in A New Century Chinese-English Dictionary (2016). *Foreign Language and Literature, 2*, 11–22.

Wang Renqiang, & Yang Xu. (2017). The Word Class of "Publish" and the Endocentric Construction Controversy: A Study Based on Dual-Layer Categorization Theory. *Chinese Linguistics, 4*, 26–35, 95–96.

Wang Shiyuan. (2011). The Evolution of Evolutionary Linguistics. *Contemporary Linguistics, 1*, 1–21, 93.

Wang Shouyuan, & Liu Zhenqian. (2003). Metaphor and Culture in Language Teaching. *Foreign Language Education, 1*, 48–53.

Wang Tao, & Yang Yiming. (2017). An fMRI Study on Neural Substrates of Nouns and Verbs in Late High-Proficient Chinese-English Bilinguals. *Foreign Language Research, 6*, 60–66.

Wang Tianyi, & Wan yin. (2010). From "Meaning as Use" to "Usage-Based Models". *Foreign Language Education, 6*, 6–9.

Wang Tianyi, & Wang Yin. (2017). Embodied-Cognitive Linguistics in the Viewpoint of Postmodernism. *Foreign Language Education, 4*, 12–17.

Wang Tongwei. (2009). A Cognitive Perspective on Chinese Synonyms. *Social Scientist, 1*, 145–148.

Wang Wenbin. (2001). *English Lexical Semantics*. Zhejiang Education Publishing House.

Wang Wenbin. (2015). A Figure-Ground Analysis of Cross-linguistic Polysemy: Case Studies of "Eat" in Chinese and "Make" in English. *Foreign Languages and Their Teaching, 5*, 36–41.

Wang Xin. (2012). *Montague Grammar and the Study of Function Words in Modern Chinese*. Beijing Language and Culture University Press.

Wang Yagang. (2010). Semantic Shifts in the Grammaticalization of "Thanks to". *Foreign Language and Literature, 27*(3), 165–170, 184, 216.

Wang Yiguang. (2015). The Semantic Extension Path of the "V-kai"—Based on the Conceptual Structure. *Chinese Language Learning, 1*, 38–46.

Wang Yin. (2014a). Embodied-Cognitive Linguistics in the Viewpoint of Postmodernism. *Foreign Language and Literature, 6*, 61–67.

Wang Yin. (2014b). *Semantic Theory and Language Teaching* (2nd ed.). Shanghai Foreign Language Education Press.

Wang Yin. (2019). Metaphtonymy in Translation: A Case Study of English Film Title Translation into Chinese. *Shanghai Journal of Translators, 3*, 7–12.

Wang Yu, & Sui Mingcai. (2015). A Masked Priming Experimental Study of Recognition of Lexical Ambiguity of Second Language. *Foreign Language Research, 6*, 116–122.

Wang Yuying. (2013). *Studies of Counterfactual Elements in Chinese*. China Social Sciences Press.

Wang Yuan. (2011a). A Critical Review of Semantic Studies on the Progressive Aspect. *Journal of Foreign Languages, 3*, 31–39.

Wang Yuan. (2011b). *Event Decomposition and the Semantics of Durativity* (Doctoral Dissertation). Peking University, Beijing.

Wang Yue, & Zhang Jijia. (2017). Cross-Language Recognition of Ambiguous Words by Chinese EFL Learners in Translation. *Foreign Language World, 4*, 71–78, 87.

Wang Zhiying. (2014). The Construction of "Xiaoxin bie VP" of Strengthening the Negation. *Chinese Language Learning, 4*, 66–72.

Wang Naixing. (2002). General Methodologies in Semantic Prosody Research. *Foreign Language Teaching and Research, 4*, 300–307.
Wei Qingguang, & Qu Zongde. (2008). Semantics, Framing, and Translation Pedagogy. *Journal of Hebei Normal University, 12*, 103–107.
Wei Zaijiang. (2010a). Conceptual Metonymy and Discourse Coherence:The Interface Between Discourse and Cognition. *Foreign Language and Literature, 2*, 57–61.
Wei Zaijiang. (2010b). Three Perspectives on Presuppositions: Representation, Reception and Interaction. *Foreign Language Research, 6*, 49–52.
Wei Zaijiang. (2010c). Presupposition Mechanisms and Cognitive Construal in Object Ellipsis. *Foreign Language Education, 6*, 20–23.
Wei Zaijiang. (2011a). The Textual Appraisal Functions of Pragmatic Presupposition: A Study of the Interface Between Discourse and Pragmatics. *Foreign Languages in China, 2*, 23–29.
Wei Zaijiang. (2011b). A Constructional Approach to Pragmatic Presuppositions—Take Chinese Real Estate Advertisements as Examples. *Foreign Language Research, 3*, 19–23.
Wei Zaijiang. (2011c). A Constructional Approach to Presuppositional Meaning in Zeugma: Contrastive Studies of English and Chinese. *Foreign Languages and Their Teaching, 5*, 5–8.
Wei Zaijiang. (2012). A Study of Pragmatic Presupposition: Its Receptive Psychology and Cognitive Expectation—From the Perspective of Philosophical Hermeneutics. *Foreign Language Research, 5*, 31–36.
Wei Zaijiang. (2013). Pragmatic Presupposition and the Study of Syntactic Construction—Take the Chinese Intransitive Verbs+Objects as Examples. *Foreign Language Research, 4*, 63–67.
Wei Zaijiang. (2016). The Embodied Philosophical View of Conceptual Metonymy. *Modern Foreign Languages, 3*, 358–368, 438.
Wei Zaijiang. (2019). A Metonymic Study of Chinese Idioms: Embodied-Cognitive Linguistics Perspective. *Foreign Languages in China, 6*, 26–33.
Wen Binli. (1997). Donkey Sentences" in English and "Wh-...Wh- Construction in Chinese. *Modern Foreign Languages, 3*, 1–13.
Wen Binli. (1998). A Relative Analysis of Mandarin 'Wh-...Wh-' Construction. *Modern Foreign Languages, 4*, 1–17.
Wen Weiping. (2006). *Studies on Donkey Sentences in English and Chinese* (Doctoral Dissertation). Beijing Language and Culture University, Beijing.
Wen Weiping. (2013). The Licensing of the NPIs Any and Renhe. *Foreign Language Teaching and Research, 2*, 185–199.
Wen Weiping, & Fang Li. (2008). A Study on Chinese Donkey Sentences. *Language Teaching and Research, 5*, 323–331.
Wen Xu. (1998). Introduction to Grammaticalization. *Contemporary Linguistics, 3*, 15–18.
Wen Xu. (2019). Sociocognitive Linguistics Based on Social Cognition. *Modern Foreign Languages, 3*, 293–305.
Wen Xu, & Kuang Fangtao. (2016). English Vocabulary Instruction: From the Perspective of Categorization. *Journal of English Studies, 1*, 111–120.
Wen Xu, & Xiao Kairong. (2019). *Cognitive Translatology*. Peking University Press.
Wen Xu, & Yang Kun. (2015). The Diachronic Study of Construction Grammar—A Basic Introduction to Diachronic Construction Grammar. *Foreign Languages in China, 1*, 26–34.
Wen Xu, & Yang Xu. (2016). Constructionalization: A New Approach to Diachronic Construction Grammar. *Modern Foreign Languages, 6*(5), 5–15, 146.
Wu Anqi. (2004). The Influence of Language Contact on Language Evolution. *Minority Languages of China, 1*, 1–9.
Wu Baoan. (2011). The Semantic Evolution of *Tou* (头) and *Shou* (首). *Studies in Language and Linguistics, 31*(2), 124–127.
Wu Chunxiang, & Cao Chunjing. (2018). On the Semantic Evolution from Sequence to Degree of "*zui Gaoji*" in Contemporary Chinese. *Chinese Language Learning, 2*, 15–24.
Wu Fuyun, & Li Liyuan. (2015). Processing Scope Relations in Chinese: An Online Study on Universal Quantifiers and Negation. *Contemporary Linguistics, 4*, 400–413.

Wu Fuxiang. (2014). Language Contact and Semantic Replication: On Contact-Induced Semantic Change. *Journal of Soochow University, 1*, 113–119.

Wu Fuxiang. (2015). Studies on Semantic Changes in Chinese: Retrospection and Prospection. *Research in Ancient Chinese Language, 4*, 2–13.

Wu Shiyu, & Ma Zheng. (2015). Research on the "Facilitation-Without-Inhibition Phenomenon" in Second Language Lexical Semantic Processing. *Modern Foreign Languages, 5*, 646–655.

Wu Shiyu, Ma Zheng, & Hu Qingqing. (2017). The Development of Lexical and Conceptual Representation in Chinese EFL Learners: Evidence from Mixed-effects Linear Modelling. *Foreign Language Teaching and Research, 5*, 767–779.

Wu Shiyu, & Yang Feng. (2016). Research on the "Cross-Lexical" Effect in Second Language Lexical Semantic Processing. *Foreign Language Education, 3*, 45–50.

Wu Shixiong, & Chen Weizhen. (2004). Development of Category Theory and Its Contributions to Cognitive Linguistics. *Journal of Foreign Languages, 4*, 34–40.

Wu Shuqiong. (2019). Recent Developments in International Cognitive Lexical Semantics. *Foreign Language Education, 3*, 19–25.

Wu Shuqiong, & Liu Dilin. (2020). Quantitative Corpus Methods for Lexical Semantic Studies: Behavioral Profile Analysis. *English Studies, 11*, 153–164.

Wu Shuqiong, & Qiu Huan. (2017). A Study on Syntactic and Semantic Features of Chinese Antonym Co-occurrence Construction *X de Y de*. *Journal of Southwest University of Political Science & Law, 6*, 129–135.

Wu Weishan. (2003). Disyllabification Grammaticalization and the Analyse about Prosodic Word. *Chinese Language Learning, 2*, 8–14.

Wu Weishan. (2012). Polysemy and the Isomorphic Analysis of the Construction "$NP_{patient}$ + VPt + QM." *Chinese Teaching in the World, 2*, 147–157.

Wu Xiaofang, & Xiao Kunxue. (2016). A Corpus-Based Cognitive Linguistics Study on Discrimination of English Verb Near-Synonyms. *Foreign Languages Research, 5*, 46–51.

Wu Yicheng, & Zhou Yong. (2019). Towards a Unified Account of *Dou* in Mandarin Chinese: Implicit and Explicit Domains. *Contemporary Linguistics, 2*, 159–180.

Wu Sijing, & Liu Longgen. (2012). Semantics-Pragmatics "Interface": Misleading or Enlightening? *Foreign Languages in China, 4*, 34–39.

Wu Sijing, & Zhang Jingxin. (2018). Further on Semantics-Pragmatics Interface. *Foreign Language Research, 3*, 7–14.

Wu Guangjun, & Wang Ruiyang. (2019). An Eye-Tracking Study of Cognitive Efforts in Translating English Metaphors Into Chinese: With the Translation of Marriage Metaphors in Economic Texts in Focus. *Foreign Languages in China, 4*, 95–103.

Wu Jihong. (2010). On the Representation of Metaphor in Learner's Dictionaries. *Lexicographical Studies, 2*, 69–77.

Xia Nianxi. (2006). From DRT to SDRT: New Developments in Dynamic Semantic Theory. *Philosophical Trends, 6*, 52–56.

Xia Nianxi. (2010). Logic Explanation of Anaphora from the Perspective of DRT and SDRT. *Journal of Chongqing University of Technology, 7*, 8–11.

Xia Yang, & Li Jia. (2017). Interface Studies Between Semantics and Pragmatics: An Overview of Key Issues in Lexical Pragmatics Research. *Journal of Fujian Institute of Education, 1*, 117–120.

Xiao Jiayan, & Li Hengwei. (2010). A Study of Metaphor Translation from the Perspective of Conceptual Metaphor. *Foreign Languages in China, 5*, 106–111.

Xiao Kairong. (2013). Knowledge System and Cross-Lingual Transmission of Chinese Marital Arts Culture: A Frame Theoretic Approach to the Translation of Louis Cha's Martial Arts Fictions. *Journal of Southwest University, 4*, 94–101.

Xiao Kairong. (2017). *Frame Operation in Poetry Translation: A Cognitive Approach to English Translation of Classical Chinese Poetry*. Science Press.

Xiao Zhiye, & Shen Jiaxuan. (2009). Three Domains of the Sentence-Final Particle Le_2 ($了_2$) in Mandarin Chinese. *Studies of the Chinese Language, 3*, 518–527, 576.

Xie Huiquan. (1987). *On the Grammaticalization of Notional Words, Discourse Studies Forum* (Vol. 4). Nankai University Press.

Xin Xianyun. (2010). Constructing Cognitive Frames in Literary Translation in the Light of Frame Semantics. *Journal of Zhejiang International Studies University, 6*, 54–60.

Xiong Liyan, Zhao Yi, Huang Weichun, Zhong Maosheng, & Huang Xiaohui. (2016). Chinese Name Disambiguation Based on Analysis of Sentential Semantic Structure. *Application Research of Computers, 10*, 2898–2901.

Xiong Zhongru. (2008). *Dou*'s Rightward Semantic Association. *Modern Foreign Languages, 1*, 13–25.

Xiong Zhongru. (2016). The Differences of Quantificational Objects Between *Zong* (总) and *Dou* (都). *Studies of the Chinese Language, 3*, 276–288.

Xu Liejiong. (2014). Is *dou* (都) a Universal Quantifier? *Studies of the Chinese Language, 6*, 498–507.

Xu Liejiong, & Shen Yang. (1998). Thematic Theory and Valence Issues in Chinese. *Contemporary Linguistics, 3*, 3–5.

Xu Shenghuan. (1993). "Presupposition": A New Theory. *Foreign Language Research, 1*, 1–8.

Xu Shenghuan. (2001). Methodology in Linguistics Research: An Open-to-Discussion Syllabus. *Journal of Foreign Languages, 5*, 1–10.

Xu Shijing. (2017). The Constructionalization and Diachronic Evolution of Chinese Adverbial Clauses of Condition. *Research in Ancient Chinese Language, 3*, 29–40, 103.

Xu Zhilin. (2012). Strategies for Semantic Differentiation and Diachronic Investigation of Ambiguous Double Object Constructions. *Linguistic Research, 3*, 24–28.

Xu Jiajin. (2020). Multifactorial Contextual Co-selection: The Recent Development of Corpus Linguistics. *Foreign Languages and Their Teaching, 3*, 1–11.

Xu Yulong. (2010). *Contrastive Linguistics*. Shanghai Foreign Language Education Press.

Xuan Yue. (2010). Is Jiàn in V-jiàn a Grammaticalized Resultative Complement?—On the Differences Between Semantic Change and Grammaticalization. *Chinese Teaching in the World, 24*(1), 46–58.

Xue Mei. (2019). A Study on the English Translation of Novel Metaphors in Chinese. *Shanghai Journal of Translators, 1*, 25–29.

Yang Lili. (2020). Three Quantitative Means of Collostructional Analysis: A Cluster Analysis of "Reason-Purpose" Class Structure Type. *Journal of xi'an International Studies University, 1*, 43–47.

Yang Mingxing, & Zhao Yuqian. (2020). Strategies for Translating Diplomacy-Serving Metaphors with Chinese Characteristics. *Chinese Translators Journal, 1*, 151–159.

Yang Quan, & Feng Zhiwei. (2015). Study of Game Theory Model of "n+n" Structural Ambiguity and Disambiguation. *Linguistic Sciences, 3*, 250–257.

Yang Shiqiao. (1999). A Comparison of Pragmatic Presupposition and Information Focus Between English and Chinese. *Foreign Language Research, 4*, 27–33.

Yang Wei. (2011). An Analysis of the Dictionary Effects of Prototype Theory and Related Cognitive Theories. *Foreign Language Education, 1*, 29–32.

Yang Wenying. (2015). Research on the Interpretation and English Translation of Chinese Poetic Imagery from the Perspective of Conceptual Metonymy: A Case Study of "Leaning on the Railings." *Foreign Languages and Their Teaching, 2*, 75–79.

Yang Yanning. (2019). The Change of Constructions in Old Chinese and Old English: A Study from the Perspective of Non-compositionality. *Foreign Language and Literature Studies, 5*, 451–464.

Yang Zi. (2017). Reapproaching the Negative *Chadian'er* (差点儿) + *Mei* (没) + VP Structure. *Studies in Language and Linguistics, 3*, 31–36.

Yao Mingjun, & Song Bei. (2012). Sentence Meaning and Utterance Meaning. *Journal of Language and Literature Studies, 5*, 52–53.

Yao Yao, & Shi Dingxu. (2015). Background Proposition and Its Trigger: The Case of *Genben* in Affirmative Sentences. *Foreign Language Teaching and Research, 5*, 709–720.

Ye Zinan. (2013). *A Course in Cognitive Metaphor and Translation*. Peking University Press.

Yong Qian. (2014). A Typological Research Towards Counterfactual Conditionals. *Journal of Foreign Languages, 2*, 59–70.

Yong Qian. (2015). The Typological Stage of Morphology in Chinese Counterfactuals. *Journal of Foreign Languages, 1*, 30–41.

Yong Qian. (2017). The Nature and Origin of Counterfactuality. *Foreign Language Teaching and Research, 2*, 227–239.

Yong Qian. (2019). Tense, Aspect and Mood in Counterfactual Clauses. *Journal of Foreign Languages, 2*, 11–23.

Yu Linlong. (2010). The Issue of Meaning Understanding in Formal Pragmatics: From the Perspective of Deep Hermeneutics. *Foreign Language Education, 4*, 44–47.

Yu Xiaomin, & Lin Mingjin. (2018). Prototype, Embodiment, Metaphor: Insights from Prototype Theory for Definitions in English-Chinese Learners' Bilingual Dictionaries. *Journal of Fuzhou University, 1*, 90–94.

Yu Xiujin. (2013). A Tense-aspect Unified Logical Model Based on S-R-E. *Journal of Foreign Languages, 1*, 32–44.

Yu Xiujin, & Jin Lixin. (2019). Cognitive Typology: A Cognitive Interpretation of Cross-Linguistic Diversity and Unity. *Foreign Language Education, 4*, 13–19.

Yu Xiujin, & Zhang Hui. (2017). The Semantic-Syntactic Relevance of TLA with Tense in English and Chinese: Isomorphic Principle vs. Semantic Compatibility Principle in Operator Scope. *Journal of PLA University of Foreign Languages, 2*, 24–32.

Yu Gaofeng. (2011). Cognition and Translation of Metaphor. *Academics, 1*, 159–164, 287.

Yu Lina, & Zeng Dongjing. (2007). The Application of Frame Semantics in Bilingual Online Dictionary Compilation: A View of Semantic and Grammatical Annotation from FrameNet. *English Studies, 4*, 46–52.

Yu Jianliang. (2017). Categorization of Syntactic Construction and Its Polysemy. *Foreign Language Research, 2*, 36–40.

Yu Jue, & Zhang Hui. (2019). A Neurocognitive Investigation of English Phrasal Verbs Processing by Chinese English learners. *Foreign Language Teaching and Research, 6*, 838–849.

Yuan Mengxi. (2017). Analyzing Chinese Adverbs of Emphasis Under Presupposition Theory. *Modern Foreign Languages, 6*, 731–742, 872.

Yuan Yulin. (2000). On the Focus, Presupposition and Territorial Ambiguity of Negative Sentences. *Chinese Language Learning, 2*, 99–108.

Yuan Yulin. (2005). The Summative Function of "dou" and Its Distributive Effect. *Contemporary Linguistics, 4*, 289–304.

Yuan Yulin. (2012). *Focus Structure and Semantic Interpretation of Chinese Sentences*. The Commercial Press.

Yuan Yulin. (2015). Chinese Counterfactual Expression and Its Thinking Characteristics. *Chinese Social Sciences, 8*, 126–144.

Yuan Yujiao, Luo Senlin, Lin Meng, & Pan Limin. (2015). Research on Short Text Recommendation Merging Sentential Semantic Structure Model. *Information Security Research, 1*, 67–73.

Zeng Fangui, & Mao Tiaoyuan. (2010). An Overview of the Development of Formal Pragmatics. *Foreign Language Research, 1*, 67–70.

Zhang Di, Xie Nan, Miao Jing, & Xu Qianli. (2020). The Role of Sentence-Final Particles in Young Children 's Selective Trust of Cognition: A Study Based on Corpus and Experimental Investigation Technology Enhanced. *Foreign Language Education, 1*, 110–116.

Zhang Dong. (2019). Application of Corpus Quantification Method in Construction Grammar Research. *Modern Foreign Languages, 1*, 134–145.

Zhang Han, Luo Senlin, Zou Lili, & Shi Xiumin. (2015). Cross-document Personal Named Disambiguation Merging Sentential Semantic Analysis. *Journal of Zhejiang University (Engineering Edition), 4*, 717–723, 775.

Zhang Hui, & Zhan Weiwei. (2011). Dynamic Construction of Multimodal Metonymy and Metaphor in Advertising Discourse. *Foreign Language Research, 1*, 16–23.

Zhang Hui, & Zhang Tianwei. (2012). A Cognitive Metonymic Perspective of Critical Discourse Analysis. *Foreign Language and Literature, 3*, 41–46.
Zhang Jijia, Liu Xiang, & Wang Yue. (2014). On the Semantic Satiation of Chinese-English Bilinguals. *Foreign Language Teaching and Research, 3*, 423–434.
ZhangJijia, & Lu Aitao. (2010). Automatic Activation of Speech and Glyph in Semantic Processing of Action Pictures. *Studies of Psychology and Behavior, 1*, 1–6.
Zhang Jidong, & Liu Ping. (2005). A General Method of Corpus-Based Synonym Discrimination. *Journal of PLA University of Foreign Languages, 38*(6), 53–28, 159.
Zhuang Jiahua. (2013). Semantic Presupposition and Double Negation. *Foreign Language Research, 3*, 1–7.
Zhang Jianli. (2000). Lexical Field, Semantic Field and Semantic Frame. *Journal of Zhejiang University (Humanities and Social Sciences Edition), 6*, 112–117.
Zhang Jianli. (2010). A Double-Layer Network Model of Polysemy on OVER. *Journal of Zhejiang University (Humanities and Social Sciences Edition), 4*, 179–188.
Zhang Jinzhu. (2015). The Status of Antonymous Compounds in Modern Chinese Vocabulary System. *Language Teaching and Research, 6*, 89–97.
Zhang Jinzhu. (2018). Internal Semantic Structure and Conceptual Hierarchy of Antonymous Compounds in Modern Chinese. *Chinese Language Learning, 4*, 60–66.
Zhang Keding. (1995). Pragmatic Presupposition and Information Center. *Foreign Language Education, 2*, 15–20.
Zhang Keding. (1997). Presupposition and the Emphasis of Split Sentences. *Foreign Languages and Their Teaching, 4*, 24–81, 148.
Zhang Keding. (1999). Presupposition, Nucleus and Focus. *Foreign Language Research, 4*, 22–26.
Zhang Lei, Li Baolun, & Pan Haihua. (2009). Sum Operator suǒ yǒu and Universial Quantification in Chinese. *Chinese Teaching in the World, 4*, 457–464.
Zhang Lei, Li Baolun, & Pan Hiahua. (2012). The Semantic Requirements of Dou: A Study of Its Rightward Association. *Studies in Language and Linguistics, 2*, 63–71.
Zhang Lei, & Pan Haihua. (2019). A Reanalysis of the Semantics of Mei "Every." *Contemporary Linguistics, 4*, 492–514.
Zhang Li. (2010). A Cognitive Typological Explanation of "Le" in Modern Chinese. *Chinese Language Learning, 6*, 12–21.
Zhang Lili. (2012). *Research on the Grammaticalization of Content Words in Oracle-Bone Inscriptions and Bronze Inscriptions: Taking Common Monosyllabic Function Words in Modern Chinese as Examples* (Master's Thesis). Hebei University, Baoding.
Zhang Linying, & Qiu Zhijing. (2012). The Application of Metaphor Theory in English Teaching. *Educational Exploration, 12*, 45–46.
Zhang Ling. (2016). Research on the Presupposition Mechanism of Generalization Sentences. *Foreign Language Education, 4*, 30–33.
Zhang Min. (2010). *Semantic Map Model: Principles, Operations and Application in the Study of Chinese Multifunctional Grammatical Forms*. Editorial Board of *Essays on Linguistics*. Essays on Linguistics (42nd Issue, pp. 3–60). The Commercial Press.
Zhang Minghui, & Cui Xiangning. (2017). A Review of Domestic Studies on Cognitive Semantics. *Journal of Liaodong University (Social Science Edition), 4*, 90–98.
Zhang Peng. (2011). Polysemy Structure and Semantic Expansion Mechanism of Japanese Passive Auxiliary Verb "RERU/RARERU." *Foreign Language Education, 2*, 31–34.
Zhang Ren. (2012). The Semantic-Pragmatic Interface and the Hierarchy of Meaning. *Journal of Changsha Railway Institute (Social Science Edition), 2*, 184–185.
Zhang Renxian. (2008). *Introduction to Formal Pragmatics*. Fudan University Press.
Zhang Shaojie. (2008). The Two-Sided Nature of Generalized Conversational Implicature and Issues over Inferential Models of Implicature. *Foreign Language Teaching and Research, 3*, 196–203.
Zhang Shaojie. (2010). The Theoretical Orientation in Post-Gricean Pragmatics: The Rising of Semantics-Pragmatics Interface Study. *Studies in Foreign Issues, 1*, 3–11.

Zhang Shaoquan. (2010). Lexical Semantic Change: Its Motivations and Cognitive Mechanisms *Foreign Language Research, 1*, 31–35.
Zhang Wei, Liu Xiaobin, Zhou Rong, & Li Manna. (2014). An Empirical Study of Multimodal Metaphor's Application in College English Vocabulary Teaching. *Modern Educational Technology, 7*, 63–70.
Zhang Weiding. (1996). A Psychological Cognitive Study of Ambiguity. *Shandong Foreign Language Education, 2*, 62–66.
Zhang Weiyou. (2005). New Trends in Lexical Studies and Their Implications for Contrastive Analysis between English and Chinese Vocabulary. *Journal of Hubei University (Philosophy and Social Science), 5*, 590–593.
Zhang Weiyou. (2010). *A Comparative Study of English and Chinese Vocabulary*. Shanghai Foreign Language Education Press.
Zhang Weiwei. (2019). Discussion on the Hot Issues and Methods of Conceptual Metaphor and Metonymy. *Foreign Language Education, 4*, 20–27.
Zhang Weiwei, & Nian Liu. (2015). The "Empirical Cycle" of Cognitive Linguistics Research. *Foreign Language Research, 3*, 18–23.
Zhang Weiwei, & Liu Nian. (2016). Advanced Quantitative Methods in Cognitive Linguistics Research. *Journal of Foreign Languages, 1*, 71–79.
Zhang Wenpeng, & Tang Chen. (2011). An ERP Study of Chinese-English Bilingual Processing of Ambiguous Words in Sentence Context. *Foreign Language Education, 4*, 31–35.
Zhang Xin, & Zhang Feng. (2011). A Study on the Relationship Between Sentence Meaning and Utterance Meaning. *Private Science and Technology, 10*, 67–69.
Zhang Xinhe, & Yang Wanbin. (1996). Semantic Field Theory and Translation Practice. *Chinese Translators Journal, 2*, 647–650.
Zhang Xiufang. (2014). Cognitive Rationale for the Polysemy of the "V lai and V qu" Construction. *Journal of Tianjin Foreign Studies University, 5*, 23–28.
Zhang Yanfei. (2012). An Overview of Scalar Implicature in Post-Gricean Pragmatics. *Modern Foreign Languages, 1*, 95–101.
Zhang Yanjun. (2015). Lexicalization of "Later" and Its Meaning Evolution. *Chinese Translators Journal, 4*, 25–31, 95.
Zhang Yisheng. (2004). *Exploration of Adverbs in Modern Chinese*. Xuelin Publishing House.
Zhang Yisheng. (2011). On the Superimposition for Presuppositional Negation. *Chinese Language Science, 5*, 497–510.
Zhang Yu, Meng Lei, Yang Bo, & Zhang Hui. (2012). Study on the Event-Related Potential of Semantic Initiation of Familiar and Unfamiliar Idioms-One of the Cognitive Studies of Idiom Representation and Understanding. *Foreign Language Research, 1*, 21–30.
Zhang Yuan. (2015). The Cognitive Grammar Analysis on the Antonymous Adjectives Co-existing in One Construction. *Foreign Language Research, 1*, 44–49.
Zhang Zhenhua, & Yin Xiangling. (1992). On the Study of Sentence Semantics and the Rise of Sentence Semantics. *Journal of PLA University of Foreign Languages, 4*, 1–14.
Zhang Zhiyi, & Zhang Qingyun. (2001). *Lexical Semantics*. The Commercial Press.
Zhang Zhiyi, & Zhang Qingyun. (2012). *Lexical Semantics* (3rd ed.). The Commercial Press.
Zhang Caiyun. (2010). Pragmatic Ambiguity, Pragmatic Perspective and Literary Text Analysis. *Journal of PLA University of Foreign Languages, 4*, 21–25.
Zhang Caiyun. (2011). From the Perspective of Viewpoint: Pragmatic Ambiguity, Pragmatic Vagueness and Their Pragmatic Values. *Hubei Social Sciences, 4*, 140–142.
Zhang Yihua. (2001). On Sufficient and Necessary Condition and the Definition Function of Prototype Theory. *Dictionary Research, 4*, 47–53.
Zhang Yihua. (2009). *Semantics, Cognition and Definition*. Shanghai Foreign Language Education Press.
Zhang Yihua. (2010). Cognitive Semantics and the Multi-Dimensional Definition for a New Generation of Bilingual/ Bilingualized Learner's Dictionaries. *Foreign Language Teaching and Research, 9*, 374–379.

Zhang Yihua. (2018). Theoretical Background and Research Framework of Cognitive Lexicography and An Introduction to Cognitive Lexicography-Also on Osterman's Cognitive Lexicography. *Dictionary Research, 6*, 1–9.

Zhang Yihua. (2019). A Preliminary Discussion on Cognitive Lexicology. *Foreign Language and Literature, 3*, 1–10.

Zhao Chen. (2010). The Representation of Ambiguous Words in Chinese EFL Learners' Mental Lexicon: A Developmental Model. *Modern Foreign Languages, 1*, 55–63, 109.

Zhao Chen, & Hong Aichun. (2015). Chinese Learners' Interpretation of Ambiguous N + N Combinations in English. *Journal of PLA University of Foreign Languages, 2*, 77–84, 161.

Zhao Chunli, & Shi Dingxu. (2012). Ambiguity Analysis of "NP1 +in NP2 + V + NP3." *Chinese Studies, 4*, 36–42.

Zhao Mi, & Chen Lianfeng. (2011). Context: The Dividing Line Between Semantics and Pragmatics. *Out-of-School Education in China, 4*, 51.

Zhao Xiufeng. (2011). New Development of Conceptual Metaphor Studies: Multimodal Metaphor: Also on Forceville & Urios-Aparisi's Multimodal Metaphor. *Foreign Language Studies, 1*, 1–10, 112.

Zhao Xiufeng, & Feng Dengzheng. (2017). The Construction of China's Image by Multimodal Metonymy: A Case Study of The Economist's Political Cartoon Discourse on China. *Journal of xi'an International Studies University, 2*, 31–36.

Zhao Yanchun. (2003). *Explorations in Cognitive Lexicography*. Shanghai Foreign Language Education Press.

Zhao Yanchun. (2010). A Diagnosis of the Category Theories—Criticism of Cognitive Linguistics Theory III. *Foreign Language and Literature, 6*, 57–63.

Zhao Yongfeng. (2019). A Study on Language Intersubjectivity from Embodied-Cognitive Linguistics: Taking the Evolution of First Pronouns in Chinese as an Example. *Chinese Foreign Languages, 6*, 50–56.

Zhao Yushan & Yang Jie. (2012). On the Equivalence of Deep Logical and Semantic Relations of Sentences in Scientific Translation. *Exam Weekly, 39*, 16–17.

Zhen Fengchao. (2017). Exploring the Integration of Valency Pattern and Meaning: A Corpus-driven Approach. *Foreign Language Research, 4*, 13–18.

Zhen Fengchao, & Yang Feng. (2015). Verb Valence in Learner English: A Corpus-Driven Study of CONSIDER. *Journal of Foreign Languages, 6*, 57–67.

Zhen Fengchao, & Yang Feng. (2016). The Application of Valence Structure and Collocation Valence in English Vocabulary Teaching: Thoughts and Methods. *Foreign Language World, 4*, 35–42.

Zheng Qiuxiu. (2011). On Valence, Actant and Sentence Pattern. *Foreign Language Research, 1*, 90–93.

Zhong Lanying, Chen Xihui, & Zhao Mengjuan. (2013). The Interface Between Metaphor Identification and Sense Treatmentin Corpus-based Learner's Dictionary Making. *Chinese Foreign Languages, 5*, 101–106.

Zhong Shouman, & Wu Anping. (2015). Research on Semantic Relations and Its Analysis Method of Cross-Border Perspective of Disciplines. *Foreign Language Education, 3*, 9–12.

Zhong Jingyao. (2010). Chinese Learners' Errors in English Verbs: Valency and Semantic Roles— A Study Based on CLEC. *Foreign Language Research, 1*, 100–103.

Zhong Weiwei. (2020). How Images and Texts Work in the Translation of Narrative Picture Books. *Journal of Jining University, 5*, 25–32.

Zhou Mingqiang. (2011a). A Cognitive Analysis on Lexical Ambiguity Resolution. *Language Teaching and Research, 1*, 62–68.

Zhou Mingqiang. (2011b). Several Ways of Cognition of Chinese Syntactic Ambiguity. *Zhejiang Academic Journal, 4*, 92–99.

Zhou Qiqiang, & Xie Xiaoming. (2009). Cognitive Lexical Semantics: Important Theories and Their Applications. *Journal of Foreign Languages, 3*, 52–55.

Zhou Rong, & Ran Yongping. (2007). A New Approach to Pragmatic Research—Experimental Pragmatic. *Journal of Foreign Languages, 5*, 2–15.

Zhou Shaoheng. (1978). Some Theories and Research Methods of European and American Semantics. *Linguistic Dynamics, 4*, 11–19.

Zhou Simin, & Zhang Shaojie. (2019). Diachronic Investigation and Methodological Reflection on the Study of Chinese Counterfactual Sentences. *Social Science Front, 12*, 245–249.

Zhou Simin, Zhang Shaojie, & Wu Yan. (2018). An Empirical Study of How Features of a Hypothetical Conditional Sentence Facilitate Generating the Counterfactual Meanings in Mandarin Chinese. *Foreign Language Research, 5*, 80–86.

Zhou Tongquan. (2011). Verb Valence Continuum: Pragmatic Law of Chinese Verb Valence. *Journal of Huazhong Normal University (Humanities and Social Sciences), 5*, 73–81.

Zhou Ying. (2008). Metaphor Translation under Frame Theory. *Foreign Languages and Literature, 2*, 117–120.

Zhou Yong, & Wu Yicheng. (2018). The Intensification Function of "dou" in Mandarin Chinese: An Interactive Perspective. *Foreign Languages and Their Teaching, 6*(26), 35.

Zhou Yong, & Wu Yicheng. (2020). A Contrastive Study of Universal Quantification in Chinese and English. *Modern Foreign Languages, 3*, 293–305.

Zhu Jianxin, & Zuo Guangming. (2012). On the Difference and Relationship Between Cognitive Metaphor and Metonymy. *Foreign Language and Their Teaching, 5*, 59–62.

Zhu Qingxiang. (2019). On the Counterfactual Reading of *yinggai Øde*. *Chinese Language, 1*, 61–73.

Zhu Yan. (2016). Image Schema and Polysemous Categorization: A Case Study on Chinese Verb *Gan*. *Contemporary Linguistics, 1*, 38–50.

Zhu Yongsheng, & Miao Xingwei. (2000). Discourse Functions of Pragmatic Presupposition. *Journal of Foreign Languages, 3*, 25–30.

Zhuo Ru. (2010). On the Semantic Anomaly in Inverted Songs. *Journal of Southwest Agricultural University (Social Science Edition), 1*, 153–154.

Zong Shouyun. (2011). The Path and Motivation of Classifiers' Categorization. *Journal of Shanghai Normal University (Philosophy & Social Sciences Edition), 3*, 109–116.

Zong Shouyun. (2014). The Categorization Function and Its Hierarchical Sequence of Classifiers. *Journal of Shanghai Normal University (Philosophy & Social Sciences Edition), 1*, 120–128.

Zou Chongli. (1995). *Logic, Language and Montague Grammar*. Social Science Literature Press.

Zou Chongli. (1996). Situation Semantics. *Philosophical Studies, 7*, 62–69.

Zou Chongli. (1998). A Review of Discourse Representation Theory. *Contemporary Linguistics, 4*, 20–31.

Zou Chongli. (2000). *Research on Natural Language Logic*. Peking University Press.

Zou Chongli. (2001). The Diversified Development of Natural Language Logic and Its Influence on Information Science. *Philosophical Studies, 1*, 48–54.

Zou Chongli. (2014). Natural Language and Its Implication on the Perspective of DRT. *Journal of Chongqing University of Technology: Social Science, 10*, 5–10.

Abbot, B. (1999). A Formal Approach to Meaning: Formal Semantics and Its Recent Development. *外国语, 1*, 2–20.

Allan, K., & Robinson, J. A. (2012). Introduction: Exploring the "State of the Art" in Historical Linguistics. In K. Allan & J. A. Robinson (Eds.), *Current Methods in Historical Semantics* (pp. 1–13). Mouton de Gruyter.

Allwood, J. (1999). Semantics as Meaning Determination with Semantic Epistemic Operations. In J. Allwood & P. Gärdenfors (Eds.), *Cognitive Semantics*. Benjamins.

Anttila, R. (1972). *An Introduction to Historical and Comparative Linguistics*. Macmillan.

Arlotto, A. (1972). *Introduction to Historical Linguistics*. Houghton Mifflin.

Arppe, A., & Järvikivi, J. (2007). Every Method Counts: Combining Corpus-Based and Experimental Evidence in the Study of Synonymy. *Corpus Linguistics & Linguistic Theory, 3*(2), 131–159.

Arppe, A., Gilquin, G., Glynn, D., Hilpert, M., & Zeschel, A. (2012). Cognitive Corpus Linguistics: Five Points of Debate on Current Theory and Methodology. *Corpora, 5*(1), 1–27.

Asher, N. (1993). *Reference to Abstract Objects in Discourse.* Kluwer Academic Publishers.

Asher, N., & Lascarides, A. (2003). *Logics of Conversation.* Cambridge University Press.

Atlas, J. (1989). *Philosophy Without Ambiguity: A Logico-Linguistic Essay.* Oxford University Press.

Atlas, J. (2005). *Logic, Meaning and Conversation: Semantic Underdeterminacy, Implicature, and Their Interface.* Oxford University Press.

Bach, E. (1989). *Informal Lectures on Formal Semantics.* State University of New York Press.

Bach, K. (1984). Default Reasoning: Jumping to Conclusions and Knowing When to Think Twice. *Pacific Philosophical Quarterly, 65*, 37–58.

Bach, K. (1994). Semantic Slack: What Is Said and More. In S. L. Tsohatzidis (Ed.), *Foundations of Speech Act Theory: Philosophical and Linguistic Perspectives* (pp. 267–291). Routledge.

Bach, K. (2002). Semantics, Pragmatics. In J. K. Campbell, M. O' Rourke, & D. Shier (Eds.), *Meaning and Truth* (pp. 284–292). Seven Bridges Press.

Bach, K. (2004). Minding the Gap. In C. Bianchi (Ed.), *The Semantics/Pragmatics Distinction* (pp. 27–43). CSLI Publications.

Bach, K. (2006). The Excluded Middle: Semantic Minimalism Without Minimal Propositions. *Philosophy and Phenomenological Research, 73*, 435–442.

Bach, K. (2007). Regressions in Pragmatics (and Semantics). In N. Burton-Roberts (Ed.), *Pragmatics* (pp. 24–44). Palgrave Macmillan.

Bach, K. (2010). Implicature vs. Explicature: What's the Difference? In B. Soria & E. Romero (Eds.), *Explicit Communication: Robyn Carston's Pragmatics* (pp. 126–137). Palgrave Macmillan.

Bach, K. (2012). Context Dependence. In M. García-Carpintero & M. Kölbel (Eds.), *The Continuum Companion to the Philosophy of Language* (pp. 153–184). Continuum Publishing Corporation.

Barwise, J., & Perry, J. (1983). *Situations and Attitudes.* MIT Press.

Bloom, A. H. (1981). *The Linguistic Shaping of Thought: A Study in the Impact of Language on Thinking in China and the West.* Lawrence Erlbaum Associates.

Borg, E. (2004). *Minimal Semantics.* Clarendon Press.

Borg, E. (2007). Minimalism Versus Contextualism in Semantics. In G. Preyer & G. Peters (Eds.), *Context-Sensitivity and Semantic Minimalism: New Essays on Semantics and Pragmatics* (pp. 546–571). Oxford University Press.

Borg, E. (2010). Semantic Minimalism. In L. Gummings (Ed.), *The Pragmatics Encyclopedia* (pp. 423–425). Routledge.

Borg, E. (2012). *Pursuing Meaning.* Oxford University Press.

Bybee, J. (2006). Language Change and Universals. In R. Mairal & J. Gil (Eds.), *Linguistic Universals* (pp. 179–194). Cambridge University Press.

Bybee, J., Perkins, R., & Pagliuca, W. (1994). *The Evolution of Grammar: Tense, Aspect, and Modality in the Languages of the World.* University of Chicago Press.

Bynon, T. (1977). *Historical Linguistics.* Cambridge University Press.

Cappelen, H., & Lepore, E. (2005). *Insensitive Semantics.* Blackwell.

Cappelen, H., & Lepore, E. 2006. The Myth of Unarticulated Constituents. In O' Rourke & Washington (Eds.), *Essays in Honor of John Perry* (pp. 199–214). MIT Press.

Carston, R. (2002). *Thoughts and Utterances: The Pragmatics of Explicit Communication.* Blackwell.

Carston, R. (2004a). Relevance Theory and the Saying/Implicating Distinction. In L. Horn & G. Ward (Eds.), *The Handbook of Pragmatics* (pp. 633–656). Blackwell.

Carston, R. (2004b). Truth-Conditional Content and Conversational Implicature. In C. Bianchi (Ed.), *The Semantics/Pragmatics Distinction* (pp. 65–100). CSLI Publications.

Carston, R. (2009). The Explicit/Implicit Distinction in Pragmatics and the Limits of Explicit Communication. *International Review of Pragmatics, 1*, 35–62.

Carston, R. (2010). Explicit Communication and Free Pragmatic Enrichment. In B. Soria & E. Romero (Eds.), *Explicit Communication: Robyn Carston's Pragmatics* (pp. 217–287). Palgrave Macmillan.

Charles, W. G., & Miller, G. A. (1989). Contexts of Antonymous Adjectives. *Applied Psycholinguistics, 10*(3), 357–375.
Chen, P. Y. (2015). *What Do Counterfactuals Do in Language? A Comparison of English and Chinese* (Unpublished MA Thesis). National Chiao Tung University, Hsinchu.
Cheng, L. L. S. (1995). On *dou*-quantification. *Journal of East Asian Linguistics, 4*, 197–234.
Cheng, L. L. S., & Giannakidou, A. (2013). The Non-Uniformity of Wh-indeterminates with Polarity and Free Choice in Chinese. In K. H. Gil, S. Harlow, & G. Tsoulas (Eds.), *Strategies of Quantification* (pp. 44–123). Oxford University Press.
Cheng, L. L. S., & Huang, C. T. J. (1996). Two Types of Donkey Sentence. *Natural Language Semantics, 2*, 121–163.
Chierchia, G. (1992). Anaphor and Dynamic Binding. *Linguistics and Philosophy, 15*, 111–183.
Chierchia, G. (1995). *Dynamics of Meaning. Anaphora, Presupposition and the Theory of Grammar*. University of Chicago Press.
Chierchia, G. (2000). Chinese Conditional and Theory of Conditionals. *Journal of East Asian Linguistics, 9*, 1–54.
Chierchia, G. (2013). *Logic in Grammar: Polarity, Free Choice, and Intervention.* Oxford University Press.
Chomsky, N. (1957). *Syntactic Structures.* Mouton.
Croft, W. (2009). Toward a Social Cognitive Linguistics. In V. Evans & S. Pourcel (Eds.), *New Directions in Cognitive Linguistics* (pp. 395–420). John Benjamins.
Cruse, D. A. (1986). *Lexical Semantics.* Cambridge University Press.
Dąbrowska, E., & Divjak, D. (2019). In E. Dabrowska & D. Divjak (Eds.), *Cognitive Linguistics: Foundations of Language* (pp. 1–10). Mouton de Gruyter.
Davies, M. (2013). *Opposition and Ideology in News Discourse.* Bloomsbury Academic.
Deese, J. (1965). *The Structure of Associations in Language and Thought.* The Johns Hopkins Press.
Diessel, H. (2019). Usage-Based Construction Grammar. In E. Dąbrowska & D. Divjak (Eds.), *Cognitive Linguistics: A Survey of Linguistic Subfields* (pp. 51–80). Mouton de Gruyter.
Divjak, D. (2010). *Structuring the Lexicon: A Clustered Model for Near-Synonymy.* Mouton de Gruyter.
Divjak, D., & Gries, S. Th. (2006). Ways of Trying in Russian: Clustering Behavioral Profiles. *Corpus Linguistics & Linguistic Theory, 2*(1), 23–60.
Divjak, D., Levshina, N., & Klavan, J. (2016). Cognitive Linguistics: Looking Back, Looking Forward. *Cognitive Linguistics, 27*(4), 447–463.
Durkin, P. (2009). *The Oxford Guide to Etymology.* Oxford University Press.
Engberg-Pedersen, E. (1999). Space and Time. In J. Allwood & P. Gardenfors (Eds.), *Cognitive Semantics: Meaning and Cognition.* John Benjamins.
Evans, G. (1980). Pronouns. *Linguistic Inquiry, 11*, 337–362.
Evans, V. (2019). *Cognitive Linguistics: A Complete Guide.* Edinburgh University Press.
Evans, V., & Green, M. (2006). *Cognitive Linguistics: An Introduction.* Edinburgh University Press.
Evans, V., & Pourcel, S. (2009). *New Directions in Cognitive Linguistics.* John Benjamins.
Fillmore, C. J. (1988). The Mechanisms of Construction Grammar. *Proceedings of the Fourteenth Annual Meeting of Berkeley Linguistic Society* (pp. 35–55). Berkeley Linguistic Society.
Firth, J. R. (1957). *Papers in Linguistics, 1931–1951.* Oxford University Press.
Freeborn, D. (2009). *From Old English to Standard English: A Course Book in Language Variation Across Time.* Shanghai Foreign Language Education Press.
García-Carpintero, M., & Kölbel, M. (2008). *Relative Truth.* Oxford University Press.
Garrett, M., & Harnish, R. (2007). Experimental Pragmatics: Testing for Implicature. *Pragmatics & Cognition, 1*, 65–90.
Garrett, M., & Harnish, R. (2009). Q-phenomena, I-phenomena and Impliciture: Some Experimental Pragmatics. *International Review of Pragmatics, 1*, 84–117.
Geeraerts, D. (2006). Methodology in Cognitive Linguistics. In G. Kristiansen, et al. (Eds.), *Cognitive Linguistics: Current Applications and Future Perspectives* (pp. 21–49). Mouton de Gruyter.

Geeraerts, D. (2010). *Theories of Lexical Semantics*. Oxford University Press.
Geeraerts, D. (2015). Lexical Semantics. In E. Dabrowska & D. Divjak (Eds.), *Handbook of Cognitive Linguistics* (pp. 273–295). Mouton de Gruyter.
Geeraerts, D., Grondelaers, S., & Speelman, D. (1999). *Convergentie en Divergentie in de Nederlandse Woordenschat. Een onderzoek naar kleding-en voetbaltermen*. Meertens Instituut.
Gilquin, G., & Gries, S. Th. 2009. Corpora and Experimental Methods: A State-of-the-art Review. *Corpus Linguistics and Linguistic Theory, 1*, 1–26.
Glynn, D. (2009). Polysemy, Syntax, and Variation: A Usage-Based Method for Cognitive Semantics. In V. Evans & S. Pourcel (Eds.), *New Directions in Cognitive Linguistics* (pp. 77–106). John Benjamins.
Glynn, D. (2010). Lexical Fields, Grammatical Constructions, and Synonymy: A Study in Usage-based Cognitive Semantics. In H. J. Schmid & S. Handl (Eds.), *Cognitive Foundations of Linguistic Usage Patterns* (pp. 118–189). Mouton de Gruyter.
Glynn, D., & Fischer, K. (Eds.). (2010). *Quantitative Cognitive Semantics: Corpus-Driven Approaches*. Mouton de Gruyter.
Glynn, D., & Robinson, J. (Eds.). (2014a). *Polysemy and Synonymy: Corpus Methods and Applications in Cognitive Semantics*. John Benjamins.
Glynn, D., & Robinson, J. (2014b). *Corpus Methods for Semantics: Quantitative Studies in Polysemy and Synonymy*. John Benjamins.
Goldberg, A. E. (1995). *Constructions: A Construction Grammar Approach to Argument Structure*. Chicago University Press.
Grice, H. P. (1975). Logic and Conversation. In P. Cole & J. L. Morgan (Eds.), *Speech Acts* (pp. 41–58). Academic Press.
Grice, H. P. (1978). Further Notes on Logic and Conversation. In P. Cole (Ed.), *Syntax and Semantics 9: Pragmatics* (pp. 113–127). Academic Press.
Grice, H. P. (1989). *Studies in the Way of Words*. Harvard University Press.
Gries, S. Th., & Deshors, S. (2014). Using Regressions to Explore Deviations Between Corpus Data and a Standard Target: Two Suggestions. *Corpora, 1*, 109–136.
Gries, S. Th., & Divjak, S. D. (2009). Behavioral Profiles: A Corpus-Based Approach Towards Cognitive Semantic Analysis. In V. Evans & S. S. Pourcel (Eds.), *New Directions in Cognitive Linguistics* (pp. 57–75). John Benjamins.
Gries, S. Th., & Hilpert, M. (2008). The Identification of Stages in Diachronic Data: Variability-Based Neighbor Clustering. *Corpora, 3*(1), 59–81.
Gries, S. Th., & Hilpert, M. (2012). Variability-Based Neighbor Clustering: A Bottom-Up Approach to Periodization in Historical Linguistics. In T. Nevalainen & E. C. Traugott (Eds.), *The Oxford Handbook of the History of English* (pp. 134–144). Oxford University Press.
Gries, S. Th., & Otani, N. (2010). Behavioral Profiles: A Corpus-Based Perspective on Synonymy and Antonymy. *ICAME Journal, 34*, 121–150.
Gries, S. Th., & Stefanowitsch, A. (2004a). Extending Collostructional Analysis: A Corpus-based Perspective on "Alternations". *International Journal of Corpus Linguistics, 9*(1), 97–129.
Gries, S. Th., & Stefanowitsch, A. (2004b). Covarying Collexemes in the Into-causative. In M. Achard & S. Kemmer (Eds.), *Language, Culture and Mind* (pp. 225–236). CSLI Publications.
Gries, S. Th. (2001). A Corpus-Linguistic Analysis of English -ic vs -ical Adjectives. *ICAME Journal, 25*, 65–108.
Gries, S. Th. (2010). Behavioral Profiles: A Fine-grained and Quantitative Approach in Corpus-based Lexical Semantics. *The Mental Lexicon, 5*(3), 323–346.
Groenendijk, J., & Stokhof, M. (1990). Dynamic Montague Grammar. In L. Kálmán & L. Pólos (Eds.), *Papers from the Second Symposium on Logic and Language* (pp. 3–48). Akademiai Kiado.
Groenendijk, J., & Stokhof, M. (1991). Dynamic Predicate Logic. *Linguistics and Philosophy, 14*(1), 39–100.
Gronder, D., Klein, N., Carbary, K., & Tanenhaus, M. (2007). *Experimental Evidence for Rapid Interpretation of Pragmatic Some*. Paper presented at XPRAG, Berlin.

Gross, D., Fischer, U., & Miller, G. (1989). The Organization of Adjectival Meanings. *Journal of Memory & Language, 28*(1), 92–106.

Hall, A. (2008). Free Enrichment or Hidden Indexicals? *Mind & Language, 23*, 426–456.

Hall, A. (2014). "Free" Enrichment and the Nature of Pragmatic Constraints. *International Review of Pragmatics, 1*, 1–28.

Halverson, S. (2013). Implications of Cognitive Linguistics for Translation Studies. In A. Rojo & I. Ibarretxe-Antuñano (Eds.), *Cognitive Linguistics and Translation: Advances in Some Theoretical Models and Applications* (pp. 31–73). Mouton de Gruyter.

Hanks, P. (1996). Contextual Dependency and Lexical Sets. *International Journal of Corpus Linguistics, 1*(1), 75–98.

Hanks, P. (2007). *Lexicology: Critical Concepts in Linguistics.* Routledge.

Harder, P. 2010. *Meaning in Mind and Society: A Functional Contribution to the Social Turn in Cognitive Linguistics.* Walter de Gruyter.

Heim, I. (1982). *The Semantics of Definite and Indefinite Noun Phrases.* University of Massachusetts.

Heim, I. (1990). E-Type Pronoun and Donkey Anaphor. *Linguistics and Philosophy, 13*, 137–177.

Heine, B., & Kuteva, T. (2002). *World Lexicon of Grammaticalization.* Cambridge University Press.

Hilpert, M. (2006). Distinctive Collexeme Analysis and Diachrony. *Corpus Linguistics and Linguistic Theory, 2*, 243–256.

Hilpert, M. (2008). *Germanic Future Constructions: A Usage-Based Approach to Language Change.* Benjamins.

Hilpert, M. (2012a). Diachronic Collostructional Analysis Meets the Noun Phrase: Studying Many a Noun in COHA. In T. Nevalainen & E. C. Traugott (Eds.), *The Oxford Handbook of the History of English* (pp. 233–244). Oxford University Press.

Hilpert, M. (2012b). Diachronic Collostructional Analysis: How to Use It, and How to Deal with Confounding Factors. In K. Allan & J. A. Robynson (Eds.), *Current Methods in Historical Semantics* (pp. 133–160). Mouton de Gruyter.

Hilpert, M. (2013). *Constructional Change in English: Developments in Allomorphy, Word Formation, and Syntax.* Cambridge University Press.

Ho-Abdullah, I. (2010). *Variety and Variability: A Corpus-based Cognitive Lexical-semantics Analysis of Prepositional Usage in British, New Zealand and Malaysian English.* Peter Lang.

Hock, H. H. (1986). *Principles of Historical Linguistics.* Mouton de Gruyter.

Holmqvist, K. 1999. Conceptual Engineering. In J. Allwood & P. Gardenfors (Eds.), *Cognitive Semantics: Meaning and Cognition.* John Benjamins.

Horn, L. (2009). WJ-40: Implicature, Truth, and Meaning. *International Review of Pragmatics, 1*, 3–34.

Huang, S. Z. (1996). *Quantification and Predication in Mandarin: A Case Study of dou.* University of Pennsylvania.

Huang, S. Z. (2005). *Universal Quantification with Skolemization as Evidenced in Chinese and English.* Edwin Mellen.

Huang, Y. (2013a). Micro- and Macro-Pragmatics: Remapping Their Terrains. *International Review of Pragmatics, 5*, 129–162.

Huang, Y. (2013b). *Unarticulated Constituents in Neo-Gricean Pragmatics.* Papers presented at the 1st International Pragmatics Conference of the Americas.

Huang, Y. (2014). *Pragmatics* (2nd ed.). Oxford University Press.

Hudson, G. (2005). *Essential Introductory Linguistics.* Peking University Press.

Israel, M. (1996). The Way Constructions Grow. In A. Godlberg (Ed.), *Conceptual Structure, Discourse and Language* (pp. 217–230). CSLI Publications.

Jansegers, M., & Gries, S. Th. (2017). Towards a Dynamic Behavioral Profile: A Diachronic Study of Polysemous "Sentir" in Spanish. *Corpus Linguistics and Linguistic Theory, 16*(1): 1–43.

Jaszczolt, K. M. (2005). *Default Semantics: Foundations of a Compositional Theory of Acts of Communication.* Oxford University Press.

Jaszczolt, K. M. (2007). The Syntax-Pragmatics Merger: Belief Reports in the Theory of Default Semantics. *Pragmatics & Cognition, 3*, 41–64.

Jaszczolt, K. M. (2008). Semantics and Pragmatics: The Boundary Issue. In K. von Heusinger., P. Portner, & C. Maienborn (Eds.), *Semantics: An International Handbook of Natural Language Meaning* (pp. 15–24). Mouton de Gruyter.

Jaszczolt, K. M. (2010). Default Semantics. In B. Heine & H. Narrog (Eds.), *The Oxford Handbook of Linguistic Analysis* (pp. 193–221). Oxford University Press.

Jaszczolt, K. M. (2011). Salient Meanings, Default Meanings and Automatic Processing. In K. Jaszczolt & K. Allan (Eds.), *Salience and Defaults in Utterance Processing* (pp. 11–33). Mouton de Gruyter.

Jeffries, L. (2010). *Opposition in Discourse: The Construction of Oppositional Meaning*. Continuum.

Jones, S. (2002). *Antonymy: A Corpus-Based Perspective*. Routledge.

Jones, S., Murphy, L., Paradis, C., & Willners, C. (2012). *Antonyms in English: Construals, Constructions and Canonicity*. Cambridge University Press.

Kamp, H. (1981). A Theory of Truth and Semantic Representation. In J. Groenendijk, T. Janssen, & M. Stokhof (Eds.), *Formal Methods in the Study of Language: Proceedings of the Third Amsterdam Colloquium* (pp. 277–322). Mathematisch Centrum. Reprinted in Groenendijk, J., Janssen T. M. V., & Stokhof, M. (Eds.). (1984). *Truth, Interpretation and Information* (pp. 1–42). Foris Publications.

Kamp, H., & Partee, B. (2004). *Context-Dependence in the Analysis of Linguistic Meaning*. Elsevier.

Kerremans, D., Stegmayr, S., & Schmid, H. J. (2010). The NeoCrawler: Identifying and Retrieving Neologisms from the Internet and Monitoring Ongoing Change. In K. Allan & J. A. Robinson (Eds.), *Current Methods in Historical Semantics* (pp. 59–96). Mouton de Gruyter.

King, J., & Stanley, J. (2005). Semantics, Pragmatics, and the Role of Semantic Content. In G. S. Zoltan (Ed.), *Semantics Versus Pragmatics* (pp. 111–164). Oxford University Press.

Kölbel, M. (2008). Introduction: Motivations for Relativism. In M. García-Carpintero & M. Kölbel (Eds.), *Relative Truth* (pp. 1–38). Oxford University Press.

Koptjevskaja-Tamm, M. (2012). New Directions in Lexical Typology. *Linguistics, 50*(3), 373–394.

Kostić, N. (2015). The Textual Profile of Antonyms: A Corpus-Based Study. *Linguistics, 53*(4), 649–675.

Kristiansen, G., & Dirven, R. (2008). *Cognitive Sociolinguistics: Language Variation, Cultural Models, Social Systems*. Mouton de Gruyter.

Kuryłowicz, J. (1965). The Evolution of Grammatical Categories. *Diogenes, 13*(51), 55–71.

Leech, G. N. (1983). *Semantics* (2nd ed.). Penguin Books.

Levinson, S. (2000). *Presumptive Meanings: The Theory of Generalized Conversational Implicature*. MIT Press.

Levinson, S. C. (1983). *Pragmatics*. Cambridge University Press.

Levinson, S. C. (1995). Three Levels of Meaning. In F. Palmer (Ed.), *Grammar and Meaning* (pp. 90–115). Cambridge University Press.

Levinson, S. C. (2000a). H. P. Grice on location on Rossel Island. In S. S. Chang, L. Liaw, & J. Ruppenhofer (Eds.), *Proceedings of the 25th Annual Meeting of the Berkeley Linguistic Society* (pp. 210–224). Berkeley Linguistic Society.

Levinson, S. C. (2000b). *Presumptive Meanings: The Theory of Generalized Conversational Implicature*. The MIT Press.

Lewis, D. (1972). General Semantics. In D. Davidson & G. Harman (Eds.), *Semantics of Natural Language* (pp. 169–218). D. Reidel.

Li, X., & Xiang, M. (2019). Semantic Evolution at the Microscopic Level: The Case of suoyi. *Language Sciences, 74*, 110–126.

Lin, J. W. (1998). Distributivity in Chinese and Its Implications. *Natural Language Semantics, 6*, 201–243.

Liu, D. L. (2013). Salience and Construal in the Use of Synonymy: A Study of Two Sets of Near-synonymous Nouns. *Cognitive Linguistics, 24*(1), 67–113.

Lobanova, A., Van der Kleij, T., & Spenader, J. (2010). Defining Antonymy: A Corpus-Based Study of Opposites by Lexico-syntactic Patterns. *International Journal of Lexicography, 23*(1), 19–53.

Lyngfelt, B. (2018). Introduction: Constructions and Constructicography. In B. Lyngfelt, L. Borin, K. Ohara, & T. T. Torrent (Eds.), *Constructicography: Construction Development Across Languages* (pp. pp. 1–18). John Benjamins.

Lyons, J. (1995). *Linguistic Semantics: An Introduction.* Cambridge University Press.

MacFarlane, J. (2007). Semantic Minimalism and Nonindexical Contextualism. In G. Preyer & G. Peters (Eds.), *Context-Sensitivity and Semantic Minimalism: New Essays on Semantics and Pragmatics* (pp. 240–250). Oxford University Press.

MacFarlane, J. (2009). Nonindexical Contextualism. *Synthesis, 166*, 231–250.

Montague, R. (1974). *Formal Philosophy: Selected Papers of Richard Montague.* Yale University Press.

Muehleisen, V., & Isono, M. (2009). Antonymous Adjectives in Japanese Discourse. *Journal of Pragmatics, 41*, 2185–2203.

Murphy, M. L., Paradis, C., Willners, C., & Jones, S. (2009). Discourse Functions of Antonymy: A Cross-Linguistic Investigation of Swedish and English. *Journal of Pragmatics, 41*, 2159–2184.

Nerlich, B., & Clarke, M. (1992). Outline of a Model for Semantic Change. In G. Kellermann & M. D. Morrissey (Eds.), *Diachrony Within Synchrony: Language History and Cognition* (pp. 125–141). Peter Lang.

Noël, D. (2007). Diachronic Construction Grammar and Grammaticalization Theory. *Functions of Language, 2*(14), 177–202.

Noveck, I. A., & Reboul, A. (2008). Experimental Pragmatics: A Gricean Turn in the Study of Language. *Trends in Cognitive Sciences, 12*, 425–431.

Noveck, I. A., & Sperber, D. (2007). The Why and How of Experimental Pragmatics: He Case of Scalar Inference. In N. Burton-Roberts (Ed.), *Pragmatics* (pp. 184–212). Macmillan.

Ohara, K. H., Fujii, S., Saito, H., Ishizaki, S., Ohori, T. & Suzuki, R. (2003). *The Japanese FrameNet Project: A Preliminary Report.* Proceedings of Pacific Association for Computational Linguistics.

Palmer, F. R. (2001). *Mood and Modality* (2nd ed.). Cambridge University Press.

Panizza, D., & Chierchia, G. (2008). *Two Experiments on the Interpretation of Numerals.* Papers presented at Workshop on Experimental Pragmatics/Semantics, the 30th Annual Convention of the German Society of Linguistics.

Panther, K. U., & Thornburg, L. 2012. Antonymy in Language Structure and Use. In M. Brdar, M. Z. Fuchs, & I. Raffaelli (Eds.), *Cognitive Linguistics Between Universality and Variation* (pp. 161–188). Cambridge Scholars.

Paradis, C. (2012). Lexical Semantics. In C. A. Chapelle (Ed.), *The Encyclopedia of Applied Linguistics* (pp. 3347–3356). Wiley-Blackwell.

Paradis, C., Löhndorf, S., Van de Weijer, J., & Willners, C. (2015). Semantic Profiles of Antonymic Adjectives in Discourse. *Linguistics, 53*(1), 153–191.

Parikh, P. (2010). *Language and Equilibrium.* The MIT Press.

Park, J., Nam, S., Kim, Y., Hahm, Y., Hwang, D., & Choi, K. S. (2014). *Frame-Semantic Web: A Case Study for Korean.* Proceedings of the 2014 International Conference on Posters & Demonstrations Track.

Partee, B. H. (1975). Montague Grammar and Transformational Grammar. *Linguistic Inquiry, 6*(2), 203–300.

Partee, B. H. (1991). Topic, Focus and Quantification. In S. Moore & A. Wyner (Eds.), *Proceedings of Semantics and Linguistic Theory 1* (Cornell Working Papers in *Linguistics* 10, pp. 159–187). Cornell University.

Partee, B. H. (1995). Quantificational Structures and Compositionality. In E. Bch, E. Jelinek, A. Kratzer, & B. H. Partee (Eds.), *Quantification in Natural Languages* (pp. 541–601). Kluwer Academic.

Partee, B. H. (2011). Montague Grammar. In J. van Benthem & A. ter Meulen (Eds.), *Handbook of Logic and Language* (2nd ed., pp. 3–94). Elsevier.

Partington, A. (1998). *Patterns and Meanings: Using Corpora for English Language Research and Teaching*. John Benjamins.
Perek, F. (2016). Using Distributional Semantics to Study Syntactic Productivity in Diachrony—A Case Study. *Linguistics, 54*(1), 149–189.
Perek, F. (2018). Recent Change in the Productivity and Schematicity of the *way*-construction: A Distributional Semantic Analysis. *Corpus Linguistics and Linguistic Theory, 14*(1), 65–97.
Perek, F., & Hilpert, M. (2017). A Distributional Semantic Approach to the Periodization of Change in the Productivity of Constructions. *International Journal of Corpus Linguistics, 22*(4), 490–520.
Perry, J. (1986). Thought Without Representation. *Supplementary Proceedings of the Aristotelian Society, 60*, 268–283. Reprinted In Perry. J. (Ed.). (1993). *The Problem of the Essential Indexical and Other Essays* (pp. 205–218). Oxford University Press.
Perry, J., et al. (1998). Indexicals, Contexts and Unarticulated Constituents. In D. Westertahl (Ed.), *Computing Natural Language* (pp. 1–11). CSLI Publications.
Predelli, S. (2005). *Contexts: Meaning, Truth and the Use of Language*. Oxford University Press.
Recanati, F. (1993). *Direct Reference: From Language to Thought*. Blackwell.
Recanati, F. (2001). What Is Said. *Synthese, 128*, 75–91.
Recanati, F. (2002a). Does Linguistic Communication Rest on Inference? *Mind & Language, 17*, 105–126.
Recanati, F. (2002b). Unarticulated Constituents. *Linguistics and Philosophy, 25*, 299–345.
Recanati, F. (2004a). *Literal Meaning*. Cambridge University Press.
Recanati, F. (2004b). Pragmatics and Semantics. In L. Horn & G. Ward (Eds.), *The Handbook of Pragmatics* (pp. 442–462). Blackwell.
Recanati, F. (2005a). What Is Said and the Semantics/Pragmatics Distinction. In C. Bianchi (Ed.), *The Semantics/Pragmatics Distinction: Proceedings from WOC 2002* (pp. 45–64). The University of Chicago Press.
Recanati, F. (2005b). Literalism and Contextualism: Some Varieties. In G. Preyer & G. Peter (Eds.), *Contextualism in Philosophy: Knowledge, Meaning, and Truth* (pp. 171–196). Clarendon Press.
Recanati, F. (2010). *Truth-Conditional Pragmatics*. Oxford University Press.
Recanati, F. (2012). Contextualism: Some Varieties. In K. Jaszczolt (Ed.), *The Cambridge Handbook of Pragmatics* (pp. 135–149). Cambridge University Press.
Robinson, J. A. (2010). Awesome Insights into Semantic Variation. In D. Geeraerts. G, Kristiansen, & Y. Peirsman (Eds.), *Advances in Cognitive Sociolinguistics* (pp. 85–109). Mouton de Gruyter.
Sandra, D., & Rice, S. (1995). Network Analyses of Prepositional Meaning: Mirroring Whose Mind-The Linguist's or the Language User's? *Cognitive Linguistics, 6*(1), 89–130.
de Saussure, F. (1916). *Course in General Linguistics*. Payot.
de Saussure, F. (1974). *Course in General Linguistics*. P. Owen.
Sennet, A. (2011). Unarticulated Constituents and Propositional Structure. *Mind & Language, 4*, 412–435.
Sperber, D. & Wilson, D. (1986/1995). *Relevance: Communication and Cognition*. Blackwell.
Stanley, J., & Szabó, Z. G. (2000). On Quantifier Domain Restriction. *Mind & Language, 15*, 219–261.
Stanley, J. (2002). Making It Articulated. *Mind & Language, 1*, 149–168.
Stanley, J. (2005). Semantics in Context. In G. Preyer & G. Peter (Eds.), *Contextualism in Philosophy: Knowledge, Meaning, and Truth* (pp. 221–253). Clarendon Press.
Stanley, J. (2007). *Language in Context: Selected Essays*. Oxford University Press.
Stefanowitsch, A., & Gries, S. Th. (2003). Collostructions: Investigating the Interaction of Words and Constructions. *International Journal of Corpus Linguistics, 8*(2), 209–243.
Storjohann, P. 2010. *Lexical-Semantic Relations: Theoretical and Practical Perspectives*. John Benjamins.
Sullivan, A. (2015). The Future of the Proposition. *Language and Communication, 40*, 14–23.

Sun, C. (1996). *Word Order Change and Grammaticalization in the History of Chinese*. Stanford University Press.
Sweetser, E. E. (1988). Grammaticalization and Semantic Bleaching. In S. Axmaker, A. Jaisser, & H. Singmaster (Eds.), *Berkeley Linguistics Society 14: General Session and Parasession on Grammaticalization* (pp. 389–405). Berkeley Linguistics Society.
Sweetser, E. E. (1990). *From Etymology to Pragmatics: The Mind-as-Body Metaphor in Semantic Structure and Semantic Change*. Cambridge University Press.
Taylor, J. R. (2017). Lexical Semantics. In B. Dancygier (Ed.), *The Cambridge Handbook of Cognitive Linguistics* (pp. 246–261). Cambridge University Press.
Traugott, E. C. (1999). The Rhetoric of Counter-Expectation in Semantic Change: A Study in Subjectification. In B. Andreas & K. Peter (Eds.), *Historical Semantics and Cognition* (pp. 177–196). Mouton de Gruyter.
Traugott, E. C. (2002). From Etymology to Historical Pragmatics. In D. Minkova & R. Stockwell (Eds.), *Studying the History of the English Language: Millennial Perspectives* (pp. 19–49). Mouton de Gruyter.
Traugott, E. C. (2003). From Subjectification to Intersubjectification. In R. Hickey (Ed.), *Motives for Language Change* (pp. 124–139). Cambridge University Press.
Traugott, E. C. (2010). Revisiting Subjectification and Intersubjectification. In K. Davidse, L. Vandelanotte, & H. Cuyckens (Eds.), *Subjectification, Intersubjectification and Grammaticalization* (pp. 29–71). Mouton de Gruyter.
Traugott, E. C. (2012). Linguistic Levels: Semantics and Lexicon. In A. Bergs & L. J. Brinton (Eds.), *English Historical Linguistics: An International Handbook* (Vol. 1, pp. 164–177). Mouton de Gruyter.
Traugott, E. C., & Dasher, R. B. (2002). *Regularity in Semantic Change*. Cambridge University Press.
Traugott, E. C., & Hopper, P. J. (2003). *Grammaticalization* (2nd ed.). Cambridge University Press.
Traugott, E. C., & Trousdale, G. (2013). *Constructionalization and Constructional Changes*. Oxford University Press.
Travis, C. (1985). On What Is Strictly Speaking True. *Canadian Journal of Philosophy, 2*, 187–229.
Travis, C. (2008). *Occasion-Sensitivity: Selected Essays*. Oxford University Press.
Trousdale, G., & Norde, M. (2012). Degrammaticalization and Constructionalization: Two Case Studies. *Language Sciences, 36*, 32–46.
Trousdale, G. (2013). Multiple Inheritance and Constructional Change. *Studies in Language, 37*(3), 491–514.
Ungerer, F., & Schmid, H. J. (1996). *An Introduction to Cognitive Linguistics*. Longman.
Ungerer, F., & Schmid, H. J. (2008). *An Introduction to Cognitive Linguistics* (2nd ed.). Foreign Language Teaching and Research Press.
Van der Auwera, J. (2013). Semantic Maps, for Synchronic and Diachronic Typology. In A. Giacalone, R. C. Mauri, & P. Molinelli (Eds.), *Synchrony and Diachrony: A Dynamic Interface* (pp. 153–176). John Benjamins.
Wilson, D., & Carston, R. (2007). A Unitary Approach to Lexical Pragmatics: Relevance, Inference and Ad Hoc Concepts. In N. Burton-Roberts (Ed.), *Advances in Pragmatics* (pp. 230–260). Palgrave Macmillan.
Wilson, D., & Sperber, D. (2002). Truthfulness and Relevance. *Mind, 111*, 583–632.
Wilson, D., & Sperber, D. (2004). Relevance Theory. In L. Horn & G. Ward (Eds.), *Handbook of Pragmatics* (pp. 607–632). Blackwell.
Wu, S. Q. (2014). The Metonymic Interpretation of Chinese Antonym Co-occurrence Constructions: The Case of *You X You Y*. *Language Sciences, 45*, 189–201.
Wu, S. Q. (2017). Iconicity and Viewpoint: Antonym Order in Chinese Four-Character Patterns. *Language Sciences, 59*, 117–134.
Wu, S. Q. (2018). A Corpus-based Study of the Chinese Synonymous Approximatives *Shangxia, Qianhou and Zuoyou*. *Corpus Linguistics and Linguistic Theory*, 1–31.

Xiang, M. (2008). Plurality, Maximality and Inference. *Journal of East Asian Linguistics, 17*, 227–245.

Yang, R. (2002). *Common Nouns, Classifiers, and Quantification in Chinese.* Rutgers University.

Yang, T. H., Huang, H. H., Yen, A. Z., & Chen, H. H. (2018). *Transfer of Frames from English FrameNet to Construct Chinese FrameNet: A Bilingual Corpus-based Approach.* Proceedings of the Eleventh International Conference on Language Resources and Evaluation.

Zenner, E., Backus, A., & Winter-Froemel, E. (Eds.). (2018). *Cognitive Contact Linguistics.* Walter de Gruyter.

Zlatev, J. (1999). Situated Embodied Semantics and Connectionist Modeling. In J. Allwood & P. Gardenfors (Eds.), *Cognitive Semantics: Meaning and Cognition* (pp. 173–194). John Benjamins.

MIX
Papier aus verantwortungsvollen Quellen
Paper from responsible sources
FSC® C105338

If you have any concerns about our products,
you can contact us on
ProductSafety@springernature.com

In case Publisher is established outside the EU,
the EU authorized representative is:
Springer Nature Customer Service Center GmbH
Europaplatz 3, 69115 Heidelberg, Germany

Printed by Libri Plureos GmbH
in Hamburg, Germany